ADVANCED
STRATEGIC
PLANNING

Also by Aubrey Malphurs

Being Leaders

Biblical Manhood and Womanhood

Building Leaders (coauthor)

Church Next (coauthor)

A Contemporary Handbook for Weddings, Funerals, and Other Occasions (coauthor)

Developing a Dynamic Mission for Your Ministry

Developing a Vision for Ministry in the 21st Century

Doing Church

The Dynamics of Pastoral Leadership

Leading Leaders

Maximizing Your Effectiveness

Ministry Nuts and Bolts

Money Matters in Church (coauthor)

A New Kind of Church

The Nuts and Bolts of Church Planting

Planting Growing Churches for the 21st Century

Pouring New Wine into Old Wineskins

Strategic Disciple Making

Strategy 2000

Values-Driven Leadership

Vision America

third edition

ADVANCED STRATEGIC PLANNING

A 21st-CENTURY MODEL
FOR CHURCH AND MINISTRY LEADERS

AUBREY MALPHURS

BakerBooks

a division of Baker Publishing Group
Grand Rapids, Michigan

© 1999, 2005, 2013 by Aubrey Malphurs

Published by Baker Books
a division of Baker Publishing Group
P.O. Box 6287, Grand Rapids, MI 49516-6287
www.bakerbooks.com

Printed in the United States of America

Library of Congress Cataloging-in-Publication Data

Malphurs, Aubrey.
   Advanced strategic planning : a 21st-century model for church and ministry leaders / Aubrey
Malphurs. — 3rd edition.
      pages cm
   Includes bibliographical references and index.
   ISBN 978-0-8010-1455-0 (pbk.)
   1. Church management. 2. Strategic planning. I. Title.
BV652.M3563 2013
254—dc23
                                                               2012046707

The internet addresses, email addresses, and phone numbers in this book are accurate at the time of publication. They are provided as a resource. Baker Publishing Group does not endorse them or vouch for their content or permanence.

20   21   22   23   24   25   26   14   13   12   11   10   9   8

Contents

Introduction

I spotted the creature sitting off in the distance almost by itself. With long arms that looked like a tangle of dark blue steel tentacles, it reminded me of a large octopus that had crawled out of the ocean nearby. It was nothing of the sort. It was one of several rides operated by a small, traveling carnival that happened to pass through our town close to where my family and I lived. I was alone with my daughter, Jennifer, who at the time was around the impressionable age of four or five. I decided to live a little and have a good time that would make a lasting impression on my little girl. She would discover that Dad wasn't afraid to try something new.

We boarded the monster, and soon it was spinning around at breakneck speed while the tentacles frantically lashed up and down. It was frightening. I began to worry that one of the tentacles—the one that held us—could possibly tear loose with all the contortions it was going through. We would not survive if it did. I silently prayed and made a vow to God as I held Jennifer tightly against my chest. It went something like this: *God, if you get us off this ride alive and in one piece, I promise never to get on another ride for the rest of my life!* God answered my prayer, the octopus let go, and I have kept that vow.

More than at any other time in history, North America, along with much of the world, is exploding with change—fast, frightening change. I refer to it as megachange. It has affected every institution—business, government, the schools, and the church—and it is occurring at a number of levels: national, corporate, and individual. The result is a revolution taking place all around us that is likely to be as profound as any in the past. Some wrongly advise us just to be patient, that in time it will all pass. The reality is, however, that there is no end in sight. We have climbed on board the octopus only to discover that it will not let go.

What is the explanation for this megachange? What is happening? Peter Drucker sums it up best:

> Every few hundred years throughout Western history, a sharp transformation has occurred. In a matter of decades, society altogether rearranges itself—its world view, its

basic values, its social and political structures, its arts, its key institutions. Fifty years later a new world exists. And the people born into that world cannot even imagine the world in which grandparents lived and into which their own parents were born.[1]

Drucker's point is that we are living at one of those rare points in time when an old worldview (modernism) and many of its trappings are dying and another (postmodernism) has been born. The consequence is a massive shift in our culture, science, society, and institutions. This change is enormously greater than the world has ever experienced, and we are caught in the middle of it. We are living at a frightening point of absolute, chaotic discontinuity, watching the old die off and the new rush in to fill the vacuum.

Where is the church in all this? How is it doing?

The Problem

The answer is, not well. In an earlier book, I noted that in 1988 between 80 and 85 percent of churches in North America had either plateaued or were in decline (dying).[2] Now in the twenty-first century, that figure has not changed appreciably despite a valiant surge in church planting. The number of unchurched people across America continues to be high, possibly as high as 70 to 80 percent. Penny Marler comments that if the Gallup surveys over the past thirty years that estimate the unchurched to be only 57 percent of the population were accurate, then people would be flocking to our churches. But this is not happening.[3]

Based on my research and consulting ministry with churches, I am convinced that the typical church does not understand the full implications of megachange. Even when a church has some understanding of the implications, it doesn't know how to respond in effective ministry to those becoming immersed in the postmodern paradigm. I believe that the majority of seminaries that prepare people for ministry sit in the same boat with the churches. They are still preparing future pastors for ministry to a modern—not a postmodern—world. Most training equips pastors for one hour on Sunday morning but ignores the other forty-plus hours of the week that demand such things as leadership gifts and abilities, people skills, and strategic thinking and doing. My research, pastoral experience, and church consulting indicate that pastoring a church is a leadership-intensive enterprise. It is imperative that a pastor be able not only to preach to a congregation but also to lead and relate well to that congregation.[4]

The Explanation

The information above indicates that the North American church is not on a plateau but in decline. It is facing a major growth challenge. It is over the life-cycle hump and moving downward. Before venturing to offer a solution to the problem,

The Life Cycle of a Church

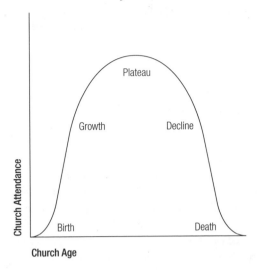

I want to look at an explanation for the problem. I believe an understanding of the reason the problem exists is a major step toward solving it. As someone once said, a problem well defined is a problem half solved.

Experts have put forth numerous explanations for why the North American church is struggling. Many lay blame. Based on the information above, you could blame the church for not doing a better job of evangelism and edification. If 65 percent of the people in the churches are either plateaued or declining in their spiritual growth, it is no wonder that so many churches are struggling.

You might also blame the seminaries and colleges that train the church's leaders. A scan of the typical seminary curriculum would reveal that far too many are not aware of what is taking place in North American culture and its impact on the typical church. Though many seminaries and Christian colleges have begun to use the new technology, they are typically business as usual when it comes to the curriculum.

My view is that the problem is not what evangelical seminaries teach but what they do not teach. Many evangelical seminaries teach the Bible and theology, and it is imperative that they do so. However, they often do not provide strong training in leadership, people skills, and strategic thinking skills, and this is poor preparation for ministry in today's shrinking world, which is undergoing intense, convoluted change.

The Sigmoid Curve

It is easy to lay blame, and many need to wake up or pull their heads out of the sand. However, a bigger, more fundamental explanation of the problem is represented by the sigmoid curve. We can better understand much of what is taking place in North American Christianity in general and churches in particular if we understand the concept of the sigmoid curve.

The term *sigmoid* simply means "S-shaped." The S-shaped curve represents the natural development of one's personal life and relationships. It also represents the natural development of biological systems, institutions, worldviews, civilizations, and organizations including the church.

The S-curve depicts how virtually everything in life begins, grows, plateaus, and then ultimately dies. It is true of human beings. It also may be true of relationships such as marriage. It is true of one's leadership and it is true of civilizations, as proved by the Greek and Roman empires in the past and the Russian empire today. The Fortune 500 companies demonstrate that it is true of businesses, as a number of companies who made the list one, two, or more years ago are not on that list today. In physics it is the second law of thermodynamics. In biology it is extinction. In terms of worldview it is the shift from theism to deism and then to naturalism or modernism. And today it is the shift from modernism to postmodernism. Not even the church is an exception to the pattern. In short, the world and everything in it are all somewhere on the S-curve.

As it relates to the church, the S-curve represents essentially its life-cycle pattern. Like people, churches have a life cycle. In general, a church is born and over time it grows. Eventually it reaches a plateau, and if nothing is done to move it off that plateau, it begins to decline. If nothing interrupts the decline, it will die. Each stage represents a growth challenge for the church. Growing, plateaued, and declining churches all face growth challenges. Some are alike, but most are unique to the church's particular situation and where it is on the S-curve.

The Message

The message or lesson of the sigmoid curve is that all good things (and even some bad things) end. In a world of constant, turbulent change, many relationships

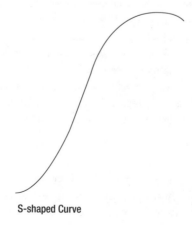

S-shaped Curve

and most organizations do not last. The pattern is that they wax and eventually wane. Even brand-new institutions and organizations such as a church will, in time, plateau and then die. No matter what institution it is, organizational "dry rot" sets in. The institution becomes brittle, ceases to function, and expires.

This concept has been true since the fall of mankind as recorded in Genesis 3. The bad news for the twenty-first century is that today decline is happening faster than ever before. In the first three-quarters of the twentieth century, for example, decline was a relatively slow process. It took time for things to change and eventually die. You had some advance warning and time to address the changes. However, writing in 1994, Charles Handy warns, "Those units of time are also getting depressingly small. They used to be decades, perhaps even generations. Now they are years, sometimes months. The accelerating pace of change shrinks every sigmoid curve."[5] I would add that it has shrunk not only to years and months but in some cases also to days.

While it does prove helpful to examine specific reasons for the decline of churches, the lesson is that it will happen anyway. We can learn from this information and try to discover what to do as well as what not to do. Regardless, in time the end is inevitable. This was true of the spiritually strong and not so strong churches of the first century. Those ministries live on today in the churches of the twenty-first century. However, the original churches are no longer. If you travel to the Middle East, you will not find any of them.

The Solution

The concept of the sigmoid curve raises a critical question for the North American church. Is there anything a church can do to circumvent or at least put off eventual decline and death? The answer is yes, and it is twofold. First, gifted leaders of churches and denominations must start new S-curves. They need to launch out in new directions. Second, they need a strategic planning process that helps them start new sigmoid curves. They need to know how to think and act in the twenty-first century.

Starting New S-Curves

The answer to the problem of church decline is to start new S-curves. This should occur in several contexts: church planting, church growth, and church revitalization. You would be wise to pay close attention to the context that describes your ministry situation.

Church Planting

The first context in which to start new S-curves is new church starts. Birthing new churches was the early church's response to Christ's Great Commission. The church's three missionary journeys found in Acts 13:1–21:26 involved church planting.

A number of organizations and denominations have caught a vision to parent Great Commission churches all across North America. They refuse to bury their heads in the sand and ignore all that is taking place around them. The Assemblies of God and the Southern Baptists launched bold church-planting programs at the end of the twentieth century. A number of smaller denominations such as the Missionary Church, Lutheran Church–Missouri Synod, Evangelical Covenant Church, Church of the Nazarene, and others have followed suit.

Church planting involves starting a new or first S-curve. The new church has no prior history. It is at the very beginning of the church life cycle. While this can be a very disorganized time in the church's history, it is also a time of great excitement and anticipation. The core group is asking, What is God going to do? To what extent will God use us to make a difference in our world in the twenty-first century? Typically, churches at this early stage are very evangelistic and reach out to people in the community and beyond.

The concept of the S-curve teaches us that for the universal church to survive, it must plant churches. Since every church in time will wane and die, it is imperative that we start new churches, or the church as a whole will cease to exist.

Church Growth

The second context for new S-curves is the growing church. The key to continued growth and renewal is not only to start new first-curve churches (church planting) but also to start a new second curve in the existing church before it plateaus.

A proactive response. Like church planting, this is a proactive response. The church starts the second curve while it is still virile and growing. It is at this stage that the ministry has the time, resources (people and finances), energy, spirit, and drive to launch the new curve. Many in the church, however, will view this response as foolish if not insane (they have not learned from companies like IBM that made the exact same mistake and as a result don't have the market share they

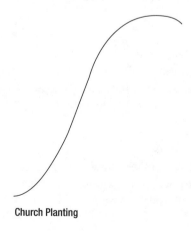

Church Planting

once had).[6] The problem and number one enemy is complacency. Why start a new course when the present course is so successful? Someone will quip, "If it ain't broke, don't fix it!" This calls for a strong leap of faith, as the need for and evidence in support of a new direction will not be obvious. This is a paradox. Leaders must push ahead in spite of the seeming evidence that the current ministry is doing well. This move is tantamount to letting go of the trapeze with no net in sight. It takes leaders of strong faith and vision to pull it off.

A reactive response. Most leaders wait until the church has plateaued or is in decline before they seek renewal. This is the crisis or reactive mode. But people do not lead and respond well in a crisis context for several reasons. One is that the leaders are discredited. They are the very ones who led the organization into its state of decline, so they are not considered competent as leaders or worthy of trust.

People will also respond poorly because of lack of resources. Declining ministries are like sinking ships. Some people are quick to abandon them and take their money with them. There will also be poor esprit de corps. People are down emotionally, which drains them of the energy needed to be involved in renewal.

Knowing where we are. At this point two important questions for growing churches are, How can we know where our church is on the first curve, and When it is time to start the second curve? The answer to both questions is that you cannot know for sure. However, the following hints may prove helpful. First, it is always safe to assume that you are close to a plateau. If you are not close, you can be sure that one is lurking somewhere off in the distance. Handy points out candidly that an organization needs a new direction every two to three years.[7] This is because not only is there more change today, but also it happens in a shorter amount of time.

It may be helpful to ask an outsider (another pastor or consultant) for his evaluation of where the church is, because he will be more objective than people within the ministry. Younger people in the church and younger leaders will often be more aware of where the church is than older members. The older and established leaders may hold assumptions, views, or paradigms that blind them to the real situation. This is why I along with others advise older leaders and retiring pastors not to stay in the church. It is imperative that those who cannot embrace the new curve step aside and, usually, leave the church. This may seem harsh, but the church as a whole is more important than a handful of former leaders. These older leaders could move to other churches where they would be able to serve with less influence as lay leaders or as ministers in small group communities.

Some second-curve issues. Not only is it difficult to convince people in a growing church of the need to start a second curve, but it is also difficult to accomplish the new direction. For a time, various currents will be pulling in different directions. The old and new curves will coexist, causing much confusion. Conflict will surface between leaders and their followers invested in the first curve and those invested in the second curve. In addition, as the second curve starts up, it may wane before it takes over. The result will be even more criticism of the leaders of change, making it easy for them to lose heart, give up on the new curve, and return to the old or resign. The answer for leaders of change is to exercise great patience with the process. Do not be too quick to decide it's not working.

Some second-curve events. How do growing churches launch new S-curves? What are some second-curve events? One is a church relocation. Lakepointe Baptist Church was a growing Southern Baptist church located in Rowlett, Texas (a suburb of Dallas), with an average of two to three thousand attenders. They relocated to a larger facility that is located four or five miles away, facing a four-lane interstate highway, and attendance has jumped to around seven thousand.

Another way to initiate a second curve is to implement some or all of the concepts in this book—discovering your core values; developing a mission, a vision, and a strategy; and so forth. For those who have already discovered and developed these concepts, begin a second curve by revisiting and updating or rethinking them.

Other second-curve events are the addition of a more contemporary worship service, transitioning the traditional church service to a contemporary service, adding a service to attract and win seekers, redesigning the traditional Christian education program, launching a vibrant small group ministry, and challenging all the people to go through a process of discovering their divine design and then investing their lives in some aspect of church ministry.[8]

Warning. Every church is unique. Consequently, what works for one church may not work for another. Relocation worked well for Lakepointe—a healthy church. It could prove disastrous for you. The same is true for transitioning from a traditional to a more contemporary format, adding a service, and so on.

Some events result in deeper changes than others. A relocation or transition in style may bring changes only at the church's edges. This depends on the church and its particular culture, needs, and problems. Usually the kinds of events that launch new S-curves result in substantial changes at the organization's heart and not just around its edges. Often they involve a change in paradigm. While a church relocation or transition from one style to another is optional, discovering core values and developing a mission, vision, and strategy are not. When an entire church concurs and decides to pursue these, the result, most likely, will be a new S-curve.

Church Revitalization

The third context for starting a new sigmoid curve is the revitalization of plateaued or dying churches. The hope is that it is not too late for the church to be revived. A plateaued church can move in a new direction, starting the new S-curve while on the plateau. New problems may arise, however. When enough new people are coming into the ministry to offset those who are exiting, the leaders may find themselves dealing with some of the same challenges as those of growing churches.

If a church waits until it is dying to make changes, it finds itself in a reactive not a proactive mode. At this point it may be too late to start a new sigmoid curve. The church may have used up most of its resources in trying to keep the sinking ship afloat. Some people are willing to invest in a ship that is listing badly, but many head for the lifeboats. Those who decide to stay with the ship find themselves constantly

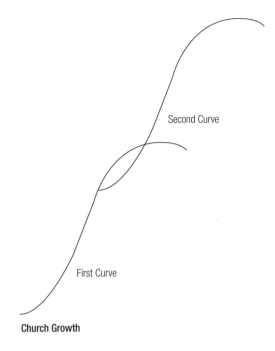

Second Curve

First Curve

Church Growth

wrestling with discouragement. As difficult as church planting and starting a new curve in a growing church are, revitalization of a declining ministry is more difficult and less likely to succeed.[9] However, if a plateaued church is to survive, it must start a new S-curve as soon as possible and trust God to chart a new course.

Strategic Planning

The answer to the problem of church decline is to start new S-curves. This necessitates a strategic planning process along with leaders or navigators who can effectively lead their churches through the process. It is imperative that strategic planning be at the heart of starting new S-curves. The following provides an overview or a synthesis of the strategic planning process, which is developed in this book. It will help you see where each part fits and how all the parts work together to accomplish congregational development. You may find it helpful to consult the table of contents as you read the following. The strategic envisioning process or navigational compass is made up of three distinct parts, each of which has several elements that work to envision the church's future.

The process begins in part 1—the ministry's preparation for envisioning the future. Remember that preparation precedes process. It consists of three elements that prepare the ministry for what is to come. The first addresses the preparation of the lead navigator. It presents the rationale for strategic planning (chap. 1). It challenges leaders to address such vital issues as their definition of strategic

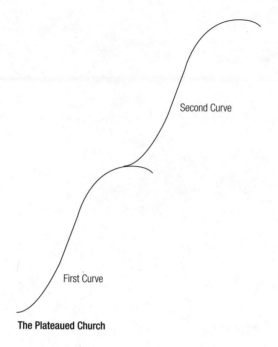

Second Curve

First Curve

The Plateaued Church

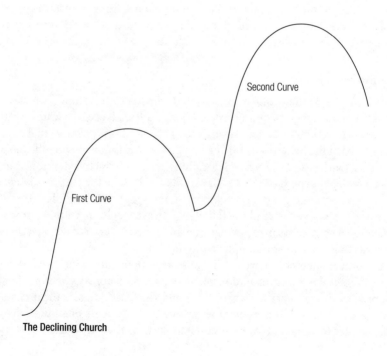

Second Curve

First Curve

The Declining Church

planning and what they believe is its importance, the need for it, and its purpose. Most important, it asks if the navigator is the kind of leader who can lead the church through change. In addition, these issues are in a twelve-item checklist to aid navigators in deciding on and developing their rationale. The second element addresses the ministry's preparation of the crew (chap. 2). It helps navigators prepare their team for the process. The third focuses on the boat or development of the strategy as the team works through the process (chap. 3).

Part 2 provides the process phase when the team begins to chart out their future. They will discover who they are, where they are going, and how they will get there. This part consists of four elements that guide leaders and their teams through the process of envisioning the ministry's future: developing a mission, developing a vision, discovering core values, and developing a five-part strategy that accomplishes the mission-vision (chaps. 4–12).

Part 3 provides the practice phase when the navigational team continues the journey. It is made up of two elements (chaps. 13–14) that accomplish the results of the process phase. The first is launching the boat, which involves the implementation of the developed strategy. The second element is evaluation, which changes and fine-tunes the results of the process.

Strategic Leadership

The key to strategic planning is competent strategic leadership. You may develop the finest strategic plan in the history of the church. It may be featured in the major journals on leadership. You might publish it in a book that sells thousands of copies. However, it will not happen without competent, gifted leadership. In a way, this is a disclaimer. I have designed this book to help you develop a plan that "touches all the bases" and makes a significant difference in your church. However, it will not likely come to fruition without good leadership, especially at the senior pastor level.

Regardless of how new S-curves in a church are started—through church planting, growth, or revitalization—two interrelated pieces must always be present. One is a congregation that is ready to grow or be revitalized. The other is a competent pastor who is able to lead the ministry through change. So who are these pastors and what does this kind of leadership look like? What are the characteristics of pastor-leaders who can lead their churches to grow or be revitalized? Because of the critical nature of these questions and the importance of leadership to the entire process, I will address them at the beginning of chapter 1, "Preparing the Navigator."

Some Final Comments on the Process

First, the problem that I have experienced with this process as with all processes is that things do not necessarily unfold as neatly and orderly as it suggests. On some occasions, a strategic leadership team or a leader will come up with the vision at the beginning of the process or even some of the strategy, and that will not necessarily

part one

Prepare to Sail!

The Preparation for Strategic Planning

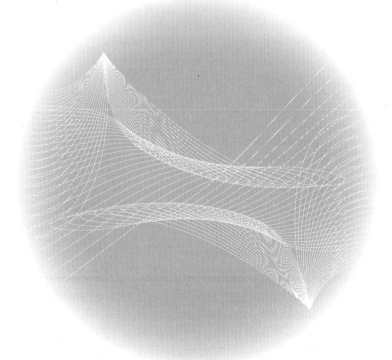

1

Preparing the Navigator

A Prelaunch Checklist

To alleviate our fear of flying, the various airlines assure us that traveling in one of their aircraft is safer than driving to the airport in your car. As a ministry consultant and trainer, I find that information comforting since I spend much time on airplanes flying to different places in North America and abroad. One of the reasons for the safety record of airlines is that pilots and mechanics carefully work through a preflight checklist. I have watched the captain walk around the plane, examining the engines and the flaps. On occasion I have even seen the captain kick the tires. When the flight personnel leave the cabin door open, you can watch them as they busily flip switches, check gauges, examine various digital and modular instruments, and review their charts and flight plans. I have also observed mechanics running test programs to make sure that the plane's electronics are working properly. To do otherwise could prove disastrous.

In the same way, good navigators prepare carefully before launching their boats. They have to get ready and prepare to sail. They use a prelaunch checklist to check out their boats to make sure that they are shipshape and safe. For example, they check every piece of equipment on board—especially safety equipment—to make sure that it is in good working order. They never know what is ahead and often face storms and other problems that are survived only because of their preplanning.

Leaders, like airline pilots, mechanics, and navigators, must also do some prelaunch work before attempting the strategic planning process. It will save the team countless hours and money that could make the difference between success and failure, and it will make the process much smoother and faster. Part 1 of this book is designed to help leaders prepare for strategic planning, which will launch their ministry ships into the future.

This chapter serves as the leader-navigator's twelve-item prelaunch checklist. The problem is that some leaders struggle with taking the time to work through checklists. They do not like to dabble in the details. They prefer to get on with the job. Thus they skip what they believe to be the appetizer to get on to the entrée. However, I would argue that it is vital for all leader-navigators to know what they are doing (definition) and why they are doing it (purposes) along with a number of important issues that could make the difference between success and failure. For example, if the leader does not establish the reason the team is doing strategic planning, some will fail to see the need for it, which will adversely affect the total effort. So it is imperative, at the beginning of this journey, that the leaders discipline themselves, if necessary, to work through these critical issues with their team so they are all prepared to launch the ship together.

Strategic Planning	
Part 1.	**Preparation for strategic planning**
Part 2.	Process of strategic planning
Part 3.	Practice of strategic planning

1. Determining If One Is a Lead Navigator

First, sailors need to determine if they are lead navigators. They could be much better at something else. Thus this determination comes at the top of the prelaunch checklist—it is the most important item on the list. If the senior or lead pastor is not the kind of leader whose leadership results in seeing a plateaued or decling church begin to grow numerically, then you need go no further.

Strategic planning, as I am presenting it in this book, will bring about a church turnaround or revitalization. (The term *strategic planning* includes the idea of church revitalization.)

Near the end of the introduction to this book, I mentioned under strategic leadership that there are two necessary elements in successful strategic planning that result in a church's revitalization. One is a church that is ready to be revitalized, and the other is a gifted, competent leader who can take the church through the process. Here in chapter 1, I will focus on the kind of leader who is competent to lead a church through strategic planning. This information is most important to those who believe that God wants them to pastor a church and to those who are looking for a pastor for their church. The rest of this book will focus attention on strategic planning that brings about a revitalization of the church.

The Characteristics of Turnaround Pastors

First, how can a pastor know if he will be competent at leading a church through the revitalization process? How can he know if he is a turnaround pastor-leader? What are the characteristics of such a person? Pastor Gordon Penfold has researched the topic of turnaround pastors and discovered the following.[1] First, at a time when most churches are plateaued or declining, turnaround pastors are men whose current ministries demonstrate in worship attendance at least a 2.5 percent average annual growth per year for five years, regardless of the size of the church. Second, he discovered that, as a group, these pastor-leaders evidenced the following common characteristics. They scored a 4 or higher on either the D or I or both on the Personal Profile or DiSC temperament tool. They are clear, passionate vision casters. Not only are they visionaries but they also cast vision for their churches with both clarity and passion. Their congregations clearly see and feel the church's vision. The majority have had coaches or mentors for much of their ministries. They have seen the wisdom in seeking out people who are ahead of them in ministry and can help them fill in any gaps in their leadership. They have a distinctive leadership style. They are self-starters who are more outgoing, innovative, and energetic than other pastors who aren't turnaround leaders. They are team players who are good at delegation and training new leaders. In addition, they are focused, directive (not domineering) leaders who relate well with people. Finally, they are better than average communicators with above-average conflict resolution skills.

Are You a Turnaround Pastor?

So the question is, Are you or is your pastor-leader a turnaround pastor? Do the characteristics above describe you or the pastor of your church? The Turnaround Pastors Audit at the end of this chapter will help you answer these questions.

What if you discover through all this that you are not a turnaround pastor? What does this mean? In most cases it means that if you are a senior or lead pastor your church most likely will plateau or be in decline. Do you find this to be the case in your situation? Yes, there are exceptions, but these are truly exceptions, not the norm. God can use anyone to revitalize a church, but most often he uses those whom he has wired to be turnaround leaders.

Can You Become a Turnaround Pastor?

Can a pastor who does not naturally have the characteristics of a turnaround pastor become one? This is difficult to answer and takes us back to the old nature versus nurture debate in leadership circles. Does a person have to be born a leader, or can he or she learn to be a leader? My intuitive read on this is that it is not one or the other but that both are true. A person can be born with a unique leadership gift, and the spiritual gift of leadership is one that is given to Christians

(Rom. 12:6–8). However, a person without this gift can also grow and develop as a leader. This is the reason we attempt to develop leaders in our churches and seminaries. I have mentioned a number of characteristics above that are skills associated with the leadership styles of turnaround pastors, and skills by their very nature can be learned.

The problem is more with temperament. Temperament is God-given, and I do believe that while one cannot change his temperament, he can adapt to another temperament with varying results. It is a bigger adjustment for some than for others. Some can adapt to the temperament that is expected of them in a ministry situation, but since it is not natural, it can prove somewhat difficult and uncomfortable for other leaders. Also, in a pressure or stressful situation, the natural response is to default to your God-given temperament. Thus the answer to the question if a leader can become a turnaround pastor is, it depends. It depends on the person and how comfortable he is adapting to another, different temperament. Some can do it, and some cannot.

2. Understanding the Importance of Strategic Planning

The second item on the leader's preplanning list is understanding the importance of having a strategic planning process for ministry. The following four reasons should catch the ministry navigator's attention.

Strategic Planning Makes a Difference

One reason for strategic planning is that it really makes a difference in a church's effectiveness. Researcher Kirk Hadaway writes, "Does a planning process which involves evaluation and a long-range plan correlate with church growth? The answer is yes. Survey results show that 85 percent of churches which have grown off the plateau have reevaluated their programs and priorities during the past five years, as compared to 59 percent of churches which have remained on the plateau. Similarly, 40 percent of 'breakout churches' have developed a long-range plan, as compared to only 18 percent of continued plateau churches."[2]

My experience as well has been that many if not most churches that are making a difference for the Savior are led by or at least staffed with strategic thinkers who, if they don't have a plan in hand (articulated on paper), have one in their heads. A case in point is my pastor, Steve Stroope. He is the pastor of Lake Pointe Church in Rockwall, Texas. We served on the board together and I was able to observe him up close. He was called to pastor the church when it consisted of only seventeen people, and he has remained to navigate the church through several strategic relocations and numerous capital funds projects in the context of a clearly articulated mission and vision. Today the church has several thousand attenders, and its strategy includes a multicampus approach.

Strategic Planning Addresses Three Organizational Questions

Another reason for strategic planning is that it enables leaders to answer three basic organizational questions. The first is the identity question, Who are we? This gets at the church's core values, or DNA. The second is the direction question, Where are we going? This identifies the church's mission and vision. A third is the ministry strategy question, How will we get there? This addresses how the church will accomplish its mission and vision. Clearly weighing and articulating answers to these questions will have a more profound impact on your ministry's future than attempting any long-range plan.

Strategic Planning Affects the Long-Term Life of the Church

A third reason for strategic planning is that it is the key to the long-term survival of the church, where ministry circumstances are constantly changing. To survive, churches must change and adapt their ministry methods, using strategic planning as their vehicle. Two metaphors will help us to understand this.

The church is a ship that attempts to cross a body of water, destined for some port. Just as a ship encounters numerous navigational hazards along the way (tides, currents, wind, flotsam, low water levels, false buoys, and so on), so a church encounters its own navigational hazards (difficult people, a changing community, lack of leadership, poor congregational mobilization, and so on). Church leaders, like a ship's navigators, must have a process (compass) to plan strategically (chart a course) to reach the church's destination (port). Though a limited few can do this intuitively (they are natural born navigators), most cannot. They need training to be navigators.

Leaders need a map to find the way for the church. If you are trying to drive to a particular location in your town or city and you do not know the way, you need an up-to-date map or you may get hopelessly lost. Lots of leaders in our churches are navigating their terrain with outdated maps (those drawn up in the 1940s and 1950s), and they are totally lost. Some of the people in their churches advise that they simply need to redouble their efforts—to work harder. The result, however, is that they get hopelessly lost faster. Others advise that they simply need to sit back and give it a little time because eventually everything will return to the way it was. The result is that things change even more and waiting merely increases the odds against survival. Strategic planning is the map that directs the church into the future.

Strategic Planning Addresses Alignment Issues

Strategic planning addresses a number of concepts that require alignment. You will discover in this book that strategic planning is a process that involves the critical alignment of a number of elements, such as a church's values, mission, vision, and so forth. I have observed many churches that have failed to make proper alignments and have suffered diminished returns as a result. For example, churches engage in capital funds projects to raise monies for a new facility or for adding on to an existing facility. Without knowing it, many of these churches are following what I refer to as a "Kevin Costner theology"—build it and they will come (the theme of the actor's 1989 movie *Field of Dreams*).

They do not realize that understanding and articulating strategic planning concepts is the critical first step to funding and building. Before taking out their wallets, people need to know who they are, where they are going, why they are going there, and what that looks like. To ignore this often results in falling short of funding goals and erecting facilities that become nonfunctional and obsolete in just a few years. I should note that those in the construction phase (the design-build side) are increasingly becoming aware of their need to help churches do strategic planning before building. I suspect that churches will see strategic planners working closely with architects and contractors in the future as they attempt to translate vision and mission into facilities.

3. Defining Strategic Planning

What is strategic planning? I have argued that it is important but I have not defined the concept. *Strategic planning is the fourfold process that a point leader, such as a pastor, works through regularly with a team of leaders to envision or reenvision and revitalize his church by developing a biblical mission and a compelling vision, discovering its core values, and crafting a strategy that implements a unique, authentic church model.* The following addresses several of the key ingredients that make up this definition.

A Process

First, strategic planning is a process. It is not an event that a team works through and finishes. Instead, it is ongoing. (That is why I use the term *regularly* in the definition.) The team will come up with an initial model that will forever be critiqued throughout the life of the church if it is to stay relevant to and have an impact on its culture. Note that it is a fourfold process the pastor leads his team through that involves *developing a biblical mission and a compelling vision, discovering its core values, and crafting a strategy that implements a unique, authentic church model.*

The Point Leader

Strategic planning requires a strategic point leader, a lead navigator. Someone has to take charge, to captain the ship. This does not mean that the captain attempts to do all the work or tells everyone what to do. He works closely with and through a team. However, someone has to be in charge and responsible for the process, its day-to-day implementation, and the ultimate outcome. A group of people cannot do this. Should the ship hit an iceberg, the captain does not have time to make a conference call or have a meeting to debate the issues and decide what to do. There will be times when this person must act quickly and wisely on behalf of all, making the critical decisions that result in survival. This person will challenge the team to dream and contribute to what could be, as well as to what is. He will influence them, not attempt to control or dominate them.

The Leadership Team

Vital to strategic planning is the leadership team. I refer to them as the strategic leadership team (SLT). The new leadership paradigm is the same as the old leadership paradigm, but it accomplishes ministry through a team approach. Gone are the days when everyone expected the pastor to come up with all the good ideas and then pass them on to the congregation for implementation. Excellent leaders understand that they can accomplish far more through the wisdom of a gifted and committed strategic team of staff and lay leaders.

Moses certainly understood this as he wisely followed the counsel of Jethro and formed a team to work with him in his wilderness ministry (Exod. 18:24–26). Jesus understood this as he recruited a team of disciples to be with and minister alongside him (Mark 3:13–14). And Paul understood the significance of a team as he led and ministered through numerous teams (Acts 11:22–30; 13:2–3, 5; 15:40; 16:1–3). I will say more about the concept of a strategic leadership team in chapter 10.

An Envisioning Process

Strategic planning is an envisioning process that results in the revitalization of plateaued and dying churches. Rather than start with the present and work forward incrementally toward a mission and vision, you start with a clearly articulated, compelling mission and vision and work backward to where you are (see the introduction to chapter 7). You envision the future and then ask, How will we get there?

This is what makes it so different from conventional strategic planning or a long-range planning exercise. Long-range planning is too incremental and simply doesn't work anymore. You cannot edge forward when things around you are changing quickly. You plan for five years out, and all has changed in six months, requiring a new plan.

God uses a strategic envisioning process that does more than plan a hoped-for future; it helps you begin to create that future now. You are making strategic decisions today that affect tomorrow, which in fact begins today. The old is conventional strategic planning. The new is visionary strategic planning or strategic envisioning. And there is a huge difference between the two that I will explore later in this chapter. (Also, see the chart at the end of this chapter that compares the two.)

In the definition, I use the two terms *envision* and *reenvision*. The first addresses envisioning the future from the perspective of church planting. The second addresses the same from the viewpoint of church revitalization. The question here is which are you? Regardless, both are the key to the future of the church in North America and both involve the envisioning process.

Four Core Concepts

Just as a navigator cannot guide a ship from port to port without a compass, so strategic leaders cannot guide their ministry ships toward their desired destination without a ministry compass. This compass consists of four core concepts: the ministry's mission, vision, values, and strategy that make up the strategic planning process, resulting in a revitalized church. *The Savior determined the church's mission more than two thousand years ago. It is found in the Bible in Matthew 28:19 and other places, where he commands his church to "make disciples!"*

The church's vision is what the church will look like in the next five to ten years of its life as it accomplishes the mission. It should excite and attract people to want to be a part of the church as it pursues this vision.

The church's *core values* function much like the engine and rudder of a boat. *They empower and guide the church as it pursues its mission and vision.*

The strategy accomplishes the church's mission and vision and includes five key elements or steps: reaching out to the community, making mature disciples, building a ministry team (congregation, staff, and possibly a board), assessing the ministry's setting (location and facilities), and raising the necessary finances to carry out the mission and vision. All of these together make up the process that the pastor leads his church through.

Churches in general and leader-navigators in particular will regularly use these core concepts throughout the life of the ministry. All they do should be viewed through the lens of these concepts. In time using them should become second nature.

For the sake of clarity and direction, I have included the following outline with chapters of the four concepts as they make up the strategic planning process:

I. Development of the Mission (4)
II. Development of the Vision (5)
III. Discovery of the Core Values (6)
IV. Design of the Strategy (7–12)
    A. Outreach into the Community (8)
    B. Making Disciples (9)
    C. Building the Team (10)
    D. Assessing the Setting (11)
    E. Raising Finances (12)

A Unique, Authentic Ministry Model

The strategic planning process produces a product—a unique ministry model. It takes all kinds of churches to reach all kinds of people. When leaders ask and answer the proper process questions, they will come up with a product or model that aligns with who they are and reaches the people in their particular ministry community. As leaders continue to apply the process, they will continually redesign the model to reach their community as it changes. Thus over time they are designing and redesigning how they do church.

Strategic planning produces a unique ministry model and it leads to the church's own authentic ministry model. Far too many well-intentioned pastors find a ministry that God is blessing somewhere, attend its pastors' conference, and attempt to replicate the model back home. "After all, if it worked for them, it will work for me!" These pastors are trying to franchise someone else's model. And the problem with franchising church models is that what works in one part of the country does not necessarily work in another part of the country. Snyder, Texas, is different from Southern California or Chicago. Rather than adopt or copy some other church's model, this fourfold process aids leaders in discovering and developing their own authentic model that is true to who they are (identity—DNA), when they are (the twenty-first century), and where they are (location). I will say more about this later.

> **The Definition of Strategic Planning**
>
> 1. Strategic planning is a process.
> 2. Strategic planning involves a point leader.
> 3. Strategic planning involves a leadership team.
> 4. Strategic planning is an envisioning process.
> 5. Strategic planning involves four core concepts.
> 6. Strategic planning produces a unique, authentic ministry model.

4. Understanding That Strategic Planning Is Biblical

Though not exactly a part of the definition, I must point out that strategic thinking and acting or strategic planning can be found in the Bible; it is biblical. References to and examples of it are generously sprinkled throughout the Old and New Testaments. Numerous leaders in the Old Testament thought and acted strategically. Moses in response to God's mission to lead Israel out of Egypt led them strategically through the wilderness, as recorded in the Pentateuch. In Exodus 18 Moses's father-in-law, Jethro, challenges him to think and act strategically in his counseling of individual Israelites. The leadership of Moses's successor, Joshua, was most strategic (Josh. 6:1–7; 8:3–23; 10:6–9). The writer of 1 Chronicles notes that the men of Issachar "understood the times and knew what Israel should do" (12:32). Nehemiah thought and acted strategically as he led God's revitalization project in Jerusalem (Nehemiah 3–6). Proverbs presents God's wisdom and role in planning (14:15, 22; 15:22; 16:3–4, 9; 19:21; 20:18; 21:30).

In the Gospels Christ informs the church of its mission—the Great Commission (Matt. 28:19–20; Mark 16:15). In Acts 1:8 he gives the church its geographical strategy and direction. The book of Acts records how the Holy Spirit used the church strategically to implement this mission, especially through the missionary journeys (13:1–21:26). Paul did not wander aimlessly but appears to have carefully and strategically selected the cities he visited for ministry while on his missionary journeys. For example, he located in Ephesus because it was the gateway to Asia Minor (compare Acts 19:1 with 19:10). According to Luke, the Godhead thinks and acts strategically (see Acts 2:23; 4:28). In Ephesians 5:15–16 Paul encourages the Ephesian church to live strategically.

It becomes obvious, then, that God has sovereignly chosen to work through strategic thinking and acting to accomplish his divine will on earth. Accordingly, churches must be careful of those who advise them to ignore any planning and simply "let go and let God." On the other hand, we must not trust our strategies and ignore the role of the Holy Spirit in the process. Proverbs 19:21 is clear that God's purpose will prevail regardless of our plans. And Proverbs 21:31 reminds us that, while it seems like we are the ones doing the planning, it is God who is working behind the scenes to grant us success. John 15:5 warns that without Christ we can accomplish absolutely nothing. In Zechariah 4:6 the prophet reminds us as well as Zerubbabel, "'Not by might nor by power, but by my Spirit,' says the LORD Almighty." Letting go and letting God must work in conjunction with strategic thinking and acting. I tell my seminary students and my readers to hold their plans in an open hand before the sovereign God of the universe.

5. Understanding the Need for Strategic Planning

I have compared the typical church in North America to a ship without a compass, drifting aimlessly on the ocean. It doesn't know where it is or where it's going. And if that is not bad enough, the winds of change and the currents of postmodernism are relentlessly blowing and pulling the church even farther off course. I have argued that the compass the church is missing is a good visionary strategic planning or envisioning process. Without it, the typical sailor—today's pastor—will find it difficult to navigate in any situation.

I came to this conclusion as a result of my own pastoral and consulting experience and after writing books on the concepts of vision, mission, core values, and strategy.[3] Early in the process of writing these books, I began to ask myself how each concept related to the other concepts and, if I put them all together, what the resulting product would be. The answer quickly became evident. I would have a visionary strategic process that would help church leaders think through the core issues of ministry and then implement their conclusions.

Too Few Church Leaders Understand Strategic Planning

Not enough church leaders understand and practice visionary strategic planning. According to an article in *American Demographics*, Gary McIntosh of the American Society for Church Growth estimates that only 20 percent of America's 367,000 congregations actively pursue strategic planning. In the same article,

George Hunter, professor of evangelism and church growth at Asbury Theological Seminary, warns that churches without plans for growth invariably stagnate.[4]

Some churches have pursued strategic planning with the help of godly Christians who have been trained and have consulted mostly in the corporate world. The problem is that strategic planning pursued correctly is deeply theological, as I will show in part 2. Thus a vital tool in any consultant's toolbox should be theological preparation.

Some Church Leaders Do Not Value Strategic Planning

In some circles, strategic planning is not held in high regard. A number of business writers and consultants play down the importance of and even the need for strategic planning.[5] Karl Albrecht, for example, writes, "In the Western business world most *conventional* thinking about 'strategic planning,' that is, setting goals and making plans to achieve them, is misguided and obsolete."[6]

In his book *Thriving on Chaos*, Tom Peters presents a more balanced position that touches the heart of the problem: "Sound strategic direction has never been more important—which is why the strategic planning process must be truly decentralized. Yet strategic planning, as we conventionally conceive of it, has become irrelevant, or worse, damaging. What is a good strategic *plan*? There is none. But there is a good strategic planning process."[7]

The conventional or traditional concept of strategic planning, as practiced up to the present, has become somewhat obsolete and irrelevant. The problem is not with "strategy" but with the particular concept of strategy that predominates in most companies and churches that attempt it. A growing number of critics are rejecting strategy that is a pedantic, incremental planning ritual that assumes tomorrow is just a long-term extension of today. Peters is correct. It is not about a strategic plan; it is about a strategic process, an envisioning process. Ritualistic planning fails to provoke the deeper fundamental questions and debates about why the organization is, what it is, what drives it, where it is going, and how it will get there. Answering these questions is vital to an organization's health. Most often an organization's strategy begins with discussing what is and never gets around to asking what could be. It does not find room for dreaming dreams—God's dreams of what could be. For too many, a strategic plan means going through the motions of an annual planning event or slavishly following a long-range plan while ignoring the profound, cataclysmic transformation of the world outside.

Early in the twenty-first century, we at The Malphurs Group (my consulting ministry) believe that strategic planning isn't all about pedantic, incremental, long-range planning rituals. After all, in a world that is exploding with change, who can plan long-range anymore and who has time to be obsessively pedantic? I'm aware of one organization that plans no farther out than ninety days. You don't have to know or control the future to prepare for it and be successful as Christ's church and to accomplish his purpose. The key is to know who you are and what you are about. These are the kinds of ships that are weathering the storms of the early twenty-first century.

6. Addressing the Purpose of Strategic Planning

What is the purpose of strategic planning? What is the potential "payoff" for your ministry? Following are twenty-six purposes for strategic planning. I know that twenty-six is a lot, but they are really important to your church and worth the read. As you read them, check those that you feel are particularly important to your ministry. Circle those that are critical and demand immediate attention.

 1. *To discover the church's strengths, limitations, and weaknesses.* Every organization, whether Christian or not necessarily Christian, has strengths, limitations, and weaknesses. Out of all that it needs to accomplish for effective ministry, its strengths are what it accomplishes well and its weaknesses are what it does not accomplish well. Its limitations are those areas of ministry that it is not qualified to do and likely should not even attempt. The process of planning in this book asks the church's strategic leadership team to take some kind of ministry analysis (The Malphurs Group has designed and uses an online Church Ministry Analysis) in the preparation stage so that it will know what its limitations are.

 2. *To build on a ministry's strengths and minimize its weaknesses.* Some believe that leaders should seek to improve or at least minimize their ministry's weaknesses to become strong. This is not correct. To become strong, you must maximize those areas where you are strong and either work around or hire others to address the weaknesses.

 3. *To facilitate congregational communication and build the congregation's trust.* One of my oft-repeated statements to leaders and strategic planning teams about a congregation is, "If they do not trust you, you cannot lead them!" And one of the most important ways to win that trust is through truthful communication. When you fail to communicate what you are planning, people become suspicious. I will address this area in the preparation for planning stage.

 4. *To understand and implement spiritually healthy, Christ-honoring change.* To do this involves a theology of change. We must know what the Bible says about change so that we can know what must change and what must never change.

 5. *To get your people—leadership team and congregation—on the same page.* While this is impossible on every issue, it is possible on the major issues that really matter, such as who you are, where you are going, and how you will get there. As people agree on these issues, many others will fall into place as well, promoting church unity.

 6. *To encourage and promote spiritual revival.* While all churches need to experience spiritual revival, those that are tired, discouraged, and struggling needed to address it yesterday. Regardless, this is a vital step in assessing your ministry's

readiness for strategic planning. This establishes a spiritual foundation for the rest of the process.

7. *To discover and articulate your ministry core values.* This gets at your core identity, your DNA, or who you are as a church. The importance of core values is that you act on the basis of who you are. All the decisions you make are values-driven. Values are the key to knowing why you do what you do or do not do what you should do.

8. *To develop and communicate your God-given mission.* In addition to knowing who you are—your identity as a church—you need to know where you are going. This is a directional issue. Navigators use their compasses to get them to a port. Do you know your Christ-given direction? Do you have a ministry port?

9. *To develop and articulate an inspiring, compelling vision.* A dream—like a mission—addresses a ministry's direction and paints a picture of that destination. The result of a powerful dream is that people get excited about the church's future. Vision fuels a passion in your people to want to be a part of the future.

10. *To understand and relate more effectively to the community.* Every church is located in a community and is responsible to minister to that community. Acts 1:8 has geographical and ethnological implications. Where is your neighborhood? Who lives in your neighborhood? Who is unchurched and without Christ? To minister effectively to the community, you must know and understand your community and its culture, especially those who are unchurched.

11. *To develop a disciple-making process for the entire church.* The mission of the church is to "make disciples" (Matt. 28:19–20). The question is, How will your church accomplish this? The answer is to design a unique disciple-making process, using the maturity matrix in chapter 9 developed by The Malphurs Group (TMG) especially for churches.

12. *To assess, recruit, and develop a strong staff team.* Whether your staff consists of one person or one hundred, you must help them know who they are—their DNA (core values), their divine design (gifting, passion, and temperament), and where they fit best in ministry. You must constantly encourage them and put in place a leadership development process to help them grow deeply as leaders.

13. *To mobilize the congregation to serve and do the work of the ministry.* According to Ephesians 4:11–13, the congregation, not the pastor or staff, is to accomplish the church's ministry. This entails a three-step process of discovery, consultation, and involvement that launches the believer on a lifetime of ministry fruitfulness.

14. *To make wise decisions about the facilities and their location.* Churches must meet somewhere, and we have discovered that their care and the location of their facilities are strategically important to ministry to the community. Churches must determine if they are best positioned to reach their community or if they need to relocate for maximum effectiveness.

15. *To inventory and assess current giving.* What does the congregation think about giving? Do they understand what the Bible says about stewardship? Do they feel that the pastor preaches too much on giving or not enough? Are they willing to

give more or less? Church leadership needs to know what their people know and think about these core financial issues.

16. *To explore new streams of giving to increase current income.* Most churches are ministry-limited due to a lack of financial resources. The problem is that they depend on only one or at the most two sources of income when God provides others as well. Does your church know what these other sources are? How can you discover and explore these other sources?

17. *To design a stewardship strategy to help people be good stewards of their finances.* Churches must build good stewardship into their very fabric. People do not give what they should because most churches do not have in place a good strategy of stewardship that touches every ministry in a Christ-honoring way.

18. *To analyze and evaluate the church's budget, looking for ways to best handle congregational finances.* Simply because a church has a budget does not mean that it handles its funds wisely and biblically. Churches need to know how much money to direct toward personnel, programming, missions, and facilities. They need to discern whether the budget is outreach or in-reach oriented and where there is unnecessary waste.

19. *To raise additional funds and direct capital funding projects.* In addition to their normal giving, every church needs an occasional "kick in the pants." Churches need to explore ways and means of encouraging people to give sacrificially.

20. *To know how to implement the entire strategic plan.* A church can design the finest, most biblically oriented plan that never happens. Doing must follow thinking, and doing involves ministry implementation.

21. *To regularly evaluate and improve the church's ministries.* How does a church keep from growing stale and becoming brittle? How does a church improve what it does? The answer is ministry evaluation. Churches that constantly evaluate all phases of their ministries not only improve those ministries but also innovate well.

22. *To discover the ways God is blessing churches across America and abroad and why.* Most churches realize that it is not "worldly" to know what is going on in society and churches across America and the world. This helps them understand people as well as observe what God is doing.

23. *To know and work with the latest technology (internet, website, and other).* Churches must keep up with and employ technology in their ministries to best serve the Savior. Otherwise, they lag behind in needed technological development.

24. *To empower the governing board and pastor to lead with excellence.* It is imperative that pastors and their governing boards work together for effective ministry. This involves a policies approach that provides role guidelines and proper distribution of power.

25. *To build a lay and staff leadership development process.* All churches must develop their lay and staff leadership if they are to minister with impact. Many are talking about it, but few are doing it.

26. *To develop a marketing strategy that will best position the church in the community to glorify God.* The purpose of the church is to glorify God, especially among the unchurched, unbelieving people who make up the church's community.

7. Determining the Number of People Involved in Strategic Planning

I used to argue that the fewer people involved in the strategic planning process the better. It was the "too many cooks spoil the broth" mentality. And many would agree. However, I have changed my mind about this, based on my consulting ministry experience. When I help a church through the envisioning process, I ask that they select fifteen to twenty-five leaders if possible to work on the process. Smaller churches may have fewer people, depending on how many of their congregation are leaders.

Here are some of the reasons I like to work with a larger strategic leadership team:

- I have discovered that leaders miss meetings occasionally due to travel, vacations, family matters, children's involvement in sports, and so forth. On a larger team you will miss them, but you will still have enough people so that you can proceed without canceling or rescheduling the meeting.
- The more people you have, the better will be the representation of various church viewpoints.
- With a larger group there is less chance that the team will be made up of those holding to extreme or minority viewpoints that fail to represent the entire church.

In addition, there will be times when you will involve the entire congregation in the process. One such time is when you conduct various online surveys that we use, for example, in The Malphurs Group to discover what the church thinks about a particular issue, such as congregational giving.

8. Considering the Time for Strategic Planning

The two most frequently asked questions regarding the strategic process concern time commitment and cost. A characteristic of most people in the twenty-first century, especially in urban North America and urban centers abroad, is busyness and limited discretionary time. Consequently, people's time is a major factor that leaders and pastors must consider in attempting the strategic planning process.

How Long Will It Take?

The question on many people's minds is, How long will it take? I would allow from six months to a year to work through the initial envisioning process. (The use of a good consultant will speed this process so it may take only six to nine months.) During this time, the team meets every third to fourth week. To wait longer than this between meetings diminishes the team's momentum, which is most difficult to regain. People tend to forget what they have accomplished and the excitement rubs off. This is the reason I ask for a strong commitment up front, which I will say more about at the end of this chapter.

The SLTs that I work with often like to meet on Friday evenings—from around 6:00 to 9:00 p.m.—and Saturday mornings from 8:00 a.m. to noon. There are three benefits to these times. First, it breaks up an eight-hour, intensive, exhausting session into two sessions with time to rest and recuperate between. Second, these are the times of the day when people are at their best and can give their best mentally (though some struggle with the Friday evening session). Finally, not only do the team members not give up their weekends, but they also have much of their Saturdays left for families or other personal matters. The only conflict I have experienced is with children's or adults' sporting events that take place on Saturday mornings.

Here is what is generally covered during the first six monthly meetings:

First meeting: preparation for strategic envisioning, including the results of the online church analysis (chaps. 1 and 2) as well as implementation (chap. 3)

Second meeting: mission and vision (chaps. 4 and 5)

Third meeting: values, introduction to the ministry strategy, and reaching the church's community (chap. 6)

Fourth meeting: a strategy for disciple making (chap. 9) and building a ministry team (chap. 10)

Fifth meeting: ministry setting (chap. 11)

Sixth meeting: raising finances (chap. 12)

Keep in mind that I am a professional consultant who uses various time-saving tools that speed up the process. So be sure to give yourself some room and add a few more weeks to your schedule.

You are not finished when you have completed the initial process and begin implementing the results. The process will continue for the life of the church. When the leadership of a ministry ceases to think and act strategically, the ministry will not survive times of chaotic and overwhelming cultural change. After completing the initial process, however, the leadership may or may not continue to use the SLT. My advice is to continue to use the team but not meet as frequently and address only major ministry issues.

Other Time Factors

Some other factors that affect planning time are the degree of initial agreement on core issues such as values and mission, the availability of data, and the use of creative, time-saving techniques such as storyboarding. I will say more about the latter at the end of this chapter.

9. Weighing the Cost of Strategic Planning

Another concern for most ministries as they consider strategic planning is cost. Can we afford to do strategic planning? It is a legitimate concern because several cost commitments may be involved. However, they are not exorbitant.

There may be an expense for the personnel who are responsible for doing the primary crafting of the process, unless the staff are already on the payroll. Should the church decide that it is best for the strategists to get away periodically for their planning sessions, their travel, meals, and lodging would be additional expenses.

If a church follows my advice and uses a consultant, this will, of course, entail a fee. But the difference a good, qualified consultant makes to the process may be the difference between success and failure. A few denominations have consultants on staff and provide their services at little cost to the church. Independent consultants charge from five hundred to several thousand dollars a day. Usually, the better consultants charge the higher fee. But it is critical for you to consider the value of a consultant who can serve your needs. What is it worth, not only in terms of money but also in terms of saving people's time? Churches that use a good consultant usually see their giving increase to the point that it more than covers the consultant's remuneration. This happens because the consultant helps them understand and implement good financial stewardship programs. Also, as the consultant guides the church toward good spiritual health, people tend to give more. An example would be the church's application of the information in chapter 12 of this book on raising finances. In some churches that I have consulted with, a congregant has stepped up and covered my costs. (Perhaps pastors should approach such gifted people in their churches and ask them to cover the expense.)

There may also be some cost for good research. Those who do strategic planning must do some research—especially in the community phase—and possibly an environmental analysis. This research looks at trends in both the secular world and evangelical churches by using demographic and psychographic materials. However, those who provide these research materials charge nominal fees for the information. I will say more about this in chapter 8.

If your ministry is on the plateaued or downward side of the organizational growth cycle (see the figure in the introduction), then the question likely is not, Can we afford to do strategic planning? The better question is, Can we afford not to?

Strategizing Cost Factors

- Cost of ministry personnel
- Cost of any travel, meals, and lodging
- Cost of a qualified consultant
- Cost of research (demographics and psychographics)

10. Deciding on the Location for Strategic Planning

The strategic planning team will need a place to do its work, a place that allows for the best thinking and acting.

The Church Facility

As long as it has all the items that a team needs to do planning, such as a whiteboard with markers or at least a chalkboard, the church facility will be a good place to accomplish much of the work. In fact that is where I do most of the work with my teams. I like to arrange the tables in a U shape, with chairs around the outside (see the diagram under storyboarding later in this chapter). Hopefully the church can provide a light breakfast, lunch, or supper, and coffee, water, and snacks between sessions.

The Team Center

Taking a cue from the people at Disney World, innovative companies are developing team centers where their people gather to do some of their most creative work. Team centers are resource-rich rooms where people work together, using creative thinking and planning techniques.

A church could create a team center within its own facility. The ideal is a room with the most current technologies, such as internet access and video equipment, and ample wall space for visualization techniques, whiteboards, and proper projection for computer presentations. If such a center is not available, a classroom will suffice. What a team needs is sufficient room for a group of about fifteen to twenty-five people to meet comfortably around a table. I do some of my most creative church work in a classroom with an LPC projector, dry erase markers, and spacious whiteboards.

Other Facilities

Though the team will accomplish much of its work at the church, it would be wise to get away periodically and use other facilities for longer planning sessions. Often these meetings prove to be highly creative with few interruptions. Teams have used such places as a large private house, a conference center, a private club, a lake house or mountain cabin, a hotel or motel meeting room, and the boardroom of a bank or other professional organization. Some teams accomplish more by spending the night at a conference center or motel. However, I prefer not to travel too far because sleeping in one's own bed and seeing one's family makes for more productive work the next day.

11. Using Creative Tools for Strategic Planning

I divide the creative tools needed for strategic planning into two categories: functional tools and process tools.

Functional Tools

Functional tools are those items that a leader needs simply to function well and accomplish the process. I have already mentioned most of these above. They consist of the following: a whiteboard and dry erase markers or a chalkboard, a large paper pad and an easel, an LPC or similar quality projector for PowerPoint presentations plus a screen, and possibly an overhead projector.

Process Tools

In my consulting and training ministry and at my church, I use several helpful creative tools that save time and enhance the planning process as well as other leadership activities. I refer to them as process tools.

I discovered some of these tools in Mike Vance and Diane Deacon's book *Think Out of the Box*.[8] They have created them or collected them from others, and Vance popularized them at the Disney Company. However, I have personalized and altered the tools so that they match my style and best facilitate the particular activity I happen to be conducting. I want to focus on four process tools: brainstorming, storyboarding, scale of 1 to 10, and consensus.

BRAINSTORMING

Use: I use brainstorming when a group needs to generate as many ideas as possible over a short period of time. It works well anytime during a session except at the end, for it does not bring closure.

Participants: The participants are usually teams, such as a board, planning group, or church-planting core group.

Setting: Brainstorming takes place best in a semiformal environment where there will be no interruptions.

Purposes: Brainstorming accomplishes several purposes. It stimulates a quick, free flow of numerous ideas. It generates and often captures important preliminary concepts. And it gives ownership of these concepts to the participants.

Characteristics: Brainstorming is fast paced, positive, smooth running, and nonconfrontational. The leader will need to establish and enforce the following ground rules: no confrontation or criticism of ideas (defer any negative thoughts or feelings), no speeches, and quantity is more important than quality. For later thought and use, the various concepts should be recorded.

Process: I conduct brainstorming sessions by gathering the group together, explaining the purpose for the session, and announcing the topic, often in the form of a question. Examples of topics are: How can we find more space for our crowded children's ministry? What could we do to reach out to some of the ethnic groups in our community? Then I announce the ground rules given above. As people voice their ideas, I ask one member of the group to write them down. When people run out of ideas, it is time to stop the exercise.

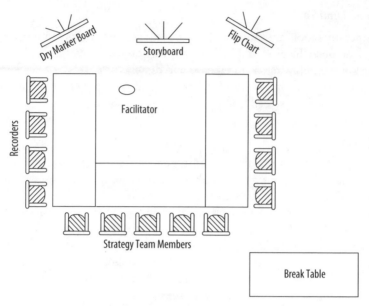

Storyboarding Room Arrangement

Storyboarding

I have used storyboarding more than any other tool in my leadership toolkit, and more leaders have asked me to teach them the storyboard process than any other tool. I always use it when discovering core values. Some refer to it as compression planning because it condenses planning processes into a short period of time.

Use: Storyboarding helps teams accomplish a number of different tasks but is especially helpful in planning. Unlike other tools that are used as part of a bigger process, storyboarding is a complete process in itself.

Participants: As few as five people or as many as twenty-five to thirty people may be involved in storyboarding. The figure above shows you how to arrange the tables where the participants sit in relation to the storyboard and the facilitator. The facilitator is responsible for guiding the process, encouraging participation and idea development, and keeping the group on track. I suggest that a group have at least two recorders, depending on the number of people who will write down words and ideas on the 8-by-6-inch Post-it notes as the participants call them out.

Setting: Storyboarding should take place in a location where there will be no interruptions.

Purposes: Storyboarding helps teams do planning in a shorter period of time than by using other methods. It also accomplishes problem solving. A third purpose is to help a ministry discover its core values.

Characteristics: Storyboarding involves creative thinking (brainstorming) and critical thinking (a workout, described below).

Process: First, you will need to purchase the proper supplies—four 8-by-6-inch Post-it notepads, a package of one-quarter-inch red dots (Avery products are excellent), and three to four blue, felt tip, dry erase markers.

I begin storyboarding by explaining the four rules, presented on a PowerPoint slide or Post-it notes. The four rules that apply to only the brainstorming part of storyboarding are the following:

1. Suspend all judgment
2. Quantity, not quality
3. Please, no speeches
4. No killer phrases

Examples of killer phrases are: *We have never done it that way before. That's not in the budget. It cannot be done.* You may want to give each participant three small foam balls to be thrown at people who violate the rules. This serves to break tension and facilitate fun. (If you are a very serious person, and the thought of throwing foam balls at one another is appalling, then don't do it.)

I explain what we hope to accomplish in the storyboarding session. I have written this on a Post-it note that is placed below the four rules. One example could be "to discover our core values." Another is "to develop a mission or a vision statement."

The first part of the exercise is a brainstorming or creative thinking session. If the group is discovering the church's core values, for example, the participants call out what they believe are the church's values—strong leadership, evangelism, celebrative worship, and others. The recorders write the responses on Post-it notes, and a volunteer places them on a 4-by-8-foot whiteboard. This part may go on for fifteen to twenty minutes.

When the facilitator senses that the group has exhausted their ideas, then it is time to shift to part two. This is the workout, or critical thinking, process. During this time the group will prioritize ideas, look for trends and recurring themes, remove any duplicates or false concepts, refine and collate concepts, and tie up any loose ends. If the group is discovering core values, they will debate and eliminate values that are not true of the ministry, toss duplicate values, and identify items that are not actually values.

I have found it helpful in prioritizing ideas to give each participant a limited number of one-quarter-inch red dots. Then I ask them to come up during the break and stick the red dots on the Post-it notes with the most important ideas. If we are discovering core values, they would place the dots on the statements they believe are the actual values of the organization. Then we can quickly eliminate any ideas without dots.

A wonderful feature of the storyboarding process is that no one has to take notes. When you are finished, you merely collect the Post-it notes and give them to a secretary who will compile and record them for future use.

Do not allow all the detail to discourage you from using this tool. Once I learned how to do it, I began to use it all the time. And the only way to learn how is to practice it until you become proficient. It is a very visual and creative process that will save you much time in strategic thinking and acting and any other work you may attempt for the Savior. If you wish to know more about storyboarding, check out the website of the McNellis Company (www.mcnellis co.com).

Scale of 1 to 10

A quick way to discover where people are on a particular decision or issue is to use the scale of 1 to 10 (see the scales in the preplanning checklist at the end of this chapter). If the leader of a group such as a board wants to know where people stand on an issue, he or she can ask each one for a number between 1 and 10. A 1 says the person is strongly against the issue, and a 10 indicates that he or she is adamantly for it. A 5 or 6 means not sure.

If all those in a group give a 10 to a particular issue, such as a change of worship style from traditional to contemporary or hiring a new staff person, then the leader can move forward without unnecessary discussion. The leader knows that the group is convinced of or behind the proposal or decision. If most of them give a 1, this signals that they do not support the issue. Since it is obvious that the group is decidedly opposed, the leader will not want to spend time discussing the issue any further. When most members of the group give a 5 or 6, it shows that they are undecided and need to spend some time in discussion.

Consensus

Some argue that church boards and committees should not take action unless they are unanimous in their decision. However, a unanimous decision is a rare occurrence in the real world of church boards and committees. Often church people do not see issues the same way. This is one of the reasons for working in teams—to get other people's viewpoints. But to come to a decision, two options are available: compromise and consensus.

Some leaders pursue compromise when a unanimous decision is needed. They encourage everyone to give a little or a lot for the sake of the entire church. This prevents gridlock and supposedly promotes unity. However, my experience is that when people have to compromise their views, no one is happy or supportive, regardless of the decision.

A second and much better option is consensus. To best understand consensus decision making, we will first probe what it is and then what it is not.

What consensus is: Team or board members approach a decision with the attitude that they will attempt to support the decision of the team—even if they disagree with it—because their view has received a fair hearing. If they feel that for the sake of conscience they cannot agree with the majority decision, then they agree to disagree and to not cause a disturbance or talk about it with others in the congregation. The point is that they have had their "day in court" and were not able to convince the jury (the rest of the team).

What consensus is not: Consensus decision making, as I am using it here, must not be confused with majority rule as practiced by the typical church. Many churches practice majority rule by asking the congregation to vote on various matters, from the color of the new carpet to a new pastor. Sometimes you want the majority to rule, for example, when you want to know if people will financially support a new building proposal. If you begin a building program and your people are against it, the church will incur an insurmountable debt from which it might never recover. The problem with majority rule is that most churches have more immature believers than mature believers. Thus the spiritually immature could control the direction or lack thereof in the church. This happened with the majority and minority reports from the twelve spies that Moses sent in to spy out the Promised Land (Numbers 13). Contrary to God's direction, the majority (ten leaders) voted not to enter the land (Deut. 1:26).

The difference between consensus, as I am using it, and majority vote is the people involved. The people who make up the ministry teams, leadership boards, and staffs of many congregations are usually a group of spiritually mature people and are able to make decisions by consensus. Much effective ministry in the New Testament was accomplished by such teams. The history of the church in Acts is replete with the names of various Pauline teams consisting of godly people. How might a group of mature leaders come to a decision when disagreement exists? The answer is consensus or a majority vote on the part of the spiritual leaders who make up the team. This approach will save you countless hours of fruitless discussion. Often only one person will hold a differing position, but no one knows it until someone (usually the team leader) calls for the question and people vote. I give such a person one to two or three minutes at the most to speak and then I call for a vote.

12. Using an Outside Consultant for Strategic Planning

I believe that, if possible, a church is wise to employ the services of an outside consultant for strategic planning. A consultant can make a significant difference in several ways.

A good church consultant has the experience, expertise, and time that your leadership staff simply doesn't have. The advent of ministry learning organizations, the explosion of knowledge, and the fast pace of communication make it nearly impossible for a senior pastor or an executive leadership team to remain knowledgeable of new methods and ministry paradigms that God is blessing. In addition, projects that require new skills and lots of time bombard leaders almost daily. In today's fast-paced, ever-changing world, churches have difficulty hiring enough knowledgeable people just to keep up with normal, ongoing ministries. Strategic minded churches and other ministry organizations are increasingly turning to ministry consultants to help them fill the knowledge and time gap for the many special situations that arise. These consultants bring to bear their expertise and years of ministry experience gained from other projects and other ministry organizations.

Good church consultants provide flexibility for their client churches. The typical church can bring them in for short-term knowledge acquisition, skills development, strategic planning, and other ministry projects. Much as Jethro in Exodus 18:24–27, they're there when you need them and gone when you don't. They come on the scene, serve your purpose, and then disappear. That way they do not get underfoot. Many also offer coaching on the phone or over the internet, which provides the time flexibility that busy leaders need.

A good church consultant provides a fresh, objective point of view. Most consultants have other projects under their belts, providing valuable experience in dealing with an array of ministry situations and leadership personalities. Through these they develop fresh, unbiased approaches to ministry. This "cross-pollination" of ideas and experiences from other similar ministries allows a church to tap into the brain power and strategies of those ministries. Often the pastor or leadership staff are too close to their situation to see the problems and potential solutions that a good, objective consultant recognizes almost immediately. In addition, the consultant doesn't have to tolerate but can address any internal politics or power plays that some use to short-circuit healthy, biblical change.

A good church consultant provides maximum ministry efficiency for the following reasons.

- They bring experience with similar situations or problems so that they don't need to take valuable time to get "up to speed."
- Senior pastors, other leadership staff, or volunteer leaders have to accomplish their "normal" assignments in addition to any special projects. To become knowledgeable and give attention to a special project on top of many other responsibilities is nearly impossible. Consultants, however, have the luxury of focusing all their expertise on the special projects and assignments for which you've retained them.
- They don't have to deal with the church's necessary, daily tasks, such as attending staff meetings, returning phone calls or answering emails from congregants, putting out fires, and dealing with other policies and procedures. Armed with ministry tools, such as the storyboarding process, they complete their assignments in one-half to one-fourth the time.

When it comes to the bottom line, a good church consultant is more cost effective for the ministry organization. The question is which is more cost effective, using a consultant or hiring a new staff person? Hired staff require a regular paycheck along with other benefits, such as a health package, retirement, and possibly a severance package. However, consultants serve you much as another staff person without the additional overhead. They work with you on an as-needed basis. The ministry has the benefit of an additional, specialized staff person without all the added financial overhead that comes with new staff.

A second vital question is whether a church can afford *not* to use a specialist where a specialist's expertise is needed, especially if the ministry is "stuck" and its future is hanging in the balance. If the project fails due to the use of someone in-house, some people in the church may not give the leadership a second chance.

A good church consultant brings a solid grounding in the Bible and theology to the ministry situation. Ministry with and to churches is deeply theological. It's critical that a consultant have a thorough grounding in theology that he or she brings to the ministry situation. We have discovered that good biblical, theological preparation is vital to the consulting equation. That is the reason The Malphurs Group uses only consultants who have biblical-theological training in a church or seminary context.

Finally, various leaders, ministries, and churches used consultants in the Bible. They simply didn't call them consultants. For example, in Exodus 18 Moses was at a ministry sticking point, and God brought Jethro (possibly an unbeliever) into the picture to help him get unstuck and move forward. The same holds true for Paul, Timothy, and Titus. Paul consulted with and advised both Timothy and Titus as well as numerous churches. Some mistakenly believe that Timothy and Titus were pastors. However, Paul used Timothy and Titus to go from church to church to consult with pastors and congregations. Today's consultants have a similar ministry.[9]

The Commitment to Strategic Planning

The Church Must Commit to the Process

If a church is not ready to commit strongly to strategic planning, it must not commence the process. Conventional wisdom affirms that all meaningful action flows out of a commitment. Where commitment exists, one finds an environment that is open to engaging the challenges presented by congregational development today. Where it does not exist, there is little heart to drive such an effort.

But what do I mean by a strong commitment? Two actual illustrations from my experience should help. I worked with one church that believed it was a good idea to pursue planning strategically but was not ready to commit strongly to it. Thus if it had a choice between meeting for planning purposes or pursuing some ministry in the church, the latter won out every time. When I contacted them and urged them to set up a meeting, I was met with silence. Eventually they followed through, but the meeting times became so far apart that people lost their initial enthusiasm and knowledge of what we were about, and they stopped showing up. Eventually, due to lack of interest, the whole thing died.

By way of contrast, another church informed me right from the start that they normally put on a major Easter pageant that they are known for in the community at the time when they wished to pursue the strategic planning process. However, the latter was so important that they wanted to know if it was okay to cancel the pageant so that they could give their maximum time and attention to the strategic planning process. That is the kind of commitment that churches in general and leaders in particular (especially the pastor) must make if they are to be successful. It cannot be business as usual.

The Pastor Must Commit to the Church

There is a second commitment. Not only must the church be committed to the process, but the pastor must commit to the church as it works through the process. The average pastoral tenure in America is three to four years, which has proved devastating to many churches. Before I begin to lead a church through the strategic envisioning process, I ask for a commitment from the senior pastor to the church as well as to the process. Should he leave during the process or soon after completing the process, not only would the impact on the church be traumatic, but it would also negate much of the church's strategic planning work.

On one occasion, I was visiting with a church that was considering using me as a consultant to take them through the process. The pastor picked me up at the airport. During our one-hour drive to the church, I asked him how his ministry was progressing, and he told me that things were not going well. I explained to him that he must commit to be with the church after completing the strategic planning process if the church was to benefit from it. After that visit I did not hear from him again and later learned that he was no longer at the church. He did the right thing; he did what was best for the church by leaving before beginning the process rather than during or soon after its completion.

Comparison of Conventional and Visionary Strategic Planning

Strategic Elements	Conventional Strategic Planning	Visionary Strategic Planning
1. Learning	Learns from past sources. Tends to preserve and rearrange established categories.	Learns from all sources (one's own and others' experiences plus research). Creates new categories.
2. Thinking	Analysis—breaks goals down into steps and formalizes and follows them relentlessly. It's very "neat."	Synthesis—uses intuition and creativity as well as analysis, constantly pulling things together in new ways and combinations. It's very "messy."
3. Questions	What was or what is?	What could be?
4. Time	Past orientation. It works forward from the past. It is long-term and brings the past forward with it.	Future orientation. It works backward from the future. It's more short-term and tends to break with the past.
5. Change	Assumes little change will take place.	Assumes much change will take place.
6. Future	More of the same—we can anticipate the future.	Little of the same—we can create the future.

Strategic Elements	Conventional Strategic Planning	Visionary Strategic Planning
7. Relationship	May impede visionary strategic planning.	May include some conventional elements.
8. Control	Centralized—stick to the plan.	Decentralized—add to and adjust the plan.
9. Team	Less team involvement.	More team involvement.
10. Decision making	Compromise.	Consensus.
11. Planning	Long-range.	Short-range.
12. Process	Formal (by the book).	Less formal (more open).

Preplanning Checklist

By any chance, did you fail to read the introduction to this book? If so, please go back and read it before proceeding to the next chapter. It has a lot of important information that will help you plan for strategic planning. After reading the introduction and chapter 1, you are ready to respond to the preplanning checklist that follows.

Using the scale of 1 to 10, rate how well you believe your ministry is prepared to think and act strategically. Circle the appropriate number under questions one through four (1 indicates strongly against, 10 strongly for, and 5 or 6 not sure).

1. Is the lead pastor a turnaround pastor?

Comments:

2. Is this ministry willing to take the necessary time to do strategic planning?

Comments:

3. Is the church willing to spend the necessary funds to think and act strategically?

Comments:

4. Is this organization willing to meet in the best possible place to accomplish its planning?

Comments:

5. Which of the strategic thinking process tools would help you in your ministry? Which ones will you try? Which will you not attempt? Why?
6. Do you believe that you would be wise to enlist the help of a consultant in the planning process? Why or why not? If your answer is no and the reason is that you cannot afford one, do you believe that you can afford not to use one?
7. If you desire to begin the strategic planning process, what kind of commitment are you willing to make to the process? What are you willing to do or set aside to see it done well?

Turnaround Pastors Audit

Gordon E. Penfold, DMin and Aubrey Malphurs, PhD

Directions: Circle the answer that best describes you. Then add the numbers of your answers for your score.

1. My score on the DiSC profile is a 4 or higher on either the D or I or both.

   1. True   2. More true than false   3. More false than true   4. False

2. I'm a passionate visionary who attracts followers.

   1. True   2. More true than false   3. More false than true   4. False

3. I've had in the past and have now a mentor or coach in my life.

   1. True   2. More true than false   3. More false than true   4. False

4. I'm more innovative than traditional.

   1. True   2. More true than false   3. More false than true   4. False

5. I'm outgoing and have above average people skills.

   1. True   2. More true than false   3. More false than true   4. False

6. I'm very energetic.

   1. True   2. More true than false   3. More false than true   4. False

7. When it comes to ministry, I think like a young person regardless my age.

   1. True   2. More true than false   3. More false than true   4. False

8. I prefer to work with a team as opposed to working alone.

   1. True   2. More true than false   3. More false than true   4. False

9. I'm a delegator.

   1. True   2. More true than false   3. More false than true   4. False

10. I'm good at training leaders.

   1. True   2. More true than false   3. More false than true   4. False

11. I'm focused and determined in ministry.

   1. True   2. More true than false   3. More false than true   4. False

12. I'm quick to embrace change.

   1. True   2. More true than false   3. More false than true   4. False

13. I'm good at resolving conflicts.

   1. True   2. More true than false   3. More false than true   4. False

14. I'm good at solving problems.

   1. True   2. More true than false   3. More false than true   4. False

15. People say that I am an able communicator.

   1. True   2. More true than false   3. More false than true   4. False

16. People view me as a more directive, not a passive, leader.

   1. True   2. More true than false   3. More false than true   4. False

17. I believe that it's important to have both a mission and a vision.

   1. True   2. More true than false   3. More false than true   4. False

18. I passionately communicate our mission and vision.

   1. True   2. More true than false   3. More false than true   4. False

19. I don't believe that the age of the pastor is a factor in revitalizing churches.

   1. True   2. More true than false   3. More false than true   4. False

20. I empower people to use their giftedness in ministry.

   1. True   2. More true than false   3. More false than true   4. False

21. I'm a self-starter.

    1. True   2. More true than false   3. More false than true   4. False

22. Strong relationships are important to me.

    1. True   2. More true than false   3. More false than true   4. False

23. I believe that it's important to make the gospel relevant in the community.

    1. True   2. More true than false   3. More false than true   4. False

24. I'm effective at ministering to all generations.

    1. True   2. More true than false   3. More false than true   4. False

25. My wife and I are prepared to pay the price to lead change.

    1. True   2. More true than false   3. More false than true   4. False

Total your score: _____

If your score is:

25–43: You definitely have what it takes to be a turnaround pastor/leader. God seems to have wired you to revitalize struggling churches.

44–62: You may be a turnaround pastor/leader. Chances increase the lower your score. Chances decrease the higher your score. Note areas with high scores and attempt to improve them if possible.

63–81: Chances are that you may not be a turnaround pastor/leader. The higher your score the less likely you are a revitalization pastor. Note areas with high scores and attempt to improve them if possible. Perhaps you're wired for another ministry position.

82–100: You're not likely a turnaround pastor/leader. And that's okay. God seems to have wired you to do some other ministry.

Questions for Reflection, Discussion, and Application

1. Based on the characteristics of a turnaround pastor and the Turnaround Pastors Audit, are you a turnaround or a non-turnaround pastor? How might this knowledge be helpful to you as a leader?
2. Do you believe that strategic planning is important? Why or why not?

3. Is the author's definition of strategic planning helpful? What about this definition impacted you most?

4. Do you believe that strategic planning is biblical? Why or why not? If so, does any particular biblical reference stand out?

5. The author covers several reasons why strategic planning or envisioning is needed. Do any apply to you? If so, which?

6. The author cites twenty-six purposes for strategic planning. Which ones seem most important to you and your church?

7. How many people do you plan to involve in your strategic planning?

8. How long do you think it will take you to work through the strategic planning process?

9. Do you believe that you can afford to do strategic planning? Why or why not? Do you plan to use a consultant or do it yourself?

10. Where do you plan to meet to work through strategic planning?

11. Which strategic planning tools are or will be most important to you?

12. The author makes a case for using a consultant. Did he convince you? If so, what was it that persuaded you? If not, why not?

13. Is the pastor of the church committed to the process? Why or why not? Is the church committed to the process? Why or why not?

2

Preparing the Crew

Readiness for the Process

As I said in chapter 1, it is critical that lead navigators of sailing vessels take time to prepare their boats before they attempt the process of navigating any body of water, whether a lake or the ocean. They have to prepare to sail! To accomplish this, they often use a prelaunch checklist of every item on the boat to make sure that each is fully working, from the head (bathroom for you nonsailors) to the hull and the boom to the bowsprit. The maxim is, "If you have it, it should work." This is especially true of the boat's safety equipment. Do you have a fire extinguisher, life jackets, a radio, a first-aid kit, and so on? Failure to properly prepare could result in the loss not only of the boat but of a life as well.

But it is not enough simply to prepare your boat. You must prepare the people who will be on board that boat. Are they ready to set sail and begin the journey, and if not, what needs to be done to get them ready? Primarily this involves the crew who sail the boat. They need to know where the boat is going and what it will take to get it there as well as the potential problems they may face along the way.

Sailing a boat has much in common with strategic planning, especially the preparation of people for the journey. It is imperative that leaders prepare their team for the process before venturing out of port. Consequently, this chapter covers seven steps that strategic planners must take to determine the church's readiness for the process that I will cover in parts 2 and 3—the rest of this book. They are enlisting the support of the church's empowered leadership, recruiting a strategic leadership team, improving communication with the congregation, assessing the church's readiness for change, conducting a church ministry analysis, setting reasonable time expectations, and laying a spiritual foundation for the process.

Step 1. Enlist the Support of the Empowered Leadership

My wife and I married at a young age and had all but one child while in our twenties. The result is that we are young grandparents. Our grandchild, Maria, is, of course, the most intelligent child on the face of the earth! My wife taught her how to read at the age of three and one-half. She was ready; otherwise, any attempts at teaching her to read would have been futile. The point is that each child is unique in his or her intellectual development, and not every child—no matter how intelligent—is ready or able to read at three and one-half.

The readiness of churches to begin strategic envisioning varies, just as it does with children and their learning to read. To attempt to force the process on an unwilling subject is not wise. So it's important to ask if this church is ready to pursue strategic planning. How can you know if your ministry is ready to proceed with the process? The answer begins with the church's empowered leadership. Here I am not using the term *empowered* in a negative way. There is power in every organization, including the church, and that is neither good nor bad. The question here is, Are the people with the power supportive of embracing the strategic planning process? These empowered people are the church's governing board, pastor, staff, and any matriarch or patriarch. Ultimately, they must support the process if it is to succeed.

The Board's Attitude toward Strategic Planning

The first step in preparing a church for strategic planning is to assess the openness of the church governing board toward the process. Most churches have a board or several boards that function in some capacity. In most smaller churches, the board runs things, due to their high pastoral turnover (on average every three to four years). In larger churches, especially those with more than five hundred people, the staff often runs the church, and the board's role may involve monitoring the senior pastor or it may be a diminished role. In the smaller board-run churches, if the board does not support strategic thinking and acting, it will not happen. For example, if the pastor pushes it, even if board members like him, they may drag their feet or simply fail to act. If the pastor pushes it and they do not like him, they will argue with him and vote it down.

Before taking a small church, the potential pastor who is change-oriented should use the Readiness for Change Inventory in appendix A of this book or selected questions from it to assess where the board stands on change. The pastor who finds himself in a church with a change-resistant board needs to be patient with them and not be quick to abandon them. I recommend that he take at least three to five years—preferably five—to bring them along with him in his thinking, through education (reading books together on strategy and change), through visiting change-friendly churches that plan strategically, and through personal, individual counsel. If the church is struggling and in decline, sometimes these boards will open up by taking a church ministry analysis, which may help to pull their heads out of the sand of denial and to face the reality that the ministry is in deep trouble and in need of an urgent overhaul before it is too late, if it is not too late already.

The Pastor's Attitude toward Strategic Planning

A second key to knowing if your church is ready to pursue strategic planning is the attitude of the pastor, or the senior pastor in a multistaff situation. If the pastor sees the need for and understands the importance of strategic planning, the process has a chance, depending on his ability to persuade the board and other leaders. (Most often in my consulting experience it is the pastor who first contacts us and initiates the process.) If he does not see the need, the process simply will not happen. He will not push for it, and it will die for lack of a second.

Why might a pastor oppose strategic thinking and acting? One answer is lack of awareness. He may not be aware of or understand the process. Another is he may be resistant to change. Some temperaments fear or are suspicious of change. For those familiar with the temperament tools, they tend to be the S and C temperaments on the Personal Profile (DiSC System),[1] and the SJs on the Myers-Briggs Type Indicator.[2]

A third reason a pastor may resist strategic envisioning (planning) is that he is an old-paradigm thinker who lives and ministers in the past. Much of the change that has affected ministry has passed him by. Thus he sees no need to plan strategically. He is convinced that if something seems to no longer work, the staff needs simply to redouble its efforts and work harder. (These are the people who in my map metaphor in chapter 1 get lost faster.)

A pastor may also fear failure. Making the kinds of deep changes that turn a ministry in a new direction requires the leader to take some big risks and step outside his and others' comfort zones. He has no guarantee that the church will follow him. Thus he is vulnerable as he walks into the land of uncertainty and the real possibility of failure. For many this is a terrifying choice that involves a dark night of the soul.

I have discovered that some strong, gifted, high-energy leaders—especially those with leadership gifts but no administrative abilities—find it difficult to take the time for any strategic envisioning. They neglect it at their own peril. Avoiding or rushing through strategic development is characteristic of a "quick fix" mentality. The result is a symptomatic solution that is temporary in nature because it fails to address the key issues of ministry at a fundamental level. Leaders who resist strategic planning would be wise to recruit, learn from, and work closely with those who have gifts and abilities in this area.

The Staff's Attitude toward Strategic Planning

A third key to knowing if the church is ready is the attitude of the church's staff. This may range from only one person, such as a worship leader or youth pastor, in a smaller church to one hundred or more people in a megachurch.

Regardless of the number of staff, it is important that they be on board the strategic planning boat when it sets sail, as they are the ones who will be heavily involved in the implementation of the resulting plan or a part thereof. If the board and the senior pastor support the process, most likely it will happen. However, if the staff is not on board, they can undermine the process by dragging their ministry feet. If asked why they did not implement some phase of the plan in their ministry, they may say that they are so busy that they just did not get around to it, when the real reason is that they did not want to implement it and do not support it.

Why might a staff person resist implementing the process? Here are a few reasons that have to do primarily with change: a lack of awareness of change and the change process, a fear or suspicion of change, an old-paradigm perspective that clings to the past, a fear of failure, a preference for the status quo, and not wanting to take the time to change.

In these situations, the board and senior pastor must be patient with these people, giving them some time to get on board (this assumes of course that the church is not in steep decline and has some time to help staff members change their minds). However, if they fail to come around, the senior leadership must look for new staff to take their place. While letting staff go is always an unpleasant experience, in this situation it could mean the difference between the life or death of the church. In the long term, these staff people will be happier and more productive in a ministry where they fit better.

The Patriarch's or Matriarch's Attitude toward Strategic Planning

In many small churches and some large churches, there is a patriarch or matriarch who is an empowered person. Most often it is a man or woman who was born and raised in the church's community, has been at the church since its inception, and will be there until he or she dies. What you must understand is that the typical small church has seen a number of pastors come and go over a short period of time (typically every three to four years). However, long-term members are not going anywhere and have earned the congregation's respect, so people trust them and grant them much power. The congregation knows that the patriarch or matriarch will be there long after the current pastor is gone. This person may or may not have an official leadership position, but he or she exercises tremendous influence even if the church has a pastor.

Most often this person is spiritual and committed to the Lord, but not always. Pastors who serve small churches in particular need to be aware of the presence of a patriarch or matriarch and his or her importance to the church. If the patriarch or matriarch is not for strategic planning, it will not happen. I advise any leaders who pastor churches with these people to cultivate them spiritually. Spend quality spiritual time with them. Meet with them at least once a week for prayer and relationship building. Get to know them and their hearts. Run your ideas by them first. Their response will let you know whether or not they will support your efforts, especially in regard to strategic planning.

Four Readiness Keys for Strategic Planning

1. The governing board's attitude toward the process
2. The pastor's attitude toward the process
3. The staff's attitude toward the process
4. The patriarch's or matriarch's attitude toward the process

Probing the readiness of each of these will let you know whether or not to pursue strategic planning. Again, the governing board, the pastor, the staff, and a patriarch or matriarch must generally be on board for it to happen.

Once I received a phone call from a man who attended a somewhat large church somewhere in the Northeast. He had read the first edition of this book and wanted to know if I would come help his struggling church do strategic planning. I asked if he thought the pastor would be in favor of this. His answer was no. Then I asked about the board. Again he said no. Finally, I inquired about the staff and received the same answer. I told him that he could do us both a favor by saving his money and my time. I explained that in light of the attitude of these people and their influence in the church, it was likely that strategic planning would not happen, at least not then. After hearing my comments, he was quick to agree with me.

Step 2. Recruit a Strategic Leadership Team

Critical to any church's readiness for ministry are the people who make up its leadership. A ministry is only as good as the people who lead it. Therefore the question is, Who will be involved in the strategic planning process? The answer is not those who are willing volunteers and faithful followers but who are not leaders. The tendency is to fill a team with people like these, because they are such faithful servants. But the team must be made up of as many of the ministry's leaders as possible. The more leaders you involve in the process, the greater will be their ownership of the results.

The responsibility for thinking and acting strategically rests with what I refer to as a strategic leadership team or SLT. We must understand, however, that God is ultimately doing the planning. Proverbs 21:31 says, "The horse is made ready for the day of battle, but victory rests with the LORD." Most often God works through people, in this case, the leadership team, who make the horse ready for battle. They will represent the church and lead the process. Consequently, the senior pastor must recruit the team, recruit a leader of the team, and secure a commitment from leaders to be on the team.

Recruit the Members of the Core Team

Answering the following questions will help you select and recruit the best leaders in the church for the strategic leadership team.

WHO WILL CHOOSE THE TEAM?

Most often those who choose the members of the SLT are the core leaders in the church. They are the senior pastor and one or a few other influential people, such as a board chairperson, a board member, or a key staff person. In the small church, the team might include a patriarch or matriarch.

WHOM WILL THEY CHOOSE?

The members of the SLT should be the leaders in your church. Success is dependent on leadership that knows what it is doing and is capable of doing it. You must resist the temptation to draft people who are merely willing to sit on the team, any team. Such people may be faithful saints and willing servants, but they are not necessarily people who are capable of leading. Capable leadership is critical to a robust effort.

I often refer to the SLT as the church's E. F. Hutton people. I am referring to the brokerage company that ran an ad several years ago that pictured people stopping whatever they were doing and putting their hands to their ears to listen when someone from E. F. Hutton spoke. These are the church's spiritual leadership, who have influence throughout the church and the respect of the members.

They include the senior pastor; five to ten board members, including the chairperson; all the staff in a small church and the executive staff in a large church (likely four to six people); lay teachers; small group leaders; other leaders in other key positions; and any who exert influence over the church but do not have an official position in the church (the patriarch, matriarch, and others).

Often a viewpoint that is missing in strategic thinking and acting is that of the women in the church. Whether the church has few or no women in leadership positions, it will have women leaders in the congregation. Thus it is imperative that the leadership solicit the female perspective. Otherwise the process will not have important female insight, especially in the area of women's ministries. One church that I pastored believed that women should not be elders. However, we had a women's advisor to the elder board who sat in on our meetings and regularly provided us with wisdom from a woman's perspective. (I would not hesitate to do this again in a similar situation.)

WHY HAVE THESE PEOPLE ON THE TEAM?

There are several reasons to involve these people on the team.

1. They are the leaders whose presence will generate congregational buy-in or trust in the process. If the congregation does not trust the process, it will not be realized in the life of the church. Leaders, especially those who have had deep spiritual impact in people's lives, will have their trust.

2. These leaders will be the more spiritually mature and gifted people in the church, and you will want to harness their talents and abilities for the process.
3. The team's involvement sends a message to the congregation that strategic planning is not just the pastor's idea or work but that of the leadership as well. The pastor is not merely handing down a plan he wants everyone else to follow. Others they trust have had significant involvement in developing the plan.
4. The team will know best the congregation—its traditions, culture, weaknesses, strengths, and other vital planning information—especially if the pastor is relatively new to the church.
5. Many of the leaders who make up the team will outlast the pastor. Long after he is gone, they will still be a part of the church and its ministry. This is vital to the long-term follow-through and implementation of the process.

Why Would These Leaders Want to Be on the Team?

These leaders will want to be on the team for several reasons.

1. They care about Christ's church here on earth and its future.
2. They care about their local church and its future. Their church matters to God, and it matters to them.
3. They care about the people in their Jerusalem (Acts 1:8) or their geographical ministry community and want to reach them with the gospel.
4. They are convinced that the church is the only hope of the world and that their church is the only hope for their community.
5. They want to play a major role in shaping the future of their church. They want to make a difference.

How Does the Process Help These People Create a Strategy?

1. The process gives these leaders ownership of the plan. They have their fingerprints all over it.
2. The process empowers these leaders. They have a say and can make a dramatic difference.
3. The process creates unity. In working together, the team members listen to and trust one another, and that gets everyone on the same page.

How Many Will Be on the Team?

As I stated in chapter 1, the more on the team the better. This depends to a large degree on the size of the church and the number of its leaders. When I consult with a church, I prefer around twenty-five to thirty leaders. That way people can miss, and the team can still meet.

How Often Will the Team Meet?

In chapter 1 I stated that I challenge the SLT to meet at least every four weeks or risk losing its initial inertia or ministry momentum. I have found as well that most like to meet on a Friday evening for several hours and then come back on Saturday morning for a second session from 8:00 a.m. to noon. This gives them a big rest break overnight and does not require that they give up their entire Saturday or weekend.

However, the team needs to be alert to planning around summer vacations, Easter, Christmas, Thanksgiving, and other times that people are accustomed to having off.

Recruit a Leader of the Team

In addition to recruiting a team, there must be a leader of the team, a captain of the ship or the lead navigator.

The Pastor

I am convinced that the point or senior pastor should be the primary leader and person responsible for the planning process. That is why he must see the need for and agree with the importance of strategic planning for the church. However, the question is, Is he ready to lead the process? It helps if he has skills and abilities in strategic thinking and acting, and he should also be knowledgeable about the strategic planning process. One of the reasons I have written this book is to help leaders get ready, to become more knowledgeable. The senior pastor of a large church or the sole pastor of a small church should take the responsibility for the initial development of the strategic plan.

However, it does not always work this way. My experience is that many churches are led by pastors who are not leaders. And many congregations sense this. They may be excellent teachers, even scholars or good at pastoral care and visitation, but they are not strategic leaders. Thus the board, team, or others may opt for someone else to lead the team. Several times churches where I have consulted have chosen as leaders those who have proven themselves in the corporate world.

If you are a senior pastor and you question whether you are a leader, you may want to take the Leader-Manager Audit in appendix B.

Other Potential Leaders

There are other potential leaders as well. In a large church the leader might be an executive pastor, associate pastor, a pastor of strategic planning, the board chairman, or a talented corporate person with a leadership gift. In a smaller church it could be a board member, chairman of the board, or an extremely gifted church member. My experience has been that others can effectively lead the church through the process, but still the senior pastor must be a champion of the process for it to be successful.

Explain the Expectations for the Team

A wise team person will want to know what the expectations are for the strategic leadership team. There are at least twelve that I explain to the teams with which I work:

1. To pray for the church, the team, and the process.
2. To be a positive participant who believes in and is enthusiastically supportive of the process. This means that the leader will need to give an overview of and sell the prospective team members on the strategic planning process.
3. To be a team player but not necessarily a "yes" person. In fact I think that it is spiritually healthy for team members to disagree at times and challenge one another.
4. To agree to a consensus approach to decision making. This means team members support a decision even when they do not agree with it.
5. To be at the meetings as much as possible. If a member is in town, he or she is at the meeting. Poor attenders become nonparticipants who tend not to own the final product.
6. To participate in group processes, such as storyboarding, values discovery, mission development, and so on.
7. To keep confidential matters confidential. There will not be many confidential matters, but the few there are will be held in confidence.
8. To commit to the total time necessary for the process, approximately six to nine months. A team member needs to hang in there when some of the initial excitement wears off.
9. To use his or her gifts, talents, and abilities to support and proactively contribute to the process.
10. To join a development team (DT) and be involved in the development or design process as well as its implementation that takes place throughout the process.
11. To be prepared for each team session. This involves reading book assignments, gathering information, conducting surveys, and so on.
12. To promote proactively the work of the team with the congregation.

I ask the lead navigators that I work with to pick leaders who are potential team members and invite them to a meeting where I spell all this out, present an overview of the process, and answer their questions. I encourage all who are willing to commit to these twelve expectations to pray about their involvement and consider becoming a part of the team. We give each a Covenant of Commitment (see appendix C) and ask those who will make a commitment to the team to sign and date it and return it then or within the next week. Again, the reason for this is the crucial nature of commitment to robust congregational development. This is essentially what took place in Nehemiah 9:38.

Step 3. Improve Communication with the Congregation

Whenever there is a coup in a country and the government is toppled, have you noticed that the new regime is quick to take over the radio and television stations? It is imperative that they take their message or cause to the masses, and they will win them over through communication. Otherwise they will likely lose power.

How good are you at communicating with your people? Are you ready to move on to the next step, or do you have some work to do on improving your congregational communication skills?

Communication Builds Trust

Why communicate with the congregation? One of our sayings at The Malphurs Group is, "If they do not trust you, you cannot lead them." If you conduct secret meetings behind the congregation's back, or if you conduct meetings and fail to communicate in general what happens in those meetings, you will not be able to lead the congregation, because they will not trust you. They will become convinced that you are trying to hide something from them, which will only serve to anger and alienate them. During the strategic planning process, as well as at any other time, you must communicate, communicate, and then communicate some more.

One Monday after I had consulted with a strategic leadership team on a Friday night and Saturday morning, the pastor of the church called me at home. He told me that one of the older members of the church had confronted him Sunday morning and said, "We heard about the secret meeting with the guy from Dallas!" His reply was that according to the Freedom of Information Act, he did not have to tell anyone anything. That is precisely what the team and its leadership must *not* do if they want to win congregational trust.

Who Will Communicate?

The pastor is responsible for communicating with the congregation. While he may assign this to someone else on the team, he must take ultimate responsibility to see that it happens. And if it does not, he must take responsibility for the repercussions.

Others who might communicate with the congregation are the team leader, a board chairman, or an unusually gifted, articulate communicator who is on the team. It is also important that the right information be communicated accurately. The idea is to prevent miscommunication and disinformation along with cultivating congregational trust. In essence, all the team members must be communicators or spokespersons who speak out in favor of the process and address any misinformation.

How Will You Communicate?

Perhaps the best way to communicate with the congregation is informally. The strategic planning process generates lots of excitement on the team. Consequently, I make it a point to encourage them to speak up proactively, "talking up" the process with people in the congregation, especially those within their circles of influence. At the beginning of a team meeting, you may want to take time to allow various team members to express how they are accomplishing this in their contacts with people.

The other method is formal communication. You may divide this into one-way and two-way communication. One-way communication involves the use of sermons, bulletins, newsletters, personal letters, video announcements, skits, and public testimonies from team members. Two-way communication involves online chat rooms, town hall meetings, potluck dinners, personal telephone calls, and listening groups.

Regardless of your method, every sermon, Sunday school lesson, ad, bulletin, newsletter, testimony, skit, and meeting is an opportunity to get the message across—to present the cause and thus win people's trust.

If you employ two-way communication in a large public meeting, such as a town hall meeting, you would be wise to have some rules in place. There will always be some opposition to something that the church is doing, whether strategic planning or some other ministry. Do not let one individual or a group of people turn a public session into a gripe session or venue for personal attacks. You should be prepared for this—at least at the first few meetings—and be ready to deal with it. Announce proper decorum prior to opening the meeting for discussion. Assign someone, such as the chairman of the board, a respected board member, or a patriarch, to deal on the spot with those who violate decorum. This will send an important message that will save you from problems later.

What Will You Communicate?

The pastor should alert the congregation that the church will be going through a strategic envisioning process led by the strategic leadership team. He might accomplish this in the context of a biblical message on strategic planning, using the material in chapter 1 under the heading "Understanding That Strategic Planning Is Biblical." Sunday school teachers could follow up with similar messages and studies.

Also, it would be appropriate to identify those on the strategic leadership team, the purpose of the team, and how long they will be meeting (six to nine months), along with the board's and staff's commitment to the strategic planning process. Should someone ask why he or she was not selected to be on the team, explain the expectations, especially the number and length of meetings. Most people will not pursue further involvement. If they do, consider including them on the team.

The pastor will need to communicate the results of the strategic envisioning process. Using appropriate Scripture, he should preach on the church's core values, mission, vision, and strategy, as designed by the SLT. This may have been preceded by several town hall meetings where this information was communicated and people had a chance to respond. Again, Sunday school teachers and others in teaching positions could address these matters as well.

In addition to the above, some pastors have preached through portions of Bible books that present some aspects of strategy, such as the early chapters of Nehemiah and Acts. Also, I strongly encourage pastors and Sunday school teachers to cover the material pertaining to spiritual formation in this chapter of this book, even before beginning the process.

Communicating Well

There are several very simple questions that the team must ask to assure good communication.

1. Who needs to know? Should we communicate this to the entire congregation, a portion of the congregation, the board, the staff, the public?
2. What do they need to know? What is relevant to them? What is unnecessary and might be a waste of their time?
3. Who will tell them? Should we go through normal channels (the pastor, board chairman, and so on) or have someone else do the communicating (such as a former, respected pastor)?
4. How will we tell them—formally or informally?
5. And finally, when and where will we tell them? Should it be on Sunday morning at our facility or during the week at a town hall meeting in another facility?

Establish a Biblical Grievance Process

THE PROBLEM

Scripture commands Christians not to be complainers (Phil. 2:14) but to be patient and gentle, bearing with one another in love (Eph. 4:2). This is not the case, however, in far too many churches. When people don't like something, they complain and talk about it among themselves, often spreading false rumors. This hurts the congregation more than it helps them and causes much damage to the church.

The Solution

The biblical solution is communication. It is imperative that you set up a grievance process for the congregation based on such passages as Matthew 5:23–24 and 18:15–19. The teaching here is for those who feel that they have been wronged and those who believe that they may have wronged someone to get together, one-on-one, to attempt to resolve their issues. Should this not happen, Matthew 18:15–19 includes additional steps that involve others in the resolution process that may ultimately end in discipline. Other relevant passages are Matthew 12:25–26; 1 Corinthians 10:10; Ephesians 4:29; Philippians 2:14; and James 3:2.

The Process

It is a good idea for you as the senior pastor to introduce the grievance process with a sermon on the importance of communication and recognize that at times people will have legitimate as well as illegitimate complaints. Then present the grievance process as the biblical way that the congregation is expected to handle these issues. Encourage your people not to listen to any gripes or gossip but to direct such people to pursue the proper grievance procedures. Coach them to respond to complaints with the following questions: Have you pursued the grievance process? Have you gone to the responsible party and discussed the situation with him or her? If a person pursues the process and does not get his or her way, the discussion is over. He or she has had the opportunity to be heard. You must not tolerate any further complaining or negativity. The fact that some people operate this way does not legitimize it or make it okay.

I suggest that you preach on this concern once a year. Also consider having a membership covenant and making the grievance process a part of it, asking people who desire to join the church to sign it. That way all are aware of how your church handles matters of dissent.

Step 4. Assess the Church's Readiness for Change

As we have already seen, many changes are taking place in our world that are having an impact on the church. Not only are there many changes, but they are taking place over a shorter period of time than was true in the past. The waves of change are pounding the typical church boat and are showing no signs of letting up long enough to allow the water to be bailed out. The purpose of this book and the strategic thinking and acting process is to place the church in a position where it can function at its best in preparation for and during the pounding. To accomplish this, however, the church must know where it stands on change and assess its readiness for change. Six activities are involved in this: understand how change has affected people in the church, take the Readiness for Change Inventory, discuss the results of your church ministry analysis or some other analysis, ask probing questions, address people's emotions, and embrace a theology of change.

Some older folks are convinced that your people are pushing change on the church to make them angry. Nothing could be further from the truth. Change or transformation is at the core of Christianity. Paul writes, "And we, who with unveiled faces all reflect the Lord's glory, are being transformed into his likeness with ever-increasing glory, which comes from the Lord, who is the Spirit" (2 Cor. 3:18). The purpose for changing what we do at church is to change who we are inside. The way we do church (worship forms, preaching style, teaching style, and so forth) directly impacts who we are as believers in Christ. However, we can fall into ruts in the way we do church that negatively affect how we do life.

Perhaps an exercise illustration will help. My wife works with a trainer at a local health club. He is constantly changing her routine to deal with what he refers to as "muscle memory." He believes that if you continue to do the same exercise repeatedly, the muscle will become used to it and cease to grow. I argue that the same is true for the various forms that churches practice to accomplish spiritual growth. They need to change, or people will cease to respond and grow spiritually.

Understand How Change Has Affected People in the Church

Many of the people in our churches grew up in the twentieth century at a time when stability was the norm. The prevailing motto was, "If it ain't broke, don't fix it!" However, in the twenty-first century the tendency toward change that began in the latter part of the twentieth century has become the norm. One person writes, "From the time of recorded history to 1900, information doubled. By 1950 it doubled again. Starting in 1975 it began doubling every five years. Presently, it's doubling every two years."[3] The new motto is, "It's broke, so fix it!" The problem is that even though some people are aware of this, they are still hoping for a return to times of stability. So we still hear the old motto and encounter resistance to change.

There is a second problem. Having grown up in a time when stability ruled, many of our older leaders in the church do not have a leadership legacy to help guide them through the morass of change. They desperately need help but may not realize it. A third problem is that some leaders cling to the status quo rather than risk the carnage that change may bring to the church. They must ask an important question: Is it reasonable to think that by continuing to do what we have been doing, things will be different and better in the future?

Take the Readiness for Change Inventory

How can you know where the church is in terms of its readiness to change? A Readiness for Change Inventory is in appendix A. The entire team should take this inventory as it relates to the church. Each member should total his or her score and compare it with the grouping of scores at the end of the tool. What do the resulting scores tell you about your church's chances for change?

If your church did not score well, what will you do? I encourage you as a team to have a heart-to-heart discussion about whether or not to proceed with the strategic process. Outside of a miracle, the planning process may be your only hope for a future, but only the strongest of commitments to the process will bring about revitalization. Are you as a leadership team willing to make that kind of commitment?

Discuss the Results of the Ministry Analysis

When you take the Church Ministry Analysis, the next step in this assessment, you will learn about your church's openness to change. The majority of the audits in the Church Ministry Analysis address in some way a church's readiness for change. For example, the obstacles audit asks if the church is flexible or inflexible and whether or not it is a learning organization. Questions about outreach versus in-reach and vision and mission show a church's readiness for change.

You will be able to answer these questions: Where did the life-cycle audit place the church? Is it growing, on a plateau, or spiraling downward? And if the latter, how far along is it? A church that is on a plateau or has just shifted downward can handle change much better than a church that is in a downward spiral or has been so for some time. The difference is between what I refer to as tweak change versus deep change. *Tweak change* means changing things a little here and there to improve current ministries. *Deep change* means changing much of what the church is doing in a short period of time, such as a shift from traditional to contemporary worship over a month or so. (I will say more about this in the chapter on ministry evaluation.) Churches that are spiraling downward will need to go through deep change to survive, but my experience has been that they will not do so. It is too drastic, and most people in these churches could not handle such change emotionally. It would simply overwhelm them.

You must also consider how the team responds to the results of the analysis—especially if the church does not do well. Ask these questions: Were they angry? Did they challenge the accuracy of the tool? Did they feign denial? Did they plunge their heads back into the sands of complacency? Or do they admit that they are struggling? Are they legitimately concerned? Do they see and accept the problems and genuinely want to do something about them? The last questions are also important in assessing the church's openness to change and renewal.

Ask Probing Questions

My experience is that asking probing questions plants seeds of doubt that lead to change. But what are probing questions? They are the kinds of questions that force people to think. And they can make them think about issues they would rather avoid. You can offer directions and issue ultimatums, but both invite complacent resistance. Questions serve to catalyze and challenge the thinking process.

Probing questions are no strangers to the Scriptures. God probed Adam and Eve with questions in the garden after the fall: "Have you eaten from the tree that I commanded you not to eat?" And Jesus was a master at the skillful use of questions to probe and pierce the veneer of denial to expose complacent thinking (see, for example, Matt. 22:41–46).

A good probing question is the *why* question. Constantly asking people why the church does what it does will uncover complacent thinking. In fact I will continue to ask why to each answer I get until we reach the heart of the matter. My favorite question, however, for stalled and declining churches is, "If you continue to do what you are currently doing, what makes you think that the results will be any different?"

Address People's Emotions

Already in this book I have dropped a few hints about the importance of a congregation's feelings toward change. When I consult with churches, I try to address their emotions as well as their minds. Yes, you have to provide them with a process that involves them heavily in the thinking process. But what does God use to move them to want to change and stick with it for the long term? I believe that the Holy Spirit works through the emotions as much as through the mind to accomplish this. (Have you noted that the fruit of the Spirit in Galatians 5:22–23 consists essentially of emotions? Also, Nehemiah's emotions were touched deeply when he heard about the deplorable condition of Jerusalem and its people [Neh. 1:3–4], and this led to his return and the revitalization of the city.) Later, when people think back over the planning process, the events that impacted them emotionally will be most vivid. These events evoke images that stick in people's minds.

TAP INTO EMOTIONS

When I work with a team, I try to be constantly alert to ways of tapping into their emotions. One way to do this is to have the various individuals on the leadership team interview several unchurched people as to why they do not attend church or why they would not attend their church. (The team will need to give them permission to respond honestly. Request that they tell what they think the church needs to hear, not what it wants to hear.) I asked one church to give a very brief, four-question survey to some of their unchurched friends with a church-addressed, stamped envelope. When they received the results, not even the pastor believed some of the responses. One unchurched respondent said that she had attended once but felt rejected because of her clothes. Then a team member responded that she had felt the same way when several people had shunned her because of her clothing. You could hear a pin drop!

ENGAGE THE EMOTIONS

Here are some ideas for engaging the emotions. Videotape an interview with someone who left the church because of its complacency (you may need to disguise the person's appearance and voice). Conduct a live interview with someone along the same lines. Take your people on a trip to a church in your vicinity that is having a dynamic impact for the Savior. Let them feel the excitement of the atmosphere. Use lots of illustrations and stories of churches that changed and had a dramatic impact for Christ in their communities. Interview some of your most positive, excited team members in front of the church. Let their excitement rub off on the others. Use drama. Take the team on a tour of the facility when it is empty. Explain that, if they as a church do not address their shortcomings, in one or two or more years the facility will look like that on Sunday morning. You may also want to take the team to a church in the area that has closed its doors. Perhaps one of the best books on how to touch the emotions to effect change in organizations is John Kotter's *The Heart of Change*.[4]

Embrace a Theology of Change

Change is at the very core of Christianity. The biblical term for change is not *conformation* (which is the enemy of change) but *transformation* (Rom. 12:2; 2 Cor. 3:18). (Perhaps we would be wise to use the term *transformation* in place of the C word.) The goal for every Christian is to be transformed by the power of the Spirit (2 Cor. 3:18) into Christ's likeness (Gal. 4:19) as evidenced by the fruit of the Spirit (Gal. 5:22–23). To stay the same is anti-Christ. If the goal of every Christian is transformation, then the various means that help accomplish this must change as well.

Every institution—whether for profit or not for profit—must wrestle with the vexing question of what in the organization should change and what should never change. Opinions in both contexts range from one extreme (nothing should change) to the other (everything should change). Thus it is imperative that the church and its leaders have a biblical theology of change that guides them, especially when people react adversely and it is so difficult to think clearly. This will help a congregation be more open to change. A good theology of change addresses three areas: function, form, and freedom.

FUNCTION

The functions of the church are those timeless truths that must never change. They are the same for the church of the twenty-first century as they were for the church of the first century and all the centuries in between. Some examples of functions are evangelism, worship, prayer, and fellowship. Theologian Scott Horrell argues that these are the only functions of the church and that they mark the church as a legitimate local church.[5] I tend to agree.

For the purposes of strategic planning, you must decide what in the process is timeless and should not change. I believe that the church's values, mission, to a great degree the vision, and purpose are timeless core ingredients of the ministry. They make up the congregation's heart and soul. Once the ministry has discovered and articulated its values, mission, vision, and purpose, it must not change them except to reword or rephrase them for purposes of communication and to remain culturally current. They are core ministry ingredients that will define and direct the organization's future.

FORM

The forms of the church are timely vehicles that are tied in some way to the church's culture. They implement the functions. The problem is that most churches tend to equate the church's functions with the cultural forms that express them, whether local, national, or international. For example, the cultural forms of the European churches have exerted a strong influence on many traditional North American churches. Far too many people in these churches believe that the New Testament prescribed the great hymns of the faith for worship. However, men such as the Wesleys and Martin Luther wrote these in the context of the Western European mind-set and culture. Some also believe that the first-century churches met in facilities like the great European cathedrals. Regardless, these forms must change if the church is to speak to its culture.

Theology of Change

Functions	Forms
Timeless, unchanging (absolutes)	Timely, changing (nonabsolutes)
Based on Scripture	Based on culture
Mandates (ministry precepts)	Methods (ministry practices)
All churches must choose	All churches are free to choose
Accomplish the church's purpose (the glory of God)	Accomplish the church's functions (evangelism, worship, fellowship, teaching)

FREEDOM

Again, for strategic planning purposes, you must decide what is open for change. My view is that only the core values, mission, vision, and purpose of the church are timeless. Thus everything else—the church's strategy, structures, systems, policies, and procedures—are subject to change and should regularly change. The vision expresses the church's direction in a cultural context. While the direction (to make disciples) will not change, the cultural context (who, where, when, and how) will change over time.

Strategic Planning

Timeless	Subject to Change
Values	Structures
Mission	Strategy
Purpose	Systems
Vision	Policies

This means that every church has much freedom when determining its forms (not its functions). In fact I predict that those who were in churches in the 1950s through the 1970s will question the legitimacy of many of the churches that are planted in the twenty-first century, based on the forms they use. However, theologically and biblically, the forms are not the issue. If these new organizations are functioning as churches, they are churches in a biblical sense, regardless of what people think of their forms.

Step 5. Conduct a Church Ministry Analysis

I am a visionary, and my wife, Susan, is a realist. I spend much time dreaming about what could be. She spends her time thinking about what is—reality. We have been involved in several difficult church revitalization projects. In each situation, she asks, "Do you know what you are getting yourself into? Are you sure you want to do this?" I need to hear those questions. Usually I follow them with one of my own: "But don't you see what could be?" She needs to hear that. Though this difference in our way of thinking can lead to strong disagreements, it helps us balance each other and see both sides of an issue or decision. I help her think about and envision what could be; she helps me think about and examine reality. Both are vital to any ministry situation. Conducting a church ministry analysis is about reality.

When I consult with a church, I ask the SLT to take a ministry analysis. The church's leaders make up the team, and my assumption is that they know the church better than anyone else. Thus they provide an accurate response. If the church is small, the entire church could take the analysis as well as its leadership. This may reduce accuracy but would provide an idea of what the people as a whole think about themselves.

The Importance of the Analysis

It is important in strategic envisioning that churches conduct a ministry analysis.

It Asks the Basics

The analysis invites churches to ask a basic question: How are we doing? This forces people like me to face and deal with reality. It grabs the proverbial ostrich around the neck and pulls its head out of the sands of complacency. Since no organization is perfect, it helps each leader see the need for strategizing and provides both information that informs the process and a realistic picture of the work that needs to be accomplished.

There are examples of ministry analysis in the Bible. In Nehemiah 2:11–17 Nehemiah conducted a ministry analysis when he and his leaders rode through Jerusalem, examining the walls (vv. 13, 15). He did this before communicating the mission for the Jerusalem Reclamation Project (v. 16). Then he used the results of his findings to establish the need for his mission (v. 17) and to challenge the Jewish remnant living in Jerusalem to attempt that mission.

Paul and Barnabas planned to conduct a ministry analysis in Acts 15:36: "Let us go back and visit all the brothers in the towns where we preached the word of the Lord and *see how they are doing*" (emphasis mine).

IT PROMPTS "WHAT COULD BE"

We can observe a church and how it is doing from two different time perspectives. The first is the present, so we ask, What is? It is what the ministry analysis focuses on and reveals to the church—how it is doing currently.

The other time perspective is the future, so we ask, What could be? Answering the question What is? prompts the church to think about what could be in the future. While the ministry analysis does not tell us what could be, it can be used to prompt this kind of thinking. For example, it asks the church to unearth its weaknesses, and these always lead to thoughts of correcting them in the future, which in turn lead to and facilitate the development of the church's vision for its future. The church begins to think about what could be.

IT PRODUCES THE ICEBERG EFFECT

In one of my consulting sessions, I was reviewing a church's ministry analysis. During the break a man approached me and said that doing the analysis was like discovering an iceberg. I asked what he meant. Then he compared his church to a ship out on the ocean headed toward a giant, menacing iceberg. Those on the ship cannot see the iceberg because there is a heavy fog. He concluded that the ministry analysis is like a strong wind that comes along and blows the fog away, revealing the iceberg so that the ship can change course and avoid a deadly collision. His concern was whether his church would make the necessary corrections and navigate around the obstacles in its path.

I like this image and now refer to the work of ministry analysis and what could be as the iceberg effect.

IT SURFACES COMPLACENCY

At the heart of the man's concern was his church's complacency.[6] We often fail to realize that in spite of evident church decline, most churches are steeped in complacency—everyone has an excuse for it that lets them off the hook. For example, you will hear, "We may be struggling a little, but so are most of the churches in our part of town."

The way to address complacency is to create a sense of urgency. This is how leaders handled it in the Old Testament (Neh. 2:17–18; Isa. 55:6; Hosea 10:12) and in the New (Matt. 3:2; 28:19–20; 2 Cor. 5:14–6:2). And that explains the impact of the Church Ministry Analysis on struggling churches. It is too overwhelming—it does not let people off the hook intellectually or emotionally.

IT PROMPTS CHANGE

My experience has been that when churches see the iceberg, they change course. Even the most complacent, change-resistant person will flinch when facing an iceberg. When I give the life-cycle portion of the ministry analysis, if the church is in decline, I will use the rate of decline (or percentage of decline) to figure out how long it will be before the church will have to close its doors. You can do this too. While larger churches have longer, small churches may have only a year or two before it is over. As I said above, this gets people's attention. It touches them emotionally and may be key to getting the reluctant ones on board with the process.

The Need for Objectivity

I must stress the need for objectivity as you and your team move through the analysis. At times you and others will face the temptation to distort or minimize the information you uncover, especially that which surfaces your personal failures or those of the ministry. This analysis contains some gut-wrenching questions. It pokes and prods the ministry's tender underside. Nevertheless, operate with candor, openness, and accuracy as you work through the process. Otherwise the results will be skewed and misleading.

A Ministry Analysis

The ministry analysis that I use has two parts. The first is the internal analysis. It consists of twelve audits taken on various aspects of the ministry that tell the church what it needs to know about itself. I include it here as a summary and an example. However, you may want to use it as your actual ministry audit.

Answer the following questions about your ministry as a whole.

1. The *organizational life-cycle audit* reveals where the church is on the S-curve (see the S-curve figure in the introduction).

   This audit asks the following questions: Based on the church's annual average worship attendance (worship attendance, not membership) as far back as you have records, is your church growing, plateaued, or declining? Based on the church's average annual giving, are your church's finances increasing, plateaued, or declining? (Put this information on a graph so that people can observe the church's attendance and giving history.)

   This audit will help the church determine whether it is growing, plateaued, or in decline in attendance and is a strong indicator of the church's health. Luke reflects this type of audit in Acts when he reports periodically on the effect of the gospel (Acts 2:47; 6:7; 9:31; 12:24; and so forth) and tracks the church's growth (Acts 1:15; 2:41, 47; 4:4; 5:14; and so on).

2. The *performance audit* assesses the ministry's strengths and weaknesses—spiritual and otherwise. (John is conducting a type of performance audit in Revelation 2 and 3.)

This audit asks the following question: What are your church's strengths and weaknesses?

You will determine which of the following is a strength or a weakness: senior pastor, pastoral care, worship, preaching, biblical instruction, nursery, friendliness, leaders, adult ministries, fellowship, teaching, board (elders, deacons, and others), staff, morale, women's ministries, men's ministries, location, family emphasis, Sunday school, giving/stewardship, unity, planning, small group ministries, children's ministries, organization, youth ministries, communication, reputation in the community, education ministries, lay participation in the church's ministries, follow-through, facilities/campus, world missions focus, orientation to change, young married couples, mission (direction), community ministries, leadership development, vision (direction), evangelism.

3. The *direction audit* seeks to determine if the church has a mission and vision, and if so, if the congregation knows what they are.

This audit asks the following questions: Does your church have a mission or mission statement? If so, what is it? Does your church have a vision or vision statement? If so, what is it?

4. The *strategy audit* addresses whom the church is trying to reach and how it makes disciples.

This audit asks the following question: Is the main focus of the church the congregation itself, the church's community, lost people, unchurched lost people, a combination of these?

5. The *outreach audit* determines if the church has an effective outreach into its local and international communities.

This audit asks the following questions: Does your church have an effective outreach into its local community? Does it have an effective outreach into the international community?

6. The *in-reach audit* assesses the church's worship, empowerment of leaders, lay ministry involvement, and application of Scripture to life.

This audit asks the question: On a scale of 1 to 5 (1 being low and 5 being high), how would you rate your church in terms of its worship, empowerment of leaders, lay involvement in ministry, and people's application of Scripture to life?

7. The *culture audit* identifies such things as core values, traditions, heroes, memories, and rituals.

This audit asks the following questions: What are your church's core values? What are some of its traditions? Who are its heroes (former or current pastor, missionaries, and others)? What are some of the church's memories that you or other people talk about from time to time? What are some of its rituals?

8. An *obstacles audit* seeks to determine what or who is blocking more effective ministry.

This audit asks the question: What or who might be blocking effective ministry in your church? Because the analysis is confidential, people may be more inclined to name names.

9. The *age audit* seeks to discover the age of the congregation and the need for younger members.

This audit asks the following questions: What is the age of your church? Is your current congregation made up of young people, middle-aged people, elderly people, a balance of all three? If it is made up mostly of elderly people, what might this say about the future of your church?

10. The *energy audit* measures the intensity with which people pursue ministry.

This audit asks the question: On a scale of 1 to 5 (1 being low and 5 being high), where would you rank your church in terms of the intensity with which people pursue ministry?

11. The *emotions audit* seeks to rate people's emotional level.

This audit asks the following question: Would you say that your church is mostly upbeat, discouraged, or somewhere in between in terms of where people are emotionally?

12. The *finance audit* explores the church's finances.

This audit asks the question: To the best of your knowledge, how is your church doing financially?

The second part of the ministry analysis is external. It tells the church what it needs to know about its ministry community. It consists of four audits.

1. The *community audit* seeks to determine how well the congregation knows its community and will guide its outreach to that community.

This audit asks the following questions: On a scale of 1 to 5 (1 being low and 5 being high), how well does your church know its community's demographics (ethnicity, income, education, and so forth)? How does this affect its outreach into your community?

2. The *threats audit* attempts to identify what is taking place in the church's community that might harm it in some way, such as a growing crime rate or people moving out of the community.

   This audit asks the following question: What is taking place in your community that might harm your church's ministry in and to its community?

3. The *competitors audit* identifies various events and organizations that might compete with the church for the involvement of unchurched people as well as of its own members.

   This audit asks the following question: Who are your church's competitors that might be competing with you in terms of reaching people?

   Most assume the main competitors are other churches. In my consulting, I have found this never to be the case. Usually it's sporting events, shopping malls, leisure activities, the entertainment industry, a fast-food chain (such as Pizza Hut or Burger King), and so on.

4. The *opportunities audit* addresses the many opportunities for the church to minister to and in its community.

   This audit asks the following question: What are five opportunities that your church might have or should explore in terms of ministering to your community? Some examples are adopting a school in the community, adopting a fire station, repairing rundown houses, offering ESL (English as a second language), and others.

Rather than using this church ministry analysis exclusively, I would challenge you to create your own that takes into account the uniqueness of your church. You may want to use the above analysis and tweak it to fit your needs or simply create an entirely new tool with different questions. As a feature of my consulting practice, I offer an online ministry analysis to the churches we work with. This makes it easy to tabulate the results quickly and accurately. Otherwise it would take someone several days to tabulate the results by hand.

Step 6. Set Reasonable Time Expectations

The strategic planning process provides a compass that will bring change and a new direction to your church. However, this is not likely to happen overnight. It took time for the church to get where it is, and it will take some time for it to get where God wants it to be. I describe it as a gradual process that takes place over time. It's important to think about how much time the process will take and if the congregation and the team are ready for it.

As the process progresses, change should happen regularly; some changes will happen quickly and early. The degree of change can serve as a barometer of how the process is going. However, working through growth issues, especially a plateau or downward spiral, will take longer.

My friend Randy Frazee, former pastor of Pantego Bible Church in Arlington, Texas, writes, "Experts suggest that it takes about three years for a language to become part of a culture. . . . It has taken three full years for our definition of a disciple and the language that accompanies it to become a part of the corporate culture of our church. (And there were times along the way when we wondered if anyone would get it.)"[7]

John Kotter believes that for change to take hold in organizations it must sink deeply into their culture. He states that this can take three to ten years, as new approaches are fragile and subject to reversals.[8] In *Executive Success*, Eliza Collins argues that easing a large organization into a major shift of values takes anywhere from three to eight years.[9] Consequently, while some changes occur quickly, the range of time for what I would refer to as significant change to take place is from three to ten years. However, a spiritually healthy church will always be undergoing some change.

The Problem

This time factor may present a problem for some churches. Those that are small and in deep decline or spiraling downward may not have even three years for making critical changes. I worked with one church of forty to fifty members that had one year to make significant enough changes to survive. It did not happen.

It may be that in these difficult situations the best thing for all concerned is to let the church die, as difficult as that is emotionally. Most likely the church is having little impact, and all the attenders would be better off finding new churches where they could have a more effective ministry.

The Response

The best response to the question of time is patience. Patience is a virtue and thus a fruit of the Spirit (Gal. 5:22). The problem in our culture is that when we want something, we want it yesterday. The fast-food industry, which has made millions of dollars, is proof of our society's desire for instant gratification. Here are the questions strategic leadership teams must ask: Are we willing to hang in there? When the newness and excitement of the process begin to wear off, will we still move forward? And how will we handle matters when the detractors and change resistors come after us?

My experience is that many teams are willing to hang in there but want to know if the pastor is willing to follow suit. As stated earlier, the average tenure for a pastor in North America is three to four years, and the people on the team sense this intuitively, even if they are unaware of the statistic. That is why I ask pastors to commit to the process before I agree to work with the church. Often my first questions of him are: Are you willing to stay for the long term? How will you respond when some people do not respond? What will you do when the "never adopters of change" verbally attack you? Will you run for cover or hang tough?

Step 7. Lay a Spiritual Foundation

There is one more step in preparing for the strategic planning process, that of laying a spiritual foundation. While I have placed it at the end of this chapter, it doesn't come last in the process. It is so critical that it must undergird the entire envisioning process.

My experience is that few churches are ready spiritually to begin the process, and so they launch their ministry ship, only to watch it sink to the bottom of the sea. Consequently, in this section I cover the importance of spiritual formation, include a definition and thirteen steps for pursuing spiritual formation, and discuss the implementation of spiritual formation in the life of the church.

The Importance of Spiritual Formation

It is imperative that the leadership of the church call the church to spiritual renewal and revival. There are several reasons for this.

First, spiritual formation is foundational to strategic envisioning. The latter will not be as effective without it. In Zechariah 4:6 the angel says to Zerubbabel, "'Not by might nor by power, but by my Spirit,' says the LORD Almighty." Spiritual formation connects God with the strategic planning process and then its ministry product or model, and it must undergird the entire process. If you picture strategic planning as a house or building, spiritual formation would be the foundation that supports it. Any planning for the church must begin with and be about the spiritual formation of the church.

Second, spiritual formation must not end at the beginning. It is not something that you begin with, only to forget as you take the next step. It pervades the entire process. It begins prior to step one and continues throughout the process. In a sense, it wraps up all the steps. The entire envisioning process is and must be about the spiritual forming of the church.

Third, spiritual formation of the church is what change is about. In theological terms, we call this the sanctification of one's soul. In this case, it is the church's soul! All other change is subordinate to and subsequent to this. We change the forms of our ministries to facilitate our personal, spiritual change or formation not to make people mad, as some seem to think!

The Definition of Spiritual Formation

Spiritual formation is a process through which the Holy Spirit transforms us into Christ's likeness or image. A key text to understanding this process is Galatians

4:19, where Paul says to the Galatian Christians, "My dear children, for whom I am again in the pains of childbirth until Christ is formed in you." Note two things: Christ is formed in you, and it is the work of the Holy Spirit.

CHRIST FORMED IN YOU

Paul talks about Christ being formed in these believers. I take him literally. I believe that he is saying that over time people should literally see Christ in the Christian's life. What did people see when they observed the Savior? The answer is also found in Galatians, specifically Galatians 5:22–23, which lists the fruit of the Spirit. The same Holy Spirit who indwelled Christ while on earth (Matt. 3:16) also indwells the Christian (1 Cor. 6:19) and produces the fruit of the Spirit in the believer's life. Consequently, when people observe the believer, they see what those in the first century saw when they observed the Savior—the fruit of the Spirit. In 2 Corinthians 3:18 Paul says that we are being transformed into Christ's likeness.

THE WORK OF THE HOLY SPIRIT

Note that in 2 Corinthians 3:18 Paul talks about Christ being formed in the Christian. This is in the passive voice. The Christian does not accomplish this. It is something that is done to him or her, the work of the Holy Spirit. He is the one who conforms us to Christ and produces his fruit in our lives. Paul explains: "And we, who with unveiled faces all reflect the Lord's glory, are being transformed into his likeness with ever-increasing glory, which comes from the Lord, who is the Spirit."

Paul describes this as a spiritual transformation process, and it involves not only the individual believer but the entire church. Paul is writing to the church at Corinth as much as to individual believers (1:1). In theological terms, some would also call this the progressive sanctification of one's soul. In the strategic planning process, it concerns the progressive sanctification of the church's soul.

The Process of Spiritual Formation

There are at least thirteen steps of spiritual formation that I walk a strategic leadership team through when I work with them. I cover them specifically with those who are facing growth challenges because they address most of the issues that may be causing these problems.

ACKNOWLEDGE PERSONAL SINFULNESS

First, ponder and acknowledge your individual, personal sinfulness (Ps. 51:5; Rom. 7:14; 1 John 1:8, 10). In 1 John 1:8 the author writes, "If we claim to be without sin, we deceive ourselves and the truth is not in us." He is writing to believers and underlines the fact that we continue to sin though we are saved. We are saved from sin's penalty, not its power. If we begin to think and even go so far as to claim that we no longer sin, we are guilty of self-deception and have crossed the line from truth to error. In Romans 7:14 Paul writes, "We know that the law is spiritual; but I am unspiritual, sold as a slave to sin." The term *unspiritual* is better translated *fleshly*—under the control of the flesh. Paul's point is that he still sins and is most aware of it. In fact there are times when he is sin's slave (Rom. 6:15–23).

What is the application to those in churches that are addressing growth challenges? I have a cartoon that shows an elderly lady who, as she shakes her pastor's hand after the service, says, "Your sermon hit close to home. It was perfect for my next-door neighbor." Most often the people in these churches are struggling spiritually. And there is the temptation to point the finger at others, especially those with whom they do not agree and those who are trying to change the church. Key to spiritual formation is resisting that temptation, taking your eyes off others and looking long and hard in a mirror, and remembering that you are still a self-deceived sinner who may not see his sin. This means that you will be wrong at times and on the wrong side of an issue that may divide a church. Could it be that you are the one in Jesus's story with a plank in your eye who has become preoccupied with the speck of sawdust in your brother's eye (Matt. 7:3–5)? Stop worrying about everybody else's supposed sin and deal with your own.

Confess Your Sins

Confess your sins to God (Psalm 51; 1 John 1:9). Should you look long and hard in a mirror, chances are excellent that you will find something. It may be an entire plank or just a speck of sawdust. Regardless, you need to deal with it. How? First John 1:9 teaches that when sin is confessed, there is forgiveness. A great example is David's confession of sin in Psalm 51. At a particularly difficult time in his life, David committed adultery with a woman named Bathsheba. When he tried to cover it up, God sent Nathan the prophet to confront David (2 Samuel 11–12). The prayer in Psalm 51 is the result of that confrontation and provides us with a recording of what genuine confession of sin sounds like.

David asks God to blot out his transgressions, to wash away his iniquity, to cleanse him from his sin, to hide his face from his sins, plus a number of other similar requests. He cannot forget his sin (v. 3), and he sees it for what it really is—a sin against God (v. 4). After acknowledging that he has lost the joy of his salvation—not his salvation (v. 12)—we see that he has a broken and contrite heart (v. 17). We would be wise to deal with our sin in a similar manner, asking God to forgive us and cleanse us from our sin. That is what it will take to see our churches forming spiritually—we must deal with our sin by acknowledging it with broken and contrite hearts. Who will be the first?

Forgive Others

Forgive those who have sinned against you (Matt. 18:21–22; Eph. 4:31–32; Col. 3:13–14). There is no question that somewhere along the way someone has wronged you or sinned against you. It may have been an absentee father who was never there when you needed him most. It may have been a pastor who divulged to others personal, intimate matters from your life that you had shared in confidence or a best friend who turned on you and didn't support you when you needed him or her most. It may have been some person in the church who spread false rumors about you to damage your credibility.

The real issue is not whether someone has sinned against you, as horrible as that may have been. The real issue is what you have done about it. If you are typical of most Christians, you have not done anything to resolve the situation. Instead, you may have chosen (yes, I said chosen) to become angry, even bitter toward the person. And you may have brought this baggage with you to your church.

Scripture is very clear that you are to grant forgiveness to anyone who has wronged you, no matter who they are, no matter how grievous the sin. In Ephesians 4:31–32 Paul commands us, "Get rid of all bitterness, rage and anger, brawling and slander, along with every form of malice. Be kind and compassionate to one another, forgiving each other, just as in Christ God forgave you." By the power and example of God who has forgiven us in Christ, we can genuinely forgive those who have wronged us. We can climb out of the rut of bitterness and anger with them and get on with our lives. While you may not change overnight, now is the time to begin this journey. Remember, each time you forgive another, it becomes a little easier the next time.

Pray for the Church

Spend time in intense, positive prayer for the church (Matt. 7:7–12; James 5:16). God invites us to prayer. In Matthew 7:7 Jesus commands, "Ask and it will be given to you; seek and you will find; knock and the door will be opened to you." One of our faculty at Dallas Seminary is an expert on prayer. I have heard him say on several occasions that the theology of prayer is not all that difficult. When you pray, you will always get an answer. There are three possible answers: yes, no, or wait. It is refreshing to know that more often than not the answer, according to Matthew 7:7–12, will be yes.

James illustrates the power of our prayers in James 5:16–18. In verse 16 he commands believers to pray for one another, especially those who are ill. Then he recounts the story of Elijah, whose prayers were so powerful that they stopped all rain on the land for three and a half years and then started it again.

The temptation in times of growth challenges is to take matters into our own hands and deal with them as we think best. We forget about the privilege of prayer and its power. Show me a church whose people in general and leaders in particular pray regularly and positively for the church, and I will show you a church that is being blessed of God. Regular prayer speaks for itself. Positive prayer does not include asking God to remove the new pastor because he wants to change "how we do things around here" or to help run off any newcomers who might spoil the status quo. Positive prayer involves asking God to use the church to reach the lost, to grow believers up in the faith, and to uphold his reputation in our communities, all of which will glorify God.

Be Positive

Put off any negative "stuff" (1 Cor. 10:10; Eph. 4:1–3, 29; Phil. 2:14). Have you noticed that you can listen to a church and know how it is doing spiritually? Is much of what is said by the people in your church negative or positive stuff? What is negative stuff? It is constant grumbling (1 Cor. 10:10), complaining and arguing (Phil. 2:14), gossip, and even slander at times (2 Cor. 12:20; Titus 3:1–2). Often I find that negative stuff characterizes churches that are struggling spiritually.

Paul is very clear that these things are not to be part of the believer's and hence the church's life. In Philippians 2:14 he commands, "Do everything without complaining or arguing." Then he says in Ephesians 4:29, "Do not let any unwholesome talk come out of your mouths, but only what is helpful for building others up according to their needs, that it may benefit those who listen." Constant complaining and negativity will not build others up and benefit them. This kind of talk accomplishes the opposite. In general, people involved in negative stuff are angry people. And I believe that much of this negative behavior on the part of Christians is traceable to anger that they have never addressed. Paul would seem to agree with me as he addresses unbridled anger in the context of Ephesians 4:29 (see vv. 31–32). Following the step above—forgiving others—should help with this problem. The grievance process that was suggested earlier in this chapter will also help.

Paul's words in Ephesians 4:1–3 reflect how we should behave toward one another: "As a prisoner for the Lord, then, I urge you to live a life worthy of the calling you have received. Be completely humble and gentle; be patient, bearing with one another in love. Make every effort to keep the unity of the Spirit through the bond of peace." Following is a test for negativity. See how you do. Ask someone else, such as a spouse or friend, to answer the questions about you.

Test for Detecting Negativity

1. Are you an optimist or a pessimist?
2. Do some things at church (such as changing the way things are done) upset you?
3. When you are upset, do you complain?
4. Do you express your complaints to others?

   If you answered yes to questions 2, 3, and 4, then face it, you are a negative person.

Pursue Reconciliation

Pursue reconciliation with a brother or sister (Matt. 5:23–24; 18:15–19). I find in most churches that few Christians attempt reconciliation with those who have offended them or those whom they may have offended. This is probably because they are not aware of the biblical teaching on reconciliation. However, I suspect that it may also be the fear of approaching someone over such issues. A typical response is, "Why, I could never do that!" And some who are less biblically literate would even go so far as to think that such confrontation is not Christian.

The biblical teaching on reconciliation is found primarily in two key texts: Matthew 5:23–24 and 18:15–19. In Matthew 5:23–24 the Savior commands that if we know of a brother or sister who has something against us, we are to drop what we are doing (in this context, worship), go to that person, and seek reconciliation. Reconciliation is so important to the believer that it takes precedence over worship. Indeed, how can we experience authentic worship with unreconciled relationships in our lives?

In Matthew 18:15–19 the Savior addresses those who are on the other end of reconciliation—those who believe they have been wronged. In this context, Jesus commands the offended brother or sister to pursue and seek reconciliation with the offending party.

Regardless of what the text clearly teaches, some will not follow through because they are afraid of the consequences. "What if they get angry and won't listen? It could become a bad scene." Actually, this has happened to me as I have pursued the reconciliation process with those I think I have offended. However, it has been a rare occurrence, and I would rather risk upsetting a brother or sister than miss an opportunity to win him or her back. My experience has been that most people respond positively, and these people become good friends rather than alienated persons.

Agree to Church Discipline

Agree to pursue and accept church discipline (Matt. 18:15–20; 1 Cor. 5:1–13). It is likely that you do not know of any churches that practice church discipline; they are few and far between. I believe that it is because the majority of churches are small and view themselves as families. And as families they tend to tolerate more than they would even from those who are a part of their biological families. We do not want to risk making family members mad at us or having them turn on us.

Scripture is very clear that the church is to discipline those who are caught up in sin (1 Cor. 5:1–13) or resist reconciliation (Matt. 18:15–20) if they fail to correct their situations and attempt to remain in the church. This discipline may extend to excommunication of the errant person (Matt. 18:17; 1 Cor. 5:13).

I am aware of one pastor who shortly after being called to a church was approached by two men in the church. They made it clear that they were opposed to his selection as the new pastor and that they would do everything in their power to run him off. They accomplished this within two years. In this situation, I would argue that the church's governing board should have gone to them and informed them that they were aware of what was happening and would discipline them if things went any further (and might discipline them regardless). Here the pastor was in a no-win situation—he was the one who was in their crosshairs. Whatever he said or did would be considered defensive. That is why the board needed to step in and take action.

It is important that those who are disciplined accept it, understanding that the goal is not to embarrass or hurt them but to restore them to fellowship.

Obey the Leadership

Obey and submit to the church's leadership (1 Thess. 5:12–13; Heb. 13:17). We are living in a time when it seems fashionable, even trendy, to challenge and question those in authority—the leaders of our churches—rather than follow them. Being a recognized leader in the church is almost like hanging a target around one's neck. Why? I believe that trust is the primary issue. You cannot lead people who do not trust you! This is such a problem because so many leaders in both the church and the corporate world have done much to undermine people's trust. For pastors it has largely been moral failure. For corporate leaders it has been greed. Regardless, God has gifted and provided his church with leaders who are to be followed. Hebrews 13:17 is very clear when it says, "Obey your leaders and submit to their authority."

Consequently, discontented followers must decide whether or not they can follow their leaders. If they cannot for whatever reason, they must work through the church's established grievance process (earlier in this chapter). If they still feel the same way, they need to leave the church and find someone they can obey and to whom they can submit. The worst thing a person can do is stay in the church and gripe and complain and cause trouble for the leadership (see "Be Positive" earlier). Those who do not comply leave themselves open to God's discipline and his removal of them (1 Cor. 5:9–13; Heb. 12:1–13; 1 John 5:16–17).

Listen to Others

Become a better listener (James 1:19–21). If we practice listening well to one another, we will better understand and avoid unnecessary misunderstandings in our churches. James warns, "My dear brothers, take note of this: Everyone should be quick to listen, slow to speak and slow to become angry, for man's anger does not bring about the righteous life that God desires" (vv. 19–20). All too commonly in struggling churches the reverse of James's admonition is seen. They are slow to listen, quick to speak, and too quick to become angry.

Good listening, not necessarily more talking, is the key to good communication. Failure to listen well communicates that we may not value the person talking or we may not think what he or she is saying is important enough to give him or her a hearing. It could also mean that we have already made up our mind. We owe it to our brothers and sisters in the faith to give them a hearing, whatever the topic. This is especially true if they disagree with us or stand on the side of an issue that we do not support. On the one hand, we tend not to discuss issues in the church that divide us. On the other hand, when we do, we can short-circuit the process by not listening well.

As we saw earlier in this chapter, the third step in the preparation for strategic planning is developing good congregational communication. Communicating the results of strategic planning to the congregation to gain their trust as well as listening to their thoughts and concerns are both important. The people do not have to agree with you or you with them. The point is that they will tend to respect and trust you if you give them a hearing and they feel they have been heard.

Speak the Truth

Speak the truth in love (Eph. 4:15). In Ephesians Paul prescribes our speaking the truth to one another in love. But what is truth? In context, truth seems to be sound teaching coupled with the absence of deceit, or simple truth telling. This must have been a problem for some in the church at Ephesus, or Paul would not have bothered to address it. There are those who are quick to speak the truth but in the wrong way. They bludgeon people over the head with truth. Paul's point is that there is a right and a wrong way to communicate truth to people.

The best way to communicate truth is out of a genuine love for the person who needs to hear that truth. When you address people with truth, take a moment to examine your motives. You may discern various good motives for speaking the truth to them. The question the text raises is this: Is love one of those motives?

A common example of not speaking the truth in love is gossip. A layman's definition of gossip is passing on negative information about someone or something that we do not know to be true as if it were true. This is a clear violation of Paul's admonition, and it reveals that the person who indulges in this sin does not love those who are injured by it. Participating in gossip is like pouring hydrochloric acid on human relationships. It hurts and often destroys people.

Wise leaders will address this sin and invite the congregation to confront people who indulge in it. Often in strategic planning it takes place when people feel threatened by change that will involve the loss of power or the loss of a cherished tradition. This is the reason a grievance process is necessary. When someone is approached by a gossip who is reporting about something he or she thinks is going on in the church, this person can be directed to the grievance process. I believe that if we emphasize this strongly enough and enforce it, it will eliminate much congregational gossip.

Pursue Holiness

Pursue personal holiness (Rom. 6:1–15; 12:1–2). In Romans 6 Paul carefully instructs his church in how to pursue personal holiness. My aim in this short space is to focus on Romans 6:1–15, where he writes that we need to know something, believe it, and then act on it. First, we need to know or understand that we as believers no longer have to obey sin (vv. 1–10). (In this context, Paul compares sin to a slave master.) When we accepted Christ, we died to the power of sin over our lives (vv. 2, 5, 7–8). Before we accepted Christ, we had no choice but to serve and obey sin. However, now we are in Christ and he has crucified the old self; we do not have to serve sin. We may choose to, but we do not have to. Not only did he break the control of sin over our lives, but as he was raised, so we have been raised to a whole new way of life (vv. 4, 8).

Second, Paul teaches in verse 11 that we must embrace this truth in faith. Though it happened, it is of no use to us if we do not know or believe it. Thus he commands, "Count yourselves dead to sin but alive to God in Christ Jesus."

Finally, he commands that in light of what Christ has accomplished for us (death to sin and resurrection to new life), we must neither allow sin to rule over us nor obey its desires (v. 12). Instead, we are to offer ourselves to God and our bodies as instruments of his righteousness (v. 13).

Obedience to this teaching must be expected in our churches, because we desire holiness on the part of our people. Paul affirms in verses 19 and 22 that offering our bodies in slavery to righteousness results in holiness (some versions render this "sanctification"). If our people are struggling spiritually, perhaps we as leaders need to teach more on personal holiness and provide our people with opportunities to commit to its pursuit when we gather as a body.

BE A SERVANT

Adopt a servant attitude (Matt. 20:20–28; Phil. 2:3–11). Jesus teaches clearly that leaders are to be servants. But what does a servant look like? Servant leaders display at least four characteristics: humility, willingness to serve, a focus on others, and love.

Matthew 20:25–26 says, "Jesus called them [the disciples—his SLT] together and said, 'You know that the rulers of the Gentiles lord it over them, and their high officials exercise authority over them. Not so with you.'" Jesus uses a negative example to make his point. They are to lead with humility, not ego as did the Gentile leaders.

In verses 26–28 Jesus continues: "Instead, whoever wants to become great among you must be your servant, and whoever wants to be first must be your slave—just as the Son of Man did not come to be served, but to serve, and to give his life as a ransom for many." He is teaching that the essence of servant leadership is service, not status. Combined with the first characteristic, we find that leadership is about humble service. This is the kind of service that involves giving of oneself, not taking for oneself.

A servant leader focuses on others. The objects of our service, in the context of Matthew 20:20–28, are other people, such as those in our congregations. Jesus came to serve and give his life for *many*, and so also must our service be to benefit others, not ourselves. Servant leadership is selfless. It is all about others, not us.

Another characteristic of servant leadership is love. The love of leaders for their followers is the reason servant leaders serve; it is their motivation for service. This is clear from Jesus's teaching in John 13:1–17 when he washed the disciples' feet. They had been so busy arguing over who among them was the greatest that none had lowered himself to wash the others' feet (a common practice usually done by a slave when a guest first entered a home). This act would have been an admission by one that he was not the greatest. So they all proudly reclined around the table with dirty feet. Then the Savior assumed the role of a servant and washed their feet, setting the example for them. Here is the point. We will serve others humbly only to the degree that we love them. And the dirt on their feet will test our love for them. If we do not love them, we will take up the leadership towel only to toss in that towel quickly when it gets a little dirty. If we love our followers deeply, we will not only take up the leadership towel but also wrap ourselves in it. We will not mind a little dirt.[10] Perhaps to drive this point home, you might consider having an actual foot-washing ceremony with your strategic leadership team.

REMEMBER WHOSE CHURCH IT IS

Give your church back to Christ (Matt. 16:18). It is most common to hear people refer to the place where they worship as "my church." While we think little about such expressions, people can get the idea that they own the church. They may have been there from day one, they may have also given a lot to the church, and they may be in a position of leadership, and when someone, such as a new pastor, comes in and attempts to change something in *their* church, it is comparable to his coming into their homes and rearranging their furniture or repainting the walls. Based on their false sense of ownership, they feel violated.

The truth according to Matthew 16:18 is that the church does not belong to any person. It is not "my church," and it is not yours either. It belongs to Christ. He made it very clear in this passage when he said, "I will build my church." Therefore I would encourage everyone on the leadership team to ask himself or herself to whom the church belongs. Do any of them think the church belongs to them? Regardless, it is time for everyone to give it back to the Savior, putting him back on the throne, turning the control over to him. If we want him to build the church as the passage states, then we must make sure that it is his and not ours. He will build his, not our, church.

To make this point, you could have a worship ceremony with the strategic leadership team or the entire congregation and focus on the enthronement psalms (Psalms 47, 93, 96–99). You would preach and even sing some of these psalms. Then invite those who are ready to put Christ on the throne, as head of the church, to kneel or even come forward. Follow this with a time of prayer and commitment.

The Implementation of Spiritual Formation

A chain of events that begins with the pastor and ends with the church's ministry community at large will implement spiritual formation in your church.

THE PASTOR

It is imperative that spiritual formation and renewal begin with the senior pastor of the church. My experience in churches that are experiencing growth challenges is that the pastor may be discouraged and need spiritual renewal. Most congregations look to their pastors for spiritual leadership. This is most difficult because there are times when even pastors struggle. And when a church is moving through a growth challenge, he may be questioning his leadership ability and allowing his spiritual development to slip. However, this affects the church as well as the pastor as spiritual leader.

Like Paul, we all struggle with sin in our lives (Rom. 7:14). The battle is constant and unrelenting. Therefore I challenge pastors to take the thirteen steps of spiritual formation first, as they seek their own personal spiritual renewal. They cannot lead their people through strategic planning or anything else for that matter if they are not themselves being spiritually formed. Only as the Holy Spirit revitalizes and refreshes their spirit will they be able to lead their church in transformation to Christlikeness.

The Strategic Leadership Team

Spiritual vitality is catching. As the Spirit transforms the point leader, so his life, in turn, catalyzes the leadership team to a passionate pursuit of Christ. As they pursue Christ, they experience the same revitalization and transformation of their souls that the pastor experienced.

When I consult with churches, I set aside at least one meeting to address with the team their spiritual formation and to lead them through an understanding of this process. If it is not happening at the team level, it will not happen at the congregational level, because the team members are the E. F. Hutton people—the leaders of the church who, like it or not, set the example for the congregation.

The Congregation

Spiritual vitality is infectious. From the pastor and the leadership team it quickly spreads to the congregation. They watch their leaders and follow their example. And as they catch on, spiritual growth spreads to their families and friends.

This is why fellowship, one of the church's four functions (Acts 2:42), is so important. People come into a close and deep relationship with one another, and they rub off on one another. The fruit of the Spirit rub off from those who are intently, regularly involved in the spiritual formation of their soul.

I encourage pastors regularly—at least yearly—to take time out to preach and teach the truths of spiritual formation to their congregation, because a combination of hearing truth and seeing truth is a powerful spiritual motivator. Therefore it is imperative that pastors call their people to repentance and strong pursuit of the Savior's transforming power in their lives.

The Community

Spiritual formation does not and must not stop with the congregation. Those who make up the unbelieving community are constantly watching and judging our Christianity and our Christ by our lives. They will respond to what they sense and experience as authentic.

Jesus said to his disciples that they were the salt of the earth and also "the light of the world." He added, "A city on a hill cannot be hidden" (Matt. 5:14). Thus the church becomes a lighthouse to its believing and unbelieving community. And its light, in turn, penetrates and illumines the darkness of communal unbelief.

Questions for Reflection, Discussion, and Application

1. Does the ministry's empowered leadership—the board, pastor, staff, patriarch or matriarch—support the strategic planning process? How do you know? What is the plan if some or all do not support it?

2. Do you—the pastor or lay leader—see the importance of recruiting a strategic leadership team? Who would choose this team? Who would make up this team in your congregation? Make a list of names. How many are on that list? What qualifies them to be on the list? Will you have them sign a covenant of commitment?

3. How would you rate your current communication with the congregation (average, better than average, worse than average)? Do they trust you? What are some other ways to communicate with them that will promote their trust? Does your church have a grievance process?

4. Do a church ministry analysis—use the one in this chapter or one you design for your team. What does it reveal about your church? If your church is in decline, what is its percentage of decline? Based on this percentage, how long does the church have before it will have to close its doors? Does this fact get people's attention?

5. Is your church ready for change? How do you know? If not, what will you do to help it along?

6. How long do you think it will take for your church to make significant, meaningful change? Are you willing to commit to it for this period of time? Why or why not? If not, what are your options and which will you choose?

7. Do you agree with the author regarding the importance of spiritual formation to strategic planning? If so, how will this affect your preparation?

8. Do you agree with the author's definition of spiritual formation? If not, why not? If so, why? How would you alter or add to it?

9. How would you rate your church's need for spiritual maturity on a scale of 1 to 10 (1 being low and 10 being high)?

10. If you are the pastor, a staff person, or a member of the strategic planning team, how are you progressing in your own personal spiritual formation? Are you a little discouraged? If so, why?

11. As you read and possibly walked through the thirteen steps, did some stand out to you as especially important? If so, which ones?

12. If you are the pastor or part of the leadership team, what are some ways that you might implement these spiritual formation steps in your ministry?

3

Preparing the Boat

Developing the Strategy

In chapter 1 I noted that good navigators prepare carefully before launching their boats. The prelaunch checklist makes sure the boat is shipshape and ready to launch. At the top of that list is determining if one is truly a navigator. In chapter 2 we discovered, however, that it is not enough to prepare the navigator alone; we must prepare the crew who will be on the boat so they are ready to sail. This involves using a seven-step crew readiness process. Now in chapter 3 we are ready to prepare the ministry boat. Not only must the boat be ready to sail but it also must be the right boat. The wrong boat could spell disaster. If not properly attended to, it could spring a leak and eventually head straight to the bottom rather than the proper ministry port. Thus this chapter involves developing the best strategy to get the navigator and the crew to their desired port of call.

Strategy development walks hand in hand with planning. Good development necessitates good planning. The problem is that far too many ministry leaders do not plan well, and thus their ministries are underdeveloped if developed at all. There are several reasons for this.

- The leaders do not see the need to plan, because their predecessor has left them with a plan in place, though it may be very outdated. They respond, "Shucks, if it ain't broke, don't fix it!"

91

- They have embraced and mimic the model of some successful megachurch so they feel that the megachurch has done all the development work for them. They respond, "How can you improve on what God is evidently blessing?"
- Some do not think that planning and development are important. They are good preachers and believe that preaching is most important. They respond, "Just preach and teach the Bible and everything else will take care of itself!"
- They do not know how to plan or develop strategies. This is the most prevalent reason. They did not take this course in seminary. Their response is, "Help!"

Regardless of the reason, the old adage is right on target—failing to plan is planning to fail! However, we can do something about this. We can learn how to plan and develop a strategy. Therefore in this chapter we'll briefly explore why developing a strategy is so important, what development is, who is responsible for strategy development, and a four-step process that will help you develop a ministry strategy for your church.

The Importance of Developing a Strategy

The church's Strategy (capital S) is made up of five mini-strategies (small s)—the reasons strategy development is important to a ministry.

The Strategy of Encouraging Community Outreach

The local church exists in a geographical community, and an important part of its ministry is reaching out to that community with the gospel (Acts 1:8). To accomplish this, every church must develop a strategy for community outreach. This includes determining the soft boundaries of that community and then identifying who lives within those boundaries. I refer to this as an Acts 1:8 exercise. The early church identified its community as Jerusalem and the people living in its environs. The boundaries for our churches today are determined by either drive time or distance to and from the church. These boundaries form a flexible, concentric circle with the church at the center. Then with the aid of demographic and psychographic studies, the church identifies the people who live within its boundaries. Without this outreach strategy, the church will not effectively impact its community for Christ, and so I address forming such a strategy in chapter 8.

The Strategy of Designing a Process for Making Disciples

Once the church has developed a strategy for community outreach, it needs to design a strategy for making disciples of those within its community. Such a strategy provides a clear, simple, memorable pathway for making disciples that most everyone understands and helps them know where they are in the process. The way to develop such a strategy is to take five steps:

1. Embrace a Great Commission mission.
2. Identify the biblical characteristics of a mature disciple.
3. Determine what will be the primary ministries that will ingrain these characteristics in a disciple.
4. Align the characteristics and the ministries.
5. Evaluate how well the disciple-making strategy is doing.

I address how to develop such a strategy in chapter 9.

The Strategy of Forming a Ministry Dream Team

Every church needs a strategy for forming teams to accomplish its disciple-making ministry within its community. This strategy will address two or three teams. The first is made up of the congregation and involves mobilizing them for ministry. The second consists of the staff members who develop lay leaders who, in turn, will lead the ministry workers to carry out the church's ministries. The third is a governing board, which some churches do not have. This board, along with the pastor, exercises leadership at the highest level of the church. Chapter 10 addresses developing such a team strategy.

The Strategy of Addressing the Church's Setting

Churches are wise to develop a strategy that addresses their setting—their location and facilities. The reason is twofold. A disciple-making church can quickly outgrow its facilities and this has a limiting effect on its ministry to and in its community. They simply have no place to put their people. Another reason to address setting is that the church may need to move to a more strategic location in its community. This is often the case when what was once a growing community around the church changes and begins to die. I address forming a strategy for the church's setting in chapter 11.

The Strategy of Raising Needed Finances

A fact of ministry life is that every church needs money if it is to carry out its disciple-making ministries in the community. To accomplish this, it is imperative that a church develop a strategy for raising and managing the necessary funds. Such a strategy consists of three factors: determine who in the church is responsible to raise and manage its finances, determine how much funding the church needs to make disciples, and determine how the church can raise the necessary funds. Chapter 12 will help you form a strategy for funding your church's ministries.

Five Mini-Strategies

1. Strategy of Encouraging Community Outreach
2. Strategy of Designing a Process for Making Disciples
3. Strategy of Forming a Ministry Dream Team
4. Strategy of Addressing the Church's Setting
5. Strategy of Raising Needed Finances

What Is Strategy Development?

For the sake of clarity, we need to pause and experience a brief "clarity moment" that involves answering the question, What are we talking about? This chapter addresses the development of a strategy for your ministry, and it is important that you know what *strategy development* means. In this book I am using the term to mean *the process that a church works through to determine the goals and their objectives of each mini-strategy (small s) that makes up the church's overall Strategy (big S).* It also includes the recruitment of development teams (DTs) who work through and develop the goals and objectives of these mini-strategies within a set time frame. And this process takes place in the context of who the church is, where it is, and when it is.

First note that developing a strategy involves a *process*, which means it is ongoing. You will always be assessing and developing your strategy. At the beginning of the process, as covered in this book, this will be more intense and time demanding than later on in the ministry.

Next, strategic development has a *direction* that consists of your objectives and their goals, which make up and are essential to each mini-strategy (community outreach, disciple making, building a dream team, setting, and finances). Together they make up your overall strategy.

Third are *deadlines*. You will need to determine when the development of these objectives and their goals for each mini-strategy should be completed and ready to be implemented in the life of the congregation.

Finally, there will be a *leader* for each strategic objective or mini-strategy who will recruit a development team (DT). These teams, in turn, will develop the strategies and meet the deadlines for their development work.

All this takes place in a ministry context that consists of three factors: who the church is, its identity (mission, vision, and values); where the church is or its location (urban, suburban, or rural); when it is (the time or year when the development takes place). All three context factors must be taken into consideration if the church is to strategize authentically. I would discourage a church from mimicking another church, such as a successful megachurch. What works in one part of the country may not work in another.

Responsibility for Strategic Development

The Senior Pastor

The leadership in general (the staff, a board, and strategic leadership team) and the senior pastor in particular are responsible for developing the strategic plan. This is the reason the pastor is so important to the entire process. Here are some factors that the pastor must consider as he develops the strategic process:

1. He must not only commit to the process but also plan to stay at the church through the process. For a pastor to leave early during the development step would spell disaster. It would so disrupt the process that it would likely unravel. I ask senior pastors to make a commitment to the entire strategic planning process before it is begun.

2. He must be patient with the process, as development will not happen overnight. He must focus on the process in light of the many distractions cited earlier, including his personal passions. This takes a great deal of discipline. Successful strategy development requires a focused commitment of one's attention and energy.

3. He will need to reassess his ministry or job description. If he has learned anything, he has learned the importance of leadership. If seminary trained, he may have placed undue emphasis on preaching and teaching the Bible. They may consume an inordinate amount of his time. This is not to say that preaching and teaching the Bible are not important. They are. However, leadership is as crucial today as it was in the early church, as seen in the book of Acts. Preaching and teaching the Scriptures are essential to his leadership. They go together.

4. He needs to create a "stop doing" list. He must ask, What am I currently doing that I should not be doing? What is the 20 percent of what I do that produces the 80 percent of what gets done? What am I doing that I should have delegated to someone else long ago? This frees up the leader-pastor to do what he needs to be doing—what God wants him to be doing—strategically leading and developing and redeveloping the strategy.

5. Keep your goals where you can see them so you won't forget them. Keep them with your schedule or calendar. Make them part of your to-do list. Post them in your office or on the bathroom mirror, anyplace where you will see them often.

The Staff

While the senior pastor and not the staff is responsible for the overall design of the strategic plan, the staff will be a part of the process. Obviously, even in the smallest churches the pastor cannot do it by himself. He will need the help not only of the strategic leadership team but also of any full-time or lay staff persons.

Some larger churches may have an executive pastor, an administrative pastor, or even a pastor of strategic planning who will help the senior pastor by shouldering much of the load. However, the senior pastor is ultimately responsible. And many of the factors above that apply to the senior pastor will also apply to him.

There will be some aspects of development that only the staff will accomplish. And there will be other aspects that the staff will accomplish along with the strategic leadership team.

Regardless, the staff will want to be involved because much of development will affect what they do and will be doing in the church, and they need to have a voice in this (see chap. 10).

The Governing Board

If the church has a governing board, it will be involved in the development of the strategic plan. It will be involved not only because most if not all of the board members are on the strategic leadership team but also because the board itself has leadership responsibilities. Its primary responsibility is to monitor and make sure that the pastor and staff follow through. This is one of the accountability features or safeguards of the process.

The Strategic Leadership Team

The strategic leadership team (SLT) is also involved in and responsible for much development. This needs to be understood up front and was stated in the Covenant of Commitment (see appendix C) that each signed at the beginning of the process. Sometimes the team as a whole will be involved. At other times only certain gifted, talented individuals will be needed in their areas of expertise. The SLT will break up and work on development teams, each focusing on and developing one of the mini-strategies and taking responsibility for it.

Responsibility for Development

Senior Pastor

Staff

Board

Strategic Leadership Team

Developing a Strategic Plan

Now that we know why development is important, what it is, and who is responsible to make it happen, we turn to the practice of strategic development. It will tell us how to design the Strategy plan (big S). This involves pursuing a four-step strategic development process.

Anytime you attempt to execute a process, there will be certain barriers that get in the way and attempt to block it. I define them as embedded practices, policies, or persons (anything or anyone) that block the effective activation of your strategic plan. You will run headlong into them both in the development process and especially in its implementation, when you launch your developed strategic plan. Thus I have included some information on how to identify and deal with these barriers in chapter 13 under "Some Important Implementation Practices." Should you encounter barriers as you take the following steps, use the information there to deal with them.

Step 1. Formulate Development Objectives with Goals

The very first part of the process is to formulate the objectives and their specific goals needed to effectively develop the mini-strategies that make up the overall ministry Strategy. We at The Malphurs Group have come up with eleven objectives. They are prayer, congregational communication, community outreach, disciple making, congregational mobilization, staffing, board development, setting (location and facilities), finances or stewardship, creativity and innovation, and leader development. Each of these objectives could have five to twenty or more goals. To see the goals for each of these objectives, turn to the Strategic Development Worksheet in appendix D. You may need to adjust each objective and its goals to your particular context. In your context you may want to come up with other objectives.

Before formulating specific goals, it is wise to understand the characteristics of good goals. There are at least five. They are clear—people understand what they are. They are urgent, important to the ministry, and need to have been accomplished yesterday. They are visible—people can see something taking place right before their eyes. They are meaningful and important to people. They are timely and can be accomplished quickly. Thus they lead to short-term as well as long-term wins.

Five Characteristics of Good Goals

1. Clear
2. Urgent
3. Visible
4. Meaningful
5. Timely

Step 2. Recruit Development Team Leaders and Teams

Ministry is only as good as the people who lead and carry it out, and this needs to be kept in mind in this step—recruiting the teams and their leaders. Most people have a profound inner desire to accomplish something of significance with their lives. Our job as leaders is to assist our people in accomplishing this for Christ, and it can be done when people are put in positions for which they are wired. Then their gifts, passions, and temperament will help them accomplish the goals. A person with the gift of evangelism might connect with the community outreach development team (DT). Another indication is one's profession. For example, a realtor might join the community outreach DT, or a contractor, architect, or carpenter might be on the ministry setting DT (facilities and location).

First, you will need to determine which DTs are needed and then recruit the team members. We at The Malphurs Group recommend teams for each of the objectives listed above, along with a lead development team. Thus in addition to the lead team, we recommend the following: prayer team, congregational communication team, community outreach team, disciple-making team, congregational mobilization team, staff team, ministry setting (location and facilities) team, finance or stewardship team, and creative and innovative team, which can help the church adapt quickly to change in the culture. An optional team is one that develops a governing board. This objective is optional because some churches do not have a board. Another optional team is a church leadership development team.

The pastor and others, such as the leader of the lead development team (who may be the pastor), will select and recruit from the SLT the leader or champion for each development team listed above. Do not make the mistake of asking for volunteers. It's okay to ask for volunteers to be on a team but not for leading a team. When you ask for volunteers to lead, you may get people who are not able or competent to lead. I suspect this may be the reason Jesus selected and pursued the disciples he knew would be good leaders (see Mark 1:17–20).

Next, the DT leaders will, in turn, select their teams (at least two but no more than nine people) from those on the SLT, who are not leading or on another team, and from people in the congregation.

Once you have in place the DT members, the team members will divvy up the goals among them. How might they know which goals each should pursue? One, as mentioned above, is the person's divine design (gifts, passion, and temperament). A second indication might be a personal interest. Someone may not have gifting or experience in a particular area but simply be interested in the area of ministry.

Step 3. Determine Development Deadlines

Decide when the goals must be accomplished. This means setting completion dates, which are the benchmarks for success. I have discovered that in ministry, like almost everything else, some people are doers and some are procrastinators. While I suspect that all people have a little procrastinator in them, the leaders of the teams need to be doers. Doers as well as procrastinators need deadlines, for deadlines signal not only when they have to be finished but also when they have to begin the launch or implementation phase.

Keep in mind that time is of the essence in strategic design. We are looking for short-term wins as much as long-term wins. For some people to do their best work, however, plenty of time will be needed. They prefer not to be too rushed. They like some time to think and be creative. Others do their best work when under pressure. When things come down to the final out in the final inning, they can step up to the plate and hit the ball out of the ballpark. In either case, a deadline is essential and exerts necessary pressure.

Deadlines may vary. They may be staggered deadlines. This is because some teams, such as the community outreach development team, start the development process several weeks to a month earlier than the others. Either way, we set a benchmark of 120 days for the teams to complete their planning objectives, understanding that some teams may require more time while others require less.

On the other hand, deadlines may be the same. This means that all the teams finish on the same date. In this case, the teams that begin the process earlier may have a little more time (120 days) to develop their goals than the later teams that may have 90 or 60 days. So far my experience has been that this is not a problem as long as the teams with less time are aware of this. They can expand or contract the time periods, depending on the amount of time they have.

And there may be special deadlines. Some teams are intrinsically different from the others and may require special deadlines. An example would be the prayer team. Rather than develop a strategy for prayer, its goal is to pray for the development process and those involved in it. This goal would need to be met from day one.

Finally, you will need to develop a time line that will help you follow each team's progress. I recommend that you employ a Gantt chart to accomplish this. A Gantt chart is a bar chart that illustrates a project schedule that includes the beginning and end of each goal.

Step 4. Develop Strategy Goals

How will your goals and ultimately your objectives be developed? Here there will be some overlap with step 2 because we will need to revisit the team leaders and their teams. This is because who affects how. In addition, keep in mind the importance of regularly communicating your progress in goals development to the congregation. Remember, they will often be down on what they are not up on.

Team Members

At this point the teams have been formed, and each team has the needed number of members. I recommend that people not join more than one team unless they have loads of time at their disposal. And just because a person is retired does not mean he or she has loads of discretionary time. The basic tasks of the team members are the following.

1. Determine the goals you want to develop. As stated earlier, you would be wise to pursue the goals that call for your special giftedness and abilities as well as interests.

2. Be sure to attend the session where either a staff person or a consultant presents the material that you need to know to develop your goals. Essentially, this is the material found in chapters 8–12. Also, take copious notes and be sure to ask any questions you have.

3. Strive to become an expert in your area of goals development. For example, read voraciously and interview people in the community who are experts in your area.

4. Meet with your team as determined by the team leader in accord with the team. It could be once a week or once a month. Some team members will be able to work by themselves, while others work best with a group.

5. Direct any questions you have to your team leader. Should he or she not have the answer, the questions should go to the lead development team (LDT).

6. Pray for the process, the team as it works through the process, and the leader of your team.

Team Leaders

At this point team leaders in conjunction with the lead development team have selected the team that they desire to lead. (It is very possible that the LDT recruited them with a specific team in mind.) As with the members, this choice should be based on their gifts, abilities, and interests. The following are the basics tasks of team leaders.

1. Work with your team members to determine the development goals of the team.

2. Like the team members, you will need to select the particular goal or goals of the team you want to help develop.

3. Schedule team meetings based on the makeup of the team and the need for such meetings. Again this will likely vary from team to team. It could take place by actually coming together at a specific location or it could happen over a conference call or some other method such as Skype.

4. Answer any questions from your team members. Should you not know the answers, take them to the LDT.

5. Coordinate the team's goal development with the LDT. Make sure they are aware of what you are doing and the decisions you make.

6. Monitor the progress of each of your team members.

7. Be ready to intervene should there be any problems between members or any problems as they relate to those outside the team.

8. Be an encourager. Your team members will need tons of it.

9. Celebrate the team's accomplishments as they develop their goals.

10. Pray for the people who are on your team.

The Development Process

Step 1: Formulate Development Objectives with Their Goals

Step 2: Recruit Development Team Leaders and Teams

Step 3: Determine Development Deadlines

Step 4: Develop Strategy Goals

Questions for Reflection, Discussion, and Application

1. Are you convinced that development of the strategic plan is important? Why or why not? If so, did you come up with some reasons that the author did not mention?

2. Who in your ministry will take responsibility for strategy development? Will this include the senior pastor, any staff, and board members? Do you anticipate any problems with any of these people? What other people will play a role?

3. What is your definition of strategy development? What is the author's? Do you agree or disagree? Why?

4. What are some of the things that the pastor needs to delegate to someone else? Create a "stop doing" list.

5. Do you have a list of development goals for each objective? Have you reviewed appendix D? Are your goals much the same as those in appendix D?

6. Do you anticipate any development barriers? If so, what or from whom? Do you need to address how to deal with them now rather than waiting until the implementation or launch phase?

7. What are the actions necessary to accomplish your goals? Who will be responsible for each goal? What deadlines should you assign each? Will they be staggered, the same, or special deadlines? What kind of resources will team members need (money, equipment, facilities, and so on)?

part two

Set the Course!

The Process of Strategic Planning

Developing a Biblical Mission

What We Are Supposed to Be Doing

I explained in chapter 1 that strategic planning is a fourfold process that consists of the development of a biblical mission (chap. 4), the development of a compelling vision (chap. 5), the discovery of the church's core values (chap. 6), and the design of a strategy that accomplished the mission and vision (chaps. 7–12). I will introduce the strategy design in chapter 7 and then cover the steps that make up the design of a good strategy in chapters 8–12. I have given each step its own separate chapter because each is so important to forming the strategy. Thus Step 1 is reaching out to the church's community (chap. 8). Step 2 is making mature disciples (chap. 9). Step 3 is building a ministry team (chap. 10). Step 4 is assessing the church's setting (chap. 11). Step 5 is raising and managing the church's finances (chap. 12).

Now it is time to work on the first core concept that makes up this fourfold process: developing a biblical mission for the ministry. The Savior believed this to be important, for after his resurrection and before his ascension he gave the church its mission (see Matt. 28:19–20; Mark 16:15; Luke 24:45–49; Acts 1:8). In *The Seven Habits of Highly Effective People*, Stephen Covey writes, "One of the most important thrusts of my work with organizations is to assist them in developing effective mission statements."[1] That is my goal in this chapter—to help ministry navigators address the ministry boat's port of destination.

The development of an effective, biblical mission should be the goal of every church leader. Warren Bennis writes, "The task of the leader is to define the mission."[2] In addition, Peter Drucker, in *Managing the Non-Profit Organization*, states, "What matters is not the leader's charisma. What matters is the leader's mission. Therefore the first job of the leader is to think through and define the mission of the institution."[3] Obviously the church's mission is vital to its ministry. The mission answers the first fundamental question of the ministry: What are we supposed to be doing? or, Where are we going? People on board the ministry ship want to know where it is heading, where it is going to land. In this chapter we will learn why a mission is so important to a church, define the mission, discover the different kinds of missions, and show how to develop and then communicate the organization's mission.

Strategic Planning	
Part 1.	Preparation for strategic planning
Part 2.	**Process of strategic planning**
Part 3.	Practice of strategic planning

The Importance of the Mission

The ministry's mission is important because it affects the church in a number of essential ways. Here are nine of them.

Dictates the Ministry's Direction

Before embarking on a cruise, most people want to know where their boat is going. Otherwise, as Yogi Berra, the former New York Yankee catcher, once said, "If you don't know where you're going, you might end up somewhere else." A ship without a clear direction finds itself hopelessly adrift, not going anywhere. Leader-navigators and their churches must have a direction, and it is the mission that provides that important direction. It answers the question, Where are we going? Thus the ministry's mission provides a compelling sense of direction, a target for everyone to aim at, a port to land at, and it serves to focus the congregation's energy.

> **The Fourfold Process**
>
> **Mission Development**
> Vision Development
> Values Discovery
> Strategy Design

Leaders in the Bible demonstrated a strong sense of direction. God gave Adam and Eve their mission in Genesis 1:28. Moses pursued with a passion his mission to lead Israel out of bondage to the Promised Land (Exod. 3:10). The same is true of Joshua (Josh. 1:1–5), David (2 Sam. 5:2), Nehemiah (Neh. 2:17), and others. The Savior's mission directed his ministry (Mark 10:45), and Paul was passionate about his direction throughout his ministry (Acts 21:12–14; Rom. 15:20).

Defines the Ministry's Function

You will never do ministry that matters until you *define* what matters. Besides direction, the mission helps a ministry formulate or determine its biblical function. It answers the strategic, functional questions: What are we supposed to be doing? What function does the organization exist to perform? What is the primary or main thing that God has called us to accomplish? What are we attempting to do for God and our people? In short, what matters?

Therefore the mission is an expression of strategic intent. It summarizes and provides the church with its biblical task, and it defines the results that it seeks to obtain. When leaders communicate a meaningful, biblical mission to their people, it rings true. The people nod and think, *Yes, that is what we must be about.* Someone has pointed out that America's rail system has failed largely because it did not realize that it was in the transportation business. The most effective organizations know and understand what business they are in or what function they perform. The same holds true for the church that proclaims Jesus Christ.

Focuses the Ministry's Future

Both the directional and functional questions above address the church's future. That is because the mission, like the church's vision, has everything to do with its future. Though we cannot predict the future (except for biblical prophecy), we can create it, and that is the job of the mission. A clear, biblical mission serves to bring into focus the church's ministry future. The converse is also true: no mission, no future.

In addition, by focusing on the future, the mission helps the ministry not to live in and focus on the past. Paul put his past behind him and pushed forward to experience Christ. In Philippians 3:13–14 he writes, "Brothers, I do not consider myself yet to have taken hold of it. But one thing I do: Forgetting what is behind and straining toward what is ahead, I press on toward the goal to win the prize for which God has called me heavenward in Christ Jesus." Living in our ministry's past is like trying to drive a car by looking only through the rearview mirror. We must learn from and periodically celebrate the past but not live there.

Provides a Guideline for Decision Making

Every day church leaders have to make decisions. It comes with the ministry territory. Not only does a dynamic mission or intent focus the church's future, but it also sets important boundaries. It guides what the church will and will not attempt. It provides direction for when to say yes and when to say no. Mission is to the ministry what a compass is to a navigator or a template to a machinist. It provides a framework for critical thinking, a standard or criterion for all decision making.

Sincere (and sometimes not so sincere) people often approach a church board or pastor with suggestions for new areas of ministry that could potentially lead the church away from its divine direction. However, a clear, shared mission will protect the pastor and the board from involvement in numerous tangential activities. Their response can be, "Thanks so much for your interest, but that would lead us away from our mission."

Inspires Ministry Unity

Scripture is clear about the importance of unity among Christians. In John 17:20–23 the Savior prays for you and me and all who believe in Christ to be one. The result of this unity is that the world we seek to reach will believe that the Father has truly sent the Son. Paul stresses the importance of Christian unity in the local church. In Ephesians 4:3 he urges the church to "make every effort to keep the unity of the Spirit through the bond of peace."

Unity is another function of a well-constructed, shared statement of intent or mission. A clear direction communicates a unifying theme to all the members and draws them together as a team or community. It broadcasts, "Here is where we are going. Let's all pull together and with God's help make it happen." Thus it serves to get everyone on the same page. At the same time it encourages those with a different intent or another ministry agenda to look elsewhere. Just think of what your people could accomplish if everyone agreed with what you are trying to do!

Shapes the Strategy

A dynamic mission tells the church where it is going. It is the strategy, however, that gets it there. Though the two are mutually dependent, the mission leads and shapes the church's strategy. The mission tells what, and the strategy tells how. The mission always comes first—it is found at the front end of the strategy. The strategy is only as good as the mission that directs it. If you do not know where you are going, then any expressway or any body of water will take you there.

What amazes me is that so many churches today have a strategy, as expressed in their programs, but they have a vague, unclear mission. This does not make sense. Peter Drucker writes, "Strategy determines what the key activities are in a given business. And strategy requires knowing 'what our business is and should be.'"[4]

Enhances Ministry Effectiveness

When the people understand what the church is trying to accomplish, they become more effective in their efforts. Drucker has observed the effectiveness of a corporate mission in the marketplace: "That business purpose and business mission are so rarely given adequate thought is perhaps the most important single cause of business frustration and business failure. Conversely, in outstanding businesses . . . , success always rests to a large extent on raising the question 'What is our business?' clearly and deliberately, and on answering it thoughtfully and thoroughly."[5]

If you took time to investigate effective, God-honoring churches across North America, large or small, you would discover that each has a significant, well-focused mission. They know what business they are in. This is because all good performance starts with a clear direction. People who know where they are going are more willing to go the extra mile.

Ensures an Enduring Organization

It is rare that any one pastor lasts the entire time that a spiritually healthy church exists. Pastors come and they go. This is not necessarily bad. Once a pastor reaches retirement age, he serves his ministry best by leaving. This may be sad, but it makes room for a younger person who will be more in touch with the current culture and the ministry paradigms that God is blessing.

The goal of every ministry leader should be to leave behind a mission that will continue after he is gone. The mission, like the values, must not change appreciably over time. It is the Great Commission regardless of who is the pastor. A biblical, dynamic mission can help ensure the continuity of an enduring and great church.

Facilitates Evaluation

When you know what your mission is, you know how to evaluate your progress. For example, the church's mission is to make disciples. Thus the evaluation of the mission demands, Show me your disciples! In 2 Corinthians 13:5 Paul instructs the church at Corinth, "Examine yourselves to see whether you are in the faith; test yourselves." Throughout his second letter to the Corinthian church, Paul subjected both himself and his ministry to close scrutiny.

I have pastored three churches and served as an interim pastor in countless others. I suspect that during those ministries some unhappy congregants examined me and questioned whether I was in the faith. However, few have ever formally evaluated my leadership or the church's ministry. The church that fails to examine its people and its effectiveness as a ministry in light of its mission does itself an injustice. Otherwise, how will the church know if it's fulfilling its mission? How will it improve without formal evaluation? What you evaluate not only gets done but also gets done well.

While no organization enjoys living under the lens of careful scrutiny, evaluation will improve any ministry and the work of its people. I will say more about this in the last step of the strategic planning process that addresses ministry evaluation.

> **Why a Mission Is Important**
>
> It dictates the ministry's direction.
> It defines the ministry's function.
> It focuses the ministry's future.
> It provides a guideline for decision making.
> It inspires ministry unity.
> It shapes the strategy.
> It enhances ministry effectiveness.
> It ensures an enduring organization.
> It facilitates evaluation.

The Definition of a Mission

What is a mission? Let us assume you agree that a mission is important and you desire to develop a clear, consensual, effective one for your church. Precisely what is it you are trying to construct? What is the definition of a congregational mission? When defining a concept, it helps to clarify what it is not as well as what it is.

What a Mission Is Not

People have confused several concepts and used them synonymously with the mission concept. The most common is purpose. For example, Allan Cox defines a mission statement as "an organization's brief, compelling statement of purpose."[6] However, the purpose of a church as an organization is very different from its mission in a number of ways.

First, the purpose answers different questions. It answers the *why* questions: Why are we here? Why do we exist? What is our reason for being? The mission, however, answers the *what* questions: What are we supposed to be doing? What is our divine, strategic intent? What does God want us to accomplish while we are here on earth? You can discover your ministry purpose by asking the *why* question. First, state your mission. It may be to make disciples. Then probe it with the *why* question, Why do we want to make disciples? The answer—to glorify God—is your purpose.

Purpose is different from mission because it is broader in scope. The mission of a church, as well as its values, vision, strategy, and other concepts, is subsumed under its purpose.

The third difference is that the purpose of the church is doxological: to honor or glorify God (Rom. 15:6; 1 Cor. 6:20; 10:31). Thus it is abstract. The mission of the church is practical: to make disciples (Matt. 28:19). It is more concrete. When we make disciples (our mission), we glorify God (our purpose).

The focus of purpose and mission is different. The purpose focuses on God. He is the object of our glory, not ourselves or another. The mission focuses on people. We are to disciple people.

Finally, the purpose is for those within the church and those living in the community, whereas the mission is only for those in the church. On one occasion I used Willow Creek Community Church's mission statement ("Our mission is to turn *irreligious people* into fully devoted followers of Christ") with a group of church planters. One asked if those in the church's community knew that Willow viewed them as irreligious people. The question assumes that the mission statement is for the community. It is not. It is an internal document for the church's members, attenders, and those who are considering becoming a part of the church. It is the church's, not the community's, marching orders.

However, the church's purpose, to glorify God, is both internal—for the church—and external—it includes the community. How does it include the community?

The church's purpose helps it to position itself in the minds of those who live in the community and reach out to it. They should know not only that the church is located in the community but also why it is there. The answer for the church is to glorify God, that is, to live and minister in such a way that his excellent reputation is upheld before that unbelieving world. The answer for the community is that the church is there to make a difference—a positive difference that contributes to the community.

At the essence of positioning your church in the community is communicating well a positive, God-honoring image. When your image is good, this glorifies God and his reputation is good, since you represent him to the community. When your image is bad, his is bad—you misrepresent him to the community.

How do you develop your community image and glorify God? Actually, if you are an established church, you already have a reputation in your community. What is that image? Is it good or bad? A great example of a positive image in the community was the Jerusalem church. Luke notes in Acts 2:47 that the church enjoyed "the favor of all the people." And again in Acts 5:13 the Jerusalem believers were "highly regarded by the people." Does your church's image glorify God, or is there a need for some damage control?

Next, you should ask what you want your image to be. This involves your outreach and ministry into the community. What are you as a church doing to minister to the community? Some churches allow the community to use their facilities free or at a reduced cost, depending on the organization. Others minister to the police, firemen, and other public servants. And still others volunteer time in the public schools, hospitals, and public and charitable organizations.

The Difference between Purpose and Mission

	Purpose	Mission
Question	*Why* do we exist?	*What* are we supposed to be doing?
Scope	Broad	Narrow
Intent	To glorify God	To make disciples
Focus	God	Man
Use	Internal and external	Internal

Every ministry must know its purpose as well as its mission. The purpose is part of the ministry's congregational heart and soul. It is why the ministry exists, but it is not the mission. Let's go on to see what the mission is.

What a Mission Is

I define *a mission as a broad, brief, biblical statement of what the ministry is supposed to be doing ("Make disciples!")*. This definition has five key elements.

A MISSION IS BROAD

The first element of the definition expresses the expansiveness of a mission. A good mission must be broad, comprehensive, and overarching. It is the primary goal, mandate, or charge that is over all other goals or mandates of the ministry. They are subsumed under the mission. It is the predominate thrust that directs all that the church does, the umbrella that is over all the ministry's activities. And, most important, every ministry in the church must advance in some way the mission. The question we must constantly ask of our ministries is, How and what do they contribute to the church's mission? And the same applies to someone who wants to start a ministry in the church. At this point I would challenge you to do a quick inventory of your ministries, asking what each contributes to realizing the church's mission, if there is any overlap, and if the people involved in these ministries know and understand the question.

It is possible for a mission to be too expansive, so broad that it doesn't say anything. An example is a mission statement that says that the church will glorify God. Glorifying God is the church's purpose, not its mission, and the concept, without explanation, does not communicate what the church will actually do. The average parishioner as well as many pastors do not know what it means to glorify God.

A MISSION IS BRIEF

The statement of a mission should be brief. Cox says that it should be no more than seventy-five words.[7] Others allow for it to be longer.[8] The mission statements in the Bible are short—no longer than a sentence. For example, Moses's mission was to lead God's people, Israel, out of bondage in Egypt (Exod. 3:10). David's mission was to shepherd Israel and become their ruler (2 Sam. 5:2). Nehemiah's mission was to rebuild the wall of Jerusalem (Neh. 2:17). From a hermeneutical perspective, we must remember that mission statements in the Bible are generally descriptive, not prescriptive.[9] Neither Moses's, Nehemiah's, nor David's mission is our mission. So in most cases Scripture does not mandate our mission, with the exception of the Great Commission.

The one-sentence mission statements in Scripture, though descriptive and not mandatory, are good models for us. Actually most of them are just one word in the original languages. For example, the command "make disciples" in Matthew 28:19 is one word in the Greek. The leadership of a ministry should be able to catch the church's mission statement in a single, concise sentence. Drucker says that the statement should be able to fit on a T-shirt.[10] The leadership at Pantego Bible Church in Arlington, Texas, argue that the mission should be able to pass the "T-shirt test." I would state that it must be short enough to fit on a business card and pass the business card test. The reason is simple. If the mission is not short, people will not remember it.

A MISSION IS BIBLICAL

The third part of the definition means that a mission for a church must be based on the Scriptures. God determines the church's mission. Our triune God is by nature a missionary God. He has sent the Son (John 3:17), the Son has sent the Holy Spirit (John 16:7), and the Son has sent us (John 20:21). The mission first and foremost is God's mission, and we are to join him in mission. The question is, What does God say the church's mission is? The answer is the Great Commission. But what is the Great Commission? I provide that answer in the chart below that brings together all the biblical passages on the Great Commission. In Matthew 28:19 Jesus instructs his disciples, "Therefore go and make disciples of all nations." The Great Commission proactively involves the church in making and maturing disciples at home and abroad. This was the church's mission in the first century and continues to be its mission in the twenty-first century. Making disciples involves the church in proactively pursuing lost people (the "go" in Matt. 28:19), evangelizing them (Mark 16:15; Luke 24:46–48; Acts 1:8), and helping these new Christians to mature (Matt. 28:19–20), to become like Christ. The church is to accomplish this both at home and abroad (Mark 16:15; Acts 1:8). Finally, the church's mission is incarnational more than invitational. It involves the church going out into and ministering to the community, not waiting for the community to come to it.

The Great Commission

Scripture	Directed to Whom	What	Ministry to Whom	How	Where
Matt. 28:19–20	Disciples	Go, make disciples!	All nations	Baptizing and teaching	—
Mark 16:15	Disciples	Go, preach the good news!	All creation	—	All the world
Luke 24:46–48	Disciples	You are witnesses	All nations	Preaching repentance and forgiveness of sins	Beginning in Jerusalem
Acts 1:8	Disciples	You will be witnesses	—	With power	Jerusalem, Judea, Samaria, and all the world

A MISSION IS A STATEMENT

The fourth element of the definition says that a mission is a statement. The church must articulate and communicate its mission edict to the congregation. This takes the form of a statement, both verbal and written. Christ expressed the Great Commission in a verbal statement, and Matthew recorded it as a written statement. Mission developers would be wise to express their thoughts not only verbally but also in writing. This forces them to think and express themselves clearly. If they cannot write it, then they probably do not yet have a clear, articulate mission. Also, the mission will not have the authority to be a leadership statement until you can write it down.

A MISSION IS WHAT THE MINISTRY IS SUPPOSED TO BE DOING

The final element of the definition focuses on the *functional* question, What are we supposed to be doing? As we just discovered, more than two thousand years ago,

Christ predetermined the church's mission: "Make disciples." This is his mission mandate. This is what the church is supposed to be doing. This is God's will for your church, which raises the question, Can your church be in God's will if it is not obeying the mandate? Research indicates that far too many North American churches have drifted away from or missed entirely Christ's Great Commission mandate.

Good questions for a candidating pastor to ask of a church are, What is this church's mission? What is it supposed to be doing? I use these and three similar questions as diagnostic questions when I consult with churches on their mission. Pastors would serve their churches well if they too asked these questions. Here are the four questions to use:

1. What is this church supposed to be doing?
2. What is this church doing?
3. Why are you not doing what you are supposed to be doing?
4. What will it take for you to change and do what you are supposed to be doing?

The first question causes leaders to think biblically. They must ask what the Scriptures teach about the church's mission mandate. The second question assumes that the ministry has missed Christ's directive (a reasonably safe assumption). If you are not making disciples, then what are you doing? Some churches function as Christian retirement centers; others are evangelistic ministries; and others are mini-seminaries. The third question is very convicting. The room will get silent on this one. The last question is the most difficult and important because the answer reflects the church's willingness to obey Christ and ultimately exert an influence in the community.

> **The Definition of a Mission**
>
> A mission is broad.
> A mission is brief.
> A mission is biblical.
> A mission is a statement.
> A mission is what the ministry is supposed to be doing.

Various Kinds of Missions

When we cover the ministry's core values in chapter 6, you will discover that there are various kinds of values: conscious and unconscious, shared and unshared, and so forth. Most of those same categories hold true for the church's mission. Five of them are given here.

Conscious versus Unconscious

Most churches have a mission whether or not they know or can verbalize it. As I say in the chapter on values, your actual values will drive or take you somewhere. This is also true of the mission. The ministry ship is moving toward some ministry port, and this is the church's mission. The church, however, may not realize this or be aware of where its mission is taking it. Thus it needs to move the mission from an unconscious to a conscious level so that it can know what its mission is. It must discover and articulate its actual mission.

The way to accomplish this is to look at the church's values and determine where they are taking the church. When consulting with a church, I list its core values on a whiteboard and ask the SLT where these values have taken them. The answer is the church's ministry mission. Next, I ask the team to articulate that mission in a written statement so they can hold it and work with it at a conscious level.

Personal versus Organizational

While the church as a whole has a mission, whether they know it or not, most individuals have a mission in mind for the church as well. The first is the organizational or congregational mission, and the second is a personal mission. Most personal missions are formed early in life. Often mission formation takes place in the church when people come to faith. They may have embraced the church's mission as their own. Or it may have occurred later when the person was involved in a church or ministry that was vibrant for Christ. Regardless of the circumstances, the mission has marked them for life, and they bring this mission with them to their current church and will use it to judge all churches.

The same is true for the pastor of a church and his staff. Most have a personal ministry mission that they bring with them when the church hires them. Some may not be aware of their personal mission.

I encourage every church to address this issue. People must know that their personal missions may be in conflict with the church's mission and that the latter must prevail, or the church will attempt to move in many different directions at the same time, pulling apart rather than together. I will say more about how to do this in the following section. Concerning a senior pastor and any staff, the church must work with them and attempt to discover what those personal missions are before inviting these people to pastor and minister to the church. And to maximize your ministry placement, those of you who are pastors and staff must consider whether your mission and that of the church agree.

Shared versus Unshared

Some churches have consciously developed and articulated a mission statement, but most have not. Once the church has articulated such a statement, it may discover that some or even many of its people do not share the same mission. They lack mission alignment. People join churches for different reasons, and as stated above, many bring their own personal mission with them, which dictates their reasons for joining.

A shared ministry mission is essential to the church's effectiveness. Unshared ministry missions lead to disunity and hold potential for disaster, pulling people apart, not together. Therefore it is most important that a church address this issue with its congregants. I suggest that a good time and place to do this is when a person joins the church. It is my conviction that every church should have a new members class where it orients its new people to its values, mission, vision, and strategy as well as other matters such as doctrine. The idea is to get as many people as possible on the same page at the very beginning of their church experience to achieve maximum ministry effectiveness.

Correct versus Incorrect

While most or all churches have a ministry mission, it may not be the correct mission. My experience is that most churches fall into this category. More than two thousand years ago, the Savior predetermined and gave the church its biblical mission. It is the Great Commission—to make (evangelize) and mature (edify) believers (Matt. 28:19–20; Mark 16:15; and others). A church that pursues any other mission is pursuing the wrong mission, no matter how noble it may be. For example, the mission of some teaching churches is to preach the Bible. The mission of some worship-oriented churches is to worship God. And some churches' mission, often but not always smaller churches, is fellowship. Do not misunderstand what I am saying. These are all good things that are found in the Bible, but they, by themselves, are not the Great Commission! They may lead to the Great Commission but are not the totality of it.

Therefore it is imperative that once a church discovers its mission, it ask itself, Is our mission the correct mission? Is it the Great Commission? If the answer is fuzzy or an outright no, the church will need to change its mission from whatever it is to what the Savior has determined that it be—the Great Commission. To continue to pursue the wrong or incorrect mission is a violation of Scripture and disobedience to God's will for the church.

Actual versus Aspirational

A church may have an actual as well as an aspirational mission. The actual mission is where its values are taking it as described above. However, if this is an incorrect mission, the church will need to embrace a Great Commission mission. When the churches where I consult discover this, they quickly adopt a Great Commission mission. However, it is imperative that a church understand that when they adopt the new, correct mission, it is only aspirational—it is what they want their mission to be, not what it actually is.

The problem is that many assume that the new mission is now their actual mission when in fact it is still aspirational. It will not become their actual mission until the church changes its goals and owns the mission, which takes time. How can the church accomplish this kind of change so that it embraces the new, correct, biblical mission? The answer is to examine their actual values. They may need to change some values or, better, embrace those that will lead it to the correct mission.

A list of these values is found in Acts 2:41–47, and the key value in that list is evangelism, which actually serves as bookends for the other values (see verses 41 and 47). I would go so far as to argue that if a church does not hold evangelism as a core value, it cannot become a Great Commission church. Correct core values are the key to adopting in time the correct, biblical mission.

Developing a Mission

Once you see the necessity of having an effective and biblical congregational mission, you are ready to move to the next step. This involves immersing yourself and your team in the crafting of a dynamic, strong, memorable mission for your church. This section begins with selecting the right personnel to develop the mission, addresses several guidelines for developing your mission, and then walks the team through the development process.

The Personnel for Developing the Mission

Which people in an organization should craft a mission statement for the church? The answer is easy. It is the strategic leadership team. They are tasked with developing the mission as well as developing its vision and discovering the church's core values.

The Mission Guidelines

There are four guidelines for developing your mission statement.

1. DETERMINE THE CHURCH'S MISSION

In the business world a leadership team asks, What business are we in? Though not a business, essentially the church is asking the same question: *What business are we in?* The answer in the business world varies from company to company and will change. The answer for the ministry must neither vary from church to church nor ever change. As already stated and fully developed above, God has mandated what he wants his church to do: make disciples (Matt. 28:19).

2. WRITE YOUR MISSION STATEMENT

Next, you must put your newly developed mission down on paper, as a written statement. In his book *Learning to Lead*, Fred Smith writes, "In my view, nothing is properly defined until you write it down. Writing forces you to be specific; it takes the fuzz off your thinking."[11] If you cannot write it down, you probably do not have a well-thought-out mission.

3. CLARIFY AND SIMPLIFY YOUR MISSION

How do you clarify and simplify your mission? Ask and answer the following questions.

What words communicate best with your target group? Mission drafters must be wordsmiths. Their job is to think and rethink, shape and reshape, draft and redraft the statement. They do this with meaningful words. Think about the words that will best communicate with your congregation. Are the people more traditional, contemporary, or a combination? Will older clichés communicate best or fresh, contemporary terms? Also take into account the part of the country you live in. What terms are native to this locale and would communicate well to these people? Note the following statement as an example:

> Our mission is to colonize the greater commonwealth of Northwest Boston with the gospel of Christ so that it may be liberated from the rule of darkness and adopt a new spiritual constitution that passionately embraces the revolutionary teachings of Jesus Christ.

This statement could serve the people in and around Boston and other parts of New England. It is regional, however, and would not fit or communicate well in other parts of North America. In addition, it is far too long.

Do people understand what you have written? How well do the words that you have selected communicate? Do people understand them? Do they know what you are saying? Be sure to avoid unfamiliar biblical terms such as *glorify, holy, kingdom, disciple,* and others. These terms represent what I refer to as christianeze or temple talk. Some will understand them, most won't. Some have asked, If the mission statement is the Great Commission, then why not just quote Matthew 28:19–20; Mark 16:15; or Acts 1:8? You could, but many parishioners will not understand the terminology used in the New Testament. These words are not clear to them. For example, the term *disciple* that Jesus uses in Matthew 28:19 may seem ambiguous. What is a disciple? Is making disciples a reference to evangelism only or sanctification or both? Even the average seminarian struggles to answer this question. Willow Creek Community Church has done an excellent job of mission clarity by including their definition of a disciple in their statement: "Our mission is to turn irreligious people into *fully devoted followers of Christ*." However, do not be surprised if you have to explain this statement as well.

Therefore I encourage mission crafters to personalize the Great Commission so that it is clear to their particular congregation. We did this in the mission of my last church:

> The mission of Northwood Community Church is to be used of God in helping people become fully functioning followers of Christ.

The words "used of God" imply we could not do it alone. God is the one who makes disciples. And the words "in helping people" mean that we would not take all the responsibility ourselves. We could only aid people—they must assume individual responsibility for the process. We substituted "fully functioning followers" in place of "disciple." Because our people understood these words, we had clearly defined for all what we meant by the term *disciple*. We were making it clear that a disciple is a Christ-follower, not a follower of Allah or Buddha, and that a disciple is a functioning follower of Christ. That means that he or she is authentically involved in the five functions of the church: worship, fellowship or community, biblical instruction, evangelism, and ministry or service as opposed to being parked somewhere on the sidelines. Finally, that involvement is a full or deep involvement. Christ-followers are not just busy but have made deep commitments of their lives to the Savior. I also believe that repeating the *F*s (fully functioning followers) is catchy and memorable.

4. Make Your Mission Brief

The power of the mission statement is in its brevity and its simplicity, even though it is difficult for it to be both. Often we want to cram too much into the statement. Two questions will help.

Does the mission statement pass the T-shirt or business card test? Is it short enough to fit on a business card? If not, you have committed the sin of information overload. You would do well to remember the statement: "Say more by saying less" or "Less is more!" The most common error is to include a *how* statement along with the mission statement. Here is an example:

Faith Community Church exists to make disciples by loving Christ, loving one another, and living to reach our world for Christ.

The mission statement is "Faith Community Church exists to make disciples." The *how* statement, signaled or flagged by the preposition *by*, is not necessary to the statement of the mission. It provides the strategy for accomplishing the mission. It is important and should be stated but not in the mission statement. Instead, put it in a separate document or statement of strategy. The problem with including the strategy with the mission statement is that it unnecessarily lengthens the mission and renders it less memorable.

Is your mission memorable? A good mission statement is both meaningful and memorable. This is because it is well worded and short. The goal is to be able to walk up to anyone in the church, ask the person to tell you the church's mission statement, and he or she is able to do it.

You should be able to read it, then turn your head away or close your eyes and remember it. Here is one that is not memorable:

Trinity Church is a deeply committed community composed of caring men and women who desire to have an impact on southwest Collin County for eternity. We will accomplish this to the glory of God by reaching out to the lost and passionately loving the saved.

This statement would be most difficult to remember. Following is one that is most memorable.

Our mission is to know Christ and make him known.

The Process

With the four guidelines in hand, you are ready to develop your mission statement. You have at least four options.

OPTION 1: IDENTIFY YOUR CURRENT MISSION STATEMENT

This first option is to identify and, if necessary, correct your current mission statement. You will be focusing on the mission you have been using. To catalyze your thinking, there are two questions to ask.

What is your actual mission? You will begin by attempting to discover what your current actual mission is. You will recall from my discussion earlier in this chapter that a church will have an actual mission, whether it is aware of it or not. Now your goal is to unearth or discover that mission.

The key to discovering and articulating your mission is to ask where your actual core values are leading you (see chap. 6). They will point to the church's actual current mission. Even if you have articulated a mission statement in the past, it may be aspirational, not actual. It's wise to determine what your mission will be in light of your core values. If a leading value is teaching the Bible, that may also be the church's mission. If it is the worship of God, that may be the church's mission.

Is it the correct mission? You have learned that there is a correct mission for the church. It is the Great Commission. You are probably tired of hearing this by now, but do not be. It is too important.

Guidelines for the Mission Statement

1. Determine your church's purpose.
   Whom will you serve?
   How will you serve these people?
2. Write your mission statement.
   What words communicate best with your target group?
   Do people understand what you have written?
   Does your format convey well your mission?
3. Make your mission statement broad but clear.
   Is the statement broad enough?
   Is the statement clear?
4. Make your mission statement brief and simple.
   Does the mission pass the business card test?
   Is your mission memorable?

Compare your current actual mission with the Great Commission, as stated in Matthew 28:19–20 or in one of the other commission passages. If it reflects well the Great Commission, then you are finished with this part of the process, unless you desire to fine-tune the statement. If so, you may want to follow option 2 or 3, remembering the guidelines for developing your mission in the preceding section. If you discover that your current actual mission is not the Great Commission, you need to follow option 2 or 3.

OPTION 2: DEVELOP A NEW MISSION STATEMENT

The second option is to develop a new mission statement that is unique to your ministry. It focuses on your future mission or "what should be." To do this, you will need to address your current values and follow the Great Commission model.

Address your current values. For the majority of churches across America, their mission is aspirational. If your core values do not sustain your mission or move your church toward your mission, you will not accomplish it. This means that you will need to determine what values are necessary to sustain a Great Commission mission and begin to embrace these values in your church through your primary activities. (I will say more about primary ministry activities in chapter 7 on ministry strategy.) The way to spot these values is to examine the ones given in Acts 2:41–47. Luke lists at least four that are key to pursuing a Great Commission mission: Bible doctrine, worship, fellowship (possibly community), and evangelism. My experience is that few churches are actively pursuing evangelism. Thus I would begin there.

Use the Matthew 28:19 model. I have taken this passage and developed the following model that will enable you to craft a Great Commission mission statement unlike any you would write from scratch.

1. What is a disciple? In Matthew 28:19 Jesus commands his church to make disciples, but we need to ask, What is a disciple? One outstanding answer is found in Willow Creek Community Church's mission: they aim to turn irreligious people into fully devoted followers of Christ. Note that rather than using the term *disciple*, they have defined it to make sure their people understand what they mean by the term. What term will you use that will be meaningful to your congregation? Your choices are limited. As I asked myself this question, I came up with the following choices. If you can think of any others, add them to the list. Your assignment is to discuss these with your strategic leadership team and choose one.

   - a follower of Christ
   - a Christ-follower
   - a Christian
   - a believer
   - a learner

2. Further refine this term. I believe that Jesus had in mind mature disciples. The goal of any congregation is to take a person, wherever he or she is (belief or unbelief), and lead him or her to maturity in Christ. Willow Creek reflects this in their mission statement by putting the words "fully devoted" in front of "follower of Christ." This could be expressed in other ways:

   - a devoted follower of Christ
   - a fully devoted follower of Christ

- a functioning follower of Christ
- a fully functioning follower of Christ
- a developing follower of Christ
- a fully developed follower of Christ
- a committed follower of Christ
- a completely committed follower of Christ
- a totally committed follower of Christ

Be sure to substitute in these phrases the other terms listed in number 1. Ask which would be most memorable to your church and would capture the biblical text. As you read and think about these, which ones grab your attention? Which terms seem to communicate maturity? If you do not like these, you will need to come up with one of your own.

3. What verb best expresses what you want to accomplish? We started at the end of the mission statement to define what we mean by a disciple. Now we will move toward the beginning of the statement. In Willow Creek's mission, note their use of the verb *to turn*. This is a key term describing what they want to accomplish for those in their community who are "irreligious." They want "to turn them into fully devoted followers of Christ." What do you want God to accomplish in the lives of people in your community or congregation?

   The key is the verb you choose to convey this information. Here are a few I have spotted in various mission statements.

to assist	to make
to develop	to make and mature
to empower	to mature
to encourage	to present
to establish	to promote
to follow	to provide
to fulfill	to pursue
to help	to transform
to influence	to turn
to know	to win
to lead	

If none of these captures what you want to accomplish, come up with some of your own. You and your team will need to select the one that works best in light of your mission. Some people say that we cannot do any of these things. While I discussed this earlier in this chapter, I will probe it a little further here. The Holy Spirit must accomplish the mission through the church, but keep in mind that Christ commanded the disciples to "make" disciples. It was understood that he would accomplish this through them. If you still struggle, you could say something along the lines of "to be used of God to develop fully functioning Christ-followers."

4. With or for whom will you accomplish this activity? Answering this question is optional. Who or what will be the object of your activity (receive the action of the verb)? For example, the objects of Willow Creek's verb (to turn) are irreligious people. Your objects may be people, unchurched people, churched people, irreligious people, religious people, unsaved people, saved people, ordinary people, everyday people, all people, your community, your city, your town, and so on. Choose the one that best fits your situation. Once you have completed these four steps, you should have a mission statement that is tailor-made for your congregation as well as your community.

Option 3: Adopt an Existing Mission Statement

You may decide your best option is to adopt a mission statement that has been created by another church. I have included below some mission statements from my collection. Some are excellent and some aren't. Critique them using the mission test in the next section. Several are similar to the Matthew 28 model. Read the following and let them inspire you and encourage your creativity. You may want to adopt one or tweak one of them so that it becomes yours. As Rick Warren has said, why go to all the trouble to create something new when you have something that already says it best?

Our mission is to make and mature believers at home and abroad.

Anonymous

Our mission is to know Christ and make Him known.

The Navigators and several churches

Our mission is to present Christ as Savior and pursue Christ as Lord.

Ikki Soma

Our mission is to follow and make followers of Christ.

Emmanuel and Jelena Ralevich
(two Serbian Christians)

Our mission is to passionately follow and make followers of Christ.

Anonymous

Our mission is to help our community find real life in Christ.

Anonymous

Our mission is to provide the best opportunity for people to become fully devoted followers of Christ.

Valleydale Baptist Church

Our mission is to lead ordinary people to extraordinary life in Christ.

Hillcrest Baptist Church

Our mission is to be people who provide living proof of a loving God to a watching world.

Sagemeont Church

Our mission is to connect the disconnected into Christ-centered community.

First Church Pasadena

Our mission is to lead all people into a life-changing, ever-growing relationship with Christ.

Mobberly Baptist Church

Our mission is that every man, woman, and child in Greater Austin hear the gospel from the lips of someone at Hill Country Bible Church.

Hill Country Bible Church

Sharing Christ • Building Believers

Lakepointe Church

OPTION 4: TWEAK AN EXISTING MISSION STATEMENT

A number of the churches I work with like the option of tweaking the church's current mission or the mission of another church. The mission seems to be just about right, but something is missing. By tweaking the statement, they preserve the old that they like, while adding the new that makes it just right.

An example is the following:

Our mission is to follow and make followers of Christ.

One church liked this statement but felt that something was missing. Thus they added the word *passionately* and the statement they adopted was:

The mission of our church is to passionately follow and make followers of Christ.

They loved it.

The Mission Test

Now that you have a completed mission statement or are well into the process of mission development, submit your work to the mission test. The mission test uses the definition of a mission in question format.

Question 1: Is the mission broad enough? (Will all the ministries fit under and contribute to its accomplishment?)

Question 2: Is the mission brief? (Is it short enough to fit on a business card?)

Question 3: Is the mission biblical? (Does it align with Scripture or contradict it?)

Question 4: Is the mission what the church is supposed to be doing? (Is the Great Commission—make disciples—at the heart of the mission?)

The Mission Question

The mission question asks, Will you be a church with a mission statement or will you be a missional church? At this point you are either a church with a mission statement or you are about to become one with a mission statement. While that is a good start, the goal is to become a missional church, that is, a church that follows or practices its mission in its geographical community. That is the point of having a mission.

You will know that you are a missional church because people will be sharing their faith. There will be lots of new, happy faces around the church. There will be a growing number of people whom you do not know. The church will conduct a large number of baptisms. And a few people will be upset and threaten to leave the church.

The Mission Challenge

The mission challenge is not only to develop a biblical mission but also to remain focused on that mission. There will be many distractions! Satan does not want your church to be on mission, so do not be surprised when all kinds of obstacles surface, including well-meaning people, when you attempt to communicate and focus the church on the mission. Stephen Covey's words are wise advice at this point: The main thing is to keep the main thing the main thing!

How might you accomplish this? I believe that passion is key. A growing number of consultants, including me, believe that the strategic leadership team, the staff, and especially the senior pastor must be passionate about the mission statement to fulfill the Great Commission. Passionate people begin to live and breathe the mission. Passion is the decided difference between ministry mediocrity and ministry excellence. So how passionate are you over your mission statement? If the response is lukewarm or less, then the problem may lie with the final mission product, and you need to try again.

If the mission is a good one, and the problem is with you, you will need to reassess your passion or passions. It is possible that in time you will passionately embrace the church's mission. Many pastors have a passion for preaching. It is even more important that they have a passion for a Great Commission mission, or they should make room for someone else who does.

Finally, it is important that you consider your mission in all that your church does. For example, the decisions you make must be done with the mission statement in mind. The question to ask always is how will this decision affect our mission? Does it support Christ's mission or detract from it?

Communicating Your Mission

It is important that you communicate or propagate the mission. Even though you have a statement that is clear and memorable, if you fail to make it known to your people, it accomplishes little beyond the efforts of the strategic leadership team.

Following are some methods for imparting the mission: the leader's example, sermons, formal and informal conversation, stories, the bulletin, a framed poster, a church brochure, training materials, a slide-tape presentation, audio- and video-tapes, skits and drama, a newcomers class, a newsletter, your website, and the performance appraisal. You may want to put the mission on a business-type card that would fit in a man's wallet or a woman's purse. Or put it on a T-shirt. When working with a leadership team, I ask them to take out a small scrap of paper (about half the size of a business card). Then I instruct them to write their mission statement on it. Finally, I ask them to put it in their wallets so that every time they go there for money, they see it and are reminded of their church's mission.[12]

Questions for Reflection, Discussion, and Application

1. Did this chapter convince you of the need for your church to have a biblical mission statement? Why or why not?
2. Does your church already have a written mission statement? If not, why not? If yes, what is it? Is it a good one? Does it reflect your congregation's values? Has someone written it down? Does the congregation know what it is? Why or why not?
3. What is your church supposed to be doing? What is your mission mandate? Is that what the ministry is doing? Why or why not? What would it take to change what you're doing and pursue Christ's mission for the church? Would you anticipate any resistance to such a change?

4. Does your church know what its purpose is? If yes, what is it?

5. Use the mission test to evaluate your actual mission statement. Will you need to make any changes? If so, what ones?

6. If you decide to start over in developing a mission statement, or if you have decided to revise the current one, who will be involved in the process? Will you invite evaluation of the mission statement? Whom will you ask for this evaluation?

7. Is your church at a place where it is ready to craft an effective, correct, biblical mission statement? If not, why not? If so, when will you begin?

8. Will you be a church with a mission statement or a missional church? How would you know? What is the difference?

9. Which methods for communicating the mission statement appeal to you? Why? Will you use them to propagate your mission? Why or why not?

10. Make a list of all your ministries. What does each contribute to the realization of Christ's mission. Do any not contribute? What will you do about them?

5

Developing a Compelling Vision

The Kind of Church We Envision

The second step in the strategic planning process is creating the church's vision. While I like putting vision here for developmental purposes, envisioning takes place throughout the process. And in my ordering of the process, it could fit well in several places, such as before developing the mission or after developing a strategy. I will say more later in the chapter under "The Vision Process" about where it may fit.

Like the ministry's mission, vision is essential to the organization. It is the ministry's port of call. However, unlike the mission, the vision is more subject to change. It is dynamic, not static. Over time the vision must be renewed, adapted, and adjusted to the cultural context in which the congregation lives. Although the vision changes, the changes take place only at the margins of the vision, not at its core. The core—the Great Commission—does not change, but the details of the vision and the words used to convey them will change. The vision provides us with a picture of what the mission will look like as it is realized in the life of the community, a picture of the port where our boat is headed. Both mission and vision address the ship's direction. The mission states the direction and the vision supplies a picture of it.

The vision concept is found in Scripture. You will find visions sprinkled throughout the Old and New Testaments. For example, God caught Abraham's attention with his vision for him in Genesis 12:1–3 (the Abrahamic covenant). God used Moses to communicate his vision for his people, Israel, expressed in Exodus 3:7–8 and Deuteronomy 8:7–10. It is possible that the "joy" that Jesus looked forward to while enduring the cross was the vision of his return to the presence of his Father in heaven (Heb. 12:2).

The purpose of this chapter is to help leaders understand the vision concept and how to develop a unique, compelling vision for their ministry. It answers the fundamental questions: What kind of church would we like to be? If we could have it our way, what would we look like? Whereas the ministry analysis, in the preparation stage, uncovered "what is"—reality—the vision step probes "what could be."

This chapter consists of four sections. The first covers purpose or why the vision is so important to a church. The second provides a definition of a vision so that we know what it is we are talking about and are attempting to develop. The third section helps visionary leaders develop a vision for their organization, and the last presents several practical ways they can communicate their vision to their people.[1]

> **The Fourfold Process**
> _____
> Mission Development
> **Vision Development**
> Values Discovery
> Strategy Design

The Importance of a Vision

The information that is available indicates that pastors and congregations are struggling with the vision concept. For example, in commenting on pastors and their visions, George Barna writes, "But when we asked these pastors, 'Can you articulate God's vision for the ministry of your church?' we found that roughly 90 percent of them could articulate a basic definition of ministry. But only 2 percent could articulate the *vision* for their church."[2] David Goetz writes, "In *Leadership*'s study, however, pastors indicated that conflicting visions for the church was their greatest source of tension and the top reason they were terminated or forced to resign."[3] Clearly, vision is of utmost importance to leaders and their ministry. Here are seven reasons why.

Provides Energy

Not much happens without an inspiring, compelling vision. Not much was happening in Nehemiah's day. The people had no vision. Jerusalem lay in ruins, and no one was motivated to do anything about it (Neh. 1:3). Then along came Nehemiah with a vision from God to rebuild the gates and walls of the city. Visions are exciting and they energize people. They ignite a spark—the excitement that lifts a ministry organization out of the mundane. They supply the fuel that lights the fire under a congregation—leaders are able to stop putting out fires and start setting a few. A vision from God has the potential to turn a maintenance mentality into a ministry mentality. And when your vision resonates with your values and mission, it generates the energy that fuels the accomplishment of the ministry task.

Creates Cause

The right vision creates meaning in people's lives, providing them with a cause and giving them a sense of divine purpose. They are a part of something bigger than themselves, something great that God is accomplishing at this time and place in history. They are a part of God's cause. With a shared vision, people see themselves not just as another congregant or a "pew warmer" but as a vital part of a church that is having a powerful impact on a lost and dying world. They are not simply in a church; they are on a crusade. They are part of a revolution that has the potential to change this world, to have a wonderful impact for Christ. For example, a wide gap exists in terms of commitment and dedication to God and a sense of personal significance between one member who, when asked what he or she does, replies, "I am a teacher" and another, who may have the same ministry, who answers, "I am changing the life course of a class of adolescents who will someday accomplish great things for Christ."

Fosters Risk Taking

A shared vision fosters a congregation's willingness to take risks. This is especially true in church-planting situations. When the point person or lead pastor casts the vision, everyone knows what needs to be done. But the question is, How will we do it? Sometimes we know the answer, but most often we do not. Consequently, ministry for Christ becomes an exciting adventure into the world of the unknown. We attempt something for Christ and it does not work. We attempt something else and it does work. Though much of what we are doing is experimental, it is not ambiguous. It is perfectly clear to all involved the reason we do it. It is for God and the Savior. People are not asking for guarantees of success. They all know that no guarantees exist, yet people are committed anyway. The risks are great, but so is the God we serve and the vision he has given us. How else can we explain the early church and what God accomplished through them or those believers who make up the faith hall of fame in Hebrews 11?

Legitimizes Leadership

Bill Hybels writes, "Vision is at the very core of leadership. Take vision away from a leader and you cut out his or her heart."[4] If leaders cannot see where they are going, maybe they are not leaders, at least not yet. Not only do true leaders know where they are going, but they can also see where they are going. That is key to leadership. They have a vision of where they are going as well as a sense of mission. Like navigators who may carry around a picture of their port of call in their wallet, so leaders carry in their mental wallet a picture of the church that could be. The vision helps them and their people focus on and follow their dream of where God is taking them and what that looks like.

Energizes Leadership

Bill Hybels also writes, "Vision is the fuel that leaders run on. It's the energy that creates action. It's the fire that ignites the passion of followers."[5] When people see the vision, they can feel it. Developing a vision and then living it vigorously are essential elements of leadership. A leader is a godly servant who sees as well as knows where he or she is going, and that wins followers. That describes not only the Savior but also his disciples and those who ministered in the early church, as recorded in Acts. They moved with God-given passion. They led with fire in their bones. They were on fire with visionary, Christlike passion, and this in turn ignited followers. When a congregation has a leader who owns and inflames a vision and lives that vision in a Christlike, passionate manner, they will follow that leader to the ends of the earth.

Sustains Ministry

Ministry can be very difficult, even painful. Discouragement and disappointment often lurk in the ministry hallways and boardrooms of the typical church. It is not beyond the enemy to incite persecution against Christ's church (Acts 8:1). Spiritual warfare comes with the ministry territory (Eph. 6:10–18). Many have risked or given their lives for the Savior and the furtherance of the gospel. The list of martyrs for the cause of Christ is extensive.

What has sustained Christians from the beginning of the church in the book of Acts up to today? One answer is a biblical, compelling vision. It encourages people to look beyond the mundane and the pain of ministry. It keeps a picture in front of them that distracts from what is and announces what could be. It is the glue that holds the church together in turbulent times. All the trouble and grief that we experience in this world while serving the Savior are trivial compared to the importance of what we are attempting for him. That picture, carried in our mental wallets, is one way God sustains us in the worst of times.

Motivates Giving

This last reason for a vision always gets people's attention—especially pastors. It takes money to do ministry, and it is the leader's responsibility to raise that money. My seminary students do not like it when I stress this in class. Many of them want primarily to teach the Bible. Their response is, "My gift is teaching. Can't somebody else do that!" The problem is that the congregation looks to its leader to raise the necessary finances for the ministry to function as God intended.

What most leaders have discovered is that it is vision that motivates giving. We at Dallas Seminary understand this. Few contributors donate to pay the light bill or my salary. They donate to what they see the seminary accomplishing for Christ in the coming years, based on what he has accomplished in the past. Again Hybels writes, "When leaders who understand this take the time to paint pictures for people and to help them imagine the kingdom good that will result from their collective efforts, then people are free to release their resources joyfully. And generally, the grander the vision, the greater the giving."[6]

What Is a Vision?

If a vision is so important, we need to know what it is. First, let's look at what it is not.

What a Vision Is Not

People confuse vision with a number of other concepts, such as purpose, goals, objectives, and mission. In the following I want to stress the difference between a vision and a mission.

A church's vision is not the same as its mission. The concepts of vision and mission are confused more than any of the other concepts in strategic planning. They are similar in some ways: they are both based on the Scriptures, focus on the future, are directional (tell people where the ministry is going), and are functional (address what the church is supposed to be doing). However, the differences are greater than the similarities.

SOME DISTINCTIONS

I make ten distinctions between a vision and a mission.

1. The mission is a statement of what the church is supposed to be doing, while the vision is a snapshot or picture of it.
2. The mission is used for planning where the church is going; the vision is used for communicating where the church is going.
3. A mission statement must be short enough to fit on a business card. The vision statement, however, goes into detail and can range from a single paragraph to several pages in length.
4. The purpose of the mission is to inform all of the ministry's functions. The purpose of the vision is to inspire people to accomplish the ministry's functions.
5. The mission involves knowing. It helps your people know where they are going. The vision involves seeing. It helps people see where they are going. If people cannot see a goal, it probably will not happen.
6. The mission comes from the head—it is more intellectual in origin. It supplies knowledge. The vision comes from the heart—it is more emotional in origin. It supplies passion.

7. Logically, the mission precedes the vision. In their development, the vision grows out of and develops detail around the mission, fleshing it out.
8. The mission has a broad, general focus, while the vision has a narrow focus. It singles out the details and specifics of the ministry community.
9. Mission development is a science—it can be taught. The vision, however, is an art—it is more caught. Either you catch it or you miss it altogether.
10. Finally, the mission is communicated visually; it is written down somewhere. The vision is communicated verbally. You hear it preached. An example is Martin Luther King's "I Have a Dream" vision. Hearing him preach it has much greater impact than reading it off the page.

My friend Will Mancini uses the following to distinguish the two. He says they are comparable to taking a vacation to some scenic place like the Swiss Alps. The mission is simply where you are going. The travel company, however, provides you with a compelling vision, found in a brochure full of pictures of what your destination looks like. This makes you want to go there.

Mission and Vision Distinctions

	Mission	Vision
Definition	statement	snapshot
Application	planning	communication
Length	short	long
Purpose	informs	inspires
Activity	knowing	seeing
Source	head	heart
Order	first	second
Focus	broad	narrow
Development	taught	caught
Communication	visual	verbal

BIBLICAL EXAMPLES

One of many biblical examples of a mission statement is God's mission for Moses:

So now, go. I am sending you to Pharaoh to bring my people the Israelites out of Egypt.

Exodus 3:10

Note that it meets the above criteria for a mission statement.

A biblical example of a vision statement is God's vision for Israel communicated through Moses:

> For the LORD your God is bringing you into a good land—a land with streams and pools of water, with springs flowing in the valleys and hills; a land with wheat and barley, vines and fig trees, pomegranates, olive oil and honey; a land where bread will not be scarce and you will lack nothing; a land where the rocks are iron and you can dig copper out of the hills.
>
> Deuteronomy 8:7–10

Note that it meets the above criteria for a vision statement. Also observe the differences between the two.

What a Vision Is

I define *a vision as a clear, challenging picture of the future of the ministry, as you believe that it can and must be.* This definition contains six elements.

CLEAR

We cannot expect people to act on information that they do not understand. Vision clarity is as essential as mission clarity. My paraphrase of Paul's words in 1 Corinthians 14:8 is: "If the bugler muffs the call to arms, what soldier will know to prepare himself for battle?" Then we will have lost the battle before it has begun. A vision accomplishes nothing if it is not clear and precise. If the congregation or people who make up the ministry do not know what the vision is, the ministry has no vision, only empty words on a piece of paper or vague sounds—a noise—proceeding from the leaders' lips. It is much like Alice's destination in *Alice in Wonderland*:

> "Would you tell me, please, which way I ought to walk from here?"
>
> "That depends a good deal on where you want to get to," said the Cat.
>
> "I don't much care where—," said Alice.
>
> "Then it doesn't matter which way you walk," said the Cat.
>
> "—so long as I get *somewhere*," Alice added as an explanation.
>
> "Oh, you're sure to do that," said the Cat, "if only you walk long enough."[7]

We have discovered that people fear the future. It frightens them to the extent they prefer to live in the present or, worse, the past. So to succeed, leaders must address that fear. By far the most effective way is vision clarity—to picture the future with such vivid terms that a congregation can see where it is headed.

Apparently Nehemiah's vision for Israel and the rebuilding of Jerusalem was clear and specific. He and his followers must have seen in their heads new walls with gates hanging from them. Note the people's response in Nehemiah 2:18: "They replied, 'Let us start rebuilding.' So they began this good work." That is vision clarity—the most effective antidote to congregational anxiety.

Compelling

Visions often face a quick, untimely death. A pastor hears that he is supposed to have a vision for his church, so he quickly develops something that he hopes will do. However, he is only going through the motions, may not be convinced in his heart, and does not feel it in his bones. He has not read the previous section on the importance of vision. Consequently, he conceives and births something he calls a vision only to see it quickly die and be placed in some ministry graveyard, such as a church filing cabinet.

A good vision is compelling. It ignites passion that moves people to action. It excites people and gives birth to focused ministry activity. It is challenging when people need a challenge. It is that compelling challenge that penetrates the deep resources of the mind and touches the human spirit. And the challenge serves the vision by pulling people out of the pews and into the arena of effective, passion-driven ministry.

A Picture

Passion is a feeling word that plumbs the depths of our emotions. *Vision* is a seeing word that probes the imagination and creates visual images. Our vision is our ministry snapshot. It is what you see when you envision your ministry two, five, or ten years from now, the picture of the future you believe God is going to create. Seminary professor and author Haddon Robinson recounts, "Soon after the completion of Disney World, someone said, 'Isn't it too bad that Walt Disney didn't live to see this!' Mike Vance, creative director of Disney Studios replied, 'He did *see* it—that's why it's here.'"[8]

Again, a vision is comparable to the brochures that a travel company uses to provide interested travelers with pictures of what some exotic destination will be like when they get there and makes them want to go there.

Visionary church planters will tell you that from the very beginning they had a picture of what the church would look like when it was up and running, when the dream—their vision—was in place. When I work with a strategic leadership team, I like to use a cartoon to make this point. The cartoon is a picture of three frogs out on a desert with shovels in their hands. Situated next to them is a cactus, in front of them is a scorpion, and off in the distance are some mountains and another cactus. One frog announces to the others, "We'll put the swamp here!" I like to ask the team the question, "What do you see?" They proceed to identify the objects that I have mentioned. Then I ask them, "What do the frogs see?" The answer of course is a swamp. And that is the point. Visionaries, like the frogs, see what others do not see. They see beyond what others see. They see pictures not of what is but of what could be. Note that the frog cartoon uses very few words to communicate the frogs' vision. Instead, it creatively uses a picture—a cartoon—to convey it. If instead of using words you were asked to convey your vision by painting a picture, drawing a cartoon, or taking a picture with a camera, what would it be? What would it look like?

I suspect that in the concluding chapters of Deuteronomy, when God took Moses up on Mount Nebo, he was showing this great leader the reality of what he had carried around and seen in his head for all those years of wandering in the wilderness—a land flowing with milk and honey. It was assurance that, though Moses would not enter the land, the dream was about to become reality.

Not only does vision affect what leaders see, but it affects what their people see as well. You must ask, Do my people see what I see? If they cannot see the vision, it is not likely to happen.

The Future of the Ministry

The vision is a picture of the future we seek to create. It depicts the church's preferred future. While, outside of biblical prophecy, we cannot predict the future, we can create the future. That is the function of the vision. It pictures the end of the ministry at the beginning. The best way to create what you really want is by visualizing the outcome that you are trying to achieve.

Also, the vision serves to bridge the past and the future. The right vision provides the all-important link between what has taken place, what is now taking place, and what the organization aspires to build in the future. A strong vision changes the orientation of the church from the past to the future. It takes people's eyes off the greatness of the church in its prime and helps them see how great it can be. Vision announces that our best days are ahead of us!

It Can Be

A good vision drips with potential because it is constructed on the bedrock of reality. The dream involves seeing something that is not yet but is possible. The visionary leader is convinced that the vision is attainable. It is what Robert Kennedy had in mind when he said, "Some people see things the way they are and ask why; I see things the way they could be and ask why not."

It Must Be

The vision goes beyond what can be. It concerns what must be. Somewhere toward the end of the "can be" stage, it grabs hold and will not let go. Now not only does the visionary believe that it can be, but he is also convinced that it must be. A critical sense of urgency along with a heavy dose of passion drive him in his quest to achieve the vision. It may keep him awake at night.

Three things have happened. First, the leader is convinced that God is in the vision, that God himself has placed it in his heart. It is a "God thing"; it is God's doing, not his. Thus he will not find rest until the church has embraced the vision. Second, the leader believes that he is God's person to see the vision through. God has chosen him to pilot the vision ship through his church's ministry waters, whether they are smooth or choppy. Finally, he is certain that the vision is the very best thing for people—both lost and saved. Because the leader cares about people, he knows that they will be so much better off when they embrace and own the vision. They will experience eternal life and spiritual renewal. This was the attitude of Martin Luther King Jr. He knew what his vision had to be if African American people across America were ever to experience deliverance from racism and intolerance.

How to Develop a Vision

It is imperative that leaders not only carry their vision around in their head but also put it in writing. One of the elements in the definition of vision is clarity. Writing a vision statement forces vision clarity from the vision navigator. This process requires the right people to create a unique product—the vision.

The Vision Personnel

In my discussion of mission development in the last chapter, I identified the strategic planning team plus the lead pastor as those tasked with drafting a clear mission statement for the congregation. The same people should also draft the vision statement. I believe that the pastor should take primary responsibility for developing and implementing the vision. Thus he is the "keeper of the vision"—the chief vision caster who regularly casts and recasts the vision. However, the wise pastor-leader will involve others in the process. My experience is that white-collar people want much involvement in vision development, while blue-collar people may look to and depend more on the pastor to lead in vision development.

Vision development begins with a visionary pastor or leader or whoever is leading the planning team, and it is promoted by those who make up the team, especially the visionaries. How do you know if you are a visionary? One way is to take the Myers-Briggs Type Indicator (MBTI) or the Kiersey Temperament Sorter.[9] These tools measure whether a person is sensing (S) or intuitive (N). Sensing-type people are the practical, hands-on realists. They can have a vision; however, they go about it in a different way. Whereas intuitive-type people see the vision naturally in their heads, sensing types have to see it literally with their eyes. They perceive it through their five senses. Thus they "catch" a vision by actually visiting a church where they can see, smell, and touch the vision. They are able to form the vision as they walk the church's corridors and experience its ministries. The intuitive types are the abstract, imaginative, natural visionaries. For them, vision is a sixth sense. They seem to create a vision and carry it around in their head.

Another way to discover how you relate to vision is to take the Vision Style Audit in appendix G. It will tell you your vision style or how you go about forming a vision.

The Vision Process

It is not enough to have the right personnel in place. The vision process is also critical to the final product. The process has two steps: a preparation step and a process step.

STEP 1. THE PREPARATION STEP

The preparation step is exactly what it says. It gets you ready to develop your vision. It prepares and aids your thinking for the actual process. It has six aspects.

Envisioning prayer. The visionary leader must bathe the entire vision process in prayer. Envisioning prayer must be at the beginning of the development process and remain a part of it throughout. As the leadership prays, God will open their eyes to his Word and its application to the people in the world.

In Nehemiah 1:4–11 Nehemiah prays an envisioning prayer. Word got back to him about the desperate plight of his people and their city, Jerusalem. His response was to fall to his knees for confession and prayer. And it was during this time that God placed his vision on Nehemiah's heart. God wanted him to return to Jerusalem and lead his people in rebuilding the city (2:5).

Thinking big. In Matthew 28:19–20 Jesus challenged a small band of itinerant, nonclassically trained disciples to reach their world with the gospel. As you examine the scope of Jesus's Great Commission from its first proclamation after the resurrection, through the book of Acts, and up to today, you quickly realize that he was a person of no small vision. He was the visionary of visionaries.

Consequently, visionary pastors should not hesitate to think big. Do not let current realities constrict your dreaming. Someone has said, "Make no small plans, for they have not the power to stir the souls of men." In his doxology in Ephesians 3:20 Paul challenges the Christian community at Ephesus, and us as well, to ask (pray) and think (envision) big: "Now to Him who is able to do far more abundantly beyond all that we ask or think, according to the power that works within us" (NASB). Indeed, this seems to be a light slap on the wrist for not asking and thinking big enough. Paul says that God is able to do much more than we are asking or even thinking about. Therefore vision developers must ask, Is this vision big enough?

Discovering your passion. Passion is at the very core of vision and is key to discovering your vision. Your passion is what you feel strongly and care deeply about. It has to do with your emotions—it is an emotional concept. To get at your passion, you must tap into your emotions, asking what particular emotions move or motivate you when it comes to ministry and leading the church. Which experiences excite you and make you feel alive? Which bring focus and meaning to your life and ministry?

These emotions function as signboards, pointing to your passion for your ministry. And this passion lies at the core of your vision. It gives meaning to your ministry and breathes life into your church. Discover your passion for your church and you will begin to unearth your vision.

Experiencing the dream. You must never underestimate the power of your emotions in shaping your vision. As the vision begins to take shape, give yourself permission to experience or feel it as you see it. As the vision seed grows within you, focus on what it would be like to live the vision now. Visualize and begin to experience the feelings as if you were there already. The way to do this is to employ your five senses. Move into your vision. Then ask and answer the question, What do you see, hear, smell, feel, even taste as you immerse yourself in the emerging vision?

The more you experience your dream in your head, the more you live your dream in your life before your congregation. Dream living is essential to vision casting. Not only must you discover and develop your vision, but you must also communicate your vision, for if you cannot communicate your vision, you might as well not have one. Effective dream casting in the future happens in direct proportion to your living and experiencing the dream in the present. You must begin to live the dream to best cast the dream.

This kind of vision casting will have a powerful impact on your people. They will sense the passion and pick up on the dream. They will resonate with it because they see and feel it in your life. As you help them experience in the present what the ministry will be like in the future, the vision becomes compelling.

Questioning the dream. As you picture your vision, probe it with numerous questions. Use the definition of the vision as a test of the quality of the vision statement. First, ask, Is it clear? Do I understand it; is it clear to me? As Professor Howard Hendricks of Dallas Seminary says, "A mist in the pulpit is a fog in the pew!" Then ask, Will it be clear to my people? The only way to know the answer is to observe and ask. Think about the response of the strategic leadership team as they developed the vision. Did it move them? Present it to a random sampling of your congregation and note their response.

Then ask, Is it challenging? Does it challenge me? And if so, Will it challenge my people? You'll know the answer if you watch the emotional response of your people as you present your vision to them. Do they get excited? Do they respond with passion?

The next question is, Is the dream visual? Does it create mental pictures of the future of the ministry? Then, Do I believe this vision can be realized? Is it feasible? Finally ask, Am I convinced that it must be? Does it ignite passion within me?

Demonstrating patience. You must be patient with the vision development process. You cannot rush it; give it whatever time it takes. Sometimes a vision will pop fully formed into the visionary's head in a matter of days. Nehemiah's vision in Nehemiah 1 came to him fully formed. However, he did not have much time. More often, a vision takes weeks and even months to develop fully. A vision could even take years of cooking on the back burner of the leader's mind as is the case for some pastors while in seminary.

However, visionary thinking tends to be a way of life for visionaries. They spend much of their waking time envisioning their future and that of their ministry. For most, when it comes time to develop a written statement, they simply record what has been on their mind since they first began their ministry.

STEP 2. THE PROCESS STEP

In the vision process step, there are four potential processes: expand your mission statement, build on your core values, model your vision after another's vision statement, or build on the strategy. Examine each and ask yourself which speaks to you. With which do you feel an affinity? Then pursue that process.

Expanding the mission. With this approach, the leader returns to the mission statement that he has already developed (see chap. 4). The vision statement is an expansion of that mission statement—make disciples! (Matt. 28:19–20). The visionary immerses this disciple-making mission in the ministry community, where the vision will be implemented, and asks, What do I see? The vision involves developing and adding details to the mission, such as the church's purpose, some core values, and later the ministry strategy. Again, the question that is repeated throughout is, What does this look like? Give yourself permission to explore, feel, dream, be creative, and be daring. Get away by yourself and spend some relaxed time dreaming and imagining what could be.

When working with a strategic leadership team, I have used the following approach. I divide them into groups of two to four people. I give them a copy of their mission statement or write it on a whiteboard where all can see it. I ask each group to choose a recorder, and I give that person one or two 4-by-6-inch cards. Then I ask the groups to describe what they envision when their church begins to realize its mission. The recorder writes down the results, and I ask this person to read to the entire group what his or her group said. When finished, they pass these cards to the pastor or leader of the team, who incorporates them into the final statement. If the pastor is a strong, creative visionary, he serves as the final editor of the vision statement so that he has his visionary fingerprints all over the final product.

Building on the core values. A second approach to vision development is to build on your core values, which you will discover and articulate when you get to chapter 6. Here is an example that was developed by one of my students (Paul Srch) for church planting. The first statement is his articulation of one of his core values; it is followed by a vision for that value.

Value: A Commitment to Creative Evangelism

Unchurched people matter to God and thus must matter to us as well. Therefore, we will provide opportunities for them to hear the Good News of Jesus Christ in creative ways through a variety of means and media so that they respond in faith.

But what does this look like? What will people see when the church begins to put this value into action, to live it out in its ministry community? The answer is the following vision:

We see friends bringing friends to a Sunday morning seeker-focused service because they will hear the Good News presented clearly and creatively in an atmosphere of acceptance. . . .

We dream of a church communicating the message of Christ to lost people, using multimedia, the arts, and the Internet. . . .

We hear believers sharing their faith at work over coffee, at home around the dinner table, at the park while their kids are playing. . . .

We see new believers being baptized as a testimony to lives changed by God's grace. . . .

We envision forming a network of healthy churches, which in turn plant other churches, throughout McHenry County and beyond!

If you were presenting these statements to your congregation, you could either combine the values credo with the vision statement or separate them into different documents.

When working with an SLT, I follow a similar process to that of expanding the mission statement. However, I assign each team one value and ask them to expand it into a vision statement.

Modeling after another vision. The third approach is to model your vision after another's vision. I suspect that when most of us read or hear various vision statements, we have our favorites. Some click with us. They ignite our passion, while others do not. We may even wonder why a leader has chosen and developed a particular one. Nonetheless, God is able to use the ideas of different leaders and people in different contexts.

This approach challenges you to find a vision statement that grabs your attention. When you hear or see it, you take a second look. It will not let go. It moves you deeply and inspires you. Use it as a pattern or working model to develop your own statement, changing the wording as needed. It will get you started in the process.

There are a number of vision statements in appendix F. Most but not all are for churches. One, for example, is a statement that Will Mancini designed for a children's ministry when he was on the staff at Clear Lake Community Church in Houston, Texas.

When working with a strategic leadership team, I give each group a copy of the vision statement rather than a 4-by-6-inch card. I ask them to discuss it in light of what they see two, five, ten, even twenty years from now and write their responses on the copy. After sharing some of their ideas with the entire team, the leader collects them and edits and collates their work into the final vision product.

Building on the strategy. The fourth approach is to build your vision on your ministry strategy. While I have used all of the above processes at some point to develop a vision, I have found this approach works best for the teams I train and for me. When using it, I delay intentional vision development until after designing the church's strategy. Thus after the team develops the mission, we move next to core values discovery rather than to vision, because with this approach strategy design is key to vision development.

As you will see later in this book, the strategy consists of five key ingredients: reaching the church's community, making mature disciples, building a ministry team, assessing the ministry setting, and raising ministry finances. I believe that a church's vision should address each of these.

Each of five development teams is assigned one of the five aspects of strategy to develop. One of their goals is to develop a one-paragraph vision statement for their specific strategy ingredient (I will provide examples when I cover strategy design). Once the DTs design and complete their strategies, they move on to develop the vision, which involves editing and combining all five vision statements together in a single one- to two-page document. The teams may also add other items to the vision statement, such as the mission, core values, and so forth.

Before any work on the four approaches to writing the vision begins, I ask the pastor to develop his mission for the church and share and discuss it with the teams.

The Vision Product

Someone has said that a picture is worth a thousand words. I suspect that it was Adam while in the Garden of Eden. Whoever said it must have been a visionary. Pictures and visions walk hand in hand, because a vision is a picture or image in one's head. Not only are mental pictures important to vision, but actual vision statements are as well. They help people picture the vision. The culmination of the work of the vision personnel through the vision process is a unique product—the vision statement. Not only does it serve as one way to communicate the vision to the congregation, but it also records the thinking of the strategic leadership team. Should there be any discrepancy or should someone attempt to launch a different vision, the SLT's work is on paper.

Articulating the vision in a written statement is a valuable experience that encourages ministries and leaders to discuss and come to agreement on their vision for the organization even before they write it for public scrutiny. A vision, however, is so much more than a written statement; it is an ongoing conversation. It is the way we think, individually and collectively, about the community that God is using us to build. It is what is important to us. It is why we want to be together.

The Vision Test

Once you have developed your vision, it is important to examine it to see if it is a good one. Again, as with the mission statement, use the vision definition to test it. Ask yourself, your team, and your congregation the following questions.

Question 1: Is the vision clear and compelling?

Question 2: Does it paint a picture of our future and where we think God wants us to be in the years to come?

Question 3: Is it a snapshot of the church's future? Is it future-oriented or is it merely a picture of the past?

Question 4: Do we believe that this can be? Do we believe that it is really possible?

Question 5: Are we convinced that it must be?

In my experience with churches, I have found that after they use this test, they know if they have a good vision. If you have a good one, you will feel it. You will experience an emotional connection. It will enflame you and your people with passion, and all will be excited about it. However, if it is lacking in any way, this test will help you determine where it needs some work.

How to Communicate the Vision

In addition to developing a compelling, biblical vision, it is most important that you communicate the vision, as well as the mission and values, to the people. All is lost if you do not or cannot communicate the vision. While I encourage you to write it down on a piece of paper, that is not the way you communicate it. You communicate it verbally.

I refer to this process as casting the vision. Like a fisherman who casts a lure into the water, hoping that as he reels it in some fish will follow, so the visionary casts the vision into the congregational waters, hoping that when he reels it in his people will follow. Vision casting is fishing for men. However, nothing happens if the vision isn't cast, because nothing is communicated.

The Leader's Example

The leader's example is critical to communicating the vision. His or her actions must reflect belief in the vision. If the leader does not live the dream, no one else will. People watch what leaders do as well as what they say.

The Sermon

The sermon is the primary verbal means for casting the vision. Whereas the mission communicates well on paper or written on a business card, the vision is best expressed through spoken communication. The power of the vision is in hearing it preached, not reading it. You can discern this by reading Martin Luther King Jr.'s great vision message and then listening to it. He communicates with great passion and conviction. That is key!

Today's preachers who believe in their visions should demonstrate passion and conviction. If the pastor struggles as a vision caster, the church may be in trouble. That is the bad news. The good news is that he can learn and grow in his vision-casting ability. To do this, he must first discover his passion—he will communicate best what he is passionate about! It is his passion that motivates him. And he must be sure he is embracing the right passion. My research and experience as a church consultant have shown that a passion for the Great Commission must be at the core of the pastor's vision. The thought of people accepting and then growing in Christ should deeply move the leader. If it does, he will not have difficulty communicating his vision.

Other Methods

Most of the other methods used for communicating the values and mission can also be used for casting the vision. They include the following: formal and informal conversation, stories, the bulletin, a framed poster, a church brochure, training materials, a slide-tape presentation, audio- and videotapes, skits and drama, a newcomers class, a newsletter, having the congregation vote on it each year, the performance appraisal, and a cartoon, picture, or photograph. Each ministry will need to discover which method is best for them. What works well in one context may not work in another.

Questions for Reflection, Discussion, and Application

1. This chapter presented seven reasons a vision is important. Did any one reason seem more important than the others? If so, which one? Would you add any other reasons to the list? If yes, what?
2. Does your ministry already have a vision statement? If not, why not? If yes, what is it? Does it meet the criteria in the definition of the vision statement? (Use the vision test: Is it clear, compelling, a picture of the future of the ministry, feasible, a must?)
3. What kind of visionaries are represented on the strategic leadership team? How many are vision catchers? How many are vision creators? Is the senior pastor a vision catcher or creator? What effect will this have on the envisioning process?
4. Have you spent any time praying for a vision? Why or why not? If no, when will you start? If yes, what thoughts have come to mind?
5. Do you tend to think big or small? How might this affect your vision?
6. What is your passion? What do you feel strongly and care deeply about when it comes to your ministry? What is at the very core of your being that motivates you and gives your ministry meaning?
7. At this point in your thinking about vision, which of the four processes for developing a vision appeals most to you?
8. Peruse the vision statements in appendix F. Do any excite you or elicit some kind of emotional response? If so, which ones? How might they help you structure and develop your vision statement?
9. Draw or paint a picture or draw a cartoon or take a photograph that conveys your vision.
10. What methods for casting the vision appeal most to you? Why? Which will work best with your congregation?
11. Do you have a passion for the Great Commission? How do you know? Do you live and breathe a ministry that strongly pursues both evangelism and edification?

6

Discovering Core Values

Why We Do What We Do

Navigators not only sail ships, they also have a soul. That catches only the most robust atheist by surprise, for belief in a soul is old news. What some do not understand is that churches, like people, have a soul—a collective soul.[1] Congregational or corporate soul is at the very heart of the organization. It is a leadership concept that embraces the church's unique values. What sets successful congregations apart is their discovering and tapping into that soul, making contact at its deepest levels. This chapter is all about tapping into a church's soul.

In this chapter we continue on the course of strategic planning through values discovery, which follows the steps already taken of mission and vision development. The final step will entail the crafting of a strategy.

Keep in mind that these steps form a ministry compass, like the compass on board a ship. They are a process that leads to a product or ministry model that fits your particular ministry community. Having observed a number of churches that God is using and blessing, I am convinced that most if not all have worked intentionally or intuitively through this process or one very close to it. Again, this approach sails against the popular current of church franchising and asks leader-navigators to think carefully through the fourfold process so as to tailor a model that fits their particular ministry—one that is authentic to their church. With this important distinction in mind, let our cruise continue.

This chapter is step 3 of the strategic envisioning process. It asks and answers the values question: Why do we do what we do? I have designed it to help you tap your ministry's heart and soul, specifically discovering what is conceivably the most important element—core values. Core values explain who you are—your identity. They are the very building blocks (DNA) of your ministry and explain why you do what you do or don't do what you should do. They form the foundation on which the mission and vision are built, and along with them form the church's core ideology. In navigational terminology, they function like the GPS (global positioning system) that tells the navigator where the ship is and where it is headed. Here is the point—the bad news is that beyond biblical prophecy, no one can know the future. The good news, however, is that you do not need to know the future to prepare for it. You need to know yourself and your culture. Discovering your values is the basis for knowing and understanding your identity, because they are at the core of the church's culture.

> **The Fourfold Process**
> Mission Development
> Vision Development
> **Values Discovery**
> Strategy Design

The Jerusalem church considered core values important, for Luke states that the church "devoted themselves" to its core values, which he lists in Acts 2:42–47.[2] After stating that a mission and values are at the foundation of an effective organization, Ken Blanchard and Michael O'Connor write, "Perhaps more than at any previous time, an organization today must know what it stands for and on what principles it will operate. No longer is values-based organizational behavior an interesting philosophical choice—it is a requisite for survival."[3] Lyle Schaller writes, "The most important single element of any corporate, congregational, or denominational culture, however, is the value system."[4] In this chapter we will explore why values are so important. I will provide a definition and then help you discover, develop, and communicate your congregational core values.[5]

The Importance of Values

Just as personal values speak to what is most important in our lives, so a congregation's values speak to what is most important in the church's life. Following are nine reasons why core values are so important to the life of a church.

Determine Ministry Distinctives

No two churches are exactly alike. Each is unique in a number of ways. Some churches are very traditional, while others have adopted a more contemporary format. Some devote their attention to strong Bible preaching and teaching, others to evangelism, reaching seekers, counseling, or children's ministries. What makes each church unique is its culture, and the most important ingredient in that culture, as Schaller noted in the quote above, is values.

If you examine the values statements or credos in appendix H, you will note many differences. Each one tells you much about the church and its distinctives. You can learn a lot about the church before you walk through the front door. For example, the credo of the church that I once pastored had eleven values. The sixth value—family—is most distinctive. It marked what was truly unique about this church. I have not found family listed as a value in any other church credo, and I have collected many.

Family

We support the spiritual nurture of the family as one of God's dynamic means to perpetuate the Christian faith (2 Tim. 1:5).

This value would catch some people's attention, specifically those with a family. It tells them that if their family is important to them, then this is a church worth considering.

The concept of values distinctiveness is so important that I will return to it shortly in the section on discovering core values.

Dictate Personal Involvement

Wisdom teaches that people who are looking for a church should look for one that has their same values. I refer to it as values alignment. It is much like a marriage. Couples with the same values pull together; those with different values are unhappy and pull apart. Just as it would be foolish for a couple with different values to marry, the same is true of a church (people and staff) and of a pastor who is looking for a church. He would be wise to know his core organizational values and those of the church before seeking a position. The church would be wise to know its primary beliefs and keep them in mind when looking for a new pastor. When a pastor marries a church with different core values, either one or both will eventually sue for a divorce. (An exception, however, is church planting. Most often the church planter's personal ministry values naturally become the congregation's core values. He holds these values, and people who share them are attracted to them. This is a real advantage for church planting and results in fewer divorces, at least early in the marriage.) Values alignment is critical for people joining the church and staff as well as pastors. One of the early criteria for joining a church or its staff must be values alignment. Studies confirm that people whose values align with those of the church will be much happier than people with values that don't align.

Communicate What Is Important

Core values signal a ministry's bottom line. They communicate what really matters. Clearly articulated values drive a stake in the ground that announces to all, "This is what we stand for; this is what we are all about; this is who we are; this is what we can and cannot do for you." The Jerusalem church communicated what was important through its values as seen in Acts 2:42–47.

A commitment to one's core values helps pastors know where to draw the line in the sand. For example, as a result of my ministry at Dallas Seminary, I have come to know many pastors in the Dallas–Fort Worth metroplex. At least once or twice a year a pastor who is having difficulty with his church will come to me, asking if it is time to move on and look for another ministry. My answer is always the same: "Does your situation force you to compromise, deny, or abandon your fundamental ministry values?" If the answer is no, and it usually is, then I encourage him to give the ministry and himself more time (James 1:3–4). If the answer is yes, then it may be time to leave.

Embrace Good Change

This book has already said much about change. The sum of it is that today more than ever before North America is reeling with accelerating, convulsive change. As the country shifts from one worldview to another—modernism to postmodernism—there is even more change, and it is happening in a shorter time than we've ever seen. No organization, especially the church, is exempt from its effects.

The problem for the church is how to know what is good and bad change. How can we know if a change will help the ministry or harm the ministry? A wrong move could prove disastrous. One answer to this dilemma is our core values. We must ask, Does this change agree with or contradict our beliefs as a ministry? We can embrace that which aligns with our values but must reject that which opposes them.

Influence Overall Behavior

A church's values or beliefs are ministry shaping. I have labeled this the *values effect*. Values dictate every decision and influence every action right down to the way we think and the manner in which we execute those actions. They beget attitudes that dictate behavior. They make up the premises of the ministry's policies and procedures. They affect everything about the organization: its decisions, goals, priorities, problems solved, conflicts resolved, spending, and much more.

In the problematic situation of Acts 6:1–7, the Jerusalem church models the values impact. The Twelve faced a potential church split over an accusation of discrimination. The Grecian Jews accused the Hebraic Jews of neglecting their widows in the daily disbursement of food. Instead of taking valuable time to wait on these widows, the Twelve assigned this responsibility to seven highly qualified people and gave their attention to the higher-value ministries of prayer and the ministry of the Word.

Inspire People to Action

A congregation's values are the invisible motivators that move its people toward meaningful ministry. The values of both leaders and followers catalyze—energize—people. For example, you can tell parishioners to evangelize the lost and urge them to support missions. However, if these are not a part of their values mix, they are not likely to happen. To truly catalyze the greatest amount of energy, to strike a resilient chord in the hearts of its people, to seize the day, each church must penetrate to a deep level. It must touch people at the level that gives meaning to their lives—the values level.

Enhance Credible Leadership

Good leadership at all levels is essential to any successful organization. As the leadership goes, so goes the church. Values drive and guide leaders as well as churches. Therefore leaders must know and articulate what they stand for—their values bottom line. Every bottom line is braced with core values, and it is imperative that these be biblical.

It is most important that leaders model a lifestyle consistent with those values. Leadership that aligns with solid beliefs invites credibility; leadership that violates or contradicts its values quickly loses all credibility and, over time, forfeits the ministry. An example of the former is the Johnson and Johnson Company, the maker of Tylenol. Several years ago the company responded to an episode of product tampering by voluntarily recalling all its product at a cost exceeding one hundred million dollars. It did so because one of its vital beliefs is the health of the customer: "We believe that our first responsibility is to our customers."[6] Consequently, to this day, I prefer Tylenol over any other product.

Contribute to Ministry Success

Any organization, Christian or non-Christian, must adhere to a sound set of fundamental values if it hopes to experience success. Not only to survive but to achieve success, it must have a solid set of values on which it premises all its policies and actions. It is the organization's ingrained understanding of its shared core values more than its technical skills that make its success possible. This is partly because shared values encourage people to serve longer hours and work harder. An inspired community of believers who are united in a common cause is enthusiastic and exerts a strong influence on its ministry constituents. This seemed to be the key to the effectiveness of the early church (Acts 2:42–47; 4:32–37).

But what is ministry success? A church is successful when through the power of the Spirit it accomplishes its ministry mission (the Great Commission, Matt. 28:19–20) without compromising its ministry values.

Determine Ministry Mission and Vision

As we have seen, the church's mission is what it is supposed to be doing. The vision is what that looks like. The mission is a *statement* of the church's direction; the vision is a *snapshot* of it. The first *tells* us where we are going; the second *shows* us where we are going. Both are vital to the life of the ministry organization and are located with the values at its very heart and soul.

<table>
<tr><td>Nine Reasons Why
Values Are Important</td></tr>
</table>

1. Determine ministry distinctives
2. Dictate personal involvement
3. Communicate what is important
4. Embrace good change
5. Influence overall behavior
6. Inspire people to action
7. Enhance credible leadership
8. Contribute to ministry success
9. Determine ministry mission and vision

I have hinted at least twice so far in this book that of all that makes up congregational heart and soul, core values may be the most important. This is because of the effect that the values have on mission and vision. The church's values are foundational to its mission and vision. The shared values influence and determine what the mission and vision are. Just because a church decides that the Great Commission will be its mission does not mean that this will be the case. If the church does not value evangelism, then in reality it will have some other mission that aligns more closely with its values, whatever they may be. Churches that are not evangelical or that do not value the Bible may have some other mission and vision based on what they do value.

What Are Values?

Now that we know the reasons core values are so important, it is time to discover what they are. I define *core values as the constant, passionate, biblical core beliefs that go deep and really, truly empower and guide the ministry*. This definition consists of five vital elements that we will look at one by one.

Constant

Values are tenacious. Like the barnacles attached to the hull of a ship, they tend to hang on tightly. In terms of our ministries, they are the constant threads that hold together the ever-changing organizational fabric. In chapter 2 Eliza Collins informed us that a major shift of values takes anywhere from three to eight years.[7] While values do change, they do not change easily and quickly.

This can be good or bad. On the one hand, it is good because values dictate congregational behavior. If organizations changed too quickly at the values level, people would be left in a constant state of confusion. Congregants would become disoriented and the church's organizational fabric would quickly unravel. On the other hand, this is bad because some values need to change and don't, or change takes forever.

Passionate

Passion is a feeling word. It describes what you care deeply and feel strongly about. A good core value touches the very heart and soul of the church and elicits powerful emotions. Passion involves the emotions more than the intellect. It affects not only what you believe but also how deeply you believe it. This is the reason the definition says that values go deep. Passion stirs people through excitement and motivation to action.

This concept will prove most helpful in the section on values discovery. You can discover your own values by reading a values statement or credo. The values that you hold will jump off the page at you. They will stand out from the rest because you feel strongly about them—they connect with your emotions.

People who share your values feel the same way about them that you do. If they hear you articulate them or if they read them in a church brochure, they connect with the ministry at a gut level. They sense a kindred spirit that draws them in. These shared values penetrate to the bone and bond people together.

Biblical

When I say that values are biblical, I mean that most of the values of a ministry are found in the Bible. We all agree that we want whatever we do to be biblical. However, we accept many things in our churches that are not found in the Bible. Some examples are air conditioning, indoor plumbing, computers, faxes, organs, pianos, kneelers, and other helpful things.

Some values are not found in the Bible, but they do not contradict or disagree with the Scriptures. Therefore not all of our values will be articulated in the Bible, but they must not disagree with or contradict it. Even in the marketplace, many of the core values of an organization are biblical. For example, Liberty Bank in Fort Worth, Texas, employed me as a consultant and trainer to help them discover their core values. They embraced five: integrity/honesty, people orientation, teamwork, excellence, and high performance. Are all of these found in the Bible? Are any unbiblical? Johnson and Johnson's first key value is responsibility to their customers. Is that one in the Bible? Does it contradict Scripture?

Core Beliefs

In several places in this chapter, I have used the term *belief* as a synonym for *value*. This could be confusing. What is a belief? Is a core belief any different from the beliefs or doctrines listed in a doctrinal statement? *A belief is a conviction or opinion that you hold as true, based on limited evidence.* You have faith or trust in that conviction. However, a belief is not a fact, by definition.

A fact is a conviction that a significant number of people hold as true, based on fairly significant and extensive evidence. The doctrines that comprise a church's doctrinal or faith statement are facts based on Scripture. The values that comprise a church's values statement or credo are beliefs. The difference is the number of people who hold a conviction and the evidence that authenticates the conviction. You may find it helpful to compare Northwood Community Church's values statement with its faith statement. Both are in appendix H.

Various churches hold numerous beliefs. When I work with a church as a consultant to help the people discover their beliefs or values, I use the storyboard process that I presented as a helpful planning tool in chapter 1. After we finish the brainstorming portion that attempts to list all the church's values, we may have as many as twenty-five that are stuck to the whiteboard. However, we are after the church's core or primary beliefs. These are the values that are central to the organization, those that they believe are at the very heart of their ministry. There may be as few as four or five or as many as ten or eleven core values. In the storyboard process, I limit them to six. Thus I give each participant six one-quarter-inch red dots (see chap. 1) and ask him or her to place them on the Post-it notes that contain the six primary values. When all have finished, I simply look for the values with the most dots to discover the organization's core values. In the discovery phase, I encourage you to follow this procedure.

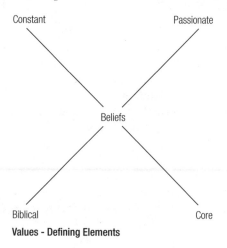

Values - Defining Elements

Empower and Guide the Ministry

Core values drive and guide the church. Like a ship out on the high seas sailing toward some port, churches are on a journey toward some ministry port that is their mission and vision. The church's mission determines its port, and the vision is a picture of what it will look like when it arrives at that port. And it is the church's values, like the engine and rudder of a ship, that empower and guide the church toward that destination. At least this is how it is supposed to work. The problem is that far too many churches have neither thought through nor articulated this mission-vision concept as I am assuming for this illustration.

If the church is off course on its journey to its mission-port, then its values are not in alignment with its stated mission. As covered in the first section of this chapter under "Determine Ministry Mission and Vision," the values will drive the church toward some mission-port, but it may not be the church's stated or desired mission. A congregation's primary beliefs function much like a driver sitting behind the wheel of a car. They are the church's shaping force that influences all that its members do as well as how they do it. As summarized earlier under "Influence Overall Behavior," values comprise the bottom line for what the institution will and will not do. Therefore important questions for a church are: Where or to which mission-port will our values take us? Will it be the Great Commission or somewhere else?

Further Clarification of Core Values

My definition of core values—core values are the constant, passionate, biblical core beliefs that go deep and really, truly empower and guide the ministry—should help you understand in general what values are. However, I have found that in working with congregations, the following distinctions are also very helpful.

FUNCTIONS NOT FORMS

First, values are functions (timeless) not forms (timely). For example, community or fellowship is a timeless function and also a value of the church, whereas a small group gathering is a timely form that this function may take to express itself. The small group is not a value.

ENDS NOT MEANS TO ENDS

Second, values are ends and not means to those ends. For example, small group gatherings are means to an end and not the end itself. The end, however, could be community, and that is the value. Therefore, if you are trying to decide whether something is a value, it may help to ask, Is it an end or a means to an end?

EXPLAIN WHY YOU DO WHAT YOU DO

Third, values explain why you do what you do. Again, a small group gathering is what you may do. The reason why you do it, however, is the value, such as community. If you are trying to determine if something is a value, determine if it is what you are doing or the reason for what you are doing. The latter will be the value.

The Different Kinds of Values

Now we have a working definition of a core value. This will help us in the values discovery process. However, before we move to that process, we need to further hone the definition of core values by examining seven kinds of values that exist in tension.

Conscious versus Unconscious

The core values of every church exist at either a conscious or unconscious level. My experience is that most church members are not aware of their values—they exist at the unconscious level. Unless someone mentions them, they don't think about them. Therefore it is the leadership's job to move the church's values from an unconscious to a conscious level. This is the values discovery process. When the people in a ministry know and articulate the ministry's values, good or bad, they are aware at a conscious level of what is driving or influencing them. The people will be able to answer the critical question, Why are we doing what we are doing?

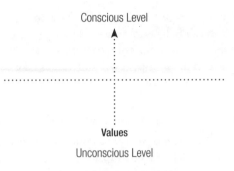

The Values Discovery Process

Shared versus Unshared

Shared values are essential to ministry effectiveness, while unshared values bring ministry demise. The former lead to a common cause; the latter lead away from it. In their book *In Search of Excellence,* Thomas Peters and Robert Waterman write, "I believe the real difference between success and failure in a corporation can very often be traced to the question of how well the organization brings out the great energies and talents of its people. What does it take to help these people find common cause with each other?"[8] Shared values are the key that unlocks the door of common cause. If the leaders and people who make up a ministry share the same values, together they will accomplish their mission and vision.

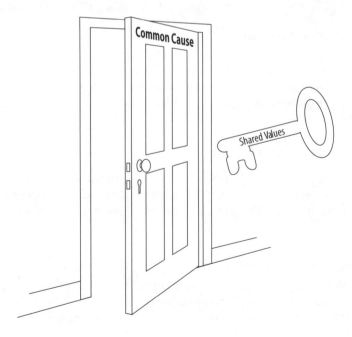

Personal versus Congregational

People have values, and the organizations of which they are a part have values. People hold various beliefs about what the church should be like. These are their personal organizational values, and they use them, for example, whenever they look for a new church. Since churches consist of people, the church's values will be the sum of the people's values. Churches that have dynamic ministries will find that their people share most of the same values. Most often churches that are struggling do not have people who share the same values, or they may share the wrong values.

The same holds true for staff. Studies indicate that when the staff's core values align with the senior pastor's as well as the church's, they are more committed to the ministry, experience less conflict, have a more positive work attitude, and experience greater job satisfaction. Consequently, if you are a pastor or a staff person, and you are struggling in these areas, most likely it is a values issue.

Actual versus Aspirational

Leaders and their ministries have both actual and aspirational values. Actual values are the beliefs people own and practice daily. They are reality. The Jerusalem church's core values in Acts 2:42–47 were actual, for Luke says that they "devoted themselves to" them (v. 42). Aspirational values are beliefs that leaders and their people neither own nor practice. For example, a church may list evangelism as one of its values because it knows it is supposed to be evangelistic. However, its people may have won no one to faith in years. For them, evangelism is an aspirational value. Around the turn of the century the infamous Houston-based Enron Company claimed integrity as one of its values. That was aspirational. The proverbial proof of the pudding is in the doing, not the wishing.

What leaders and their churches must uncover are their ministry's actual values so that they can know what is driving them. In addition, mixing actual and aspirational values leads to a loss of credibility. People can sense what is and is not a value. To say that a belief is actual when it is aspirational is an integrity issue. This does not mean, however, that you cannot communicate your aspirational values. Just make sure that you distinguish between what is aspirational and what is actual. Northwood Community Church's credo, in appendix H, is one example of how to do this. The aspirational values have an asterisk after them.

You might assume from the previous two paragraphs that aspirational values are mostly bad. That is not the case. They can have an upside or a downside. While actual values identify who the church is, aspirational values identify and signal who it wants to be or become. When a church identifies values as aspirational, not actual, it communicates to its people where it is going and why it is pursuing new ministries—to realize or implement those values. That is the upside. The downside is when a church believes or assumes that its aspirational values are actual values, deceiving itself. For example, they think that they are evangelistic when they are not. As long as they believe this, the chances are good that they will not become evangelistic.

Single versus Multiple

All organizations have multiple values. They could have hundreds of beliefs. However, it is not unusual that many have one value that dominates or towers over all the rest. In the following table, this is called a unifying value. It is a single, controlling value that serves to unify the church and communicate its central thrust. This demonstrates the power of a value. It dictates the pastor's role, the role of the people, and so forth. Who said values are not important to a church?

In the table I have charted some of these values for North American evangelical churches. Note, for example, that in the classroom church the single or unifying value is doctrine—a knowledge of the Bible. This value, in turn, affects the role of the pastor (the church's expectations of him), the role of the people (the pastor's expectations of them), the key emphasis, and so on across the chart. For those who are strongly evangelistic, the single value is evangelism.

I believe that a ministry with a single towering value is in danger of being a "niche" ministry church, and this detracts from a Great Commission vision. Such a church tends to be biblically imbalanced. For example, little evangelism takes place in most Bible churches, and little biblical information is communicated in many soul-winning churches. A spiritually healthy, biblically balanced church, however, as exemplified by the Jerusalem church in Acts 2:41–47, holds these five values in balance: worship, fellowship, biblical instruction, ministry, and evangelism.

Type of Church	Unifying Value	Role of Pastor	Role of People	Key Emphasis	Typical Tool	Desired Result	Source of Legitimacy	Positive Trait
The Classroom Church	Doctrine	Teacher	Student	To know	Overhead projector	Educated Christian	Expository preaching	Knowledge of Bible
The Soul-Winning Church	Evangelism	Evangelist	Bringer	To save	Altar call	Born-again people	Baptisms	Heart for lost
The Liturgical Church	Worship	Worship leader	Audience	To exalt	Liturgy	Committed Christian	Spirit	God's presence
The Family-Reunion Church	Fellowship	Chaplain	Siblings	To belong	Potluck	Secure Christian	Roots	Identity

Corporate versus Departmental

Much of the emphasis in this book is on the church or organization as a corporate entity, and the next section of this chapter will help you discover the core values of your church. What I am after are corporate core values—those that are unique to the entire church. The various departments or subministries, such as the adult, youth, and children's ministries of a church, will also have core values. For example, the church may corporately value unchurched, lost people. Therefore the adult ministries might value lost, unchurched adults. The youth ministries would value unsaved, unchurched youth, and the children's ministries would value unsaved children. The various ministries need to discover their core values.

Ministries	Values
Congregation	lost, unchurched people
Adult Ministries	lost, unchurched adults
Youth Ministries	lost, unchurched youth
Children's Ministries	lost, unchurched children

Good versus Bad

When I lead an organization through the values discovery process, we are looking for the ministry's good, not its bad, values. However, a ministry would be wise to look for its bad values as well, for they drive the ministry in a different direction from the good values. Some examples of the former are when a church values men above women, the wealthy over the poor, the old-timers over the young "upstarts," especially as concerns congregational leadership, the status quo, and many others.

Kinds of Values

Conscious versus Unconscious
Shared versus Unshared
Personal versus Organizational
Actual versus Aspirational
Single versus Multiple
Corporate versus Departmental
Good versus Bad

How to Discover Your Core Values

Once you know why values are important and what they are, you are ready to identify your church's set of core operating values. In this section we will probe three questions: Who discovers the values? Whose values are discovered? and, How are actual values discovered?

Who Discovers the Values?

The strategic leadership team should be tasked with discovering the organization's values. The pastor may not know the values, especially if he is new to the church. (Research indicates that it usually takes at least a year for someone to pick up on an organization's values.) Many of the leaders on the strategic leadership team have been in the church for a long time. They will be most sensitive to the church's values and thus are essential to values discovery.

It is possible that the entire church could be involved in the values discovery process if it is a small church. However, this is not necessary as long as you involve the leadership team. I also suggest that the team revisit the values one year later to determine if they were on target.

Whose Values Are Discovered?

The primary thrust of this chapter is to help churches and their leaders discover the overarching, primary core values that govern their strategic thinking and acting. However, organizational values exist on both the personal and corporate congregational levels, and the congregation's values are the sum of each individual's values. Thus we need to look at both.

PERSONAL CONGREGATIONAL VALUES

Personal congregational values are the actual core beliefs of the people who make up a ministry organization. It is essential to take these values out, dust them off, and take a hard look at them. They exist on three levels. The first level is that of the typical church attenders or members. Their personal organizational values determine whether they are happy at their current church and should dictate where they land if looking for a new church. The second level is the staff, including the senior pastor and any other paid professionals and, in some cases, volunteers. Their core beliefs determine their future at the church, their overall effectiveness, and how well they work together. The final level is the church governing board, if the church has one. Though its impact may vary from church to church and tradition to tradition, the board's essential beliefs often affect who is on the pastoral team, how long that team will minister at the church, and ultimately the general direction of the church.

The people at each level would benefit greatly by knowing their values. However, in the real world, only the pastoral staff and boards may realistically achieve this. The typical attender and member, busy with other things, will likely not make the effort to discover their values. This is all new stuff to them.

Each person on the staff should discover his or her values. One of my goals as a seminary professor is to help future pastors discover their values while in seminary. I teach them to match their values with those of a potential church to see if a marriage is even feasible. Boards would be wise to discover their authentic, overarching beliefs. Do they as board members share the same values? Are their values the same as those of the staff and those of the congregation? Are most on the same page?

This raises a most important question. What happens if board members, pastors, or staff persons find that their personal core values do not align with those of their church? There are at least four possible answers. One is that they may attempt to change their personal values to those of their church. This would take some time. They may attempt to change the church's values. This would also take some time and might prove to be more frustrating than profitable. They could leave gracefully and find a church that shares their values (what some refer to as a "blessed subtraction"). This is likely the best option. A fourth answer is to be involved in planting a church that shares their values. This could be a good option, assuming their values are the right ones, such as those in Acts 2:41–47.

Corporate Congregational Values

Corporate congregational values are the actual, not aspirational, values of the entire church. They are primarily what we are looking for in this chapter. Thus far I have not worked with an organization that could not identify a set of shared beliefs. However, the mistake many people make is to assume that a pastor or leader can set a congregation's values or instill new ones. Core values are not something that people simply buy into. They already hold them, and the job of a leader is to help his people discover or identify what they are. It is a discovery process, not a sell job. Again, these are actual, not aspirational, values. The leader's task is to discover the actual values, lead the people as they pursue these values, and let the people who do not share the values embrace new ones, which will take time, or go elsewhere.

Having said that, I do believe that people can and in many cases should change their values. At various times in our lives, we go through a period of values formation when we examine and may change our values. Often this takes place when a person attends a university or seminary. Some Christian parents fear this when they send their kids to the public state university. The strategic planning process is also a time when a church should discover and reexamine its core values. However, as I've already noted, changing values is a long process that takes time. Ken Blanchard believes that it takes no less than two to three years to adopt new values.[9] Eliza Collins argues that from three to eight years are needed. My point is that initially the leader's job is to help the people discover and agree on a set of values that they hold at a gut level. His or her job at this point in the process is not to create or shape new ones. At this time you are discovering what is, not what could be. Shaping new values where necessary comes later in the process.

Discovering Actual Core Values

There are several techniques that aid organizations in identifying their core values. One approach is to examine several values statements or credos from other churches (I've provided some in appendix H). Some may seem to jump off the page. You identify with them, and, most likely, they are your values.

Following is a second more common approach that I use with churches.

1. Ask the SLT to cover or review the material in the first two sections of this chapter—the importance and definition of core values. The first motivates people to identify their beliefs, and the second helps them know and understand what it is they are looking for. The leader-pastor may need to lead them through this material, giving the SLT time to digest it mentally.

2. Ask the SLT to take two core values audits—a personal and a congregational audit. (These can be found in appendix I.) They are exactly the same, except for the titles and instructions. The personal audit serves to identify the individual's values, and the organizational or congregational audit identifies those of the church. Then I ask each team member to compare his or her values with those of the church to check for alignment. If their values do not align, it is likely they are not happy at the church. And the opposite is true as well.

   The advantage of using the Core Values Audit is its objectivity. It is the least subjective of all the techniques I use. It also primes the group for the next technique.

3. Conduct a storyboarding session (see the section on process tools in chap. 1) Storyboarding is one of the most effective tools in values discovery. This begins with brainstorming, which involves creative thinking. The SLT verbalizes out loud the values based on the results of the organizational Core Values Audit, recorders write them on 8-by-6-inch Post-it notes, and another sticks them on a whiteboard. Then we do the workout, which involves critical thinking: the team members identify and discard values on the notes that are duplicates or similar to others, as well as any aspirational values. During a break each person places red dots on what he or she believes are the most important (core) values. Then we simply count the dots to discover the critical values and their order of priority. (The ones with the most dots win.) This plus the audit is usually more than sufficient to identify any group's actual values.

Discovering Aspirational Values

When I first began to help churches discover their values, I would not let them list any aspirational values in their final credo. My thinking was that people would know they were not actual values and write off the whole exercise as inauthentic and inaccurate. However, I have changed my mind. Now I allow them two aspirational values (sometimes more), for a total of eight values. And in a values statement, they must clearly mark the aspirational with an asterisk, footnote, or other indication, such as adding, "We aspire to value . . ."

**How to Discover
Your Actual Values**

Understand the importance and definition of values.

Take a personal core values audit.

Take a congregational core values audit.

Conduct a storyboarding session.

So how might a church discover its aspirational values?

1. My favorite way is to compare a church's actual values to those of a spiritually healthy, biblically functioning church. A great example that meets this qualification is the Jerusalem church. In Acts 2:41–47 Luke details five critical core values of this church: worship, fellowship, biblical instruction or doctrine, evangelism, and ministry or service.

   Then ask, What is missing from our values? Where do we fall short? (Most often it is evangelism and ministry.) The answer will provide the church's aspirational values. The goal is that over time these values are embraced and become actual values.

2. Another way to identify aspirational values is for team members to write one page that describes what they envision as a perfect, spiritually mature church. This is a "Have It Your Way" exercise. You ask, If you had an opportunity to plant a church for God with unlimited resources, what would it look like? What would its values be?

Your aspirational values reveal who you want to be (your future identity), not who you are (your current identity). As you think about your aspirational values, note that they will direct your church toward some new mission that is different from the current one, preferably the Great Commission. Is that the case? If evangelism and ministry are not actual empowering and guiding core values, then a Great Commission mission is an aspirational mission at best.

Two Approaches to Discovering Aspirational Values

One approach:

- Understand the nature of aspirational values.
- Compare the church's actual values with those of the Jerusalem church.
- Determine what key actual values are missing.

Another approach:

- Understand the nature of aspirational values.
- Describe a perfect, spiritually mature church.
- Identify the values of this church.

The Results of Values Discovery

The ideal result of values discovery is to find that the church holds the core values of the Jerusalem church as actual values. However, in my experience this has never been the case. There is always values work to be done.

In the section in this chapter "The Different Kinds of Values," I noted that, though not ideal, churches may have a single value (possibly more) that towers over the others and affects the role of the pastor, the role of the people, and other essential church roles. My point was that not all values are equal. One or possibly two will have priority over the others and exert more of an impact on the church. At this point in the values discovery process, if you have not done it already, go back and determine if there are any top-priority values in your church.

Also, the church may display some unique-to-the-church values. Following are some questions that will help you determine if this is the case: What is unique about your church? What makes it different from the other churches in the community? What is it that attracts people? What initially attracted you to the church? Why are you at the church? Why would people drive past other churches to come to your church? What are they looking for? With some reflection, churches can answer these questions.

Following are some examples of distinguishing values. Fellowship Bible Church has had two such values, while the other churches have one. I believe that of Willow Creek's ten core values, their love for and value of lost people—in particular unchurched lost people—is what distinguishes them from other churches. It is this value that drives them and makes them a seeker church. Note the distinguishing values for the other churches listed below.

A Philosophy of Grace
    You cannot earn God's acceptance. He accepts you now and forever through faith in Jesus Christ. The church should not focus on guilt to motivate its members, but encourage them to live good lives from a motivation of love and thankfulness toward the Lord.

A Christian Self-Image
    You can have a positive self-image, not because of who you are in yourself, but because of what God has done for you in Jesus Christ.

                                                            Fellowship Bible Church, Dallas, Texas

Lost People
    Lost people matter to God, and, therefore, ought to matter to us.

                                            Willow Creek Community Church, Barrington, Illinois

A Mobilized Congregation
    Ministry over buildings—"Every member a minister."

                                                        Heritage Church, Moultrie, Georgia

Family
    We support the spiritual nurture of the family as one of God's dynamic means to perpetuate the Christian faith (2 Tim. 1:15).

                                                    Northwood Community Church, Dallas, Texas

I cannot locate a statement of values for Fellowship Church in Grapevine, Texas, a suburb of Dallas, Texas. However, in reading their literature and the information on their website, it is evident that what is unique about this large, contemporary church is its creativity. Their desire is to reach their community creatively for Christ. And they offer weekend services that are very creative and unique as well as compelling and relevant to the lives of those people who make up the church's community. Valuing creativity may bother some. They wonder where it is found in the Scriptures. My response is in the character of God. He is a creative God (see Genesis 1 and 2).

Not every church knows or states the one or two values that make it unique. And in some cases these could be negative values. This is all the more reason for churches to discover and determine their actual core values.

The Follow-up to Values Discovery

The discovery of your actual core values reveals your DNA or identity. They describe who you are. Now you know what is key to your church culture and why you do what you do.

You should also begin to think ahead about where these values are taking you. Will they guide your church to accomplish your mission and vision or will they lead to another mission and vision? To return to my navigator metaphor, will your values guide the ship to the right port? Rate each value as to whether it is inward or outward focused. The ideal is to balance inward- with outward-focused values. My experience is that churches that are more inward focused will eventually plateau and die. Those that are more outward focused grow but often do not have spiritual depth. Spiritually healthy churches tend toward balance, as in the case of the Jerusalem church in Acts 2:41–47. For a healthy church, one of the outward values must be evangelism. I have noted that for churches strong in outreach, it takes two to three times the effort to maintain evangelism as a core value than to retain any other value.

The Development of the Core Values Statement

Once the team members have discovered their ministry's core values, the next step is to articulate them for the rest of the congregation. This will take the form of a values statement or credo much like those in appendix H. It involves both preparation and a process.

The Preparation

The preparation for articulating the values the team discovered is twofold. First, you must determine who will develop the credo. My experience has revealed that the person who should be a vital part of this process is the senior pastor on the team. He functions as the draftsman or writer of the statement—at least the final draft. However, staff people, those on the strategic planning team, and board members may function as drafters and editors. Their fingerprints need to be on the document. This allows them to provide valuable input and gain ownership.

Second, you should think through why you are writing or crafting a credo. A written values statement benefits the ministry in several ways. One is that it infuses those values with leadership authority. Also, writing out the primary beliefs gives them greater clarity. And in a multisensory culture, writing remains fundamental to good communication.

The Process

The process of developing the stated values into a credo takes four steps.

STEP 1. DETERMINE IF IT'S A VALUE OR A FORM

The first step involves making sure that the team is working with the value and not its form. For example, one of the credos in appendix H lists small groups as a value. Actually, a small group is a form that expresses or implements a value, but a small group itself is not a value. I discussed this earlier. You may value small groups as a form, but that does not make them a value. Do not confuse what you value with the actual value.[10] Remember, core values are constant, passionate, biblical core beliefs that drive or empower and guide the ministry. The value behind small groups could be fellowship, biblical community, evangelism, or some other function. Another way to determine this is to ask, Is the item in question an end or a means to an end? Small groups are not an end in themselves—they are a means to an end: biblical community or some other function. Or ask, Why are we doing what we are doing? The answer is the value.

Determining Actual Values

	Value	Form
Example	Biblical community	Small group
Purpose	End	Means to an end
Answers	Why?	What?

STEP 2: DETERMINE THE NUMBER OF VALUES

The second step is to decide on the number of values. You will need to decide how many values will be in your statement. If you use the storyboarding process, you will make this decision before you hand out the red dots because it will dictate how many you give each person. My research indicates that most churches have from five to ten values. The only exception has been Saddleback Valley Community Church near Los Angeles. This church once had as many as seventeen. In *Built to Last*, James Collins and Jerry Porras advise that you have no more than six values, and they say that most visionary companies have fewer.[11] Blanchard and Hodges write, "Research shows that people can't focus on more than three or four values if you really want to impact behavior."[12] The rule of thumb is: less is more or having fewer values is better. I too recommend six actual values.

STEP 3: DECIDE ON A CREDO FORMAT

The third step is to determine the credo format. This affects how you state the values. A glance at the credos in appendix H or in the appendix in my book *Values-Driven Leadership* (it has a broader sampling) reveals that the values statement may take several different formats. I suggest that you peruse several credos and determine which you like best. You must strive to keep the statements simple, clear, straightforward, and powerful.[13] I prefer those values statements that include some Scripture (most in the appendix do). Making application of the value, as Grace Bible Church of Laredo, Texas, does is also helpful.

> **The Credo Development Process**
>
> Determine if the statement is a value.
> Determine the number of values.
> Decide on a credo format.
> Test the credo format.

STEP 4: TEST THE CREDO FORMAT

Finally, test the credo format. Ask the following: Does this format attract interest? Is it simple, clear, straightforward, and powerful? Does it include too many values?

Communicating the Core Values

You might develop the perfect credo or values statement for your ministry, but if the ministry constituency does not see it, or no one ever communicates it, then it dies an untimely death. You should encourage everyone in the ministry to become involved in the values communication process. But it becomes the primary responsibility of the leadership team—board and staff—to see that the credo is available to all connected with the organization.

The following are some ways that churches have communicated or cast their values:

Life and example of leadership	Slide-tape presentation
Written credo	Audio- and videotapes
Sermons	Skits and drama
Formal and informal conversation	Newcomers class
Stories	Newsletter
Bulletin	Performance appraisal
Framed posters	Cartoons
Church brochure	Website
Training materials	

I have touched only the tip of the iceberg. The only limit to the way a church communicates its values is its creative abilities. Jerry Joplin, the pastor of Bacon Heights Baptist Church in Lubbock, Texas, built a rock climb in the sanctuary where each foot- and handhold was labeled with a core value.

Questions for Reflection, Discussion, and Application

1. Can you think of any additional reasons, not given in this chapter, why values are important? Is any one reason more important to you than the others? If so, which one?
2. What is the difference between actual and aspirational values? Which is the key to what drives your ministry? Why?
3. Who in your church will be responsible for discovering the ministry's values? Why? What process will they use to discover those values?
4. Do you know what your ministry's core organizational or congregational values are? If so, what are they? How many are there? If you do not know what they are, guess.
5. What mission will your values lead to? Is it the Great Commission or some other mission?
6. Is there one value that is distinct from all the rest that attracts people to the church? If so, what is it?
7. Will you list any aspirational values? If so, how many and what are they?
8. Does the church know what its core values are? If not, how will you communicate the values to them?

7

Introducing the Ministry Strategy

How We Accomplish the Mission and Vision

In their book *Flight of the Buffalo*, James Belasco and Ralph Stayer assert, "Thinking incrementally is an American disease."[1] Though I suspect that other countries struggle with it as well, Americans have been seriously infected with this disease from early in life. Our eager parents encouraged us to eat just a few more carrots and peas and then they would dismiss us from the dinner table. Our patient teachers urged us to exert a little more effort, and the coveted A would be ours the next time. Out on the practice field, the football coach admonished us to play harder next week, and we might win the close one. Belasco and Stayer indicate that thinking incrementally is not bad, but when you think incrementally, you will not be thinking in terms of the new vision and the mission. Thinking incrementally is thinking with no mission or vision or with poor ones and can also mean that you begin with the old strategy and its methods and attempt to move toward the new vision and the mission. The problem is that you bring all the problems and limitations of your present paradigm with you, clouding your vision of what could be.[2]

Navigators cannot afford to think incrementally, or they could find themselves hopelessly lost at sea, if not at the bottom of the sea. Instead, they start with their port and then determine how best to sail there. That is strategic navigation. Navigator-leaders who think strategically look forward. They begin with their mission and vision because both articulate and paint a picture of where the ministry should go. Next, they look backward only in the sense that they ask, Now that we know (mission) and see (vision) where we are going, what will it take to get there? How will we have to act? "Looking back" here means developing an entirely new strategy, not returning to the old one. Belasco and Stayer add, "It's the looking back from tomorrow that gives thinking strategically its power, because that perspective helps you escape the limitation of today's situation."[3]

In preparing to pursue the strategizing process, we conduct a careful ministry analysis. The analysis serves not to authenticate or perpetuate what is but to show its inadequacies and to motivate us to think about what could be. We leave the ineffective behind and move on to what could be. Then we ask the strategy question, How will we get to where we want to be? If we are to think strategically and not incrementally, it is imperative that we manage backward from the future, not forward from our past.

The purpose of this chapter is to teach leaders how to develop a strategy to realize the missions they have articulated and the dreams they see. Leaders in both the Old and New Testaments led and ministered according to a strategy. Moses strategically led the Israelites through the wilderness, though they wandered somewhat, due to disobedience. Nehemiah revealed his strategy to rebuild the walls and gates of Jerusalem in Nehemiah 3–6. Jesus led and ministered according to a strategy when he selected the disciples, trained those disciples, and sent them out to minister. In Matthew 28:19–20 he gave the church its mission, and in the book of Acts, Luke shows how the church strategically carried it out.[4]

In this step of the strategic thinking and acting process, the fundamental ministry questions are, How will we get to where we want to be? How will we realize our ministry dream? How will God use this ministry to accomplish his ends? How will we successfully sail to our port of call? The answer to all is a biblical, strategic architecture that will provide guidance for the operational and strategic decisions that daily affect the life and direction of the church.

> **The Fourfold Process**
> Mission Development
> Vision Development
> Values Discovery
> **Strategy Design**

In this chapter I will introduce you to the strategy concept by covering the reasons for and the definition of a strategy. In the five chapters that follow I will present the five elements that make up a good strategy.

The Importance of a Strategy

Before you develop a significant, high-impact strategy, you and others on the ministry team should be convinced that a strategy is important and that you need one. Otherwise, the effort will be halfhearted at best. A strategy is important for numerous reasons. Here are five.

1. Accomplishes the Mission and Vision

Every church has a strategy that is partially reflected in its ministries and programs. The church must ask, Is this strategy a good one? Often a bad strategy does not have a vision or a mission to implement. It is easy to spot—people are going through the ministry motions, but not much is happening beyond maintenance.

A good strategy is the vehicle that enables the church to accomplish the mission (the Great Commission) and vision. The strategy moves the congregation from wherever they are spiritually (lost or saved) to where God wants them to be (mature). Therefore a good strategy delivers; that is, it helps the church accomplish the biblical mission that God has set for it.

2. Facilitates Understanding

More than one person in the congregation has thought, *Why are we involved in these ministries? Why sit in this Sunday school class, small group, or worship service? What are we doing here?* In some of our older, struggling, established churches, no one has thought through the answers to these questions. The response often is, "We have always done it this way." The ministries of these churches have much in common with the white paint on the outside of their building—layer exists on top of layer. No one has taken the time to scrape any old layers off. But eventually the bottom layer will come loose, affecting the entire finish.

The church's strategy is the thread that runs through all the church's ministries, tying them together and giving them meaning. As you will see, leaders build ministries around strategies. They design the ministries to contribute to and accomplish some aspect of the strategy. For example, at my last church the core of our mission and vision was the Great Commission. Each of the ministries that made up our strategy contributed to realizing that commission. Our small group ministry provided biblical community. The Sunday school exposed our believers to the deeper teaching of the Bible, and the worship service provided a worship opportunity and a place for the lost and saved to hear a word from God. It was our desire that all our people understand this and know what each ministry contributed to the whole.

3. Provides a Sense of Spiritual Momentum

Bob Gilliam developed the Spiritual Journey Evaluation as an attempt to determine if today's church is making disciples. He surveyed nearly four thousand attenders in thirty-five churches in several denominations scattered from Florida to Washington. After analyzing the results, Gilliam observed, "Most people in these churches are not growing spiritually. Of those taking this survey, 24 percent indicated that their behavior was sliding backward and 41 percent said they were 'static' in their spiritual growth."[5] Therefore 65 percent of those responding indicated that they were either plateaued or declining in their spiritual growth. These Christians had no sense of moving on with the Savior. However, people who understand their church's strategy to make disciples and who get involved in that strategy experience a sense of momentum or progress in their walk with God.

Pastor Rick Warren uses a baseball diamond to illustrate his church's strategy. The church encourages each member to work his or her way around the bases from first base to home plate. First base represents knowing Christ; second base, growing in Christ; third base, serving Christ; and home plate, sharing Christ. As members fulfill the requirements of each base, they experience not only a sense of accomplishment but also a sense of spiritual movement. They are not "sitting and soaking" or treading water but are moving forward in their walk with Christ. At the same time, they know where they are spiritually and precisely where they need to go. That is spiritual ministry momentum. We might ask, Where does a congregant go when he or she has reached home plate? My answer would be to lead another person around the base paths. That too would contribute to spiritual momentum.

4. Invests God's Resources Properly

God's resources are his people, specifically their talents, time, and treasure. While God is not dependent on people, he has chosen to accomplish his purposes through people. First, he uses our talents. He has given each of us a unique design (Job 10:8–9; Ps. 119:73; Isa. 29:16; 64:8). This design consists of spiritual gifts, talents, a passion, a temperament, and other factors (see Rom. 12:3–8; 1 Corinthians 12; Eph. 4:1–16). God can use these characteristics for ministry.

Second, God uses our time. None of us feels that he or she has enough time to accomplish all that should be done each day. We always seem to be running out of time. However, God controls our time and provides us with the amount necessary to accomplish his program (Prov. 16:3).

Finally, God uses our treasure. All that we have comes from his gracious hand (2 Cor. 9:10). And he gives us the privilege of investing our finances in building his kingdom and church (2 Cor. 8–9).

So what? To invest our talents, time, and treasure in a ministry that has no disciple-making strategy and thus is not going anywhere is a poor use of God's resources. To free the members for ministry elsewhere, God may want to close a church that has no strategy. Investing one's blessings in such a church may serve to hinder God's plan by keeping the doors open. Perhaps we need to close some of our older, struggling ministries and use the gifts, time, and money to start new churches where people are excited and have a passion for making disciples.

5. Displays What God Is Blessing

In chapter 2 I presented a theology of change. I want to return to that concept and apply it to the importance of a well-thought-through strategy. There I argued that the church's functions, such as evangelism, worship, fellowship, and teaching doctrine, are timeless and should never change. They are as valid in the twenty-first century as they were in the first century. The forms that those functions take, however, that make up and flesh out a church's strategy, are time-bound and must change for the functions to be most effective. God used the camp meeting, for example, as an effective strategic form or method of evangelism in America during the 1800s. He also used the altar call that Charles Finney popularized and evangelists used with success up to the 1940s and 1950s.

Early in the twenty-first century, these forms are not as effective in North America as they once were. And we observe that other more effective forms of evangelism have replaced them. One reason for this is that our times and culture are changing—people are different now. As times change, it takes a variety of methods to reach all kinds of people. God has sovereignly chosen to work through change. Henry Blackaby has wisely encouraged us to regularly discover what is God blessing and to invest our ministries in that. We must get outside the walls of our churches and discover what God is blessing and study churches and ministries that God is using to win people to the Savior so that we can discover what strategic methods he is blessing and using in the present. This may help us to strategize better and reach people in our ministry community.

What Is a Strategy?

I define a strategy as the process that determines how your ministry will accomplish its mission. This definition relates to the mission, the process, and the answer to the question How?

A Mission

As I said earlier, every strategy needs a mission. A strategy without a mission is like a navigator without a port, and what competent navigator would set sail if he does not know where he is going? While every church will have a strategy, good or bad, it may not have a mission. This seems strange, but if you studied many of the churches across North America and beyond, you would discover that most do not have a clear mission or a strong sense of direction. Some confuse the strategy with the mission. For example, if you asked the *function* question, "What are you supposed to be doing?" they might answer, "Study the Bible." Studying the Bible is very important, but it is a part of the strategy, not the mission of the church.

As covered under the mission development step in chapter 4, Christ has already predetermined the church's mission in Matthew 28:19–20; Mark 16:15; Luke 24:45–49; and Acts 1:8. It is the Great Commission—make disciples! Therefore every church must regularly ask itself three critical questions:

1. What are we supposed to be doing?
2. Are we doing it?
3. If not, why not?

My view is that far too many churches in North America have become "niche churches" that specialize in some aspect of the Great Commission. They have good Bible teaching or good counseling or great fellowship but have missed the Great Commission as a whole. An important part of my personal mission is to call churches back to what Christ has commanded them to do—make disciples!

A Process

A strategy is the process of moving people from prebirth to Christlikeness or maturity (Matt. 28:19–20; Eph. 4:11–13; Col. 1:28; 2:6–7). This involves moving a person from wherever he or she is spiritually (lost, saved, or immature) to where God wants that person to be (spiritually mature). This process is a part of the spiritual life journey, taking place over one's lifetime. As we grow, we go through the following phases:

Phase 1: prebirth (unconverted)

Phase 2: new birth (converted)

Phase 3: maturity (committed)

When pastors and parachurch leaders speak of discipling people, they are usually referring to taking a few believers—often young, new, and energetic—through these phases or steps on a one-to-one or one-to-two basis. The strategic purpose of this book and section, however, is to take not a few but the entire church through the disciple-making process. The strategic process will attempt to put together a church-wide ministry (not *a* ministry but *the* ministry of the church) that encourages and makes it possible for all the people to become Christ's disciples.

The How

The mission and vision of the church answer the *what* questions: What are we supposed to be doing? What kind of church would we like to be? A good strategy answers the *how* question. The strategy tells how to do what we're supposed to do. It is the overall process that enables a church to accomplish its mission. It is the ministry means that accomplishes the ministry end. If the church's mission is to make disciples, the strategy directs how the church will make its disciples. It explains to all involved how the church plans to move people from prebirth to maturity.

The Kinds of Strategies

When defining a strategy, it is also helpful to note that different kinds of strategies exist. One is a personal strategy. Christians should have a personal strategy to accomplish God's purpose for their life. The church's corporate strategy does not relieve the individual Christian of his or her individual responsibility to become mature. Another kind of strategy is departmental. In addition to the church's overall, corporate strategy, each ministry department of the church needs a strategy. Each ministry department needs a strategy just as they all need to know their own core values (DNA) and develop their own missions and visions. However, they must come under the umbrella of the corporate strategy and not contradict it.

This chapter and those that follow focus primarily on the church's corporate or broad, general organizational strategy.

Developing a Strategy for Your Ministry

Now that you know the importance of a strategy to your ministry and what precisely a strategy is, it is time to develop a general, overall strategy that is tailor-made for your unique ministry situation.

The preparation for strategic envisioning and the prior steps in the strategic thinking and acting process will have a significant impact on the development of the strategy. The ministry analysis, for example, evaluates the effectiveness of the old strategy and so influences the new one. Spiritual formation provides the spiritual foundation for the building of the strategy. Your core values drive the strategy. The mission directs the strategy, determining what the strategy seeks to accomplish, and the vision energizes the strategy.

The Impact of the Prior Steps on the Strategy

Steps	Impact
Step 1: Developing a Mission	Directs the strategy
Step 2: Creating a Vision	Energizes the strategy
Step 3: Discovering Core Values	Empowers and guides the strategy

The mission, vision, and values are virtually timeless and do not change appreciably, although the vision may change around the edges but not at its core. The same is true of the general Strategy (big S). Its core elements or mini-strategies (small s)—community outreach, disciple making, team building, ministry setting, and raising finances—will not change. They will always be the key elements that make up the strategy, but they will change around the edges to stay in tune with the times. For example, the first core element or mini-strategy is community outreach. This element does not change. There must always be outreach to the community, but the community itself will change. To carry out the mission of the church in a changing world, the general strategy—including its practices made up of its structures, systems, and policies—should be changing all the time. To carry out the mission of the church in a changing world, its practices—made up of its structures, systems, and policies—should be changing all the time. When a ministry freezes its strategy practices (the fringes), it becomes brittle and begins to decay.

The general, corporate Strategy (big S) framework includes five specific core activities or mini-strategies (small s) that I will discuss in the next five chapters: reaching the church's community, making mature disciples, building a ministry team, assessing the ministry setting, and raising and managing ministry finances. Each of these asks key strategic questions:

1. Whom are we trying to reach?
2. What are we attempting to do for them?
3. Who will do this for them?
4. Where will this take place?
5. How much will it cost?

Questions for Reflection, Discussion, and Application

1. Do you agree with the author that a strategy is important to your church? Which of the reasons seem most compelling? What do your current ministries say about your strategy?
2. Do you agree with the author's definition of strategy? If not, how would you change it? What needed element does the strategy supply to the strategic envisioning process?
3. The author notes that your strategy will change in its practices at the fringes but not in its core elements. Are you open to this kind of change? Is the congregation?
4. What is the impact of the core values, mission, and vision on the strategy? Why is understanding this impact important?

8

Reaching the Church's Community

Strategy Activity 1

I can understand how, if you are a student of sociology or a social scientist, you might object to the concept of geographical community. You might ask me if I had noticed that for all intents and purposes the old parish system, popularized by the Catholic Church, is dead, and that people who live near and around churches rarely attend those churches. You might want to argue that our lives are no longer centered in places. And I would agree with you. You might also point out to me that community currently seems to consist more of one's relationships at work, one's family, the sports teams one plays with, and other social environments than it does one's geography—a person's neighborhood. In fact how many people who live in a geographical neighborhood or community purposefully, intentionally get together? I have noted the same. However, I am talking about something much bigger than geographical community. For example, if you are from Dallas, Texas, that means you live within the city's geographical boundaries or city limits. Note that Luke uses the city of Jerusalem in a similar way. On a much broader scale, Dallas County might be similar to Judea and Samaria. In addition, everyone who attends or could potentially attend a church lives in some large geographical community that is located within so many miles of the church. It could be a five-, ten-, or even a fifteen-mile radius. It could be a city, a town, or some other area. And it is this geography with boundaries that I am calling community. I hope this helps.

The Savior makes it very clear through the pen of Luke that the church is to be so much more than a holy huddle or an inward-focused family that cares for its own and no one else. Instead, the church has a God-driven Christ-given directive to be outward focused on a lost and dying world that desperately needs the Savior. This raises an important theological question: Can a church that is not and has no intention of spiritually impacting its community be in the will of God? I think not!

The fundamental question you must ask is, Is our church's impact on our community such that if it suddenly disappeared, it would leave a serious hole in the community? What would your answer be?

Note that most of the churches The Malphurs Group has worked with indicate on the Church Ministry Analysis that two serious weaknesses of their ministry are evangelism and congregational involvement in ministry (see chap. 2, pp. 72–77). This chapter addresses the former and chapter 10 the latter.

Finally, if you as a church are working through this book with development teams, this chapter provides the information the community outreach development team needs to address its goals and develop the community outreach strategy.

To design a strategy to reach your community, you must ask and answer four questions:

1. What does the Bible teach about reaching your community?
2. Who is your community?
3. What kind of church will reach your community?
4. How will your church reach your community?

Developing a Ministry Strategy

Reaching the church's community
Making mature disciples
Building a ministry team
Assessing the ministry setting
Raising and managing finances

What the Bible Teaches about Reaching Your Community

To understand what the Scriptures teach about reaching a church's community, we must revisit the Great Commission in the Gospels and Acts. The following is a chart that you first saw in chapter 4 where I addressed developing a biblical mission.

The Great Commission

Scripture	Directed to Whom	What	Ministry to Whom	How	Where
Matt. 28:19–20	Disciples	Go, make disciples!	All nations	Baptizing and teaching	——

Scripture	Directed to Whom	What	Ministry to Whom	How	Where
Mark 16:15	Disciples	Go, preach the good news!	All creation	—	All the world
Luke 24:46–48	Disciples	You are witnesses	All nations	Preaching repentance and forgiveness of sins	Beginning in Jerusalem
Acts 1:8	Disciples	You will be witnesses	—	With power	Jerusalem, Judea, Samaria, and all the world

The Gospels

We observe the Great Commission in three passages in the Gospels. The first is Matthew 28:19, where Jesus commands his disciples to go and make disciples. Thus, in effect, we have two back-to-back commands—go and make disciples.

Note that the passage clearly says that Christ's disciples are to go, not wait. Clearly the Great Commission is outreach, not in-reach, oriented. We are not to remain huddled up and focused inward in our churches as the disciples in Acts 1:13. We are to be outward focused. It's incarnational in the community, not invitational in the church. Though I see nothing wrong with inviting lost people to attend our churches to hear the gospel, fewer people are interested in attending our meetings. We must go to them rather than waiting for them to come to us. It's proactive, not reactive. The question is, Are we attempting to coax the world into the church or the church into the world?

In Mark 16:15 we have practically the same construction. Jesus commands the disciples to "go into all the world and preach the gospel" (NASB). The verbs are commands. Again, "go" means we are to take the initiative, to be proactive, not reactive. In Matthew 5:13 Jesus proclaims that we are the "salt of the earth." But how can we be the salt of the earth if we don't get out of the shaker? In Matthew 5:14 he states that we are the "light of the world." How can we be the light of the world if we are not lighting any matches?

Unlike Matthew and Mark, Luke does not address our leaving the church cocoon, but this may be inferred from the other two Gospel references. It is time to let down the drawbridges and move out of our churched fortresses into our unchurched communities.

The Book of Acts

Another reference to the Great Commission is in Jesus's last words, recorded in Acts 1:8. "But you will receive power when the Holy Spirit comes on you; and you will be my witnesses in Jerusalem, and in all Judea and Samaria, and to the ends of the earth." Luke, who wrote the Gospel of Luke, repeats here in Acts the term *witness*. In his Gospel he says, "You are witnesses of these things"; here he says, "You will be my witnesses." In other words, be who you are. Important to reaching their community is where the Jerusalem church will be witnesses.

Last words are lasting words, and here the Savior tosses a rock into the church's ministry pond that sends out evangelistic ripples across ethnic lines and in all geographical directions. Not only does this passage have the Great Commission at its core, but it also includes geography. It tells the church where it is to be a witness. It instructs us that the Great Commission comes with geographical implications. Rather than staying huddled up in Jerusalem (v. 13), the church is to move out and reach the world with the gospel of Christ.

Jesus's instruction has ethnological implications as well. In verse 8 he includes the region of Samaria. Most Jews believed the Samaritans were inferior and would not associate with them (see John 4:7–9). The shortest route from Galilee to Judea was through Samaria; however, a good Jew would walk around, not through, Samaria. Therefore I can see the look of astonishment on the disciples' faces when they heard the word *Samaria*. Jesus was telling them to go and be witnesses to the Samaritans as well as the Jews!

The Application

From Jesus's words in Acts 1:8, I would argue that today's local churches have a geographical community or "footprint" and have been tasked specifically to reach out to and minister to that community, including its different ethnicities. I would define the church's community as its geographical sphere of spiritual influence. Practically it asks, who and where are the people that your church can reach? If the early churches thought strategically about reaching out to their community, today's churches must do the same.

If we use Acts 1:8 as our guide, we discover that the church has three kinds of geographical communities where it could exert a spiritual influence. The first is our immediate or local community, which is analogous to Jerusalem. We will focus on this one. The second is our intermediate community, which compares to Judea and Samaria, and the final is our international community, which extends to the entire world. You would be wise to determine what these are in terms of your ministry's geographical community, especially your Jerusalem. They will be different for every church, because each community is different geographically.

How Are We Doing?

Scripture is clear that Christ's local churches are to reach out to and evangelize their communities. An important question at this point is, How are our North American churches doing at reaching their communities for Christ? Church growth consultant Bob Gilliam surveyed more than 500 evangelical churches in 40 denominations over a 10-year period, including more than 130,000 church members. His survey revealed that each year the average evangelical church led 1.7 people to Christ for each 100 people in attendance. If you owned an insurance company and your salespersons sold a total of 1.7 policies per year, you would be out of business in a hurry! The reason for this travesty is that too many churches have simply ignored their communities. So how might we begin to salt our community with the gospel for the cause of Christ? The answer is to draft a strategy to reach those in our community in the name of Christ. But first we need to discover who is our community.

Discovering Your Community

Pastor Rick Warren at Saddleback Church in Southern California asserts that the church ought to be an expert on its community. While Rick was attending Southwestern Seminary, his wife told me, he spent months studying census data and demographic studies before planting the church. He pinned the data to the walls of their seminary apartment. He was attempting to answer the first question, where is your community.

So how would you answer this question? You must conduct a community analysis, conduct a church analysis, compare the two, and then consider your best ministry options.

Conduct a Community Analysis

A community analysis involves asking and answering the following questions about your community.

Where is your community?

Who is your community?

How might you communicate the results?

WHERE IS YOUR COMMUNITY?

The question, Where is your community?, discovers the soft boundaries of your community. It establishes your immediate community. You cannot answer the question of who lives in your community until you have determined its general boundaries. Otherwise, you might include some who are not part of your community or exclude some who are. Following are specific questions that will help you determine your community boundaries.

1. What is the travel time to and from your church? Win Arn has conducted a study of travel time (see figure below). He discovered that 20 percent of people drive from just a few to 5 minutes to get to church. Forty percent will drive from 6 to 15 minutes. Twenty-three percent will drive from 16 to 25 minutes, and 17 percent will drive more than 25 minutes. Thus most (83 percent) will drive up to but not beyond 25 minutes to get to church.[1] Our experience at The Malphurs Group with a number of churches over

the years is that this figure is still accurate. The US Census Bureau provides mean travel time in minutes to work, which might also prove helpful here, because in some areas the drive time to church and work are similar (www. quickfacts.census.gov).

To identify and establish your immediate ministry community, if you are located in a town or city, drive out the various arteries (roads, highways, interstates, and so forth) located nearest your church and see how far you can drive in twenty to twenty-five minutes. This will likely be your city limits. If your church is located in a more rural area, you may want to shorten the time to ten to fifteen minutes. The boundary will likely be your county line. For example, I worked with a church in Lubbock, Texas, and we used the town limits as the community, based on drive time. I worked with another church located in a more rural area in Missouri, and we used the county as their community, based on drive time. I refer to these as "soft boundaries," because it is difficult to be precise; so going with your city limits or county line may work best for you. Draw on a map the geographical boundary that reflects this distance so that you have a visual to use with your people. Another approach that could prove helpful is to work with the zip codes that make up the church's potential Jerusalem. It is possible that the zip code is a better determiner of the church's boundaries.

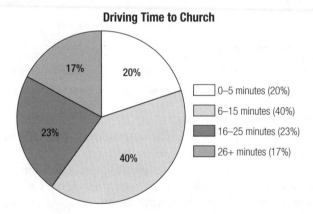

Driving Time to Church

0–5 minutes (20%)
6–15 minutes (40%)
16–25 minutes (23%)
26+ minutes (17%)

2. Is there a predominant or specific name for the community where you are located? It will usually be the name of your county, city, small town, or even a community within a city or town.

3. What are the boundaries of your immediate community? Are they geographical barriers (such as lakes, highways, railroad tracks), city limits, county lines, census tracts, zip codes, and so forth?

4. Are you located in an urban, suburban, rural, or some other kind of community?

5. Is this area old and dying, young and growing, or somewhere in between? Research has shown that younger, growing areas are easier to reach than older, dying areas.

WHO IS YOUR COMMUNITY?

Once you determine your boundaries, the next question in your community analysis is, Who is your community? The answer involves a demographic study of the community. Not only do you need to know who lives in your community but you will also need to understand who they are, which involves a psychographic study.

To identify your immediate community, you must consult demographic studies of your community. Demographics provide external information about the following: median age, occupation, income, marital status, family size, housing, gender, race, and education. In addition, demographic studies should provide you with future projections as well as current information.

Changing neighborhoods impact existing congregations. New ethnic groups move into communities, providing new opportunities and challenges for church growth and redevelopment. Churches must deal with these demographic realities. Therefore up-to-date demographic analysis is an essential tool for a robust congregational effort.

To know who the community is for churches that I work with, I collect answers to the following demographic questions for their area—usually their county or city. These are questions that most demographics studies address:

- How many people live in the community (total population)?
- Is the community growing, plateaued, or decreasing in numbers?
- What is the median (middle) age in years?
     percentage of people under 5 years
     percentage of people 18 years and over
     percentage of people 65 years and over
- What is their average level of education?
     percentage who have graduated from high school
     percentage who have graduated with a bachelor's degree or higher
- What percentage of the people are married or single?
- How many persons on average live in each household?
- What percentage are owner-occupants and renter-occupants?
- Are there more women or men?
- What is the predominant ethnic group? Give percentages of:
     White
     Black

Asian

Hispanic/Latino

Other

• What is the median (middle) household income?

The church can gather most of the above information from the latest census. Much of it applies to discovering the church's community, but you will use some of the information later when you need to look at statistics on total population. Collect the information at this point in the community analysis, though you may use some of it later.

The following is helpful information that is not likely found in the census. You will need to seek this from local community sources.

• What do most residents do for a living (white or blue collar)?
• If married, do both work?
• Do people tend to dress casually or formally?
• What are the most popular ways of spending spare time?
• What kind of music do most prefer?

A good demographics study should supply you with additional information that is important to understanding your community. Check with your denomination or other sponsoring organization to see if they have access to companies that supply this information. It is not free, but the cost is minimal and is well worth the expense in terms of what you learn about your community.

After discovering who lives in your community, you need to understand who they are if you are going to reach them. Psychographic studies of your area and your own surveys will help you do this.

Demographic information identifies your customer. Psychographic information tells why he or she buys. Psychographic information deals with attitudes, opinions, and values. It attempts to move beyond the strictly external information of demographics and into the emotions and intellect, the heart and mind of your community. It sheds light on people's beliefs and feelings as well as issues affecting them, such as their primary concerns, stress level, and resistance to change. To gain an understanding of your community, attempt to answer the following questions:

• How many people are unchurched? The way to answer this is to determine how many people attend worship services in the churches in your immediate community. (Some of the denominational agencies in the area would have this information, especially Southern Baptists). Then subtract that number from the population of the area. Express this in a percentage. The American

Religious Data Archive (Thearda) website would also have this information but likely uses membership statistics that are less accurate than actual worship attendance. Thearda will also supply you with the community's religious affiliations at no cost. You will find that in general most of the unchurched people in the community are young.

- What are their general preconceptions (or stereotypes) about churches? When asked, one person in San Francisco responded to the effect that the church is a parasite that owns the best property, pays no taxes, and helps no one. Another in Plano, Texas, responded that the church does not contribute anything to the community.
- When and under what circumstances might they visit a church?
- What are their felt needs, and which would bring them to church and with what expectations?
- Deep down what do they really want out of life? (What are their hopes, dreams, and aspirations?)
- What feelings might they experience before, during, and after a visit to your church?

The answers to these questions are more difficult to obtain. Some demographics organizations provide some psychographic information, but you will need to obtain much of this on your own through local sources, your own surveys, and general knowledge gleaned from contact with people. The more interaction that your congregation has with people in general and the lost in particular, the better they will be able to answer these psychographic questions. In appendix J there is a survey that will help your people obtain this specific information. Use it with an unchurched friend or acquaintance. If the unchurched person wants to remain anonymous, give him or her a copy with a self-addressed, stamped envelope, which can be returned by mail.

Sources for demographic and psychographic information are the Census Bureau (http://quickfacts.census.gov); denominational sources (Scan/US, Inc. at http://scanus.com); and professional providers such as Percept (http://percept.info), Free Demographics (http://freedemographics.com), and the American Religious Data Archive (http://thearda.com). Local and more accurate sources are utility companies, chambers of commerce, newspapers, libraries, and city planning offices. An excellent source for demographics in general is the publication *Advertising Age* (formerly *American Demographics*).

You will need to collect this information regularly and review it at least annually, because your community is constantly changing. Next year it will be different than it is now.

In preparation for the strategic planning process, you conducted a church ministry analysis (see chap. 2). You looked inward and asked, What is going on in here? This chapter challenges you to look outward. Seek to discover what is taking place in the world around you and what the future may hold. This is an activity that must continue throughout the life of the ministry and your life as a leader. You and the church will always need to know what is taking place "out there," because that information affects what the church does, especially its strategy.

This is the "Gretzky factor." Wayne Gretzky, the best hockey player of his generation, believed that it is not as important to know where the puck is now as to know where it will be. Good leaders have the sense of where the culture is going to be, where the organization must be if it is to grow. What is true of the marketplace is true of the church. Thus I want to challenge you and your church to be self-confessed culture watchers, to exegete the culture of a radically changing world and then respond strategically.

How Might You Communicate the Results?

How might you communicate the information about your community to your congregation? There are several ways.

The first and perhaps most obvious way is from the pulpit. Strategic pastor leaders will take time in their sermons to identify the people who make up the church's community. They can preach specifically on the community or may refer to it in sermons on other topics.

Another way is to develop a community profile. Here is the formula: your demographic plus your psychographic information equals your community profile. You could name a person to represent the resulting profile, perhaps Community Carl. This would be similar to Saddleback Church's Saddleback Sam or Willow Creek Community Church's Unchurched Harry. However, the idea of creating a typical person is more popular with the Builder and Boomer generations than with today's younger people.

Conduct a Church Analysis

With the information in hand from your community analysis, you are ready to conduct a church analysis. This involves knowing who you are, understanding who you are, finding the sources for this information, and communicating the information.

Knowing Who You Are

It is essential to know the people who are in your church. As with the community analysis, your church's demographics will give you the information you need.

- What is the congregation's median (middle) age in years?

     percentage of people under 5 years

     percentage of people 18 years and over

     percentage of people 65 years and over

- What is their average level of education?
    percentage who have graduated from high school
    percentage who have graduated with a bachelor's degree or higher
- What percentage of the people are married or single?
- How many persons on average live in each household?
- How many are owner-occupants and renter-occupants?
- Are there more women or men?
- What is the predominant ethnic group? Give percentage of:
    White
    Black
    Asian
    Hispanic/Latino
    Other
- What is the median (middle) household income?

Answering the following questions will also help you understand your congregation and serve in comparing your congregation with the people living in your community.

- What do most do for a living (white or blue collar)?
- If married, do both work?
- Do people dress casually or formally?
- What do most enjoy doing in their spare time?
- What kind of music do most prefer?

You will need to compare your church's demographics in particular with those of your community. Put them side by side. Is the church like the community or very different from the community? The more the church is different from its community, the more difficult it is to reach that community. When this is the case, the church must consider what its other options may be. I deal with this more in the next section.

Understanding Who You Are

You must understand who you as a church are. You will answer this based on your church's psychographics.

- What are our people's preconceptions about church?
- What felt needs bring them to church?

- Deep down, what do they really want out of life and out of the church?
- What are their hopes, dreams, aspirations?
- What feelings do they experience before, during, and after church?

FINDING THE INFORMATION

Here are some sources for this information: your own personal experience, the experiences of others you know well, a congregational survey, good congregational demographics, comment cards, "listening posts," random samples of the congregation, focus groups, and church records.

COMMUNICATING THE INFORMATION

How might you communicate this church information to your congregation? The pastor may cover it in his sermons. You might also want to summarize this information into a memorable format by developing a church profile similar to the one I developed earlier for Community Carl. This would involve adding together the demographics and psychographics of your church and coming up with a typical attender, perhaps Members Molly and Mike or First Church Charles.

Compare the Community Analysis with the Church Analysis

At this point you are ready to compare the people in your church (church analysis or profile) with the people in your community (community analysis or profile). The material that is most easily compared are the demographics of both groups. Place these side by side and see what you discover. What does your church share in common with your community? What does it not have in common with the community? Where are there gaps, and how big are those gaps? Compare the psychographic information as well. You can expect significant differences, because it reflects those who are believers and those who are not.

Your Best Ministry Options

You will want to investigate your church's options in light of who you are and who lives in your community. How might you respond strategically if your church is not like the community? What if the demographics in particular are different? Perhaps your church has been in the community for a long time, but most of the people who lived in the community when the church began have moved elsewhere. Most likely those who moved have been replaced by people of a different ethnicity. What does the comparison of your church with your community say about the most effective way you can minister to your community?

Here are some ministry responses. Read them through and think about which are your best options for effective ministry in the future. Consider and pray about each one to determine the direction God might have for you.

1. Remix (a merger): Would you be more effective if you merged with another church? My advice would be to consider one of the other options. Church mergers rarely work, because it is so difficult to blend the cultures of the two churches. Either they both fail or one in time takes over the other.

2. Reconfigure (an adoption): Would you have a better ministry if you asked another, stronger church to adopt you? You would become one of the campuses of a multi-campus church.

3. Reinvent (church planting): You could close your church and release your people to go to other churches. Then you could sponsor a church plant at your current site or somewhere else in the community that would have more in common with the community.

4. Retire (disband): Has an end come to your ministry in this community? There comes a time in the life of every church when it needs to close its doors. It has gone through the organizational cycle and is now dead. Perhaps you should close the church and let your people move to other, more effective churches in the community.

5. Relocation (a move): Does your ministry need to relocate geographically to a community where you would be more effective in light of who you are?

6. Revitalization (renewal): Do you need to rethink your ministry at your current site? Would your people be open to renewing and revitalizing your church? (Or should you combine a revitalization with a relocation?)

The Kind of Church to Reach Your Community

If you have decided to attempt a major revitalization of your ministry in your community, you will need to ask, What kind of church will reach our community for Christ? However, before answering this question, you must ask yourself whether your congregation is willing to adapt to reach your community. For the saved people in your church, this is a temporal preference issue. For the lost in your community, however, it is an eternal damnation issue. It is imperative that your people understand that their answer to this question will have eternal implications! Paul's answer to this most difficult question of adaption was yes, found in 1 Corinthians 9:19–23.

You should be able to answer this question based on the demographic and psychographic studies you did in answer to the question, Who is your community? (Your answers to this question will also apply to the second element of strategy that addresses making mature disciples in chapter 9.) The following questions will help you address the kind of church or churches that could reach your community for Christ.

1. The kind of pastor. Does the pastor need to be young, middle-aged, or older? Does he need to have a college degree, a seminary degree, or would

it matter? How much experience does he need? What skills, abilities, and gifts will he need? Must he be married? Must he have children?

2. The kind of staff. How many staff will it take? Should it be a multiethnic staff? What positions are needed? What education will they need, if any? What skills and abilities are required? (Some of the questions for the pastor would also apply to the staff.)

3. Style of worship. Should the worship be more traditional, such as a liturgical format, a robed choir, and handbells, or contemporary, featuring a praise and worship format with a band? Would a blended format work best? Should the church offer both styles in separate or multiple services?

4. The congregation. Will they need to be genuinely warm and friendly, inviting, and welcoming to outsiders? Should they be ethnically diverse or does this matter? Should they be diverse in age, mostly older, or mostly younger?

5. Response to seekers. First, I must define what a seeker is. Romans 3:11 teaches that lost people do not seek God. However, Acts 17:27 teaches that they can. Romans 3:11 is teaching that a lost person in his or her own attempts cannot and will not pursue God. However, when the Holy Spirit begins to work in lost people's lives, they will begin to seek God in the sense that they show interest in and pursue spiritual matters. Some clear examples are Nicodemus, Zacchaeus, Cornelius, and the Ethiopian eunuch. Thus a seeker is a lost person who through the work of the Holy Spirit is pursuing spiritual matters. Some in the emerging church movement say that the time of the seeker emphasis is past. It really does not matter what you call these people—seekers or spiritually interested unbelievers. They are still and always will be present in our culture and need to be reached for Christ.

The church's response to seekers or spiritually interested lost people will be an indication of whether it values evangelism and wants to reach lost people who are pursuing spiritual matters. I have observed at least four responses to reaching seekers that I have placed on the Seeker Matrix below. On the left are seeker churches that are outreach-oriented. Churches like Willow Creek Community Church in Chicago are seeker-driven. They make it very clear that their primary goal is to reach out to and win seekers to faith in Christ. Thus they have a separate service for seekers and design what they do around attracting and reaching seekers. Other churches are seeker-friendly. While their primary focus is not on reaching seekers, they encourage seekers' presence and design services and ministries with them in mind.

On the right are churches that are not interested in reaching seekers and are inward focused. Seeker-tolerant churches are churches with a contemporary style that attracts seekers, but they tend to ignore their presence. Other churches are seeker-resistant. They are churches that tend to be hostile toward seekers. If they do not give seekers the cold shoulder or state publicly, "We are not a seeker church!"

they at least make it clear from the design of their services and ministries that they are focused on ministering to believers.

Seeker Matrix

6. Types of ministry. You will likely need to have an excellent children's ministry. Will your community want small group ministries? Will a Sunday school class or an Adult Bible Fellowship (ABF) serve people best? (An ABF has a broader purpose than a Sunday school. It's more like a small church.) Will people expect men's and women's ministries and sports for their kids? Should the church target singles?

7. The facilities. Will nice facilities be a factor in drawing people, or will the facilities really not matter? What style of architecture will people expect, for example, western European or modern American? Will you need a multisite campus? Will you need lots of parking space?

8. Technology. Will people expect high or low technology? Do you need a website? Will you use a website to minister to those in other communities and in other countries (your intermediate and international communities)?

Your answers will help you see the kinds of changes that you need to make to be most effective in outreach to your community. While you should not attempt to make all of them at once, you will need to move in this direction long term.

How Will You Reach Your Community?

In this chapter I have addressed what the Bible teaches about reaching the community, who is your community, and what kind of church will reach your community. The last question is, How will you reach your community? While there are a number of correct answers to this question, I will articulate seven.

Set the Example

Regardless of the opinion of some, the senior pastor of a church often exerts tremendous influence on that church. In general, a ministry rises or falls on leadership. As the pastor leads, so follows the church. Consequently, if the church wants to have a powerful impact for Christ in its geographical community, the pastor will need to set the example. If he is not supportive, it simply will not happen.

And he needs to be more than merely supportive; he needs to set the example by leading the way.

An important question is, Does the pastor have a gift or passion for evangelism? I have noted that many pastors of large evangelistic churches have the gift of or a passion for evangelism. Some examples are Rick Warren, Bill Hybels, Andy Stanley, and my pastor Steve Stroope. If a pastor does not have this gift, it will be much more difficult to reach the community. Thom Rainer writes, "Effective church leaders average five hours per week in sharing the gospel with others."[2]

Cast a Compelling Vision

When I was a student at Dallas Seminary, one of the missions professors would challenge us with the question, "Have you asked God if he wants you to be a missionary and go to the mission field?" He believed that this was the first question that we should address regarding what we planned to do when we finished seminary. I can recall wrestling with the question and my openness to going on the mission field. But now as I look back at the question, I realize that his intentions were good but it was the wrong question. Scripture is clear that we are missionaries or sent ones (John 20:21) regardless of our circumstances. And the mission field starts at the front doorstep of our houses and churches.

With this truth in mind, we should discover what I refer to as our congregational self-identity. It addresses how we view or see ourselves, which affects what we will and will not do in the community. An example is the people who work at Disney World. They have been taught not to view themselves as employees but as cast—members of the Disney cast. This has a positive effect on how they do their jobs.

Churchgoers must ask who we are and how we view ourselves in the church. Far too many see themselves as members and not missionaries. Instead, I would challenge churches to view their building as a facility where they train missionaries. The staff are missionaries who are there to train others to be missionaries in their community. And the congregation must view themselves as missionaries and not just members. Actually I would like to get rid of the term *member* altogether. What does it mean? Why do we use it at all? (If anything, I think membership should mean that we are committed to a church and its ministry.) Finally, as we drive our cars out of the church parking lot, there should be a large sign with the words: *You are now entering the mission field!* This statement could make up the church's vision statement or at least part of it. It would look like the following:

The Vision for Community Outreach

We envision a building that will function as a mission's facility where missionaries are trained to passionately share their faith out in the community.

The pastor and any staff will function as trainers of missionaries. We, the congregation, will be missionaries not members.

Set a Challenging Goal

Goal-setting is essential to organizational success whether in the corporate or the church world. And it means that you, your team, and your church are set up for a major win in reaching your community. Goals provide us with a target to shoot for. They challenge, stimulate, stretch, evoke, and inspire us. They keep us on track when faced with competing forces that vie for our time and attention. Most important, goals must challenge us to excel. We at The Malphurs Group challenge churches to set not just any old goals, but challenging goals.

In terms of outreach into the community, we recommend the following goal: Each One Reach One Each Year (Goal 1:1:1). We also encourage churches to word it this way, because it is so memorable. The idea is to challenge every person in the church to set a goal of reaching one person for Christ per year. Is this doable? Are we asking too much? The answer to the first question is always yes, and the answer to the second is always no. The key is developing a redemptive relationship with someone within or even outside our community that will lead in time to sharing the gospel.

The truth is that some people will not reach anyone for Christ during that year. Floyd Bartel writes that "95% of all Christians in North America will not win one person to Christ in their lifetime"[3] much less in one year. However, I suspect that they have rarely been presented with a challenging goal to do so. And there are other congregants who will reach more than one person each year for Christ. When congregants are challenged this way, you can see how a church could double or even triple in a matter of just a few years. And I suspect that such challenging goals are the reason behind the explosive growth of our megachurches.

Pray for Your Community

We must bathe the entire community outreach ministry in prayer. In Colossians 4:3–4 Paul says, "And pray for us, too, that God may open a door for our message, so that we may proclaim the mystery of Christ, for which I am in chains. Pray that I may proclaim it clearly, as I should." We too must pray and ask God specifically to open doors in our communities so that we may proclaim the gospel clearly to our neighbors. Note that Paul's prayer is not whether to share the gospel but for opportunities to clearly share the gospel regardless of his circumstances. I would highly recommend that you make this a number one priority in your church. Not a day should go by that someone does not pray for the church's outreach into the community. This should be at the top of the intercessory prayer development team's list. The prayer team not only prays but also encourages and reminds the congregation to pray for the community. There are two high profile ways in which to do this. First, I challenge your church to take prayer walks through the community, and let people know what you are doing and why. Second, let the community know that you want to pray for them and their loved ones. Give them opportunities to communicate to you their prayer requests and then pray accordingly. And be sure to follow up. You could accomplish that by calling them or stopping by their homes. Contact them and ask what God is accomplishing through your prayers. As the relationship becomes closer, share the gospel.

Embrace Community-Specific Ministries

Discover what the needs of your community are and then address them. Following are some ministries that make a difference in communities: adopt a school, a fire or police station, or a military family or another family in need; do an on-campus sports ministry, a health fair, or on- and off-campus ESL classes; host a neighborhood crime watch; and many others. Lee Clamp, pastor of First Baptist Church in Barnwell, South Carolina, relates the following event: "A group of high school girls in our church adopted a family with four children. When they saw the children's bedroom, they decided it needed a makeover. So they hosted a spaghetti dinner that raised five hundred dollars. They went shopping at a Goodwill store, bought furniture, and painted it bright colors with polka dots. When the children saw their new room, one of them just sat on her bed and cried. It transformed them, and it transformed our girls."

One of the best sources for ministering in and to one's community is Steve Sjogren's book *Conspiracy of Kindness*. It lists more than three hundred community service projects. Also, check out his website (www.stevesjogren.com). Actually the only limit to community ministry is our creative and innovative abilities. When I'm taking a church through this material, at this point in the process I give the team the following application assignment.

Application Assignment

1. Break into groups and select a recorder.
2. Brainstorm some ways to minister in and to your community that are authentic to who you are and where you are.
3. Write them on a large pad or a whiteboard.
4. Come back together and share them.

Train Your People to Do Evangelism

The bad news is that a major limiting factor to reaching lost people in our communities is that our own people may want to but do not know how to share Christ with others. The good news is that we can do something about this. I suggest the following.

1. Arrive at a simple definition for *evangelism*. One definition is *presenting Christ to people with the intent that they accept him as Savior.*
2. Offer a premier evangelistic training course(s) a couple times a year. Two good ones are Willow Creek's *Becoming a Contagious Christian* and D. James

Kennedy's *Evangelism Explosion*. And my favorite is Howard Tryon's *Praying for You*.

3. Help people discover their style of evangelism. In their book *Becoming a Contagious Christian*, Bill Hybels and Mark Mittleberg identify the following styles with biblical references and examples: confrontational: Peter, Acts 2; intellectual/philosophical: Paul, Acts 17; testimonial: blind man, John 9; invitational: woman at the well, John 4; serving: Dorcas (Tabitha), Acts 9:36; signs and wonders: Paul, 1 Corinthians 2:1–5; and "chance conversations," based on Philip and the Ethiopian eunuch, Acts 8:26–39.[4]

4. Develop a simple, easy-to-use gospel presentation. One is the Romans Road, which presents the plan of salvation from the book of Romans.

Romans Road

- All have sinned (Rom. 3:23).
- The wages of sin is death (Rom. 6:23).
- Christ died for our sins (Rom. 5:8).
- Accept Christ and be saved (Rom. 10:9–10, 13).

Another is the bad news–good news approach.

Bad News–Good News

Bad News

- You're a sinner (Rom. 3:23).
- The punishment for sin is death (Rom. 6:23).

Good News

- Christ died for you (Rom. 5:8).
- You can be saved by faith in Christ alone (Eph. 2:8–9).

My favorite gospel presentation is Howard Tryon's prayer evangelism approach (www.prayingforyou.org).

5. Encourage your people to be intentional about spending time with lost people—especially those in your community. I like to ask, "If someone were to take a snapshot of you and your friends, would there be any lost faces in the picture?"

Plant Churches

Planting churches goes along with training your people to do evangelism. Peter Wagner writes, "The single most effective evangelistic methodology under heaven is planting new churches."[5] Depending on where you draw the lines or soft boundaries for your Jerusalem (Acts 1:8), there will be people out at the fringes who may not

> ### How Will You Reach Your Community?
>
> Senior leadership must set the example.
> Cast a compelling vision.
> Set a challenging goal.
> Pray for your community.
> Embrace community-specific ministries.
> Train your people to do evangelism.
> Plant churches.

be willing to drive to your church because of the distance or because they're not like you. Your response should be, "That's okay. If they won't come to us, then we'll go to them." Then plant a church in their area and encourage any of your congregation who live in that area to attend the new plant and use it as a launching pad to reach the lost.

Questions for Reflection, Discussion, and Application

1. Do you agree with the author that Acts 1:8 has geographical implications for the church? Do you believe that a church that is inward focused and not reaching out to its community is out of God's will? In light of where you are located, what are your immediate, intermediate, and international communities?

2. Who lives in your community? How do you know? What did you discover when you compared your church to the community?

3. What kind of church will it take to reach your community? How much change will be necessary to become that kind of church? Will you attempt this right away or over time? How much time do you have to make this kind of change?

4. Do people outside of your church know that you are located in the community? What is your current reputation in your community? Do you know? How? Are you just guessing at this? What would you like it to be? How are you currently ministering in and to the community?

5. Is senior leadership willing to set the example? Why or why not?

6. Do you have a compelling vision to be cast? Why or why not?

7. Are you willing to set a challenging goal? If not, why not?

8. Do you pray for your community? How much? Have you ever conducted a prayer walk through your community?

9. Does your church have any current involvement in the community? If so, what is it? If not, what can you do to become involved?

10. Do your people know how to do evangelism? If not, why not? What will you do about this?

11. Have you thought about planting a church in your Jerusalem or beyond? If not, why not? If so, how far along are you?

9

Making Mature Disciples

Strategy Activity 2

In chapter 7 I introduced you to the process of developing five-step or fivefold mini-strategies to accomplish your mission-vision. The question is, How will the leader-navigator guide or sail the ministry ship to the designated port? What do we want to accomplish? In the last chapter I challenged you to discover and reach out to your geographical community. Now we will look at the strategy the church will use to help people become mature disciples. More to the point, the functional question is, Does your church have a clear, simple, memorable pathway for making disciples, a pathway that most understand and know where they are along it? We in The Malphurs Group have found that most people in a church do not. You can view coming to faith in Christ as God's moving a lost person across a continuum from one extreme (little knowledge about Christ) to the other (maturity in Christ). Conversion happens somewhere in between. How will you move people from one end of the continuum to the other? What will be your pathway? The answer is to design a strategy for making mature disciples.

I believe that the best approach to such a strategy is to take the following five steps.

1. Develop a mission for the church—how you will make mature disciples. (This is what I discussed in chap. 4.)
2. Identify the characteristics of mature disciples so that you will know what they look like when they get there.

3. Determine the primary ministries that will ingrain these characteristics in people's lives, that is, a way to get these characteristics from the blueprints or navigational charts into the lives of the people.
4. Connect the appropriate primary ministries with the maturity characteristics.
5. Determine how you will measure spiritual progress.

These five steps are what is ahead in this chapter.

Note: if development teams of the church are working through this book, this chapter provides the information that the disciple-making development team will use to address its goals and develop the church's disciple-making strategy.

Developing a Ministry Strategy
Reaching the church's community
Making mature disciples
Building a ministry team
Assessing the ministry setting
Raising and managing finances

Step 1. Articulate Christ's Mission for the Church

More than two thousand years ago, the Savior gave us our marching or our sailing orders—his Great Commission, communicated in passages such as Matthew 28:19–20; Mark 16:15; Luke 24:46–48; and Acts 1:8.

By now you should have developed a broad, brief, biblical statement of what your church is supposed to be doing in your community. It should be clear, short enough to fit on a business card, personalized to the congregation, and memorable. If you have not developed and articulated your mission statement, you will need to do so before sailing any farther. If you have developed it, you are ready to move on.

In this section on mission, I will focus on what we are told to do in Matthew 28:19: "Go and make disciples." I believe that the intent of the passage is to make (evangelize) and mature (edify) disciples. This involves the process of moving people from wherever you find them (lost or saved) along a continuum toward maturity. Thus the final goal or "finished product" is not just a disciple but a mature disciple. Though I use the biblical terms *mature* or *maturity* (see Eph. 4:13; Phil. 3:15; Heb. 6:1), there are other terms or phrases that function as biblical synonyms for this goal, such as "Christ formed in you" or *Christlikeness* (Gal. 4:19), "complete in Christ" (Col. 1:28), "perfect" (fully developed, full-grown, adult, as in Matt. 5:48; Phil. 3:12; Col. 1:28), "grown up" (Eph. 4:15), and "holy" or "sanctified" (Rom. 6:19, 22).

For the sake of this chapter, let us assume that the mission statement for your church is to help people become fully devoted followers of Christ. I like this statement because it defines what a disciple is for the church and it is the description of a "mature" or "grown-up" disciple. However, do not assume that everyone will understand what this means. Its strength (brevity) can also be its weakness (clarity). It will need further clarification, so be ready to supply that clarity whenever the church's mission is being discussed or communicated. And this will be the case regardless of the mission statement that you embrace.

Step 2. Identify the Characteristics of a Mature Disciple

Now the task is to identify the characteristics of a mature disciple or a fully devoted follower of Christ. If a mature disciple were to walk through the doors of your church, what would he or she look like? These characteristics will become the goals for your people—the attributes or characteristics of an individual's life that reflect the achievement of the mission.

What a Mature Christian Looks Like

To identify the characteristics of a mature disciple of Christ, we must observe those that surface in the Bible. In doing this, you will note that it depends on which author you are reading. Some will emphasize certain characteristics, while others will stress other characteristics. For example, in Acts 2:41–47 the author, Luke, writes that the disciples were devoted to worship, fellowship, Bible study, evangelism, and service or ministry (these are also core values as well as church functions). I like these five because specifically more would be tough to remember and most all the other attributes in the Bible would seem to fit under them. For example, taking the Lord's Supper and giving would fit under worship.

If you look for the characteristics of a mature disciple in John's Gospel, you will find only three: biblical teaching (8:31), love (13:34), and fruit bearing (15:8). And Paul identifies several but seems to emphasize in Galatians 5:22–23 the fruit of the Spirit. Regardless of where in the Bible the characteristics are found, when you add them together, the result is spiritual maturity. As your people begin to embrace each characteristic in their lives, they are moving toward this goal.

Though not a requirement, every pastor-leader should consider aligning his preaching calendar with the characteristics. For example, if the church identified worship, fellowship, biblical instruction, evangelism, and ministry as the basic characteristics, the pastor would plan each year to preach in these five areas, clarifying and driving home the importance of each to Christian maturity. Thus he and his staff (such as the worship leader), as well as laypeople, would know where the sermons were going at the beginning of each church year and could plan the year accordingly. The biblical instruction and application ministry of the church could follow much the same approach, so that the Sunday school and the small group's curriculum would complement and implement the themes of the sermons.

Communicating the Characteristics

After you identify the biblical characteristics, you must decide how you will communicate them to your congregation in a way that members will remember. There are several ways to accomplish this. First, if there are five or fewer, your people may remember them as is—at least that has been my experience. Second, you might list them by using alliteration. For example, the church's mission might be to help your people become fully functioning followers of Christ. Then you would communicate that fully functioning followers have four characteristics (the four Cs):

1. Conversion—they are converted and know Christ as Savior.
2. Community—they value and are part of a biblically functioning community (small group).
3. Commitment—they have made the deepest of commitments of their lives to Christ.
4. Contribution—they are contributing to Christ's kingdom and the church by serving people, supporting the church, and sharing their faith (the three Ss).

Another approach is to create an acrostic. For example, one church that has the word *grace* in its name uses the following acrostic:

- **G**lorify God through meaningful worship.
- **R**elate together in biblical community.
- **A**pply God's truth through discipleship.
- **C**ultivate a lifestyle of service.
- **E**xpand God's kingdom through evangelism.

So if you can remember the name of the church, you will likely remember its characteristics of a mature disciple.

Step 3. Identify the Primary Ministries for Disciple Making

Once the church has identified the characteristics of spiritual maturity and a way to clearly communicate them to the congregation so that people know and remember them, the next step is to determine the primary ministries that will move the characteristics from your navigational charts into the lives of your congregation. They are the stones that make up your disciple-making pathway that you want each person to understand. This is the sanctification or spiritual transformation process that leads to maturity and Christlikeness. First, I will address who is involved in the disciple-making process and then how churches use their ministries to make disciples.

Those Involved

Who is involved in the disciple-making process? The answer is God, the individual believer, and the local church.

THE ROLE OF GOD

One of the roles of the Holy Spirit is the progressive sanctification of the believer. Paul writes in 2 Corinthians 3:18, "And we, who with unveiled faces all reflect the Lord's glory, are being transformed into his likeness with ever-increasing glory, which comes from the Lord, who is the Spirit."

We cannot accomplish this on our own. Zechariah 4:6 makes this very clear: "This is the word of the LORD to Zerubbabel: 'Not by might nor by power, but by my Spirit,' says the LORD Almighty." We are dependent on the Spirit to transform us into the very character of Christ (Gal. 4:19; 5:22–23). This is what our sanctification is all about, and this is the key to progressively growing and maturing in Christ.

THE ROLE OF THE CHRISTIAN

The believer also has a role in his or her sanctification process. What is his or her responsibility? Paul instructs us in Romans 6:12–14 to present ourselves in general and our bodies in particular to God that we might serve as his instruments of righteousness.

Christ broke the power of sin at the cross (v. 6), and we no longer have to serve sin. Before our conversion to Christ, we had no choice. Sin said, "Jump!" and our response was to jump. However, Christ has changed all that through his cross. In Christ we now have a choice. We can choose to continue to serve sin (vv. 12–13a) or to serve God (v. 13b). Consequently, the key now is our decision to present our bodies to God, to accomplish his righteousness, and not to sin as instruments of wickedness.

THE ROLE OF THE CHURCH

Not only does the Christian have a role in his or her transformation-maturation process, but the church plays a big role as well. The Christian's role is personal and individual. The church's role, however, is public and corporate. We mature together in community (Acts 2:42–47; 4:32–35). We in Christ's body need each other (1 Cor. 12:12–31). And the church's role is to design a disciple-maturing process that the Holy Spirit may use in concert with a community of believers to accomplish this process. (God does not need us to carry out his purposes. An example is a miracle where God intervenes directly to accomplish his purposes. However, I believe that he prefers to work through his people individually and his church corporately in community.)

Every believer, therefore, needs the local church (other believers). It is one of God's primary vehicles to help accomplish the maturation process. Fifty-nine times the Bible exhorts believers in the body to minister in some way to one another.

Twenty-one times (one-third) the verses exhort us to love one another. Other directives that fall somewhere under the capstone of love are the following:

"Be at peace with each other" (Mark 9:50).

"Be devoted to one another" (Rom. 12:10).

"Honor one another" (Rom. 12:10).

"Accept one another" (Rom. 15:7).

"Have equal concern for each other" (1 Cor. 12:25).

"Serve one another" (Gal. 5:13).

"Be kind and compassionate to one another" (Eph. 4:32).

"Consider others better than yourselves" (Phil. 2:3).

"Admonish one another" (Col. 3:16).

"Encourage one another daily" (Heb. 3:13).

"Use whatever gift . . . to serve others" (1 Pet. 4:10).

I do not believe that we in the body of Christ give this enough emphasis. Perhaps it is because so many are disappointed in general with the ineptitude of so many churches today. But God has neither given up on nor removed his blessing from his church. The rest of this section will focus on the church's role.

How does God use a church's ministries to make mature disciples? Two kinds of ministries—primary and secondary, which are part of every church—are involved.

The Primary Ministries

A church's ministries provide it with contexts where God works directly or indirectly through people to transform lives. All of a church's ministries can be subdivided into two kinds—primary and secondary.

CHARACTERISTICS OF PRIMARY MINISTRIES

The primary ministries are the ones that are most important in helping your congregation embrace the characteristics of discipleship and become mature. You want everyone to be involved in these activities and you tell them so. They are essentials, not electives. Primary ministries are *ordered ministries*. They are arranged in some kind of order—usually they reflect how people are assimilated into your church.

Assimilation refers to how people move from outside the life of the church into its life. If a person desires to connect with your church, how would he or she do so? What activities or relationships would he or she experience first, second, and so on? Would it first be a large-group worship service or a small-group gathering? The answer reveals your assimilation process and how people achieve spiritual momentum.

The typical, traditional format that most people encounter initially is a large-group meeting where there is worship and a sermon.[1] They are just checking things out and want to remain somewhat anonymous. If they like the experience, they may next attend a Sunday school class. If this goes well, they may begin to attend other events as well. In the past, traditional churches have offered four or five primary ministries in a week's period of time, such as Sunday school, a worship/preaching service, a Sunday night service, and a Wednesday evening prayer service.

NUMBER OF PRIMARY MINISTRIES

A number of more contemporary churches have embraced only two or three primary ministries. The idea is to do a few things well. Some have a worship/preaching event plus a small group ministry. This characterizes many in the Fellowship Bible Church movement. Others have the worship/preaching event, a small group, and a Sunday school or Bible class. The Bible study is informational and the small groups are relational in intent. At Willow Creek Community Church, they have instituted an assimilation process that has seven somewhat progressive steps.[2]

Therefore you may have as few as two primary activities or as many as seven, as in Willow Creek's case. However, the more you have, the less likely it is that people will become involved with them. Regularly and passionately you must emphasize them and their importance to the congregation, repeatedly communicating to your people that these are the primary events that they must pursue to become mature disciples. They are your essentials.

The Secondary Ministries

The secondary ministries are those that support and may back up in some way the church's primary activities. They are secondary in the sense that they are not essential to but are elective and supportive of the congregation's embracing the characteristics of maturity. They may be ministries such as men's and women's meetings, counseling ministries, a pregnancy resource center, various support groups, a twelve-step program, and so forth. (I do realize that my secondary activities may be someone else's primary activities—so I tread softly here.)

An Important Distinction

It is most important that you develop and distinguish your primary from your secondary ministry activities. You will staff and budget mostly around the primary ministries, because your primary activities will be staff-driven, in the sense that the staff or a gifted layperson will lead them. (I will say more about this in chap. 10, which deals with building a ministry team.) You will also pour most of your funding into them, and so you will budget around them. (Incidentally, they will also supply much of your income—especially the worship service, which some refer to as the church's "cash cow." I will say more about this when I cover raising the necessary finances in chap. 12.)

It is most important to understand that God has entrusted us with the responsibility of crafting the primary and secondary ministries that will accomplish his ends, the characteristics of spiritual maturity. In effect, under God's direction, we are selecting activities for the Holy Spirit's use. This is very sobering, and thus we must take this process very seriously. In all humility, we are asking God to take these ministry activities and use them as means to accomplish his ends.

No Guarantees

While the church's leadership does its best under God's guidance to develop its primary and secondary ministries, there is no guarantee that people will actively, willfully pursue them. Some could be involved in all the church's ministry processes but merely be going through the motions and not maturing. You must encourage all your people to pursue maturity, but there will be some who won't do it.

What Is Each Ministry's Purpose?

Finally, every ministry must have a purpose that answers the question, Why are you doing what you are doing? The answer should be one or more characteristics of maturity. We do nothing for its own sake. For example, if one of our activities is a small group ministry, it must have a purpose. We do not have a small group ministry just to say that we have one in place. That makes no sense. The purpose must in some way lead back to the attributes of spiritual maturity that ultimately contribute to the church's mission. Thus a small group ministry, for example, is the means to provide fellowship and a sense of community (purpose) that is vital to making disciples (the church's mission). If your church sponsors an activity that has no purpose and therefore does not contribute to its mission, you or someone needs to explain the reason this ministry was started and why it should continue.

Step 4. Align the Characteristics and the Ministries

Now that you have identified the characteristics of spiritual maturity and the primary ministries or pathway to ingrain them in the lives of your people, you need to connect the two. The question is, How do they work together to accomplish the maturation process?

This is the point where the maturity matrix can be of great assistance to you. It will help you apply and develop the very best ministries in the context of your church and its leaders and people. There are seven aspects to this process.

1. Constructing Your Matrix

Draw a matrix on a piece of paper or a whiteboard (see the figure below). Fill in the characteristics of a mature disciple along the top on the horizontal axis. Next, fill in your current primary ministries or your pathway along the side on the vertical axis in assimilation order.

	Characteristics of Maturity (Ministry Ends)				
	Conversion (Evangelism)	Community (Fellowship)	Celebration (Worship)	Cultivation (Biblical Instruction)	Contribution (Service)
Ministry Activities (Ministry Means) Worship Service					
Small Group					
Sunday School/ Bible Study					

2. Critiquing Your Maturity Matrix

Now, from a design perspective, ask, Do the primary ministries focus on and serve as means to accomplish one or more of the characteristics of maturity? The ideal is that the primary ministries help in some way to ingrain all of the characteristics of maturity. My experience with churches is that most do not. The matrix above provides a good example of what a typical church will look like—heavy in biblical instruction but weak in evangelism and ministry. (This matches as well what we see repeatedly on a typical church analysis—see chapter 2.)

3. Correcting Inappropriate Alignment

If you find that one or more of the primary ministries do not focus on and serve as means to accomplish one or more of the characteristics of maturity, you need to consider their appropriateness. If some ministries are doing a poor job of moving your people to spiritual maturity, you need to consider how to correct this. Perhaps you need to provide training for the leaders of your ministries. Do you need to drop, modify, or add a primary ministry? Do you need to design a totally new or several new ministries? There are several options as to how to correct these problems. You may want to ask or even require the small groups ministries or the Bible studies to include evangelism and ministry in what they do. For example, they might adopt as a service project a school or the family of someone in the military and focus on evangelizing them. Another option would be to creatively work a gospel presentation into the sermon/preaching event.

4. Discovering What God Is Blessing

You might benefit as well from the ministries of other churches. Randy Frazee has carefully, skillfully thought through this and has published his results in his book *The Connecting Church*. I cannot say enough good things about Randy's work and strongly advise you to read this book and understand his process, which has four ordered ministries: a worship service, a large community group meeting, a home group meeting, and an individual component.

My church has the following primary activities: build a relationship with an unchurched person, share a verbal witness, invite the person to a large-group meeting, and encourage participation in a life group. The small group is key to interactive Bible study, fellowship, care, ministry involvement, and accountability. You would be wise to investigate what other churches that God is blessing are doing in terms of ministries in general and primary ministries in particular.

The matrix will come in handy here. In addition to helping you develop your own ordered ministries, it helps you evaluate the processes other churches use in disciple making. You would look for their characteristics of a mature disciple or something similar and identify the ministries they use to develop these characteristics. This process will quickly identify strengths as well as any inadequacies.

5. Determining When You Will Meet

You must determine how often and when your activities will meet per week. Obviously you will start with the number and times of your current meetings. Then you should ask the following. Should we meet once, twice, or three or more times per week? And when should we meet? What days and times should we meet? Should we have a Saturday night meeting or Sunday morning or both? Remember that these ministries are key to becoming a disciple, so be careful about your attendance expectations. You do not want your people at the church every day or night of the week. What is reasonable? What best facilitates making and maturing disciples?

6. Remembering That "Less Is More"

The guiding principle here is that less is more. Contrary to what many believe, to make disciples you do not need a plethora of ministry activities that meet every day of the week. You need the right or best activities that meet at the best times and that best facilitate the implementation of your characteristics of maturity. Also, you will never be able to satisfy everyone's schedules. Thus you will have to make some hard decisions concerning when to meet and whether to schedule around your believers or the unchurched, unbelieving community. If possible, you want to do both. However, the group that gets priority will say much about your congregation and its mission.

7. Communicating Your Disciple-Maturing Process

If your congregation does not know what your disciple-maturing process is, then they cannot pursue it. You need to decide how to communicate your process. Some ways that we have seen in other chapters is through the sermon, a website, a brochure, some figures such as Saddleback's base paths or Andy Stanley's rooms of a house. You could use an apple with the peel, flesh, and core representing three primary ministries. Again, your creativity is key. When it comes to communicating the disciple-maturing process, remember the 7–11 principle. Your people need to hear the process, and anything else for that matter, from seven to eleven times if they are to remember it.

Step 5. Measure the Church's Spiritual Progress

There are several sayings that are most important to making mature disciples. One is, "What gets measured is what gets done!" Another is, "What you measure is what you get!" The point is that measuring spiritual progress is essential to accomplishing the maturing process. How do we know if our ministries are accomplishing their purposes or characteristics and the ultimate end (maturity)? The only way to know is to measure what we are doing, which involves articulating the problem, understanding the purpose, and designing a process for evaluation.

Articulating the Problem

The problem is that very few churches measure spiritual progress. Some may measure their offerings and their attendance, and that is helpful and good. But most churches do not measure the growth of their congregation toward spiritual maturity, which is so very important to every ministry. It is the reason—excuse the expression—they are in business. It answers the critical questions, How are we doing? Are we making disciples?

Some would argue that measurement is carnal or worldly and has no place in the church or any ministry. My experience over the years is that those who say this are most often in churches that are struggling spiritually. Should they attempt to measure how they are doing, they might be embarrassed or, worse, more discouraged than they are already. The early church measured a number of factors. Following are a few:

- baptisms—Act 2:41; 8:12–16, 36–38; 9:18; 10:47–48; 16:15, 33; 18:8; 22:16
- attendance—Acts 4:4; 5:14; 6:1, 7; 9:31, 34, 42; 11:21, 24; 14:1, 21; 16:5; 17:12
- meeting together—Acts 2:44, 46; 5:12
- sharing of possessions—Acts 2:45; 4:32
- singleness of purpose—Acts 4:32

The real key here is the church's motives. Are they playing "spiritual king of the mountain," or are they attempting to determine their disciple-making capacity in obedience to Matthew 28:19?

Understanding the Purpose

We would be wise to measure how we are doing for two important reasons.

Congregational Measurement

The church needs to know at a congregational level what is working and what is not. We must ask which primary and secondary ministries are producing fruit and which are not. The problem is that every ministry has a shelf life. (It will be effective for only so long; then it is time to change it.) So we must continually ask if an activity is still effective or if it has passed its shelf life.

Frazee addresses measurement at the congregational level: "We are able to take quarterly and annual snapshots of our congregation by means of surveying them on a particular Sunday or weekend, and then using the information in our evaluation and planning meetings so that we can focus our goals on the spiritual development of the congregation."[3]

Should we discover that what we are doing is not effective, we will need to make midcourse corrections while sailing toward our ministry port.

Individual Measurement

We also need to know at an individual level what is and is not working. Our members can evaluate their own personal growth toward maturity and the activities that best facilitate this. Frazee writes, "We ask each member . . . to evaluate his or her life in relationship to the facets of the Christian Life Profile."[4]

Designing a Process

There are at least two methods that can be used to measure spiritual maturity: counting heads and congregation-wide surveys.

Counting Heads

One method that takes us all the way back to the first-century church is "counting heads." At least Luke was counting heads according to Acts 2:41 and 4:4. Why? I believe he was updating the church regarding how they were doing spiritually.

Counting heads is a turnoff for some in today's ministries. Again, I believe that some pastors who count heads use this method to play "spiritual king of the mountain." At a meeting of pastors they will ask others how they are doing in hopes that others will return the question. Then they can brag about their church's numerical growth. The problem with rejecting this method, however, is that it throws the baby out with the bathwater. Just because a method is abused does not mean that we abandon it!

To count heads each week, someone must literally count heads and keep good records. How might this work? I mentioned earlier in this chapter that some churches have three primary ministries—a worship-preaching session, a Bible study or Sunday school, and a small group. All one needs to do is count the number of people in attendance at these three events as depicted in the figure below. Each week I would encourage those who lead and are responsible for these ministries to review the figures and compare them to the prior weeks and even the prior year.

Should the numbers be down, they are on top of the situation and have time to assess the situation and make corrections before the ministries take a serious downturn.

A CONGREGATION-WIDE SURVEY

A second method for measuring how your people are progressing in their movement along the continuum toward maturity is to develop a congregation-wide survey.

Two congregations that have developed such surveys are Pantego Bible Church, located in Arlington, Texas, and Watermark Community Church in Dallas. Pantego Bible Church's survey is called the Christian Life Profile. You may view it at www.theconnectingchurch.com. Watermark's survey is at www.watermarkcommunity.org. Watermark gives this survey during their worship time and also encourages their people to take it online. They ask their people to evaluate their progress in developing the characteristics of a disciple.

Another congregation-wide survey is one that Willow Creek Community Church has developed for its people. It asks them to indicate where they are along the following continuum: exploring Christ, growing in Christ, close to Christ, and Christ-centered.

You could design a congregation-wide survey that assesses how well your church is doing with its characteristics of maturity and its primary ministries. See the examples in the charts below.

Question: How is the church progressing in the following five characteristics?

	Weak			Strong
• Worship	1	2	3	4
• Fellowship	1	2	3	4
• Instruction	1	2	3	4
• Evangelism	1	2	3	4
• Service	1	2	3	4

Comments:

Question: How would you evaluate the church's primary ministries?

	Weak			Strong
• Worship/Preaching	1	2	3	4
• Bible Study	1	2	3	4
• Small Groups	1	2	3	4

Comments:

Questions for Reflection, Discussion, and Application

1. Has your church developed a mission statement? If not, why not? If so, is the emphasis on developing mature believers?

2. With your team, brainstorm some of the characteristics of a mature disciple as found in the Scriptures. Which ones will you identify for your congregation as indicators of Christian maturity? Will you use a particular method to communicate them to your congregation such as alliteration, an acrostic, or some other?

3. What do you believe is the role of God in the sanctification process? What is the role of the Christian individual? What is the role of the church? Do you agree with the author on the importance of the church to the believer and the selection of its ministries to accomplish maturity in the life of your congregation?

4. Why does the author use the term *ministries*? Do all of your ministries have a purpose? If not, why not? What will you do about this?

5. On a chalkboard, whiteboard, pad on an easel, or Post-it notes, list all the church's ministries. With the help of the strategic leadership team or the staff, identify all your primary ministries and write them in assimilation order. The remaining ones will be your secondary ministries. In light of the comments in this chapter, do the primary ministries make sense? Is there a clear assimilation order or process? Do you need to rethink your primary and/or secondary ministries?

6. Create a maturity matrix. Place your characteristics of maturity (ends) on the horizontal axis. Place your primary ministries (means) along the vertical axis. Does each ministry contribute to the realization of at least one characteristic? If so, which one? If not, why not? Do you need to discontinue any ministries? Do you need to develop some new ministries? How will you accomplish this? Use the maturity matrix to evaluate one other church's ministries. What does it tell you about the strengths and weaknesses of that church's discipleship process?

7. How often and when will each ministry activity take place? How did you arrive at your answers? Are you asking too much or too little from those who desire to be mature disciples? How do you know?

8. What are some of the ways that you might communicate your disciple-maturing process? Will you use a visual to picture the process? If so, what is it? What is the 7-11 principle and how will you apply it to the process?

9. Do you agree with the author that "what gets measured is what gets done"? Why? Does your ministry currently measure anything? If so, what? If not, why not? Would counting heads work for you? Look up several congregation-wide surveys online. Would any of these work for you?

10

Building a Ministry Team

Strategy Activity 3

We have seen that the ministry strategy that accomplishes the ministry mission and vision begins with the church's outreach into its Jerusalem (Acts 1:8) or ministry community. This is an Acts 1:8 exercise that strategically addresses the church's geography and determines whom the church will reach. Then the strategy includes the disciple-making and maturing processes, which clarify what the church will accomplish with those whom it reaches in its community. This brings us to the third element of the strategy—building a dream team. Here we are concerned with the ministry team, the people who will be involved in reaching our community and making them disciples. Who will help us sail our ministry ship to our ministry port?

Note: if your church is working through this book with development teams, this chapter provides the information that the board strategy development team, the staffing development team, and the mobilization development team need for addressing their goals and developing the church's staffing strategy.

The dream team is made up of three groups whose ministry is critical to the impact of the church on a lost, dying community. They are a wise, godly governing board; a highly gifted, spiritually motivated staff; and a well-mobilized congregation. Working in harmony, the three have the potential to turn many in their unbelieving, unchurched community into a band of mature disciples who will serve and glorify the Savior. In this chapter we will look briefly at four factors that address teams in general. Then the rest of this chapter will focus on the board,

209

staff, and congregational teams, which will help you develop an overall team staffing strategy for your church.

Developing a Ministry Strategy
Reaching the church's community
Making mature disciples
Building a ministry team
Assessing the ministry setting
Raising and managing finances

Two Team Factors

Who Makes Teams Work?

It is vital to remember that your church will be only as good as the people who make up the team. Peter Drucker is correct when he writes, "People determine the performance capacity of an organization. No organization can do better than the people it has."[1] The performance factor is that it takes good people to lead and build good churches. You can produce the finest study of your community and develop an excellent disciple-making process, but they will not mean much if you do not have the right people to deliver the information. The amazing thing is that God uses ordinary people to accomplish extraordinary measures if they are committed to him and his glory. These people make up your ministry team.

Two Team Factors
Who Makes Teams Work?
What Makes Teams Work?

What Makes Teams Work?

Though I am not aware of any passage that commands believers to work in teams, it is modeled by effective ministry throughout the Old and New Testaments. In Exodus 18 Jethro (Moses's father-in-law) rescued him from ministry burnout by directing him to form a team to minister to his congregation of Israelites. Jesus effectively ministered through a somewhat "ragtag" team of disciples (Mark 3:13–19; 6:7). And Paul was rarely seen without a team throughout his ministry. He served with Barnabas (Acts 11:25–26; 13:2–3); Mark (v. 5); Silas (15:40); Timothy (16:1–3); and many others. And Paul's body metaphor in 1 Corinthians 12:12–31 illustrates well the importance of a team to effective ministry.

The reason that we see teams so often in the Bible is not complex—the simple truth is that all of us can do more than one of us. There are some aspects of ministry that you can do better than I, and there are some that I can do better than you. Thus we are most effective for the Savior when we do them together. Leaders work ever so closely with a God-given team. And there are only a few exceptions to this, such as during a crisis when there is no time even to gather the team. Another exception is when the team cannot come to a consensus decision. In these situations, point leaders step out and make the decision.

When you develop a ministry team strategically and not incrementally, you need to select all your people from the perspective of your mission in general and your vision in particular. The vision is your dream of what all of you can accomplish for God. It supplies a picture not only of where the boat is sailing but also of who will sail with you, your dream team. You must select people on the basis not of who happens to be available or already on the ministry team but who should be on the team, those whom God has brought together for such a time as this. Though it may be painful, you may need to release people who are not a good fit for the team.[2] The church exists not to provide jobs for people but to provide Christ-honoring ministry through people with the right wiring in the right positions. Despite popular belief, somebody is not better than nobody. The stakes are too high for this kind of thinking that seems to permeate

Building the Team
Training the board
Developing the staff
Mobilizing the congregation

so many of our churches at the beginning of the twenty-first century. Put simply, the challenge is not finding people but finding the *right* people—the people God wants on your team.

Training the Board

A church needs a wise, godly governing board that functions in tandem with the pastor, the staff, and the congregation. Unfortunately, this is not always the kind of board a church has. Most established pastors have experienced boards that range from wonderful (spiritually mature) to awful (spiritually immature). When some hear the term *board*, they have wonderful memories of working closely with a group of wise, godly men who love the Savior. Others have recurring nightmares of how a power-hungry group rejected their leadership and ran them from the church.

Why Have a Governing Board?

Some churches have a board, while others do not. I have consulted with both kinds of churches. If I were a pastor and had my choice, I would opt for a board under most circumstances, because the role of the board is to exercise a high level of leadership. This consists of primary and occasional leadership responsibilities that make up its job description.

PRIMARY RESPONSIBILITIES

The board has four primary responsibilities:

1. The board is primarily responsible to pray for the congregation, the pastor, the staff, and itself. Boards that pray together tap into God's heart and work well together.

2. The board is primarily responsible to monitor or oversee the ministry in at least four areas (see Acts 20:28; 1 Tim. 3:2). One is to monitor the church's overall spiritual condition, regularly asking, How are we doing? Another is to monitor the church's biblical and doctrinal integrity, asking, Are we staying true to the Word of God? This was a constant concern in the New Testament. A third is to monitor the church's biblical ministry direction, which is the Great Commission. Are we doing what Jesus tasked us to do—make and mature disciples (Matt. 28:19–20)? A fourth is to monitor the pastor's overall leadership of the church. The board will provide him with supervision, accountability, and protection. (Here the board must make it clear to all that it supports the pastor and the church's direction.)

3. The board is primarily responsible for regularly making decisions that affect the life of the church. It is rare that a board will meet and not make any decisions. And much of this involves setting policy that governs the church. I will say more about this later.

4. The board is primarily responsible for advising the pastor as he leads the ministry. No single person can know it all or make the best decisions all the time. Even the best leaders often need wise counsel from a board of competent, wise, godly, spiritually directed people.

Occasional Responsibilities

The board has some occasional leadership responsibilities:

1. The board may oversee the selection process of the senior pastor.
2. The board will serve as an arbitrator in any disputes with the pastor.
3. It will enforce policy relative to the board members' functions on the team.
4. The board will provide for its own leadership development.
5. The board is responsible for church discipline. The pastor does not necessarily pursue it; the board does.
6. The board licenses and ordains qualified people for the gospel ministry.
7. It is responsible for establishing fair compensation and benefits for the pastor.

Nonfunctions

There are some functions that the board must not pursue:

1. Trying to keep everyone happy. This especially characterizes many smaller churches that see themselves functioning primarily as one happy, inward-focused family.
2. Micromanaging the church. Boards of churches with a pastor must resist the urge to take over and run the church. If the pastor is doing a poor job, they need to find a new pastor, not do his job.
3. "Keeping an eye" on the pastor. Some of us call them "guardians of the gate." This characterizes emotionally and spiritually unhealthy boards that fear change or losing control.
4. Representing particular elements in the church, such as the older people, the disenfranchised, and so forth. The church is not a representative democracy.
5. Functioning as the pastor's rubber stamp. Spiritually healthy boards will challenge the pastor when they believe that he is wrong about an issue and will not blindly go along with any and all of his ideas.

BIBLICAL BASIS

Many would argue that the church must have a board because Scripture mandates it. I do not see this anywhere in the Bible. Most argue this from the various passages in the New Testament regarding elders. However, when studied in light of the city church and house church patterns, it is likely that these elders were the pastors of the house churches that made up the city churches. If you would like to pursue this further, see my book on boards, *Leading Leaders*, and chapter 1 of *Being Leaders*.[3] I believe that the better biblical argument for a board is found in the various passages that address the wisdom of teams (for example, Prov. 11:14; 15:22; 20:18; 24:6).

Who Will Be on the Board?

I believe that the board should be made up of the board members and pastor, and there should be a board chairman and probably certain committees. The board members are responsible to lead and serve according to the primary and occasional responsibilities outlined earlier.

The senior pastor maintains three relationships with the board. First, he exercises leadership over the board as the leader of leaders. (This is his cause or ministry relationship to the board.) Second, he is equal to the other board members, a leader among leaders. (This is his community or family relationship with the board.) And third, he is an employee of the board and thus a leader under leaders. (This represents his corporate or legal relationship to the board.) These relationships are illustrated below. I will say more about the cause, community, and corporate relationships in the section to come on organizing the team.[4]

The Pastor's Relationships with the Board

```
                    Cause
                      P
        B   B   B   B   B   B   B   B
                  Community
        B   B   B   B   B   B   B   P
                  Corporation
        B   B   B   B   B   B   B   B
                      P
```

The board chairperson may or may not be the pastor. This can be a very powerful position, as he sets the board's agenda, leads the meetings, and interprets policy for the board as well as other matters. Thus the board needs to pray and think long and hard about the leader who fills this role.

A board may have ministry teams or committees that aid it in its leadership. These committees minister in an advisory capacity only, have no power, and must not attempt to exercise any power.

QUALIFICATIONS

Board members must be wise people who are spiritually qualified to lead and serve on the board. In fact the spiritual qualification is the key and only safeguard to prevent board nightmares, and it is an essential requirement for any dream team. Though likely qualifications for first-century house church pastors, those found in 1 Timothy 3:1–7 and Titus 1:5–9 would serve board members today as well. Other qualifications would be Spirit control and wisdom (Acts 6:3) and the fruit of the Spirit or Christlikeness (Gal. 5:22–23). The greatest error I have observed churches make in regard to their boards is to put immature people on them. The fact that they are "good old boys" or want to keep an eye on the pastor is unbiblical and carnal and will seriously damage Christ's church in the long term.

BOARD SIZE

Most boards tend to be too big. We have all heard about old First Church that has fifty to seventy-five deacons. My experience and research indicate that a good, functional board size is under ten people. Probably seven or eight board members is ideal. In light of this, note that though it was descriptive and not prescriptive, the apostles chose seven men (not necessarily board members) to serve the large Jerusalem megachurch in Acts 6:3. The smaller size allows the board members to get to know one another and interact at an intimate level over critical issues that face the church.

How Does the Board Lead?

One of the responsibilities of the church mentioned above is to produce and authorize written church policies that affect the board itself, the senior pastor, and the board–senior pastor relationship.

These policies dictate how the board will lead and operate—especially when it comes to making decisions. I define policies as the beliefs and values that consistently guide how the church board will make its decisions. They may be beliefs and values found in the Bible, but they do not have to be, because the Bible does not address all issues that a church faces. However, they must not contradict the Scriptures.

The Advantages of Policies

There are many advantages to using a policies approach to board leadership in general and decision making in particular. Here are seven:

1. It conserves people's time and thus allows the board to have the greatest impact in the least amount of time.
2. It addresses essential, fundamental church matters rather than ministry minutia.
3. It minimizes board interference with the pastor and any of his staff.
4. It results in consistent board decisions over time.
5. It establishes clear lines of authority between the board and the pastor.
6. It engenders trust between the board and pastor.
7. It prevents others from interfering with or controlling the decision-making process.

The Kinds of Policies

The board will operate with and make decisions based on three sets of policies:

1. Policies that govern the board itself and address such issues as its job or ministry description, chairperson's role, qualifications, conduct, operations, any board committees, evaluation, and training.
2. Policies that govern the senior pastor and address matters such as his qualifications, compensation and benefits, job or ministry description, leadership style, conduct, any pastoral committees, financial planning and budgeting, financial conditions and actions, emergency succession, staff compensation and benefits, and communication with and support of the board.
3. The most important in avoiding nightmares are the policies that govern the board–senior pastor relationship. These include such issues as the pastor's authority, his accountability, his direction, and his monitoring and evaluation.

How Will the Board Handle Power?

A question that people naturally ask is, How should a church handle power? Every organization has power, and that is not necessarily bad. The debate is over who should have and exercise that power. Obviously this is not a new issue, as the church has wrestled with it for centuries. Its answer is church polity, and it has developed three basic forms: episcopal (government by bishops), presbyterian (government by elders), and congregational (congregational rule). The key is distinguishing the difference between corporate and individual power. Here are some guidelines that should help your church with this critical issue.

Congregational Rule

First, I will address congregational rule, because the majority of churches have embraced it as their polity. Congregational rule, as the term implies, vests power in the church's congregation, usually its voting members. What this means is that the congregation has power but only when functioning corporately as the congregation, such as when it votes on an issue. Thus the congregation may have the power to vote out a pastor or vote him in and may do the same with any governing board. At the same time, in principle at least, no individual congregant has power over anyone, such as the pastor or the board. (In practice, we all have heard the horror stories of how certain individuals get power and use it for their own gain.)

In the same way, the board has power only when acting corporately as the board and on behalf of the congregation. It may be responsible to monitor the pastor but may or may not have the power to dismiss him. As the designated leader of the church, the pastor has power over all people individually but over no one (such as the board or congregation) corporately. He also has individual power over the staff and is responsible to the board and ultimately the church for their ministry. The staff will have power over those who minister under them, even if that person is a board member.

Elder Rule

Government by elders or elder rule is when power is vested in a governing board of elders and not in the congregation. Thus the congregation has no power, not even when it acts corporately, which is rare if it happens at all. However, as above, the board has power only when acting together as the board. This means that it could likely vote to dismiss the pastor. No individual elder has power over anyone else in the church, unless it is the pastor who happens also to be an elder. The pastor has individual power over all individuals in the church but not corporate power over the church or the board. Thus he can confront and be involved in the discipline and removal of any individual in the congregation but not the entire congregation or board.

Bishop Rule

With bishop rule, the power moves outside the church. Someone—a bishop who is not a member or may not even be an attender of the church—exercises exclusive authority and power over that church. This characterizes Episcopalian,

Methodist, and to some degree the Catholic Church, though the latter has the pope, who exercises his authority through bishops.

If you desire to pursue this further or learn more about board governance, see my book *Leading Leaders*.

Developing the Staff

Most often the staff is comprised of professional people involved in the church's ministry. A growing number of church staff have seminary or Bible college training, and most are remunerated in some way. The staff you want are those whom you dream about when you see yourself meaningfully involved up to your eyebrows in God's kingdom business. While the following is written more for

> **Building the Team**
> Training the board
> **Developing the staff**
> Mobilizing the congregation

churches with multiple staff members, those who lead small churches should find it instructive as well.

How Do You Define Staff?

My experience is that different churches use different terms to designate staff, which may result in confusion. Does staff include custodial and secretarial staff? My definition does not. I define *a staff dream team as two or more highly gifted, spiritually motivated, paid leaders who are deeply committed to serving together in some ministerial capacity to accomplish a clear mission and a compelling vision.*

A dream team consists of two or more people. It could range in number from a single, part-time bivocational pastor with va part-time volunteer secretary to more than one hundred men and women with plenty of secretarial and custodial backup in a megachurch.

They are leaders. This means they influence people. However, I must add that they are gifted, spiritually motivated leaders. While all Christians are gifted, these leaders bring to the team the right combination of gifts that complement those of the other team members. They are also spiritually motivated. They are leaders who want to be part of the team for the right reasons—they believe that the ministry is not all about them or what it can do for them; it is about the Savior.

They are paid people. Most ministry staff are paid and that is what distinguishes them from others in the church who volunteer their services. Jokingly I like to tell people that you pay us to be good.

They are deeply committed. They are not there simply to collect a check—their goal is more than just showing up. They have made the deepest commitment to the team, its ministry, and its direction, and they want earnestly to work together with the team. They are not the kind of people who at the slightest sign of trouble will throw up their hands and walk away. They are not waiting for a better offer—they are with the team for the long haul. In addition, they see themselves as Christ sees them—as his servants; they are servant leaders (Matt. 20:24–28).

They are committed to serve well together. I believe this is the most difficult part of working on a team—the working relationship. The team members have to get along with one another and must be committed to their working together no matter how difficult it may be at stressful times during the life of the church.

They serve in a ministerial capacity. Each member of the team functions in some ministerial capacity, such as an executive pastor, youth pastor, pastor of evangelism, and so forth, and this is what distinguishes them from secretarial and janitorial staff.

They are deeply committed to lead people to accomplish a clearly defined, biblical mission and a compelling vision. The mission and vision of the pastor or team leader have grabbed hold of them and will not let go. That is because they are God's mission and vision for the church. They are committed to the mission—God's mission—the Great Commission. Also, they hold the same dream and vision in common—his dream for the ministry is their dream for the ministry—the compelling and inspiring vision that generates excitement.

Recruiting a Staff Dream Team

How do you build a team such as this? Much of building a dream team has to do with recruiting the best available people. However, the best leaders are not always available. They are quickly snatched up. Therefore you need to maintain a recruitment mentality, constantly looking for good people. Recruiting a team involves answering a number of important recruitment questions.

WHEN DO YOU RECRUIT?

Only church planters have the luxury of recruiting a whole new team, which can have its cons as well as pros. Chances are good that most of you reading this book already have some sort of a team in place. It may be large or small, and it may or may not be a dream team. Regardless of the size of your team, your job from now on is to build that team one person at a time.

There are several indications that it is time to recruit a new team person. One is that too many things critical to the life of the church are not being done. And it is not because someone does not want to accomplish them or is not doing his job; it is because everyone is too busy with other critical ministry matters. The team is already working long hours and simply cannot do everything.

Another indication that it's time to recruit is when the church plateaus. A major reason why a church plateaus is because it does not have enough staff or the right staff to take it to the next level. As churches grow, there is a need for new and different leadership skills and abilities on the part of the staff. Not everyone, including the senior pastor, is able to grow with the church. Some staff members are small church people and some are larger church people. This needs to be taken into account in working out the staff equation.

How can you know if you have enough staff? In *Staff Your Church for Growth*, Gary McIntosh provides us with the following staff ratios that should prove helpful to your situation in answering this question.[5]

Average Worship Attendance

Attendance	Full-Time Staff	Support Staff
150	1	1
300	2	1.5
450	3	2
600	4	2.5
750	5	3

Should you be in a larger church, you would need to adjust these ratios to your size. Note that the average worship attendance increment is 150 people, the full-time staff is 1 for every 150 people, and the support staff is approximately .5 for every 150 people. Thus if your church has 900 people, you would need 6 full-time staff and 3.5 support staff. This might vary, of course, depending on a church's socioeconomic standing.

The best time to recruit someone to be a part of a dream team is before you have the need. I believe that the key for spiritually healthy, biblically balanced churches is to bring on board the necessary full-time and support staff before you reach a plateau or things start falling through the cracks. I know this sounds risky, and many would object; however, it is how you as a staff in general and a point leader in particular proactively in faith lead the church forward. (Incidentally, the right staff person will more than pay for himself or herself in just a short time, because a good staff person tends to attract new people to the church, and these people will help increase the church's revenue through their offerings.) The idea is to "play offense," to use the information in the preceding table, noting the next increment, and recruiting the necessary staff people to help lead you to that level. The other option is to "play defense," hoping that you will get to the next level, running into problems, and then hiring the necessary staff to bail you out. The latter is playing catch-up, and the problem is you may plateau before you reach the next level. And once you plateau, there is no guarantee you will be able to move on.

Whom Do You Recruit?

I separate staff into three groups in order of priority. They are the people who make up dream teams and the ones you will recruit, your staffing options. They are ministry staff, administrative or operational staff, and staff specialists. The first, ministry staff, consists of age-specific and functional staff.

Age-Specific Ministry Staff

My experience is that most churches recruit staff according to age-specific ministries. Some common examples in the typical church are children's, youth, and adult ministries, often in that order. Larger churches may break these categories down further to include preschool, middle school, and older adult ministries. The problem is that age-specific ministries by nature minister exclusively to a particular group of people and exclude the rest.

Functional Ministry Staff

Along with the age-specific staff, I would include and recruit functional staff. They lead in accomplishing the five functions of the church and include the following: a pastor of evangelism (may include missions here); mobilization, community, or fellowship (oversees the small groups ministry); service or ministry (oversees congregational mobilization); biblical instruction (this might fall under Christian education); and worship (one of the few functional staff positions present in churches characterized by the age-specific approach).

Age-specific staff minister only to a part of the church—their specific age group specialty—whereas functional staff minister to and benefit every age group. For example, the youth pastor ministers primarily to the church's youth, while the evangelism pastor ministers to all ages and trains all people in evangelism.

The age-specific staff balanced by the functional staff approach may seem like a pipe dream to the typical church that ranges in size from thirty to two hundred people. How could they afford all these staff persons? The answer is to fill these positions with gifted laypersons. Then, as the church grows, it can hire full-time staff to take the reins of leadership of each ministry area. To extend the pipe dream further, it would be exciting to continue to fill these positions with laypersons and not full-time staff. Regardless, the age-specific and functional staff approach serves to guide the future recruitment and development of the staff team. There is a blueprint for staffing later in this chapter under the section "Organizing the Team."

Summary of Ministries

Age-Specific Staff	Functional Staff
(Part of the church)	(The whole church)
Preschool	Worship
Children	Biblical instruction
Youth	Evangelism
Adults	Service
Fellowship	

Administrative or Operational Staff

The second staff group are the administrative or operational staff people. One example would be the church administrator who is responsible for oversight of the administrative matters of the church, such as banking, the budget, cash flow, human resources, and so on. This position is so necessary that most churches have someone doing this job, anywhere from a part-time layperson to a full-time staff person. Another relatively new position in a growing number of churches is the executive pastor. This person may play a number of different roles in the church. Currently, many work closely with the senior pastor and oversee the staff. Often the executive pastor is in charge when the senior pastor is away or indisposed, and some may even be a part of the preaching rotation.

Staff Specialists or Elective Staff

This third staff group is found mostly in larger churches that can afford them. Some examples are an assistant or associate pastor, gender-specific positions (men's and women's ministries), a teaching pastor (who shares the preaching and teaching load with the senior pastor), a pastor of counseling, a singles pastor, a pastor of family services, and so forth.

WHAT ARE THE DREAM TEAM CRITERIA?

Closely aligned with whom you recruit is what you look for in the people you recruit for your dream team. What are the criteria a leader must meet to make your dream team, to help sail your boat to its destination? The answer is the three Cs of recruitment: character, competence, and chemistry.

Character. The first criterion is character. It is the sum total of the qualities of a person that reflect beliefs and abilities. They may be good or bad, and a recruiter should be interested in both. I have heard Howard Hendricks say on a number of occasions that the greatest crisis in the world today is a crisis of leadership, and the crisis of leadership is a crisis of character. Character is critical to good leadership; thus recruitment begins with personal character.

Scripture provides us with several first-century character checklists for a leader that are just as relevant and binding in the twenty-first century. Lists for men (probably first-century house church pastors) are found in 1 Timothy 3:1–7 and Titus 1:6–9. Some character qualifications for women are found in 1 Timothy 2:9–10; 3:11; Titus 2:3–5; and 1 Peter 3:1–4. Character assessments for men and women can be found in appendix K.

In terms of character qualities that can prove detrimental to a team ministry in particular, be on the lookout for people with big egos, manifested by pride. Also watch for loners, people who prefer and value working alone. Finally, watch out for people who are independently successful. They have gotten to where they are by doing it their way.

Competence. A second critical criterion is ministry competence. It has to do with how well people do what they do. It consists of God-given capabilities and developed capabilities. God-given capabilities are natural and spiritual gifts, passion, and temperament. When recruiting, we must determine the gifts, passion, and temperament needed in the person who can fill a position. For example, my experience in the North American culture is that highly competent senior pastors have at least three gifts: leadership, evangelism, and communication (preaching and teaching). They are passionate about the Great Commission and have a combination of the D (dominance) and I (influence) temperaments on the Personal Profile (DiSC).

Developed capabilities include character, knowledge, skills, and emotional and physical health. Character relates to who we are. Knowledge has to do with what we know. Skills are what a person is able to do. Again, a senior pastor needs to be above reproach (1 Tim. 3:2). He needs to know a number of things, such as the Bible and theology, how to lead, and how to think and act strategically. He needs to have several skills, such as preaching, leading, vision casting, networking, and so forth. He needs to be emotionally healthy. We who train pastors have noted that far too many of our pastors have emotional issues—often from their childhood—that need to be addressed. And this is one of the reasons so many are failing morally. Finally, a senior pastor needs to be in good physical health, taking time for regular exercise, good eating habits, and enough sleep.

As you examine potential dream team candidates and design potential positions, carefully and with the input of your other team leaders, think about which God-given and developed capabilities are needed.

Chemistry. A third criterion for the dream team is your ministry chemistry. This affects several areas. First is your ministry alignment. Does a potential team person have the same core values, mission, and vision as the church? Another area is your theology or doctrine. Does the potential team person agree with your essentials and nonessentials of the faith? Your essentials are the basic tenets of orthodox Christianity. The nonessentials are areas where there is more room for divergence, such as forms of church government, mode of baptism, the role of women, and others. Disagreement with the essentials would disqualify a potential team member. And you should carefully evaluate any disagreement over the nonessentials, as one group's nonessentials may be essential to you. An example cited earlier is congregational rule. You would be wrong to join the team of a congregationally ruled church and then later try to change the system.

Emotional alignment is another aspect of chemistry. Will the person or the potential team member get along with the rest of the staff in general and the senior pastor in particular? Emotional alignment is affected by temperament, passion, and the emotional climate the leader sets for the team. This question should illustrate the latter point: would you prefer to work for Billy Graham or Adolf Hitler?

Other Cs. Some would include other Cs as well as the ones given above. One is *cause.* My pastor looks for cause-oriented people. They are passionate people—who would work for free. They have a will to win and will not take no for an answer. Finally, they get the job done with no excuses.

Two other Cs are *culture* and *call.* Prospective staff need to align with the church's culture, its unique expression of its values and beliefs. And some believe that prospective staff need to experience God's call to their particular staff.

Where Do You Begin?

The fourth recruitment question is, Where do you begin to find dream team recruits? Do you begin with the people you already have on board and design the strategy around them? Or do you begin with your strategy and look for people who will fit into it? The answer is both.

On the one hand, you can have a great team of people with a poor or nonexistent strategy, and they will still accomplish much. That is the nature of a good, dream team staff. That is what they do. On the other hand, you can have a poor staff with a great strategy, but without the right people on board, even the best strategy will not likely produce results. So the key in either case is to enlist the right people for the ministry dream team. The ideal is to have the right people involved in the right strategy. For you as the pastor, this will be your never-ending challenge—combining the right people with the best strategy, and you are responsible to craft both.

Building the right team with the right strategy involves the four Rs (see the table below). First, in light of your strategy, you will be able to *reaffirm* some or many of your current people. They are the right people in the right place at the right time, so keep them happy. Second, you will need to *redeploy* some of your people. They are the right people who are in the wrong place at the right time. So find where in your ministry they fit best. Third, you will need to *replace* some of your current people. They are the wrong people in the wrong place at the wrong time. Do them, the church, and yourself a favor by letting them go and helping them find the right place. Finally, you will need to *recruit* some people. These are the right people who need to be in the right place—on your ministry team—at the right time, which likely is now.

Building the Right Team with the Right Strategy

Four Rs	People	Place	Time
1. Reaffirm	Right people	Right place	Right time
2. Redeploy	Right people	Wrong place	Right time
3. Replace	Wrong people	Wrong place	Wrong time
4. Recruit	Right people	Right place	Right time

Where Will You Recruit?

The question is, Should you recruit potential staff from outside or inside your church? I think the best answer is both, depending on your staff needs and circumstances.

Outside the church. The advantage of recruiting people from outside the church is that the recruits bring creativity and innovation to your church. They may think differently and have other ministry exposure that could refresh and invigorate your situation. The downside is that you do not have as good a read on their character, their competence, and their chemistry or how well they will work with you as you do on current lay leaders. Add to this the fact that far too often other churches will give people a better reference than they should. They may have the best intentions but really sell the rest of the body short when they do this.

Within the church. The advantage of recruiting leaders from within the church is that you should have a good read on their character, competence, and chemistry. This assumes, of course, that you have a leadership development process in place that recruits and trains your lay leaders within the church. A disadvantage of finding leaders from within the ministry is that you miss out on the different perspective and new ideas of someone coming in from the outside. If, however, the person already in the church is creative and innovative, this may not be a problem.

Though you will likely find people from both outside and inside the ministry, a growing number of lead navigators are opting for the latter choice. For example, Bill Hybels writes, "Occasionally I'm asked where I find such great people to hire. My answer might be surprising. Almost seventy-five percent of our leaders have come right out of Willow."[6] And Larry Bossidy, the former chairman and CEO of Honeywell International, writes, "At GE 85 percent of the executives are promoted from within—that's how good the company is at developing leaders."[7]

Deploying Your Dream Team

Once you have the right person on the team, you must decide how to deploy him or her. Deployment involves placement—getting the right person in the right place. Following are several deployment steps.

STEP 1. DETERMINE PRIMARY MINISTRIES

When you developed your church's disciple-making process, you created a maturity matrix that consisted of two axes. One is horizontal and contains the characteristics (ends) of a mature disciple. The other that applies more to staff deployment is the vertical axis, which lists the primary ministries. They are the means that accomplish the ends or characteristics. You staff to your primary, ordered ministries. If you have not determined the primary ministries, then you will need to do so before you can best deploy your ministry people. If you have determined these ministries, you are ready to deploy your people.

STEP 2. ASSIGN PRIMARY STAFF CHAMPIONS

You as senior pastor will need to assign a primary staff champion for each or several of your ministries, depending on the nature of them. For example, the large group worship meeting is currently a vital and primary ministry that comes early in the assimilation process. You need to identify the person who will lead this vital ministry, the one who will be its champion. Most likely this will be you, the senior pastor and only or lead preacher. It could be a talented, gifted worship leader. You will need to work down through each of your primary ministries and determine who is to champion and take responsibility for each one. You may have a ratio of one-for-one, or you may have one champion for several ministries. It's important that all the primary ministries be covered. The leaders you choose may all be professional people who are on the payroll. In smaller churches, however, they will likely be gifted, committed laypeople.

I should pause briefly to explain the concept of a *staff champion*. Senior pastors tend to emphasize and even at times overemphasize their passion. For many, this is preaching. For others, it might be evangelism, pastoral visitation and care, and so on. The problem is that often this emphasis results in the neglect of some other vital, primary ministry, and this in turn throws the church off balance. The concept of staff champions is that each primary ministry has a champion who is passionate about his or her ministry, while still valuing the others. Employing the ministry champion concept will protect the church from the "silo effect," which may develop when the senior pastor sees certain ministries as the most important and practically the only necessary activities of the church.

Step 3. Assign Leaders for Secondary Ministries

Once you have a staff champion for each of the primary ministries, you want to address leadership for the secondary ministries. In most churches, these will be talented, committed lay leaders. In addition, you may want to consider some possible future staff positions, such as a pastor of communications, a web pastor, a pastor of strategic planning, and a pastor of stewardship.

Organizing the Team

At this point in building your dream team, you have the right person deployed as a champion in the right position. The next step is to think through how to organize these positions in a way that best supports and accomplishes your disciple-making process. You need to consider where in the organization people fit, how they will relate to one another, who is responsible to whom, and what is the "pecking order."

Job or Ministry Descriptions

The corporate world holds that organizations must be innovative and agile to accommodate change and that rigid, pyramidal organizations do not permit this. There is some truth to this. Some even mistakenly argue that the best organization is no organization. However, people do need to know who reports to whom, their authority, their boundaries, as well as their roles and responsibilities. This is the purpose and value of job or ministry descriptions. For example, at my last church, we needed a minister of Christian education. The man we wanted for the position was reluctant to accept the job because we had no job description. He wanted to know all the above regarding the position. What were our performance expectations? Exactly what were his responsibilities? For what would he be held accountable? To whom did he report and who reported to him (his span of influence)? He was a wise young man.

ORGANIZATIONAL CHARTS

The answer for us at the church was twofold. First, we developed job or ministry descriptions for every position (I have provided one example in appendix L).[8] Second, we developed three organizational charts that helped us immensely. We based them on the church's functions of cause, community, and corporation—terms I used earlier when describing the relationship between the pastor and the board. Our structures reflect these three functions.

The *cause* reflects the church's leadership structure. Our desire is that Christ be our leader (1 Cor. 11:3). Under Christ is the senior pastor, who, as primary leader and visionary, works mainly with the board and staff in large churches. With them, the pastor sets the direction for the church, and the board and staff lead and work with the congregation. In smaller churches the pastor works with the board, staff, and congregation.

Cause
(Leadership)

Christ
|
Pastor
/\
Board   Staff
\/
Congregation

The *community* function reflects how the congregation relates to one another as family. This represents the church as an organism. As family we are all brothers and sisters (Heb. 2:11–13). Therefore we are equals in Christ (Gal. 3:28).

The *corporation* function reflects the business and legal side of the church. Some do not like to acknowledge that a church has a business side, but it does. It is necessary for legal and other purposes. For example, most churches incorporate to protect individuals in the church from any lawsuits brought against the church. Ministries, like businesses, also enter into legal contracts, such as when addressing the salaries of personnel and when buying and selling a facility or property.

If team members want to know how they relate to another person on the team, they first need to determine if the context of the relationship is that of cause (a proactive leadership), community (a loving family), or corporation (a legal entity).

We also expanded the cause and corporation structures with a more detailed organization chart on page 227. This chart is for a church that has a congregational polity, because the congregation is above the pastor and below the Savior. It also reflects the position of an executive pastor who is responsible to the pastor for the staff who are identified in the boxes below but connected to his. Note that the age-specific staff are under the CE or biblical instruction staff. This would also serve the church and the staff team as a blueprint for future staffing. They have listed the staff they need to ultimately become the church they want to be. Now, as they grow, they will recruit accordingly.

Cultivating the Team

At this point in building your dream team, you have the right people deployed as champions in the right positions, and they know where they fit in the ministry

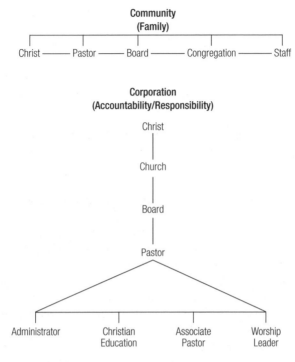

organization. The next step is to take responsibility for each person's development. This can be the most difficult thing about being on a team and the most rewarding at the same time. It has everything to do with working and ministering together in authentic community and involves serving together deeply in the most meaningful ways. Bill Hybels has described it as "doing life deeply with one another." There are at least five steps to developing such an authentic dream team.

Step 1. Cultivate a Vulnerability-based Trust

The first step in developing the dream team is cultivating a vulnerability-based trust.[9] This is when you trust others on the team to the extent that you are willing to risk vulnerability. Vulnerability means acknowledging personal mistakes, weaknesses, failures, needs, and deficiencies to each other. (I told you that this would not be easy.) An example is Paul, whose vulnerability was expressed in such places as Romans 7:14 and 1 Timothy 1:15.

The problem facing vulnerability-based trust is that most teams are not willing to take this kind of risk, because so many struggle with competition, self-protection, image, ego, and so on. This was true of the disciples throughout their ministries in Jesus's time. For example, in Matthew 19:27, after stating that they have given up everything for him, Peter asks the Savior what is in it for them. Then in Matthew 20:20–21 we read that the disciples were jockeying over who would gain positions of power, prominence, and prestige in the kingdom. If the disciples struggled in this manner, we will too.

What is the solution? How might you get beyond all this? The following group exercises will prove immensely helpful and are healthy.

- Share with the team your personal history, including the bad along with the good, as Paul did in Acts 9:22, 26.
- Share the results of a personal strengths and weaknesses audit.
- Identify and discuss the strengths, weaknesses, and limitations of your temperament.

Keep in mind that everyone on the team must participate well for these to be effective.

This first step is the most difficult one and is foundational to all the others. Key to the success of this step is the example of the pastor or ministry leader. He or she must lead the way and model well the process for the others. After they hear this person share, the rest of the team will know what is expected. If anyone feels too threatened to take this first step, it's likely a sign that something is seriously wrong with the present team makeup. It's likely that there is someone on the team who shouldn't be there, and this could include the senior pastor.

Being open and vulnerable will be most difficult for a newly formed team or for a new staff person. Before open sharing can happen, the team must spend time together getting to know one another. Depending on how often and how long the team meets together and how well the members cooperate, they may be willing to risk sharing personal histories, strengths, and weaknesses after several months.

Step 2. Engage in Robust Dialogue

The second step is to engage in robust dialogue.[10] In ministry in general and when meeting together in particular, robust dialogue attempts to get at the truth or reality through openness, candor, and informality. First, people must be open. They go into the situation with open minds, willing to consider new information and others' opinions as well as their own. Second, people must *be*. They feel free to express thoughts and emotions without there being even a hint of a threat of reprisal. Third, the meeting is informal—it invites questions, challenges, even constructive but loving debate.

The assumption of robust dialogue is that no one person has a corner on all the truth. The aim is to invite multiple views, see the pros and cons of each, and come up with the best and most accurate view. It should involve some challenges and hard questions that probe our thinking.

The problem in robust dialogue is that most people want to avoid conflict at any price, because it makes them uncomfortable. This is especially true of those with the I, S, and C temperaments on the Personal Profile. Some people fear that someone will get hurt. This is true especially of the I and S temperaments. Some people feel that engaging in robust dialogue is a waste of time and that we just need to make a decision. This is often true of the D temperament.

A general truth is that trust comes before and provides the foundation for this kind of dialogue. You will not attempt to engage in robust dialogue without having vulnerability-based trust as a team. In addition, it requires that you separate yourself from your ideas and concepts so that you do not feel personally attacked when they are discussed and critiqued. This is no easy task.

I believe that a culture where there is no debate or honest differences of opinion is spiritually and creatively sterile. Jesus differed regularly not only with his enemies, such as the Pharisees and Sadducees, but also with his friends, such as his disciples. Most important, people who avoid debate do not really trust and respect one another, and they need to understand that this lack of trust exists.

Again, as with vulnerability-based trust, the leader must model a willingness to enter into robust dialogue. If the leader will not work hard at making it happen, it will not happen.

Step 3. Lead by Consensus

Too many leaders today are still leading as "lone rangers." They make most of the decisions, especially the major ones that affect the ministry and its direction, without intentionally seeking staff input. The staff, which may be only one other person or a larger leadership team, may not agree with decisions but to avoid conflict are not willing to say so.

I've already covered consensus decision making in chapter 1. I call this consensus leadership in a team context. The wise senior pastor seeks the input of those on the team in making major decisions that affect the ministry in general and their particular areas of ministry in particular. He will bring up a matter and ask for an individual's or the team's wisdom. It's imperative that they have the freedom to express their opinions, whether pro or con. And it's most important that the pastor listen very carefully to their input, especially if it concerns their areas of ministry expertise. If he isn't comfortable with pursuing consensus leadership, he needs to determine the reason for his hesitancy. If it's simply because it's not his style and he's used to making all the decisions, he needs to change his style. If he feels he will not get good counsel from his team or someone on the team, he needs to find more competent, qualified team persons.

You will recall that in consensus decision making anyone may address an issue and pursue his or her ideas or "read" of a situation. Ultimately, the majority of the team decides the issue, especially if there is disagreement. If there is no majority, the leader makes the final decision. On occasion the pastor may make a final decision without the input of the team. An example would be in an emergency or a situation where there simply is not enough time to consult with the team. For example, the captain of a jetliner does not call for a meeting of the crew if the plane is headed down. He acts as he has been trained to do in such a situation. (It may be that the pastor's final decision disagrees with the majority of the team. This is his prerogative as the primary leader of the church. However, this will be a rare occurrence if he has the right staff people in place.) All team members commit to support the final decision (as if there were no disagreement) and work toward its success. This means that if one staff person should disagree with the decision, he or she does not go around bad-mouthing the decision behind the team's back. Working on and with a team means that you cannot always have it your way. Leading and operating by consensus is the hallmark of a team player as well as of the one who leads by securing the wisdom of the group.

Step 4. Confront Members about Inappropriate Behavior

Inappropriate staff behavior hurts and undermines the team and must not be tolerated. Inappropriate behavior includes not doing one's job, gossiping, inappropriate discussing of consensus decisions after they have been made, and other matters. These are not characteristics of a dream team.

Such situations call for confrontation. Either a team person who is aware of the behavior or the team leader will confront violators. One biblical example is Paul's confrontation of Peter in Galatians 2:11–14. Another is Peter's confrontation of Ananias and Sapphira in Acts 5:1–10.

The rules for such encounters are found in Matthew 5:23–24 and 18:15–19. In Matthew 5:23–24 Jesus instructs us that if we think there is a brother or sister out there whom we may have offended, we are responsible to go to the person and correct the situation. In Matthew 18:15–19 Jesus instructs those who have been offended by a brother or sister to go to the person in private and attempt to reconcile the matter. If that person refuses to be reconciled, he provides additional steps for the offended person and others on the team to take. While Scripture doesn't say, I suspect that Paul followed this procedure when he confronted Peter. I also suspect that the confrontation was enough to correct Peter's behavior.

Step 5. Make the Team's Interests the Priority

A major problem facing so many of us is that we look out primarily for number one. This is often based on our egos and desire for personal approbation as well as on other issues. So we pursue what we believe to be in our own best interests despite the team's interests. The example of the disciples cited in step 1 illustrates and proves the point.

The obvious solution is to put the team and its interests ahead of our own. This is essentially a spiritual issue that must be addressed spiritually. Specifically, it is a matter of sinful personal pride that needs heavy doses of humility. In Philippians 2:4 Paul writes, "Each of you should look not only to your own interests, but also to the interests of others." Then he refers us to the life of the Savior as an example of the kind of humility we are to follow and show toward the team.

Mobilizing the Congregation

A third group that makes up your dream team is a well-mobilized congregation.

The Unemployment Problem

The majority of our congregations are not involved in or not properly involved in ministry. This is what I refer to as the church's unemployment problem. As many as 80 to 90 percent of the typical congregation's members are sitting on the shore, watching a faithful few racing their boats in the ministry lake.

It seems that over the years church tradition has convinced the majority of congregations that ministry is the pastor's responsibility. As one old-timer put it, "That is what we pay him all that money for!" Others are quick to point out that it is the pastor and staff who have been trained and ordained for ministry, not them. Amazingly, many are convinced that God uses and blesses the staff's ministry more than their own. In many of these churches, the people even believe that God hears the pastor's prayers before he hears theirs.

Building the Team
Training the board
Developing the staff
Mobilizing the congregation

I am convinced that Satan has used the church's unemployment problem as much as any other to virtually cripple the church's ministry and bring it to its knees. If the employees of all the for-profit and not-for-profit organizations in America adopted this thinking, it would bring the nation to an economic standstill. If the employees at General Motors felt this way, there would be no GM cars. And if a hospital's employees felt this way, a lot of people would die.

The Solution to the Problem

The solution to the church's unemployment problem and the key to its being a vital part of the pastor's dream team is threefold: the church must understand the biblical role of the pastor and any staff, it must understand the role of the congregation, and it must develop a congregational mobilization process.

THE BIBLICAL ROLE OF THE PASTOR AND STAFF

God has provided a gifted pastor and staff as well as other laypeople for the express purpose of equipping the congregation to accomplish the church's ministry. Ephesians 4:11–12 in the New Living Translation is very clear on this. It reads, "He [Christ] is the one who gave these gifts to the church . . . pastors and teachers. Their responsibility is to equip God's people to do his work and build up the church, the body of Christ."

THE BIBLICAL ROLE OF THE CONGREGATION

God has provided the congregation for the express purpose of accomplishing the work of the ministry, which is building up the body. Again, Ephesians 4:12 in the New Living Translation says of the congregation, "Their responsibility is to equip God's people to do his work and build up the church, the body of Christ."

However, some will object and argue that they are not called to do ministry. This passage contradicts that kind of thinking. God has called all Christians to ministry, not merely a select few who pastor churches (Rom. 8:28; Eph. 2:10). The terms *call* and *calling* are used primarily in the New Testament to refer to the divine call to salvation, not to vocational Christian ministry. Should you desire to pursue the issue of a call, see my book *Maximizing Your Effectiveness*.[11]

Developing a Congregational Mobilization Process

A good congregational mobilization process seeks to mobilize all your people for ministry in the church. A well-designed mobilization process consists of three phases: a discovery phase, a consulting phase, and a placement phase.

The discovery phase. The goal of this phase is to help the people in the congregation discover their divine designs. One's divine design consists of one's natural and spiritual gifts, passion, and temperament along with other areas. This phase is made up of two parts.

1. The first part of the discovery phase is assessment. With certain tools, such as a spiritual gifts inventory, a passion audit, and the Personal Profile or the Myers-Briggs Type Indicator, people discover their design.
2. Next, beginning with their design—their God-given gifts, passion, and temperament that they discovered in the first phase—they discover their ministry direction, how they will deploy their design. They can determine their God-given competencies in light of their design. Then they pursue their development, how they will improve and grow as they use their design.

The consulting phase. There are three goals of the consulting phase.

1. Determine and confirm designs. After going through the discovery phase, most people will have lots of questions about their three Ds—design, direction, and development. It is in this phase that the church has trained people on board the ministry ship to answer questions about designs and confirm what people have discovered. A person might say that he or she has a certain gift based on an inventory. A trained lay consultant would meet with the person, ask questions, and attempt to confirm the presence of the gift.
2. Aid people in discovering their ministry mission in life in general and in the church in particular (see Acts 13:36). What is it that they do best? What are their areas of competencies?
3. In light of their designs and competencies, a consultant who knows the church and where it has needs will place people in church-related ministries that will best use them to accomplish Christ's purposes.

The placement phase. The goal of this phase is proper placement, helping people discover their ministry niche in the church. This is a twofold process that matches or pairs the person with a position. The person will bring to a position his or her ministry design. There is a preferred ministry description and design for each ministry position, the best divine design for one who works in the ministry. This would likely be found in a ministry description for the position. For example, the ministry description for the position of an adult Sunday school teacher would include a ministry profile containing the necessary gifts, passion, temperament, and any other helpful design components. It would also include a ministry summary that would list the various ministry responsibilities for the position.

If you find that you need help in establishing a congregational mobilization process, I recommend Bruce Bugbee and Associates Network Ministries International (www.networkministries.com) and Sue Mallory's book *The Equipping Generation*.[12]

On several occasions I've heard Bill Hybels say that the church is the hope of the world. I believe that Jesus would agree with him (see Matt. 16:18). Hybels goes on to say that leadership is the hope of the church. As important as congregational mobilization is to the health and life of a church, it likely won't happen without good leadership. Capable leadership understands how crucial congregational mobilization is and sees that it gets off the ministry drawing board and into the church's life.

But how are churches doing in training leaders? The answer is, not well. How many churches can you name that have an intentional leadership development process in place? A church that isn't developing leaders for the future may not have a future. A measure of how you're doing in this area is the source of your new ministry staff, as addressed earlier in this chapter. Have you intentionally trained up sufficient leaders that you can staff from within your church, or do you have to bring in staff from outside the church?

Rick Warren writes that the development of lay leaders is "the most important meeting I prepare for and lead."[13] Consequently, he takes personal responsibility for this aspect of ministry. Once a month he meets with and develops his church's leaders through his SALT (Saddleback Advanced Leadership Training) program.

I don't have the space to pursue this vital area in this book. However, Will Mancini and I have written *Building Leaders* to help you set up and conduct such a leadership training process.[14]

Questions for Reflection, Discussion, and Application

1. Do you believe in team ministry? If so, why? Do you have a biblical basis for your position?
2. What boards does your church have? Does it have a governing board? Why or why not? What are its functions? Does it perform any of the nonfunctions (micromanagement, rubber stamping, etc.) mentioned in this chapter? Are your boards functioning well or getting in one another's way?

3. How many people are on your board? Do you think this is too many? Why or why not? What are their qualifications? Most likely your board uses some kind of policies approach. Would the policies approach covered in this book help your church to do a better, more intentional job of decision making?

4. What is your church's polity? Carefully analyze and then discover where the power lies in your church. Does it rest with a governing board, the congregation, a bishop, the pastor, a staff person, a patriarch or matriarch, a family or families, or a combination of these? Is this good or bad? Is it balanced? If it is bad, what will you do about it?

5. Describe your staff dream team. How does it differ from that of the author? When does your church recruit staff people? What is your response to the author's idea of recruiting staff with the view to reaching a certain size rather than waiting until you get to that size and then playing catch-up? Does your church follow this latter approach? Should it? Would it?

6. Do you like how the author divides staff into three groups—ministry staff (age-specific or functional), administrative or operational, and staff specialists? Is your church's staff primarily age-specific? If so, what is the problem with an age-specific only approach? If your church isn't large enough to employ both age-specific and functional staff, how might you encourage both? Has your church ever considered bringing on board the ministry ship an executive pastor? Why or why not? Does your church have any elective staff, such as a woman over women's ministries, and so forth?

7. Does your church consider the three Cs (character, competence, and chemistry) when examining a potential dream team person? Why or why not? If so, which C is the most important? How do you recruit people? Do you build your strategy around the person, do you recruit him or her to fit your strategy, or both? Do you normally recruit people from inside or outside the ministry or both? Which do you prefer? If you recruit primarily from inside the ministry, do you have a leadership development process in place?

8. Do you agree with the author's concept of a staff champion? Do your primary, ordered ministries have champions? Why or why not? How is your team organized? What is your "pecking order"? Does everyone understand this arrangement? Do you have an organizational chart? Would the concepts of cause, community, and corporation help people better understand your organization and their place in it? Why or why not?

9. Is the staff currently pursuing and experiencing vulnerability-based trust? Why are some not experiencing it? Is the staff engaging in robust dialogue? Why or why not? Are you afraid to answer this question? When was the last time you had a good, healthy debate?

10. Does the team operate by consensus? Why or why not? Has anyone ever confronted or been confronted about what appeared to be inappropriate

behavior? On a scale of 1 to 10, how would you rate the staff members in terms of whether they put the team's interests ahead of their own?

11. Does your church have a congregational unemployment problem? Why or why not? What percentage of your church is involved in ministry? What excuses, if any, do people give for noninvolvement?

12. Do you agree with the author's idea that the pastor and staff are equippers for ministry as well as doers of ministry? Why or why not? Do you agree that the congregation is to be heavily involved in ministry? Why or why not? Do you have in place a congregational mobilization process? Why or why not? If not, do you plan to put one in place as soon as possible?

Assessing the Ministry Setting

Strategy Activity 4

At this point in our strategy development, we understand and are committed to outreach in our Jerusalem (Acts 1:8) or geographical community. We have designed disciple-making and disciple-maturing processes for that community, and we are bringing on board, mostly one by one, our ministry dream team who will equip us to reach our Jerusalem. We must now draft a strategy to maximize our setting.

Some may argue that we should have dealt with our ministry setting before building our dream team. So which should come first, the setting (facilities in particular) or staff? My observation has been that churches that are plateaued and struggling often opt for a new or improved facility before bringing on additional staff. They have bought into what I refer to as a Kevin Costner theology based on the maxim, "Build it, and they will come!" (from his movie *Field of Dreams*). The church is plateaued or dying and they believe that their dilemma will be resolved if they attract more people. And what attracts more people? A new facility. The problem is that they build it, but no one comes, because of other problems they have overlooked. And the congregation is left holding the financial bag long after the pastor has heard God's call to another congregation or back to seminary for an advanced degree.

In my opinion, the obvious mistake is that of focusing on setting before staffing. We discovered in chapter 10 that building a team that consists of a well-mobilized congregation; a gifted, competent, spiritually motivated staff; and a wise, godly board (depending on the church's polity) contributes most to the growth of the church.

My observation has also been that the issue of setting should come as the fourth element in the strategizing process, well after the church has determined its values, mission, vision, and much of its strategy. I have observed numerous churches that go into a building program without understanding who they are (their DNA), without a clearly articulated vision of what God wants them to do, and without a strategy to accomplish it. This makes no sense. Without a clear strategy, how can they answer design questions such as, Will the facility be multipurpose or single-purpose? Will we use a video venue approach or go a more traditional route? They are building for building's sake or merely trying to attract people, using the Kevin Costner theology approach. A facility has tremendous impact on the church's culture, so you must know what you want that culture to be. I have had church construction groups interact with me over strategic planning, because they see the need for this before a church pursues a building project. Strategic planning is the first phase that precedes the design-build phases. It is unfortunate that so few pastors and boards understand this, and the church ends up paying the price.

The functional question that begs to be asked here is, If your church were to suddenly disappear, would your community even know it? Would you be missed? And what might you do as a church so that you would be missed—terribly missed? The answer is to develop a strategy for maximizing your setting in your Jerusalem. To prepare us to develop such a strategy we must touch three bases. The first is to provide a definition of setting so that we are on the same page. The second is to discover and understand the importance of setting. The third is to present a brief theology of setting in answer to the question, What does the Bible say about setting? Then we are ready to develop our strategy to maximize our setting.

If you as a church are working through this book with development teams, this chapter provides the information that the ministry setting development team needs to develop a strategy that will maximize your church's setting (location and facilities).

Developing a Ministry Strategy

Reaching the church's community
Making mature disciples
Building a ministry team
Assessing the ministry setting
Raising and managing finances

What Is the Setting?

From the introduction to this chapter, it may appear that I am using the term *setting* to refer primarily to a church's location and facilities. And for most of us, it does. However, if we are to think and act strategically, we must understand that the setting is broader than that. I define *a church's setting as anywhere its ministry takes place, any location where there is ministry in some way in the name of Christ*. It is where your church has a ministry presence. However, in this chapter we are looking at where its primary ministry events occur, and that is at its facilities.

There are at least two kinds of ministry presence: physical and electronic.

Physical Presence

Physical presence is geographical. It is a piece of land somewhere—large or small—that has an address. It encompasses the church's location and its immediate community—where people live within driving distance. It is also the church's facilities, including where it gathers regularly and other locations, such as someone's house, a coffee shop, an office, a restaurant, a street corner, an outdoor amphitheatre, even under a bridge, wherever ministry takes place. A growing trend is to have multisite campuses that can reach beyond one's immediate community. The primary focus of this chapter will be on the church's physical presence in general, and its location and facilities in particular.

Electronic Presence

Electronic presence takes you beyond the limitations of physical presence. It focuses more on reaching the church's intermediate and international communities, wherever they may be, while including its immediate community. Primarily, electronic presence means cell and land phones, the internet, a website, and email but could also include radio and television.

This is the up-and-coming ministry thrust. Pastors such as Rick Warren and Paul Cho believe that electronic presence will have a huge impact on the future church and where it is able to minister. It is no secret that younger generations are more computer literate than the older generations, and thus they spend more time on the internet, on websites, and in chat rooms. Why would the church not use this as a viable ministry to reach beyond its four walls? If you see the value of electronic presence and would like to explore it further, see *Church Next*, a book on the subject that my son and I wrote.[1]

The Importance of Setting

Is setting important to a ministry? Following are eight reasons the answer is yes.

Affects First Impressions

A church's physical setting affects people's first impressions of the church. It's important to consider the kind of first impressions your church makes on people, because first impressions can be lasting impressions.

There was a time in my ministry when I served frequently as an interim pastor for churches who were looking for pastors. I recall my first visit to one such church. It was hard to locate because weeds were blocking the sign. When I did spot it, it was hard to read, because the paint was cracked and peeling. When I pulled into the parking lot, I noted that the paint was peeling off the building and weeds were springing up through the tarmac. As I entered the facility, I observed that the carpets were well worn and the ceiling tiles were discolored by water stains.

Later in my time at the church, when I felt that it was appropriate, I called their attention to my first impressions. They were shocked. They had become so used to these conditions that they were oblivious to them. They looked at them but didn't see them. At least initially, until I got to know the congregation, this left me with a negative impression of this church. It appeared they did not care enough about what they were doing to take care of their facility.

To find out the kind of first impressions your church makes on visitors, ask an unchurched friend to come to the church and give you his or her honest opinion. Buy the person lunch after the service and spend time talking about his or her observations.

Provides a Launching Pad for Community Ministry

The church setting provides a geographical location where the church can gather one or more times a week in community. Since the days of the New Testament, churches have gathered in a geographical location for worship purposes. Though it seems that the church met in different places, the primary meeting place of the early church was someone's home. Regardless of where the church meets, its facility provides a physical environment where the congregation can carry out the functions of the New Testament church—Bible teaching, evangelism, worship, fellowship (Acts 2:40–47) and, most important, launching ministry or reaching out to its neighboring community.

Determines Who Will and Won't Attend Your Church

The location of your setting is important because of travel time. Today time matters, whether you are saved and churched or unsaved and unchurched. People will travel only so far to attend church. In chapter 8 I wrote that Win Arn conducted a study of travel time and discovered that 20 percent of people drive from a few to 5 minutes to get to church. Forty percent will drive from 6 to 15 minutes. Twenty-three percent will drive from 16 to 25 minutes, and 17 percent will drive more than 25 minutes. Thus most (83 percent) will drive up to but not beyond 25 minutes to get to church. Our experience at The Malphurs Group with churches confirms this as well.

To establish your immediate ministry community, drive out the various main arteries (interstates, main highways, and so forth) from around your church and see how far you can drive in under twenty to twenty-five minutes. The moment you determine your location, you eliminate some people from attending your church—and include others. This can't be helped.

Can Adversely Impact Involvement

Just as travel time (how long a person is willing to drive) or distance (how far one is willing to drive) affects who will and won't attend church, travel time can also adversely impact participation in the ministries of the church. If people have decided to attend the church but the distance they travel is longer than twenty minutes, they will probably be less involved than people who live closer. The simple truth is that time on the road affects how often people are willing to travel to be involved in the church or evangelism. This is borne out by a study that Greg Hawkins and Cally Parkinson conducted. They write, "We discovered that one-third of our congregation drove more than thirty minutes to attend our services. We learned that these people were not inviting their un-churched neighbors and friends to services, nor were they significantly involved in other strategic ministries."[2]

Sends a Message to the Community

Having a church present in the community sends a subtle message, even in unchurched, pagan America early in the twenty-first century. While I believe that this message has diminished considerably, it still remains in many parts of America and abroad. And even though many people who drive by the facility each day seem oblivious to its presence, that does not mean they are completely unaware of the church—especially when they need help. When driving through parts of North America that are unchurched, we can quickly see the lack of church facilities, and this sends a message.

When churches are present but they are not well kept up, this also sends a message, a negative one. An unkempt church in a nice neighborhood unnecessarily invokes the wrath of the community. On the other hand, the presence of attractive churches in churched regions can send a positive message: spiritual things are important. Churches should want to call positive attention to their facility. They need to come up with new and creative ways to do this so that people are aware of their presence in the neighborhood.

Reflects the Church's Culture

The physical structure of the church reflects the culture of the majority of the people in the church. Traditional people tend to meet in more traditional facilities and want their church to "look like a church." Since the early church did not meet in structures like today's traditional churches, that means something similar to the churches in western Europe from the 1400s or 1500s to the present. More contemporary and younger people either do not care or favor a different, often more open architecture. For them, a converted warehouse, a rented school auditorium and classrooms, leased space in a shopping mall, a storefront, a grocery store, or a public meeting room in a bank, hotel, or movie theater will do the job. So the question becomes, What culture does your church reflect? And in terms of whom you want to reach, is that good or bad?

Reveals That Form Follows Function

Form follows function. This is at the heart of the problem I was alluding to in the introduction to this chapter—the build first and worry about the ministry later mentality (Kevin Costner theology). Function is a strategy issue, whereas form is a facilities issue. Far too many churches make form decisions with total disregard for function issues. Once a church knows its DNA and has a mission, vision, and strategy, it is ready to make function decisions. These function issues will be decided by these other concepts plus the maturity matrix, and your primary ordered activities will have a major impact on the forms you choose. For example, if you opt for a primary ministry that involves small groups, this is a function decision that will affect the church facility's form. If you decide that your small groups will meet on your campus at approximately the same time, you will likely need to construct or free up a large number of small rooms where these groups can meet.

Promotes Strategic Ministry and Outreach

We must ask two questions. First, what determines where a church should locate? The answer most often is money or the church's finances. Second, what *should* determine where a church locates? The answer is the place that best facilitates its strategic ministry and outreach to its community first and to its constituency second. Location was most important to the first-century churches. We have already discussed in chapter 8 the geographical implications of Acts 1:8. Another example is found in Acts 19:1–10, which tells that Paul located in Ephesus (v. 1). If you know the geography of the area, then you would realize that Ephesus was the gateway to Asia Minor. Everyone who traveled to Asia Minor went through Ephesus. Consequently, we are not surprised when Paul plants a church there that exposes most in the province of Asia to God's Word (v. 10). One of my seminary classmates wrote his master's thesis on why Paul chose the various churches to visit on his missionary journeys. His conclusion, based on an investigation of the cities, was that they were all located in strategic places that would promote the spread of the gospel. Thus we must think strategically about the locations of our churches.

What the Bible Says about Setting

What does Scripture teach about the church and its setting that would form our theology of setting? The answer is that where the church meets (setting or geography) is not the church. The church consists of God's people who happen to meet at some geographical location that we often refer to as the church. In 1 Corinthians 1:2 Paul writes to "the church of God in Corinth." Note the distinction between the church and where it meets. "The church of God" is people and "in Corinth" is the place where the people happen to gather—specifically in houses (see 16:19).

The view we have of the church's facility affects our theology of the church. On the one hand, some view the church facility as the "heavenly high church," that it is imbued with a sense of sacredness. Others view it from the standpoint of Puritan functionality; it's there merely to keep the rain off our heads, nothing more. So which is it? Is the church's facility sacred? The answer lies within the teaching of the Old and New Testaments on the facilities where God's people worshiped. In the Old Testament the facilities or temple was sacred because God was present in the temple (Hab. 2:20). However, in the New Testament the people, not the facility, are sacred. The temple has been replaced by God's people—the church. And God abides in a different temple, the temple of our bodies (1 Cor. 3:16; 6:19–20).

Where the church meets is not the church. However, as we've seen above and in chapter 8, where the church meets is strategically important to its ministry to its community. The Savior strategically included geography as well as ethnicity in his mandate to be witnesses (Acts 1:8). And as noted above, Paul carefully and strategically selected the cities where he planted and established churches (19:1–10).

Developing a Strategy to Maximize the Church's Setting

Now that we have an idea of what a setting is and why it is important along with a theology of setting, we are ready to develop a strategy that maximizes our setting or gets the most out of our location and facilities in terms of reaching people in our Jerusalem (Acts 1:8). Developing such a strategy involves maximizing four areas: your location, parking, general facilities, and worship facilities.

Maximize Your Ministry Location

To best maximize your ministry location, you need to address ten critical location questions, understand a key location principle, and consider nine location options.

ADDRESS TEN CRITICAL LOCATION QUESTIONS

1. *Where are your current members and attenders located in relationship to the church's main facility?* Are they located within a reasonable drive time (no more than twenty-five minutes) from the facility? Here is what happens to many churches: The church is planted somewhere in a growing, bustling suburb where there are lots of young families with children. In time the community ages and begins to decline, and these people move to a new

suburb or back to the city. They opt to drive back to the church for a while. In many cases, before long, people begin to look for a new church that is closer to where they live and thus more convenient. This is the current situation of far too many of the churches in North America at the beginning of the twenty-first century. Consequently, your answer to the question likely depends on the age of your church and where it is on the organizational life cycle that I covered in the introduction to this book.

2. *Where are the people you need to reach or will most likely reach with the gospel—your focus community?* Are they located around your members and attenders? Are they located outside a reasonable drive time to the facility? Are they located around the facility?

3. *Is your facility in the best location to serve your focus community and your current constituency?* The answer to this question is found by answering the first two questions.

4. *To whom will you give preference when deciding on location—members and attenders or your unchurched, unsaved focus community?* This is a most difficult question to answer because you need both. On the one hand, your constituency is the people who have cast their lot with the church and what they believe it stands for. They are the ones who have likely supported the church over the years with their time, talent, and money. On the other hand, your focus group is the people Christ has commissioned you to reach. So which takes precedence when it comes to the church's location?

   The church's answer to this will say much about the church, its spiritual maturity, and its future. For example, an immature response would be to focus only on current members. This does not speak well for a church. The church's answer will also reflect and be determined by the congregation's core values. If the church values lost people and evangelism and is really committed to carrying out the Great Commission, it will likely give preference to the unchurched lost. Believers must be willing to make sacrifices if they are going to reach out to unbelievers. The apostle Paul addresses this issue in 1 Corinthians 9:19–23, where he teaches this very principle. My experience has been that these kinds of issues are hard on pastors and their people and reveal as much as anything else their true spiritual level.

   On the one hand, for the saved people in your church, this is a temporal preference issue. On the other hand, for the lost in your community, it is an eternal damnation issue. It is imperative that your people understand that their answers to these questions have eternal implications!

5. *How visible is your church?* Are you located in a place where people can see you, or are you hidden away somewhere? The ideal location is near a major thoroughfare.

6. *How accessible is your church?* How easy is it for visitors to find your church? Do you provide helps, such as a map, on your website?

7. *How good is your signage?* Do you have any signs in the community, announcing your presence or directing people to your facility? Do you have signs on and around your facility that identify your church?

8. *Do you have a campus master plan?* Remember the old adage: "To fail to plan is to plan to fail." Seek out a good church architect to help you with such a plan. A good master plan takes into consideration your current campus and your plans for the future at that campus. It serves as a facilities blueprint to guide any future expansion at that site.

9. *How committed are you to your present location?* Are people ready for a move? What kind of response do you get when the topic of a relocation surfaces? Has someone designated your facility as a historic site? This affects a relocation adversely. Do the problems of remaining where you are outweigh the advantages? Is the cost of maintaining your facility exorbitant or funneling a large proportion of funds away from more important ministries, such as your primary ones?

10. *How big do you want to get?* What are your growth goals? Are these God's goals as well as your own? Are people agreed on these goals or is there broad disparity? Can these goals be realized at your present location? Another consideration is the size of church the community population can sustain in terms of church growth. If the church is at two thousand and still growing, what growth goals should it set given the number of people living in its community (city or county)? The obvious rule is that the larger the number of people living in the church's community, the more the church can reach. Lyle Schaller uses a figure of around 10 percent. If your church is at two thousand people, and its community is one hundred thousand people, the church's maximum general size would be around ten thousand people. Thus, if it set a growth goal of five to eight thousand people, the community population is large enough to sustain such a goal. Your church needs to be aware of any circumstances that might increase or decrease this number. An example is a university or a prison that is located in the area, which could raise the area head count.

The number of churches in the community should not affect your growth goal. Far too many churches are inward rather than outward focused and aren't reaching new people. Your church's competition is not other churches but the National Football League, shopping malls, coffee shops, and so forth.

Understand a Key Location Principle

The church's location or campus will determine its ultimate size. As Rick Warren has noted, the foot can get only as big as its shoe. Church architects state that the property rule of thumb is approximately 100 people per acre at one time. (Some say you can push this figure up to 150 people, but this incurs extreme overcrowding.) With this figure in mind, you can predetermine how many people your current property can support at one time and when you will max out your site. Here's what you need to do.

1. Determine how much total acreage the church presently owns.
2. Determine how much of this acreage isn't usable, such as land that is located in a floodplain and land set aside for water retention and right of way issues. The shape of your property may also render some of it unusable.
3. Subtract all of this from your total acreage. Also subtract the acres that your current facilities and parking occupy. The acreage that is left is what you have to work with for potential facilities expansion at your current site. (Remember that one acre equals 43,560 square feet.)

CONSIDER NINE LOCATION OPTIONS

You have a number of options with which to address your particular situation. The only limit is your creative/innovative abilities. Here are nine possibilities.

1. *Do nothing.* Unfortunately, this is the option far too many churches have embraced in North America. They don't know what to do, so they freeze and do nothing. Some understand that they need to do something but don't know what to do. Rather than make a mistake, they do nothing. The result of such a response is an eventual plateau if the church is growing and a decline and ultimate death if it's plateaued. I don't believe this is a viable option for a church that seeks to honor and serve Christ.

2. *Multiply your current services.* Since the rule of thumb is only one hundred people per acre at one time, then double or triple the number of times you meet at your site to accommodate more people. This multiservice approach is the most obvious solution and one that most churches adopt.

3. *Purchase property adjacent to your property.* This assumes that there is property adjacent to your church and that it's available for purchase. If this is the case, investigate the possibility of purchasing it as soon as possible. Typically, this kind of property increases in value, and the price today is better and lower than it will be tomorrow.

4. *Construct a multipurpose facility on-site.* Most often this facility is a gym that serves at least two purposes. One is an additional site where people can see the service via a video feed to that site. The other is a sports center that will not only serve the church's youth but also attract youth from the community.

5. *Use an overflow space on-site.* This assumes that there is some other place on-site where people can go to experience the service via a video feed. This place could be a smaller site that was used for worship when the church was smaller. It could simply be any other room that would accommodate people for worship.

6. *Stay where you are and plant churches.* I believe that every church should plant church planting churches. However, this may not solve space problems. You could encourage a number of your people to leave and be a part of a new church start, but most often they will be quickly replaced at your church by people who for a brief time can find a place to park and sit.

7. *Stay where you are and go multisite.* In place of or in combination with church planting is going with a multisite strategy. The difference is you start other churches at other locations that simply reproduce what you are doing at your current site. Then you encourage your people who are near one of these churches to attend it.

8. *Focus on meeting at some other site in your community.* In this approach you could keep your facility or sell it and meet in other locations in your community that might better attract the lost and unchurched who make up your community. These locations could include schools, theaters, under bridges, coffee shops, parks, and so forth. This approach appeals to a much younger generation and would not appeal to an older generation.

9. *Relocate to another site.* This solution is also a popular one but is expensive and often incurs much congregational resistance. Be forewarned. Usually there is a group in every church that does not want the church to grow and relocate. They remember and long for the good old days when the church was smaller and everybody knew everybody. One problem with this viewpoint is that churches do not remain at their current size for very long. If they don't grow, they plateau and go into decline.

   How might you accomplish a relocation? Here is one of several possible scenarios.

   • As your attendance approaches the 80 percent mark, you should begin to plan for a second worship service. It could be a duplicate of the first, or, if the first is traditional, you might want to offer an alternative service, such as a contemporary service. Be aware that adding a service places additional work and stress on your staff—especially the senior pastor who preaches and the worship team. I suggest that you consider bringing in a second preaching pastor and take a team preaching approach. At the same time, you must begin a capital funds campaign that will create a sense of excitement and expectation as well as raise the finances necessary to enlarge your current place of worship or build a new one at your current site to handle growth.

   • As you continue to grow, you will need to plan for and then add a third service. It could meet on Sunday morning with the first two or at another time of the week, such as a Saturday evening or one evening during the week. Some use their Sunday morning services for seekers and a service during the week to focus on feeding their members. However you do it, you will need to begin construction to remodel your existing facility or add a new worship center. For the sake of timing these events, keep in mind that most capital funds campaigns last from three to four years. You could use the initial campaign pledges to establish a line of credit with a lending institution and break ground before the campaign ends, or you could wait until it ends to break ground.

- When the third service is full, you should be ready to move into your new facility and start the process over again, which will last until you maximize that property. Well in advance of this time, you will need to search for another piece of property that is close to your focus community and constituency as well as one that accommodates your growth needs. Then you will launch another capital funds campaign, purchase the new property, and begin to build a new facility that will handle your growth while targeting your focus community. You should attempt to time all this so that you will move to the new location about the same time you max out your current site.

Of the nine location options, how do you know which is the best one for your ministry? For some ministries the choice is obvious. For example, you can't purchase adjacent property if there is no adjacent property available. Following is an approach any church and senior pastor should find helpful in making wise property decisions.

- Ask God for his wisdom (James 1:5).
- Consider what the facts say. Are you growing, plateaued, or declining? I refer to this as a "factual call." God may be working and communicating to you through the facts.
- What can you do as far as cost and space are concerned?
- Seek godly counsel from a mentor and/or your leaders, such as a governing board.
- What does your heart say? I refer to this as an "intuitive call."

Maximize Your Parking Facilities

The second step in the strategy to maximize the church's setting is to maximize the parking facilities. To do this you need to understand the reason parking is important to your church, discover your general and special parking needs, and know your parking options.

UNDERSTAND THE IMPORTANCE OF PARKING

In addition to having a place where congregants can park their cars, you must consider the experience of people who are not regular attenders. An example would be lost and unchurched people. Some of your congregation have been praying for and inviting lost people to visit your church. Remember that unchurched people are looking for an excuse not to attend your church, and a full parking lot provides them with that excuse to return home or try elsewhere. View a full parking lot as a missed opportunity for someone to experience your church.

DISCOVER YOUR PARKING NEEDS

To discover the general parking needs of your church, do the following.

1. Determine how many spaces you have currently. You may want to consider your offsite parking as well. Remember, however, that you could lose that offsite parking should the city rezone or someone else grab those spots.
2. Determine how many spaces you need. The answer is to divide the number of people who attend by the number of people per car. This ranges anywhere between 1 and 6 people per car. To make matters easier, we at The Malphurs Group use the figure of 2 people per car. Thus if we have 100 parking spaces, we can park 200 people at one time. So how many cars can you park?

DISCOVER YOUR SPECIAL PARKING NEEDS

There are at least six special parking needs that you should take into account in your strategy.

1. Do you have any parking reserved exclusively for your visitors or the handicapped?
2. How many spaces are reserved for visitors? (Most recommend at least 4 per 100 people in attendance.)
3. How many spaces are reserved for handicapped people? You will need to check with your city for its code requirements for handicapped parking. (Most require at least 5 spots per 100 people.)
4. Will these spaces be clearly marked? How will people find them?
5. Will there be parking attendants to help people locate a parking spot?
6. Will there be greeters in the parking lots?

KNOW SEVEN PARKING OPTIONS

It's never too soon to plan for the future. Just as you have property options, so you have parking options. And several of the property options repeat as parking options, such as going to multiple services, purchasing adjacent property, and relocating to a new site.

1. *Ask volunteers to drive one car per family*. In the early to mid-twentieth century, many families had only one car, if they had even one. Today many households drive several cars. Mom and Dad have their own vehicles, and

so do Billy and Sally. The request for each family to drive only one car will fall on many deaf ears, because we like our freedom to come and go as we please. However, you would be wise to target your more committed people who are often more willing to help out.

2. *Carpool.* If several congregants live in the same area of town or even the same neighborhood, they could take turns carpooling each weekend. Again, target your more committed people with such a request.

3. *Park and walk.* This option assumes that some kind of parking exists nearby, within walking distance of your facility. This could be the parking lot of a department store or some other business that is closed on Sundays. The obvious disadvantage of this option is inclement weather. Also, be sure to secure permission from the business to park in its lot.

4. *Park and ride.* This option is similar to the park and walk option and one that my church chose. You would locate parking somewhere in the area and provide buses to shuttle people back and forth. Some of the disadvantages are inclement weather and cost.

5. *Use public transportation.* This is likely the least feasible option because public transportation in most American cities isn't as timely and accessible as would be needed, unlike in other parts of the world, such as western Europe. Perhaps public transportation in your area is an exception to this. If so, it's a good option.

6. *Build a parking garage.* The most expensive option but a good one is to build a parking garage. This could also provide protection for people and their cars when there is inclement weather. However, the cost of such an option is prohibitive for many churches.

7. *Valet cars to and from the facility.* Perhaps the most innovative option is to operate a church valet service. Some churches provide such a service already for their elderly patrons, and it could be extended to others as well, such as single women. You could hire a professional valet service or simply create your own service. If a professional service is hired, the cost could be a disadvantage to the church.

Maximize Your General Facilities

The third step in maximizing the church's setting is to maximize the facilities. I'll address the church's facilities in general and then the worship facility in particular, because it plays such a big role in one of the church's primary ministries (the preaching/worship service).

To maximize your church's general facilities, you need to observe four guiding principles, consider the seven factors that affect church facilities, and heed a facilities suggestion.

OBSERVE FOUR GUIDING PRINCIPLES

1. *Form follows function.* As I stated earlier, the basic principle that all churches must remember is that form follows function. Your church must make the proper function decisions before it makes its form decisions. The principle teaches that once you know what your church functions will be, you are ready to make your form decisions. To ignore this or get it backwards will cost the church money and time in unnecessary design and building costs and facilities renovation. When churches have not worked through the strategic envisioning process but already have a master plan in place for their facilities, they are getting it backwards. Master planning the facilities is necessary but must follow, not precede, strategic planning.

2. *Maintenance of a facility is a stewardship issue.* Like the church I mentioned earlier in this chapter, we have all seen a facility that a church has allowed to become run-down. It costs more to repair a facility than it does to keep a facility in repair. This is a stewardship issue. Declining churches are most often facing serious physical maintenance problems due to declining funds. The church is wise to take some kind of action before its facilities are no longer cost effective to repair or before the facilities are beyond repair. Perhaps it is time to disband and leave or sell the building to someone who can maintain it.

3. *Maintenance of a facility is a testimony issue.* Perhaps you have complained to your spouse about a house in your neighborhood that someone has neglected and allowed to deteriorate. There is little difference between that homeowner and the congregation that neglects its church facilities. Both are bad neighbors. Usually churches that take good care of their facilities are still facing problems in their communities, such as parking or environmental issues. Why make the situation worse by allowing the facility to run down, which affects your neighbors' property values as well? When you adversely impact their pocketbooks, you will infuriate and alienate them.

4. *Churched people have a higher tolerance for facilities neglect than do unchurched people.* Churches that are experiencing quick, sudden growth need to make sure they do not neglect their facilities due to staffing and funding problems, which can develop with this kind of growth. Often churches that are growing are seeker churches that are doing lots of evangelism. It is important for them to remember that the congregation has a higher tolerance for facility and property neglect than unchurched lost people do. It may be that a lost person will reject you because of your message (1 Cor. 1:18, 22), but it should be unacceptable for them to reject you because of your physical appearance or presentation.

CONSIDER SEVEN FACILITIES FACTORS

The church should consider each of the following seven factors concerning its facilities.

1. *Appearance.* Is the church run-down or does it look run-down? Could it use a good coat of paint outside and inside?

2. *Church size.* Is the facility big enough for the congregation? Or is it too big, tending to dwarf the congregation?

3. *The grounds.* Are they properly landscaped, and is the grass regularly watered and mowed? Is there any trash that needs to be picked up?

4. *Cleanliness.* Is the facility, especially the bathrooms and nursery, kept clean? Remember that for most people, especially women, cleanliness is next to godliness.

5. *The playground and any outdoor equipment.* Are swings, slides, seesaws, and other outdoor equipment functioning properly and well maintained? Do any pose any kind of danger to a child?

6. *Decor.* Is the experience of entering your church's facility comparable to entering a time machine and being whisked back to a bygone era? Would some people leave the facility knowing now what life was like in the nineteenth or early to middle twentieth century?

7. *Neutral space.* Does your church provide neutral space for your people in general and visitors in particular? Neutral space includes areas such as a coffee shop, a snack bar, a lounge, the parking lot, a book store, a reading area, or bathrooms where people can go and feel safe.

HEED A FACILITIES SUGGESTION

I doubt that any church neglects its facilities purposefully. Usually problems in this area are due to budget constraints, poor congregational mobilization, overworked custodians and volunteers, and a general lack of awareness because people get used to the way things are.

If your church is experiencing such a facilities crisis, I suggest that you take your key people (governing board members, strategic leadership team, a patriarch or matriarch, and others) on a tour of the facility. Ask them to pretend that they are unchurched visitors or even a local building inspector. They should look for problems or potential problems. Consider providing them with a checklist containing some of the factors I have just mentioned. The checklist that my ministry uses with churches is in appendix M. After the tour, arrange for a time to debrief. Ask them what they observed. You will find that they will be more willing to make the needed repairs and may even volunteer to do the work themselves.

Maximize Your Worship Facilities

To maximize your worship facilities, you need to understand a key worship facilities principle, discover your worship facilities needs, and explore your worship facilities options.

Understand a Key Worship Facilities Principle

A key worship facilities principle that also serves to stress the importance of a church's facilities to its ministry is that its worship facilities determine the number of people who can attend a worship service. This is similar to the shoe telling the foot how big it can get. Here are some figures that will help you determine how many people can attend a service. If your seating consists of pews, then you will fill only 80 percent of your maximum seating capacity. If it consists of chairs, then the figure rises to 90 percent. Let's make it easy. If your seating consists of pews that will seat a maximum of 100 people, you will be able to seat only 80 people. If you have 100 chairs, you will seat 90 people. The reason is that we North Americans like our space. It's rare that we'll sit down in the seat or space next to someone we don't know. Thus much space (10 to 20 percent) stays empty and is wasted. Since visitors will not sit next to someone they don't know, which likely will be most of the people attending the worship service, you may lose them if there isn't a large enough space in a pew or a few empty chairs together where they can sit. If this isn't the case, they may opt to leave and go elsewhere or return home, and you miss an opportunity to minister to them.

Discover Your Worship Facilities Needs

It's important to know your worship facilities needs. The following will help you identify them.

1. *Determine the maximum seating capacity of your worship facility.* Include in this count any balconies, choir seating, a band or instrument area, and so forth.
2. *Do you seat people in pews, chairs, or both?* If the latter, then determine how many are in either category and if they're together or separate.
3. *Decide how many seating spaces you currently provide.* If you have only pews, multiply the number of seating spaces in each pew by 80 percent. If you have only chairs, multiply by 90 percent. If you have a combination, make both calculations and combine the results.
4. *Determine how many seats you need* to comfortably seat the number of people who come to your largest service.
5. *Decide if your seating capacity is adequate or inadequate for the present.* If adequate, then what about the future? If you are growing, now is the time to plan for the future. If it's inadequate, see the following options that may provide a solution.

Explore Five Worship Facilities Options

There are five worship facilities options that you can pursue to address a worship facilities seating problem. Some of these are the same as for the property or location options: you can do nothing, multiply your services (in this case the worship service), construct a multipurpose facility (such as a gym), use an overflow area, plant churches, go multisite, meet in places in the community, and relocate. Others are the same as the options for the parking issues. Here are five unique options for handling your worship facilities issues.

1. *Train your ushers to manage where people sit.* Worship service ushers can help you immensely in making more space available. For example, they can direct people to sit in seats where they might not normally sit such as up front. They can also note empty seats and encourage latecomers to sit in them. Along with a public announcement from the pastor, they can ask people to move together to make more room for others.

2. *Cordon off seating toward the rear of the facility.* An old "trick of the trade" is to cordon off seats that are located in the back of your worship area with a rope or seat covers. This forces people to sit in other seats that may be less popular. After the service begins, the area can be opened up for any people who come late. The problem with this approach is that it rewards latecomers. But consider that they may be the people who need to hear the message the most.

3. *Ask your committed people to sit in the front row.* In most churches few if any people sit in the front and sometimes the second and even the third rows. I suspect that it's too close to the pulpit for comfort, especially if the preacher gives "fire and brimstone" sermons. But some of your committed people may be willing to sit there

4. *Enlarge your current worship facility.* Look for ways to and places where you can enlarge your current worship space. Perhaps you could tear out some walls, add a balcony, or take out or relocate an area, such as a kitchen. There are engineers who can help you with space planning so that you can find some extra room for expansion.

5. *Build a new worship center.* This option assumes there is room on your property to do so. You may have to create some room by tearing down the current facility, a house on your property, or some other building. Of all the options above, this would likely be the most expensive.

Questions for Reflection, Discussion, and Application

1. Did the author convince you that you should delay any decisions about your setting until you have made other key strategy decisions? Why?

2. Honestly, do you now hold to or have you ever held to the Kevin Costner theology regarding facilities? Why or why not?

3. Do you agree with the author's definition of *setting* as "ministry presence"? Do the concepts of both physical and electronic setting make sense to you?

Though the author did not elaborate on electronic presence, will you take time to explore this concept further? Why or why not? How do they contribute to strategic ministry outreach?

4. After reading the section that argues for the importance of setting, are you convinced? Why or why not? If not, what would it take to convince you? If yes, which reason(s) was the most convincing? Are you using your location as a launching pad for community outreach? Why or why not? What culture is seen in your facilities? Is this good or bad? What first impressions do your facilities have on people, especially visitors? Are they good or bad? What message are your facilities sending to your community? Is it good or bad?

5. In terms of maximizing your location, what was your response to each of the ten critical questions? Using the key location principle, how many people can your location sustain at one time or event? Which options would work best in your situation?

6. Regarding maximizing your parking, are you convinced that parking is important? Why or why not? What are your parking needs? How many spaces do you have? How many do you need? Do you provide special parking for the handicapped? For visitors? What parking options work for you?

7. Concerning your facilities, did you find the four guiding principles helpful? How so? How might they affect your facilities? Of the seven critical factors, which for you were positives and negatives? Do you like the idea of taking your people on a tour of the church's facilities and grounds, using the checklist in appendix M? Would it be helpful in your situation? Why or why not?

8. Concerning your worship facilities, do you agree with the key principle? For seating, do you provide chairs or pews or both? How many people can comfortably attend a worship service at your church? Do you have enough space? If not, how much do you need? Which of the facilities options would be helpful in your situation?

Raising and Managing Finances

Strategy Activity 5

The last element in your strategy development is finances. Navigators need money to sail the high seas. It takes money to hire good sailors and officers and to keep the ship in good working order. And it's no different for the ministry navigator. The church leader must also consider cost. How much will it cost for your dream team to make mature disciples of your community in your setting, and who will raise and manage the money that's needed?

Allow me to provide a little *reality* therapy—ministry costs money! Actually, I should say that ministry costs lots of money. Bill Hybels writes, "Be as theological as you want to be, but the church will never reach her full redemptive potential until a river of financial sources starts flowing in her direction."[1] The truth is that few churches in the early twenty-first century have an abundance of money for ministry. Expenses and expectations are up while contributions are down. The church is primarily dependent on the support of its people for survival, and in most situations one out of three adult attenders donates nothing to the church. Those who do contribute give less than 3 percent of their aggregate income, despite Jesus's warning in Matthew 6:21: "For where your treasure is, there your heart will be also." This raises the fundamental question: In the midst of all this, does your church have a reputation in your community for being careful but generous with its finances?

In addition to these dire financial conditions, the typical pastor has very little knowledge of or experience with managing and raising ministry funds. The one exception could be the pastor who has worked in the corporate world, but even in that world there are no guarantees. And where or how might a pastor learn and become competent in the financial aspects of ministry? It's certainly not being taught in most seminaries. Therefore a reason for this chapter is to help pastors become competent in some financial aspects of ministry, regardless of their previous lack of knowledge or experience.

The primary reason I have included this chapter, however, is to guide churches in general and pastors in particular in developing a strategy to raise and manage the church's finances. To prepare us for developing this strategy, I will touch two bases. The first is to present a brief definition of stewardship for clarity's sake, so we can be sure we have the same thing in mind. The second is to discover and understand the importance of the church's finances to its ministry. Then we are ready to develop our strategy for raising and managing finances.

If you as a church are working through this book with development teams, this chapter provides the information that the finance or stewardship development team needs for developing a strategy that will help you raise and manage your church's finances.

Developing a Ministry Strategy

Reaching the church's community

Making mature disciples

Building a ministry team

Assessing the ministry setting

Raising and managing finances

What Is Stewardship?

Stewardship is our management of God's temporal, earthly resources in general and finances in particular with which he's entrusted us to accomplish his eternal, heavenly purposes. We see this in the Old Testament when David in his praise to God says:

> Praise be to you, LORD, the God of our father Israel, from everlasting to everlasting. Yours, LORD, is the greatness and the power and the glory and the majesty and the splendor, for everything in heaven and earth is yours. Yours, LORD, is the kingdom; you are exalted as head over all. Wealth and honor come from you; you are the ruler of all things. In your hands are strength and power to exalt and give strength to all. Now, our God, we give you thanks, and praise your glorious name. But who am I, and who are my people, that we should be able to give as generously as this? Everything comes from you, and we have given you only what comes from your hand.
>
> 1 Chronicles 29:10–14

In the classical Greek, *stewardship* was the responsibility of one (most often a slave) who managed the affairs of his master's household, especially when the latter was away. And we see this used in the same way in the New Testament, as in Luke 12:42–43 and the parable of the shrewd manager in 16:1–13.

Why Is Stewardship Important?

There are numerous reasons that finances in general and stewardship in particular are important to the functioning of the church. Here are four of them.

Stewardship Provides the Necessary Funds

For some reason unknown to us, God in his wisdom has not exempted the church from dependence on money to accomplish ministry. You would think that so-called "filthy lucre" wouldn't be necessary to advance the kingdom of God. But that's not the case. The maxim is, No money, no ministry. Someone has rightly said that the success of any church depends on its ability to raise cash and manage its use strategically to fulfill its mission. In particular we see this on the business side of the church. Funds are needed to turn on the lights, pay salaries, and purchase or rent facilities, all of which are necessary to support the church's ministries.

Stewardship Encourages People to Give

Stewardship informs people of what God expects from them in terms of their finances. It addresses our financial responsibilities to God. Hybels writes, "I firmly believe that if the right people are presented with the right kingdom opportunity in the right way at the right time, the result will be a joyful and generous outpouring of support."[2] I believe that people want to give back to God from what he has so generously given to them. And good teaching on stewardship is a major step in seeing this happen.

Stewardship Addresses Matters of the Heart

We can talk a convincing talk. We can learn Christian-speak and say all the right things, things that sound very spiritual. However, if you truly want to know where you are in your spiritual life and walk with God, then take a look at what you give back to God in terms of your finances. Whenever I'm teaching on this truth, I like to take out my wallet and point to the dollars I have attached to a clip. The point is that our giving is a better indication of our walk with God than what we profess verbally.

In Matthew 6:19–21 Jesus teaches about the things we treasure. He says, "For where your treasure is, there your heart will be also" (v. 21). In other words your heart follows what you value most. So where is your heart?

Stewardship Holds Churches Responsible for Their Finances

God wants the church to be involved in and be good at financial matters. It's imperative that the church handle its money matters well. This is illustrated by Jesus's parable about servants who are ready for their master's return in Luke 12:35–48. Jesus asks, "Who then is the faithful and wise manager, whom the master puts in charge of his servants to give them their food allowance at the proper time? It will be good for that servant whom the master finds doing so when he returns. Truly I tell you, he will put him in charge of all his possessions" (vv. 42–44).

Nothing sinks a church's reputation in the community faster than its mishandling of its finances. A church loses the trust not only of the people it serves but also of people in the community who are potential members. Strive to do everything above board when it comes to handling your finances. Be squeaky clean.

Design a Strategy for Raising and Managing Church Finances

Now that we have a definition of stewardship and understand the importance of finances, we are ready to design a strategy for raising and managing the church's finances. In this section I will address four strategic questions: Who is responsible for raising and managing the ministry's finances? How much money needs to be raised? How does a pastor raise funds? And what are the resources for fund-raising?

Who Is Responsible for Raising and Managing the Ministry's Finances?

The first question is, Who is responsible for raising and managing the ministry's finances? We must ask this question because far too many church leaders are either intentionally or unknowingly shirking this responsibility. Bill Hybels wrote of the river of financial sources that is needed for a ministry to prosper. He continues: "And like it or not, it is the leader's job to create that river and to manage it wisely. The sooner the leader realizes that the better."[3] Most leaders don't want to hear this, but the truth is that they are responsible for the church's finances. Each semester I can anticipate the shocked look on my students' faces when I inform them of this pastoral leadership "fact of life." And I know what they are thinking: *I have committed to go into the ministry to teach and preach the Scriptures, not raise and manage money!* When congregational push comes to shove, however, the church looks to no one else but the pastor to take responsibility for its finances, which involves raising and managing them.

> **Raising and Managing Church Finances**
>
> Who is responsible for raising and managing the ministry's finances?
>
> How much money needs to be raised?
>
> How does a pastor raise funds?
>
> What are the resources for fund-raising?

So what does managing the church's finances entail? The following four points supply the answer in the form of a brief primer on the pastor's financial oversight:

accepting responsibility, managing current finances, managing future finances, and raising funds.

ACCEPTING RESPONSIBILITY

The pastor. The pastor must accept the overall responsibility for managing the church's finances. Regardless of how you feel about it, if you are the leader of the congregation, you are responsible for managing its finances.

You may wonder if this is biblical. Scripture is not entirely clear on this. Paul seems to have been involved unapologetically in raising finances for himself (see Phil. 4:10–20 and possibly 1 Cor. 9:11–12) and for churches (2 Corinthians 8–9). However, he was an apostle and more a church planter than a pastor, at least in today's sense. I believe that the first-century elders were pastors, and little is said about their management of finances, and what is said is not entirely clear (see Acts 11:29–30). However, I will cite more biblical evidence of the first century pastors' involvement on page 262. In these situations where Scripture is not prescriptive, I believe that the church has freedom to decide these issues as long as they don't contradict Scripture. Nevertheless, the pastor's responsibility has been a part of the church's culture for a long time and likely will not change anytime soon, and I believe that's okay.

Rather than view this as a curse, why not view it as a challenge? In my years as a pastor, I viewed it as a necessary drudgery, because at the time I knew so little about it and had trouble even balancing my own checkbook. However, all that changed as I began to learn more about the funding side of ministry and how it is ultimately God's work, not mine. In time I have come to view it as a stewardship challenge—helping people see the importance of stewardship in their lives and the life of the church. In addition, I have discovered that raising and managing finances is not all that difficult when you know what you are doing. Thus my challenge to you is to embrace this responsibility and accept it as a challenge from the Lord.

The governing board. If there is a governing board, it has a responsibility as well. The board will assign the responsibility for fund-raising and management to the senior pastor. I think that it is important to say this, because my experience in smaller churches is that this is more assumed than assigned. And this may be true in larger churches as well. The board's role will be to monitor the pastor's fund-raising and management through such means as monthly financial reports and updates.

Though the pastor has full responsibility for funds management, that does not imply that he has to handle it all himself. He would be most wise to get some help in this area, especially when it comes to crunching numbers. There is little enjoyment in that. The larger churches may have a business administrator or manager or in some rare cases a pastor of finances who with an accountant or two will manage the funds and report to the pastor. Smaller churches can usually find volunteer help from laypeople who work with finances for a living. Plus the pastor may recruit a finance team or committee to aid him in funds management. (However, this committee will have no power. This is one of those advisory committees that I mentioned in chapter 10 when discussing board and pastor committees.)

The staff. Staff members have several responsibilities as well. They are to operate with financial integrity within their budgets. They should assist the pastor where needed and when requested. And they should be "cash sensitive," which means being aware that their actions either use or generate cash.

MANAGING CURRENT FINANCES

The pastor manages the church's current finances, which involves the following:

1. He oversees the person who handles the finances (a treasurer, business manager, or lay volunteer) and how they are handled (collecting, counting, and depositing).

2. He monitors all income and expenses. This is not difficult and basically necessitates a regular weekly, monthly, quarterly, and/or annual report. This may be in the form of a simple balance sheet, a cash flow statement, or an income statement. Some pastors create their own reporting sheets unique to their situations. A balance sheet shows the church's assets (checking, savings, value of facilities, value of land, and so forth) and liabilities (loans, mortgage, for example) at a specific point in time. The cash flow sheet focuses specifically on the church's cash and its inflow and outflow. An income statement reflects a church's revenues and expenses in addition to cash over a period of time, such as a month. The financially savvy pastor may want to design his own sheet that reports weekly on the weekend's offerings and special gifts and other forms of income along with attendance and other data that would allow him to track the church's per capita giving, which might be the best read on how the church is doing financially.

   We at The Malphurs Group suggest that churches use a flash report. It is generated weekly (Monday morning) and consists of the church's weekend attendance, revenues, and the weather, especially if it was bad. This is prepared by a staff or volunteer layperson or whoever keeps the books and allows the pastor to track how the congregation is progressing weekly in its stewardship. It is my view and perhaps the Savior's view that stewardship is one of the strongest indications of a congregation's, as well as an individual's, heart for God (Matt. 6:21).

3. He is responsible to keep expenses in line with income. He must ask, Are we living within our income or are we spending beyond our income? His primary tools for doing so are the church's budget, a cash flow statement, and an income statement.

4. He will need to account for all expenses and receipts at least monthly. Again, he should do this with the help of another and will pass this information on to the board either verbally at a board meeting or in writing. Once a year

the wise pastor will have a professional audit (not necessarily a full audit) done of the church's finances. This protects not only the church but the pastor and staff as well.

5. He manages staff compensation. The church should set up a compensation process. It could base staff compensation on such matters as the person's performance, overall staff evaluation, position on the staff, responsibilities, and so forth. The compensation package might include health insurance, life insurance, a pension plan, and other benefits in addition to salary. The staff compensation plan depends on the church's income. While the church might grant all employees a cost-of-living increase, it would not be wise to grant them a raise each year automatically. Instead, the church will give raises and possibly bonuses based on each person's ministry performance.

Managing Future Finances

The pastor plans the future use of the church's finances. A major factor in future planning is the preparation of the church's budget, which reflects the pastor's projection of income and expenses. The budget will also reflect the church's core values, because we do not spend money on what we do not value unless forced to do so.

A well-balanced budget should address at least four areas: missions and evangelism, personnel, ministries, and facilities. While I will say more about the budget later in this chapter, a few comments are appropriate here. Missions and evangelism tie to the church's mission and should evidence a core value of evangelism and that lost people matter. Much of the personnel area is staff compensation and includes staff salaries, compensation packages, annual raises, and bonuses. The pastor's input is vital here. Ministries funding is for the primary ministry activities that we developed as a part of the maturity matrix (vertical axis) in chapter 9. Finally, the facilities spending is for the current facility, including mortgage, rent, utilities, upkeep, and possibly the purchase of additional properties.

Four Budgeting Areas

Missions and Evangelism

Personnel

Ministries

Facilities

Raising Funds

The pastor assumes the responsibility for raising the church's funds. Several times individuals—usually assistant pastors—have asked me if someone other than the senior pastor could take the responsibility for and cast the ministry's vision for the church. This is usually a situation where the senior pastor is not a visionary and not able to cast the vision, whereas the assistant is a visionary with vision-casting skills. But my answer is no, because most people look to the senior pastor to be the primary vision caster, not anyone else.

The cultural evidence. The same is true, even more so, with raising the church's finances. Who else besides the senior pastor could take this role in the church? Again, in our culture people look to the leader for direction and inspiration in church funding. It is part of their package of cultural expectations. That is one of the many hats the pastor wears. While they must be strongly supportive, a board chairperson, an executive pastor, an assistant pastor, a pastor of finances or stewardship, even a patriarch or matriarch cannot perform this role. In evangelical churches, most people realize that the Bible says much about stewardship, and it is the pastor who knows the Bible best and is responsible to communicate that information to the people. The responsibility naturally falls on his shoulders. If the senior pastor is not good at or not willing to assume this function, the church is in trouble and will struggle financially.

The biblical evidence. There is also some biblical evidence, though not entirely clear, that the elders who were first-century house church pastors took responsibility for managing and raising ministry funds. One passage is 1 Timothy 3:4–5, which is set in the context of the qualifications for the pastor of a house church (vv. 1–7). There Paul states, "He must manage his own family well and see that his children obey him, and he must do so in a manner worthy of full respect. (If anyone does not know how to manage his own family, how can he take care of God's church?)" Paul's point is that if one wants to be a pastor, he must know how to manage—or lead—his family well. (The term *manage* is the same word that is translated "leadership" in Romans 12:8.) I would argue that it is likely this qualification included family finances, because they were an important, essential part of anyone's household affairs. Then he makes application to the church—in the same way they are to lead well or take care of their church. While the passage doesn't specifically mention finances, it seems that we can assume he is addressing the pastors' management of their family finances and their church finances.

In 1 Timothy 5:17 Paul writes, "The elders who direct the affairs of the church well are worthy of double honor." Here Paul is addressing the elders who were the first-century house church pastors. They are to be rewarded financially for directing well the church's affairs. While he doesn't say that these affairs included finances, I believe this is a safe conclusion, since finances would play an important role in the affairs of the church.

Acts 11:29–30 says, "The disciples . . . decided to provide help for the brothers and sisters living in Judea. This they did, sending their gift to the elders by Barnabas and Saul." Note that the elders (pastors) were involved in the handling of finances, probably in their role as leaders in the city church context.

The question. Why do pastors in general shy away from the financial side of the ministry? I suspect that there are at least three reasons.

1. They do not know how to raise and manage funds. It is rare that fund-raising is ever addressed in seminary. And we tend to shy away from what we do not know. While this is not always bad, still finances must be raised if the ministry is to thrive. So the solution is to learn how to do it. There are a few books on the topic (see some of those that I cite in the notes). Also, my pastor Steve Stroope and I have written the book *Money Matters in Church* (Baker). In addition to reading what you can find, a good approach is to find a pastor who is competent in this task and learn from him.

2. They worry too much about offending people over money or leaving the impression that all they are interested in is people's money for their own gain. Mistakenly they assume that it is a sore spot with their people, who they think will criticize them if they ask for the people's money. Then there are the people who visit—what will they think? So they just never get around to this aspect of ministry. The truth is there are some people who will complain, often vigorously, every time the pastor preachers on finances and giving. However, what pastors must realize is that the complainers are the very people who give little if anything and are under the Spirit's conviction. So don't allow them to discourage your teaching on biblical finances.

3. They are concerned about their self-image. Many have grown up in situations where they did not have to ask for money. Thus asking people to give affects their personal esteem. They believe wrongly that people will view them as they do the televangelists—as motivated more by money than ministry.

So far the response of the typical pastor's congregation is that these beliefs are unfounded. Actually they want to hear more about finances in general and to know what the Bible says in particular. I assume there are exceptions, but I have not come across one. When the pastors I work with hear this from the congregation, it has a major positive impact on their self-esteem and attitude toward raising ministry funding.

The problem with not addressing giving, at least biblical giving and raising finances, is that it mistakenly denigrates stewardship. It gives people permission not to give and to rationalize not giving. However, if we knew that people in our congregation were having a problem with gossip, would we not address it? And would we apologize for preaching on it as some leaders do finances? While we are more interested in people's souls than in their pocketbooks, we have to teach and preach about their pocketbooks, because we are most interested in their souls.

How Much Money Needs to Be Raised?

Since the pastor is the one whom the church expects to raise its funds, he must know how much to raise. The formal answer to this question is found in the church's budget. The budget is vital to funding in general and allocating funds to accomplish the church's mission and vision in particular. Therefore the budget is a strategic leadership tool in the hands of the financially savvy pastor. He must be skillful in working the church's budget, which involves building it and regularly monitoring it.

BUILD YOUR BUDGET

The church's budget should be a simple, easy tool for anyone to understand and use, especially pastors. It should conform to the KISS principles (keep it simple, Simon). To accomplish this I encourage you to be aware of accountanteze disease. Please don't misunderstand—church accountants are a gift from God. However, their budgets are often written in accountanteze, which is most difficult to decipher. I have designed the following to simplify the process.

Basically, building a church's budget involves constructing a budget blueprint that addresses where you will allocate your funds for ministry. I said earlier that there are four allocation areas: missions and evangelism, personnel, ministries, and facilities.

A church that desires biblical, numerical growth, such as we see in Acts (Acts 1:13–15; 2:41; 4:4; 5:14–15; 6:1; 9:31; 11:21, 24; 14:1, 21; 16:5; 17:4, 12; 18:8, 10; 19:26; 21:20), allocates a percentage of funds to the four key areas: missions and evangelism, personnel, ministries, and facilities. (Note that if you use a fund-accounting approach, you will need to shift that information into these four categories.)

Missions and Evangelism

Most churches realize the importance of and the need to support missions. I like to include evangelism here as well because some, such as the Builder generation, tend to replace evangelism—especially evangelism in their immediate community—with writing a check to missions. The two should work together.

I believe that a church that desires biblical, numerical growth along with spiritual health will budget around 10 percent for missions and evangelism. This sends a clear message that they value or desire to value evangelism and missions. This, however, is just a starting place. It should not be all that the church gives in this area. I would challenge any church to raise additional funds for missions and evangelism and make it a part of any capital funds project.

Missions. In regard to missions in particular, the church should develop a missions policy that governs whom they support, under what circumstances, and how much. In addition, the church should spell out its expectations and how it will know if its missionaries are delivering. This is not to suggest that missionaries would be lazy, but biblical stewardship does demand an accounting (Matt. 25:14–30). And this will help the church make sure that its missions money is being put to its best use for Christ's kingdom.

Some believe the church should spend more than 10 percent of its budget on evangelism in general and missions in particular. I worked with one church that prided itself on the fact that it gave 20–25 percent of its budget to missions alone.

However, what they didn't realize is that budget allocations are closed systems. What this means is that the additional money they were giving to missions had to come from some other part of the budget; in their case it came from personnel or staff salaries. And they couldn't understand why they were having a staff morale problem due to low salaries. The simple solution to this problem is to limit the allocation to 10 percent but do capital campaigns to raise additional funds outside and separate from the budget.

Evangelism. In regard to evangelism, it doesn't take a lot of money to be evangelistic. Normally, growing churches spend 5 percent of their entire budget on local evangelism and outreach. The allocation for evangelism includes such matters as evangelism training, outreach events, and direct mail advertising. Funding special projects for community outreach can be more expensive.

Personnel

The largest allocation of funds in most budgets is for ministry personnel. I would recommend that the church designate around 50 percent of its budget to its personnel. Often in larger churches it is a little less (40–45 percent) and in smaller churches a little more (55–60 percent).

Why so much? You will recall in the strategy section on drafting a dream team that people are God's human agents for ministry effectiveness. He could do it himself, as when he performs miracles, but he prefers to accomplish his purposes through people (Phil. 2:13) and then blesses them in return. Your ministry will only be as good as the people who serve the Lord and the church.

Fair compensation. While I suspect that only a few are out to fleece the flock or to make lots of money, Scripture is clear that the worker (in this context likely the first-century pastor) deserves his wages (1 Tim. 5:17–18). In fact Paul says those who lead well and preach and teach are worthy of double honor. I think Paul is saying to the church, "Take good care of your pastors, compensate them fairly and adequately!"

But what is fair compensation in this day and time? A number of considerations fall under fair compensation, such as the size of the church, location of the church (some parts of the country are more expensive than others), extent of responsibilities, tenure (this assumes improvement, not just longevity), specialized training (only if it increases competence), prior experience (only if it's good experience), what comparable churches are paying their staff, and so on. Fair compensation also includes benefits, such as a retirement program (typically an annuity or pension), health insurance, life insurance, disability, housing, and continuing education. In addition, some churches provide their senior pastor a cell phone, employer-paid FICA, dental and vision insurance, a health club membership, and a sabbatical.

Pay raises. The church may want to grant its employees a cost of living increase for each year that the cost of living increases. The church should not automatically grant everyone a merit raise. Merit raises should be based on good performance that likely will continue, a promotion or increase in scope of responsibility, or an employee not receiving a salary commensurate with others in similar positions. To some degree merit raises are supposed to motivate employees. If they become automatic, they fail to motivate.

Bonuses. A church may grant bonuses. A bonus is typically a one-time gift that doesn't obligate the church to give a bonus in subsequent years. When Chuck Swindoll became the president of Dallas Seminary, he granted all employees a Christmas bonus. However, we did not expect it to become a part of our salary.

It is not only unbiblical but also shameful when a church that has the means fails to take care of its staff. Many of us have heard the stories of church power struggles in which a particular group of people withheld their tithes and offerings in an attempt to "starve out" the pastor. This carnal behavior serves only to shame the Savior and invite God's discipline on these people and possibly the church.

Ministries

A church must pay careful attention to its ministries, especially its primary ones, because this is how it serves God and the people who attend. Also, the way a church cares for its ministries has a major impact on fund-raising, as people contribute through the various church ministries. I suggest that a church allocate approximately 20 percent of its funding to this vital area.

A major part of a church's ministries are the primary and secondary ministry activities that I covered in chapter 9. These make up the vertical axis of the maturity matrix. However, the church will focus on funding the primary activities first as they are so key to making mature disciples. In addition, some of them, such as the worship service, will provide the greatest funding in return. For example, in terms of return on investment (ROI), the worship service provides for much of the church's income and may fund the rest of the primary as well as some of the secondary ministry activities.

Most every other issue that does not fall under missions and evangelism, facilities, or personnel will fall in the ministries category. This includes supplies, programs, publicity, travel, vehicles, and so forth.

The church will also need to consider the congregation's ministry expectations. For example, some people believe that because they support the church financially, it should in turn provide them with Sunday school supplies and other personal materials that may be a part of the ministry. The thinking is that we give to the church and expect something in return, rather than we give to the Lord and will pay for our own personal ministry needs.

Facilities

In chapter 11 I addressed the importance of a church's setting, which covered its location and facilities. Here I want to focus specifically on its facilities. Well-meaning church planters will often start out their ministries with the idea that they will invest in people rather than in bricks and mortar. This means that they do not plan to purchase or build a facility. Their plan is to rent what they need and put the rest back into recruiting and securing competent staff along with their ministering to people. While this sounds great, unfortunately, it never works quite that way. I suspect that a part of it is culture. People want a place they can identify with and call their own ("our church"). They also grow weary of all the disadvantages of not owning, such as unclean facilities, setting up and taking down chairs and tables, and so on. The bottom line is that in time most congregations want a permanent facility.

I suggest that a church allocate around 20 percent of its budget to its facilities. Primarily, this would include such matters as a mortgage payment, rent, maintenance, insurance, and utilities. I have worked with at least one church that had paid off its mortgage and diverted those funds to another part of the budget. I do not recommend that a church do this, because it eliminates the ability to service any future notes for building purposes. If you discover that, due to growth, you need to add to or extensively renovate your current facilities, you will have no funds budgeted for this purpose and to do so either will be impossible or will place a huge strain on the current budget.

If you really plan to grow, whether or not you have a mortgage, you are wise to create a building fund and let people have an opportunity to give to it.

MONITOR YOUR BUDGET

After building your budget, you must monitor it so that you will know how you are doing. You will be able to identify funding blessings that need to be celebrated and funding problems that need to be corrected. Monitoring the budget involves asking and answering the following questions.

1. What percentage of your funds is currently allocated to the areas of missions and evangelism, personnel, ministries, and facilities? How does this compare to the author's suggested allocations of 10 percent for missions and evangelism, 50 percent for personnel, 20 percent for ministries, and 20 percent for facilities?

2. Is the church's income and budget increasing, plateaued, or declining? What does this say about your church?

3. What is your average annual per capita giving? Your answer to this question best addresses how your church is doing financially. To arrive at this figure, divide your total income (as recorded in your budget) by the number of people (age eighteen and above) in attendance. How can you know if the resulting figure is good or bad? You need a point of comparison. On the low end, in 2008 the average American gave $28.86 per week or $1,500.72 a year to charity. On the high end, churches in Leadership Network's generous churches leadership community give an average of $52.75 per week or $2,743 a year.[4] So how does your church compare with these two figures? Most of the churches that The Malphurs Group works with usually land somewhere in between the two. Keep in mind that giving depends on the people to whom your church ministers, their income status, and where the church is located in the world. It will be less if you are ministering in the

inner city, are targeting young people, or are seeker targeted (new believers tend to give less than established believers). Most people—even affluent people—give little to their church. Much has to do with the spiritual condition and growth of the church. People do not support struggling churches with little or no vision.

What about tithing? Whether or not one believes that tithing is for today, it was certainly a measure of what good giving was in the Old Testament. Thus it can also serve as a benchmark for good giving today. Great giving would occur if everyone tithed his or her income.

Finally, we must remember the story of the widow's mite. Though she gave less than the rich, she gave more from Jesus's perspective, because she had very little from which to give. Perhaps your church has a number of "widow's mite givers." The offering may be small, but still the church is giving well.

4. Are most members of your congregation supporting the church financially or only a few? Just because your giving is growing or the total amount given is a lot does not mean that all is well. It could be that 20 percent of your people are great givers while 80 percent are not.

5. Focus on every line item in the budget and ask, Why is the church paying for this? For example, Why is the church paying for materials used in Sunday school, men's and women's Bible studies, small group ministries, and so on? Why isn't the participant paying for the materials?

6. If the church belongs to a denomination and gives money to help support the denomination, you need to ask, Are we getting our money's worth? Depending on your answer, you may need to increase or decrease your support.

7. Does the church have a plan for handling a financial crisis? Does the church have from one to three months' worth of money in cash reserves?

8. Is there a line item for staff development? Remember, leaders are learners. If your staff stops learning, they stop leading.

How Does a Pastor Raise Funds?

Now that we know that the pastor is responsible to raise funds, and approximately how much, the third question is, How does he raise these funds? As I said earlier, I am convinced that many leader-navigators would focus more on raising finances for their sailing ventures if they knew how. Therefore in this section I want to address several means that pastors can use to raise the ministry's operational funds.

Understand Why People Don't Give

When it comes to fund-raising, it helps to know why people don't give to churches in general and their church in particular. Here are six major reasons.

1. The church doesn't have a vision. As you will see below, a clear, compelling vision is critical to good giving.

2. Some feel that giving to a struggling, dying church is a poor investment of God's money. Why not give it to a ministry that is spiritually strong and thriving?

3. Some are naïve and do not understand that churches, just like businesses, need income to survive. The thought never occurs to them.

4. People are selfish. We prefer to keep our money and spend it on ourselves.

5. People are in debt. A portion of our people, perhaps a large portion, have incurred massive debt due to undisciplined spending. I will address this below.

6. Far too many are simply ignorant of what the Bible teaches about finances and giving. The next point will address this problem.

ARTICULATE A BIBLICAL THEOLOGY OF FINANCES

First, you must have and be able to articulate a biblical theology of finances. I believe that the pastor should have thought through what he believes the Bible teaches about finances and stewardship. I encourage pastors to write down their views. What does the Old Testament teach us about giving? What does Christ teach us? What do the Epistles teach? A classic example is tithing. The question is, Does a mature disciple have to tithe? If so, how much is a tithe, and where does Scripture support this? The pastor will also need to preach and teach on giving and he must have a biblical theology to do so. In *Money Matters in Church*, Steve Stroope and I provide a theology of financial stewardship in appendix A. I'm convinced that it alone is worth the price of the book.

REGULARLY CAST THE CHURCH'S VISION

The pastor must regularly cast the church's compelling vision. The key to raising finances for your church's ministry is vision. My experience is that people are not that interested in paying the light bills or staff salaries, nor do they respond well to guilt trips, negativism, or needs. People give to big, dynamic visions that in turn produce passion that is vital to giving. They are more willing to invest in "what could be" (future possibilities) than "what is" (present reality), especially if "what is" is floundering or in the red. The exception is when "what is" is obviously blessed of God and growing spiritually and numerically.

To a certain degree, then, raising finances is a vision measure. What does that mean? People's giving response will often tell you something about the quality of your church's vision and the leader's ability to cast that vision. The people can know the church's vision only through the vision caster and how that person articulates and frames it. Thus a pastor who fails to or cannot cast a vision will have a negative impact on the church's income. If you have been working your way through the strategic process of this book, you now have a vision in place. What remains is for you to communicate it well and often in every way possible.

PROVIDE OPPORTUNITIES FOR GIVING

A church risks losing needed income when it fails to provide sufficient opportunities for giving. Some people will give to one fund but not another. If you give them only a few options, they may not contribute to any of them and give their money elsewhere. Multiple opportunities tend to keep these funds within the church to meet its needs. My church has addressed this by providing six "pockets of giving."

1. *The general fund,* where much of the money goes to meet the general budget.
2. *The missions fund,* which provides additional monies for missions beyond what is allocated in the budget.
3. *The benevolence fund,* which is used to help people in the church and people outside the church who have special, dire needs.
4. *The building fund.* I recommend that you provide this opportunity for giving, even if you aren't currently in a building program. Chances are you will need these funds for future expansion.
5. *The designated fund,* used for special needs or under special circumstances.
6. *The special fund* that I refer to as the "drip pan" or "catch all" category. It provides monies for any areas that aren't listed above.

IMPLEMENT A CHURCHWIDE STEWARDSHIP MINISTRY

You must implement a churchwide stewardship ministry. Of the thirteen fundraising ideas in this chapter, I believe this is the most important. Scripture has much to say about giving, and this forms the biblical basis for your stewardship ministries. Thus you must develop and implement a strategy for building biblical stewardship into your ministry. What might this look like? What are some ministry activities (the means) that will assist your people in becoming mature givers (the ends)? I would strongly encourage you to use all of the following in your church.

Sermons

It is imperative that pastors and teaching teams communicate what the Bible says about giving. As already noted, some shirk this responsibility, fearing what their people or "seekers" might think. Many pastors want to please their people and be liked. That is normal; however, a significant difference exists between being liked and being respected. Jesus did not hesitate to address people in the area of their finances (Matt. 6:19–24), and pastors must not either. Most people really do want to know what the Bible teaches about money because it is an issue that is so close to their heart. Many know that their finances are not providing true happiness, and they want to know the truth. People of God must know the Word of God, and pastors must be truth tellers.

The Malphurs Group gives the churches that we work with an online Church Giving Inventory that asks the congregation key questions, such as whether they believe the pastor preaches too much on money or not enough. It also asks if they feel that they know what the Bible teaches about finances along with a number of other issues. Our experience is that most congregations believe that the pastor does not preach enough on the topic and that they want to know more. This comes as a surprise to most pastors.

Pastors should set aside one month each year for positive, motivating biblical instruction on giving. Research indicates that the best time to preach these sermons is the month of January when people are making New Year's resolutions and attempting to develop new spending habits after Christmas. George Barna finds that pastors who preach two or more messages in a series usually see a better response than those who preach on giving only once a year or several messages spread out over the year.[5] I suggest that you approach your messages along the lines that giving is a privilege as much as it is a responsibility. Resist the temptation to bang your people over the head with biblical imperatives. Instead, assume that they want to give and you are there to help them enjoy the privilege of giving to God.

Sunday School

Take three or four sessions annually to cover some aspect of stewardship in your Sunday school or Bible class ministry. You could call it Managing Your Money God's Way. These sessions could be coordinated with the sermons or at a different time of the year. If your Sunday school follows your worship time, an alternative is to take that time to discuss the meaning of and ways to apply a sermon series on finances or giving.

Small Groups

If you have small group ministries along with or in place of a Sunday school, involve them in a Bible study on giving. They could follow up the sermon with discussion and application. However, another good option for small groups might be a twelve-week study on finances using material from an organization such as Crown Financial Ministries (www.crown.org).

New Members Class

A time when people are most interested in and committed to the church and its ministry is when they decide to join it. Wise churches provide a new members class to orient them to the church. It is critical that this class cover matters such as the church's values, mission, vision, and strategy for alignment purposes. This is also a great time for the church to communicate its giving expectations and the biblical basis for them.

Counseling

Along with the various ministries that teach on biblical giving, the church will need to provide some counseling for those who are struggling with debt and other similar financial problems. It could set up a Financial Fitness Center that helps people address any debt, establish personal budgets, and pursue financial planning.

Ministry of Deferred Giving

Early in the twenty-first century, there are more affluent people than ever before, and many of them are members of our churches. Most have estate plans but have not included the church in them. The church has a responsibility to inform them of the opportunity to have a lasting impact on the church through estate giving. I will say more about this later in this chapter when I cover the sources of income.

Workshops and Seminars

The church should consider offering quarterly or semiannual workshops on some aspects of giving, such as budgeting, investing, estate planning, retirement, and other topics of interest. Call it Biblical Money Management 101 or some other name. In addition, consider inviting unchurched people in the community to the workshops, providing them with a positive, practical exposure to the church.

Capital Funds Giving

There are times in a church's life when the people need to give over and above their normal giving for special projects, such as missions, children's ministries, and facility expansion. The congregation must learn to give sacrificially at times when the church has special, beyond-the-budget needs. Often the result of such a capital campaign is that people not only step up their giving but also keep it at the new level after the campaign is over.

CONSTANTLY COMMUNICATE WITH THE CONGREGATION

In chapter 2, on the preparation for strategic planning, I attempted to articulate how important it is that the leadership communicate constantly with the congregation. There I said that if the congregation does not trust you, you cannot lead them. The same holds true for raising funds. If they do not trust you, they will not give. Why would you contribute funds to those whom you do not trust? A leadership that keeps people in the dark for whatever reason will not be trusted by those people. Thus, if you are having problems in this area, ask yourself, Does the congregation trust the leadership?

Constant communication creates a sense of ownership that inevitably invites people to support the ministry. You tend to support that which is yours. Barna writes, "Remember: people cannot own a ministry they do not understand, and people cannot understand it if they are not kept up to date about its status."[6] In short, as Rick Warren says, people are down on what they aren't up on.

How might you practice constant communication? The answer is the same here as in chapter 2—informally and formally. Encourage the strategic leadership team or any others who might be spearheading a campaign or the regular weekly administration of funds to share with people what is going on. Formal communication can be one-way and two-way communication. One-way communication involves the use of bulletins, newsletters, personal letters, video announcements and testimonies, skits, and public testimonies from your good givers. Perhaps the best, however, is your website. Two-way communication involves online chat rooms, town hall meetings, personal telephone calls, and listening groups.

Make It Easy to Give

One way to make it easy for the congregation to give is to use an envelope system. For some this may seem a little old-fashioned. However, my church is most contemporary and finds that this system works well for it. There are several reasons this continues to be a good system.

1. We put envelopes in racks on the back of each pew. Thus the advantage is they are in plain sight and are a visual reminder to give regularly.
2. Envelopes facilitate giving. A person can put his or her offering in the envelope and drop it in the basket or plate.
3. This method provides a record of who is giving and how much for IRS purposes and tracking the church's giving.
4. It allows people to designate their giving. In our case, on the back of the envelope we have listed general fund, missions fund, and building fund, which people can check off for this purpose.

Another way to make it easy to give is to consider digital giving. Currently, this could include on-site giving (kiosk), online giving (web), and on-the-go giving (mobile), using a smart phone or tablet. You would do well to check these out at securegive.com and givingkiosk.com.

Conduct Capital Funds Campaigns

I strongly encourage churches to conduct regular capital campaigns to fund special projects, such as missions giving, the purchase of property, new construction, facility relocation, facility renovation, debt reduction, annual budget campaigns, and other key projects that require monies over and above the general fund. Though missions should already be included in the budget, you would be wise to raise additional support to expand your missions network. People seem always to find more money for missions.

I use the term *regular* when discussing conducting such campaigns. My experience is that it is okay for most churches to conduct such a campaign every three years. Remember, less time is too much, and more time is too long.

Generally the campaign goal should be in the range of two to three times the average annual budget for the past three years. An excellent campaign will raise three times that much. The campaign itself usually lasts four to six months, culminating in a commitment service when people may give an offering or at least pledge to give over and above their normal giving (it is to be sacrificial). The pledges will come in over the next one to three years. Some pastors ask their gifted givers and other generous givers to make their pledge one week in advance and announce at the commitment service the results to the rest of the congregation to encourage them to give liberally and sacrificially. The pledge approach helps churches plan when and how they will use the funds. Perhaps the best time to begin a campaign is January, because then there are fewer outside pressures on people's time and personal finances.

What I like so much about these campaigns is that they serve to provide a necessary "kick in the pants" to promote sacrificial giving on the part of the congregation. Though most of you reading this book give well, you, like me, could do even better. Thus we need an occasional prod or reminder to give a little extra.

A number of larger churches are using fund-raising organizations to conduct capital campaigns for them, because they do not know how to do it on their own. This is wise, and many of these churches report that after the campaign, general giving remains higher than before. Thus churches should consider using a fund-raising organization as a viable option. There are a number of organizations that are most helpful in planning and executing these special campaigns. However, be sure to check out any organization, asking for and checking out references. Of course, I would highly recommend The Malphurs Group.

CULTIVATE GIVING CHAMPIONS

You should identify those in your church with the gift of giving. Rather than ignore them as many pastors are inclined to do, meet with them periodically and cultivate their gift along with their relationship with God as you might someone with the gifts of leadership, evangelism, or preaching. Make sure that they understand the church's DNA, mission, vision, and strategy. Ask how the church can minister effectively to them. Do not forget to thank them for their ministry to the church.

I realize that this is controversial and questionable to some, perhaps even you. However, if we attempt to cultivate other gifts of our people, why ignore this one? The author of a *Leadership Journal* article interviewed four well-known pastors on how they handle finances in their churches. All four knew who their gifted givers were and at times asked them for financial help.[7] The key here is your motives. Are they good or bad? Are you seeking funds for your own personal benefit? How could this be an issue when the money is not necessarily going to support your salary, or, if so, it does so indirectly along with supporting a number of special projects? Usually this is more of an issue where there is low leadership trust.

Cultivating giving champions would involve your knowing how much your people give so you can spot these people. This is also controversial for some pastor-leaders, because it involves their unrestricted access to the congregation's giving records. However, Jesus makes it clear that where our treasure is, there our hearts will be also (Matt. 6:21). Consequently, if a pastor needs to know who his mature people are, the acid test is likely their giving. This would be true not only in raising funds but also in raising up leaders for board members, potential staff, and other critical positions.

At some point you will ask these champions as well as other interested people to exercise their gift of giving, perhaps toward a particular cause, such as missions or a new facility. That is okay. We expect leaders to lead, evangelists to evangelize, and preachers to preach, so why should we not expect givers to give? It is best if you ask out of a relationship that you have developed with them. They may also help you reach out to others with the gift of giving.

How might you ask people to give? Here is some guidance:

- Discover the passion and interests of your giving champions. What do they like to give to? Some like to give to missions, while others give to facilities expansion, scholarships for summer camp for needy kids, and so forth. If you're not sure, you could ask them.

- Make sure they understand the church's total giving goal and how the money will be spent. The goal might be fifty thousand dollars, with twenty thousand for missions and thirty thousand for facilities expansion and additional parking. They need this information so they can be informed givers. Also ask if they have any questions about the goal or the projects. You might want to consider asking them if they sense a special desire to give to a particular project.

- Explain how close the church is to reaching its goal. For example, "We have raised thirty thousand dollars and need only twenty thousand more."

- Determine the amount that you want to request from the champion or donor. You might base this on past giving. It could range anywhere from a few hundred dollars to a larger amount, such as one hundred thousand dollars.

- Explain how their gift can make a difference or help the church to reach its goal. For example, you could tell them, "If five people would each give four thousand dollars, we could easily raise the last twenty thousand that is needed to reach our goal of fifty thousand."

- Finally, you make the "big ask." "Is this something you would like to be a part of? Would you be one of the people who is willing to give four thousand dollars to help the church reach its goal?" If the person says no, thank him or her for the time and for helping on other occasions.

- If the answer is yes, you might ask the person when he or she wants to make this gift. For example, you could ask, "Our campaign ends in one month. When could we count on you to make your gift?" Or you could explain that you need the gift by a certain time and ask if that would be possible.

RECRUIT A PASTOR OF STEWARDSHIP

Some larger, innovative churches are hiring a pastor of stewardship or generosity. This person is on staff to help integrate a culture of generosity into all aspects of the life of the church. He could also work with people in terms of their deferred giving as well as other areas of finances. It could be that this individual is a gifted layperson. Regardless, look for someone who is working in the financial industry or someone who has retired from this line of work.

CHALLENGE THE CONGREGATION

Many people like to be challenged and respond well to challenges. However, pastors don't seem to understand this and may offer few challenges if any. I encourage pastors to challenge their people each year to give 1 or 2 percent more than last year. While this isn't a huge increase for the average person, it can add up over time if a number of people take the challenge. This challenge could form the conclusion of a series of messages on finances or biblical stewardship.

CHURCH INDEBTEDNESS

While we are discussing fund-raising and controversial issues, I should address the issue of church indebtedness. Few churches and few individuals have the ability to function debt free. Thus I believe that it is okay for a church to incur debt. However, I believe that the church's debt ratio should be no more than three times the church's income or total budget. And two times is a much better ratio. A *Leadership* survey found that median indebtedness for churches that have debt is equivalent to about 64 percent of their annual operating budget. The same survey found that churches can reasonably commit 10–15 percent of their operating budget to loan repayment and interest.[8]

When you discuss debt, there are some who always rise to the occasion and argue that a church should not incur any kind of debt. This may be understandable, but it is wishful thinking. When I probe, I find that these people have mortgages, car loans, and loans for college educations just like the rest of us. What is the difference between their incurring personal debt and the church doing the same? While I do not want to encourage church indebtedness too strongly, the attitude that a church should have no debt does seem a bit hypocritical.

What is key to me is knowing the difference between good and potentially bad debt. Good debt is that which you can cover with your current income. You know that with careful management you can make payments that will pay off the loan over time. *Potentially* bad debt is borrowing funds that you cannot cover with your current or anticipated income. Thus the church may pursue the former, but I question pursuit of the latter.

I have intentionally used the term *potentially bad debt*. I believe that there are times when God is leading a church to step out in faith as well as take God-inspired risks. This may involve the church in borrowing funds that will be covered not with current but with anticipated income. Here are some questions that should guide such a decision.

1. Is the ministry a spiritually healthy, biblically balanced church that is growing numerically? You are looking for evidence that God is in this. Numerical growth can be (with some exceptions) a sign of God's blessing on a church.

2. Do a majority of the church's key, spiritually mature leaders agree? Are they prepared to cosign for the loan if the church does not have a line of credit?
3. Can you not raise the funds from your congregation through a capital funds campaign?
4. How much time have you spent praying about this?

Finally, while I am discussing debt, I should address reserve funds. A good practice is to keep about two weeks to one month's worth of money in your cash flow reserve fund. This allows for any giving shortfalls, emergencies, and so forth.

What Are the Resources for Fund-Raising?

There remains one final question. Where will the funds come from? The church's "streams of income" provide the funds. They include current and deferred giving.

CURRENT GIVING

Current giving refers to funds that are available now. There are two kinds of current giving—traditional or typical and additional or nontypical.

Traditional funding is the typical source of income that churches have used over the years. It includes the following.

1. Passing an offering plate or taking an offering walk during the worship service.
2. Encouraging one-time large gifts from individuals at tax time.
3. Conducting capital funds campaigns for new buildings, renovation of existing buildings, debt reduction, and other special projects. This includes major, sacrificial-giving campaigns. Rick Warren has conducted three of these. The first was called "Possess Our Land" and lasted from 1987 to 1990. The goal was to raise the money to pay for their land. The second was called "Time to Build" and lasted from 1995 to 1997. The goal was to build their facility. The third was called "Building for Life" and lasted from 1997 to 2004. The goal was to fund other major projects.
4. Charging rental fees for others' use of buildings and parking lots and for various events—high school graduations, weddings, funerals, and so forth. Although you might want to provide this for free as a ministry to your community, a fee is necessary to at least cover the cost of custodial cleanup, utilities, and wear and tear on the facilities. You do not have to charge a lot.
5. Selling noncritical real estate and properties donated to and owned by the church. By *noncritical* I am referring to properties that the church will not need for expansion or any other purposes in the future.
6. Sponsoring auctions, bake sales, potluck dinners, car washes, and other such events.

Additional sources of income that you may not have considered could include the following.

1. Developing a strategy that focuses specifically on building stewardship into the very fabric of the church. I covered this earlier. The advantage is that it uses a number of different activities at the same time to increase congregational giving. It seeks to build mature disciples who desire to give back to God what he has given them. I believe that God honors this because it so focuses people's attention on Scripture.

2. Providing the congregation with good literature on stewardship. For example, my church handed out free copies of Randy Alcorn's book *The Treasure Principle*[9] along with the pastor's sermon on giving. We experienced a serious increase in giving, much of which the pastor (Steve Stroope) attributed to the book and not his sermon.

3. Addressing various "pockets of passion" in the congregation (also known as modular giving). People in your church will have areas of personal ministry passion to which they love to give, such as missions, kids, youth, AIDS prevention and treatment, and unwed mothers.

4. Providing a list of opportunities to which people may contribute on special giving envelopes in the pews. My church lists three such opportunities: the general fund, building fund, and missions fund. My pastor is convinced that this encourages additional giving to all three.

5. Charging user fees. User fees are monies charged primarily for secondary ministry activities, such as Christian day school, materials and instructor's time in midweek Bible studies, most non-weekend church ministries (except evangelistic ones), ski trips, summer camps, senior citizen trips, after-school ministries, drama classes, aerobic dance, Vacation Bible School (materials and refreshments), and others. Simply because people donate to the church does not mean that the church is responsible to provide such activities without charge. However, for some events, such as youth ski trips and summer camps, the church should offer scholarships so that kids from low-income families can participate.

6. Encouraging the giving of income from investments of people with accumulated wealth. Challenge them to give a portion (such as 10 percent) to the church.

7. Leasing space in the church for or operating its own coffee bar. In the early twenty-first century, sitting around and drinking coffee (actually experiencing community) is popular in the American culture. A number of churches have either opened and operated their own coffee shops or leased space to one of the chains. Irving Bible Church on the outskirts of Dallas invited Cici's coffee company to set up shop in the church free of charge. The purpose was to expose the lost, unchurched people in the Irving community to the church rather than to increase revenue.

8. Determining if the government is granting any monies through Faith Based Initiative programs, as it did during the George Bush administration. This is a source of income for which many inner-city ministries with strong social ministries would likely qualify.

9. Securing grants from private organizations such as a corporation for special projects. Private organizations can give tax-free monies to churches. You may have someone in your church who is in a position in one of these organizations who could legally and legitimately direct funds your way.

10. Removing from the budget any church ministries that should be funded by special projects other than the budget. These would primarily be secondary ministry activities. Leaders who pursue this will need "tough skins" as people can get upset over what they perceive to be the removing of funds from their favorite ministries. However, this is not the issue. The money should still be available, but it would come from a different funding source.

11. Setting high standards for church membership, such as asking all new members to be involved in a ministry, to give regularly to the church, and to be involved in the primary activities. Lyle Schaller observes that high expectations usually result in better giving.[10]

Deferred Giving

Today there are more affluent people, and more people have more accumulated wealth than ever before in our nation's history. Forty-one trillion dollars will pass from one generation to another over the next twenty-plus years. (This is ten million dollars a day for the next eleven thousand years.) Parachurch ministries and not-for-profit organizations are most aware of this and have trained professionals on their teams who go to these people and ask them for special gifts. We have discovered that those who ask for money will get it.

Though most donors have a will or estate plan, more than nine out of ten are not leaving anything to the church.[11] And most churches have not thought about asking their people to consider such a gift. This could mean millions in additional income for churches. Some people could leave more to the church at death than they ever gave in life. This is how your people can continue to influence the church and serve God on earth while enjoying him in heaven. Rick Warren said on one occasion that it is more than the opportunity of a lifetime; God offers you an opportunity "beyond" your lifetime.

So how can your people minister to and invest in the church's ministry through deferred giving, and what are some of the benefits from such giving? Consider the following:

1. *Wills that include bequests* (related to one's personal property) *and legacies* (related to money). This helps the person save on or avoid estate and gift taxes.

2. *Living trusts in place of wills.* This avoids all the disadvantages of probate.

3. *Retirement accounts such as IRAs, 401k plans, and others.* Should one leave the retirement funds to the church, no one (the estate, loved ones, or the church) will pay taxes on them.

4. *Charitable trusts such as remainder and lead trusts.* The remainder trust can provide a current charitable deduction for the member in addition to income for him or her during the member's lifetime with the remainder passing to the church. Estate and gift taxes can be lowered or eliminated by the use of remainder trusts. Members with very large estates can use a lead trust to benefit the church and pass principal to their family members while incurring little if any tax penalty. This involves transferring assets to a trust that makes payments to the church for a certain number of years. Then the trust principal goes to the children, grandchildren, or others free of or at a reduced federal gift and estate tax.

5. *Life insurance gifts.* By designating the church as both the owner and the beneficiary of a life insurance policy, the donor's premiums are tax deductible. This is an attractive approach for younger persons in the church.

6. *Real estate.* The donor can contribute the property but continue to reside there for his or her lifetime or the combined lifetime of the donor and his or her spouse. Donors receive a charitable deduction for the full fair market value of the property as determined by appraisal.

7. *Personal property such as paintings, jewelry, vehicles, boats, aircraft, and so forth.*

8. *Gifts of appreciated securities (stocks and bonds).* These gifts bring tax savings to the donor because he or she avoids paying capital gains taxes on the increased value of the security and receives a charitable deduction for the full fair market value of the security when the gift is made.

9. *Charitable gift annuities.* The donor makes an irrevocable gift of cash, securities, or real estate to the church in exchange for fixed payments for life. Then, at the donor's death, the remaining value benefits the church.

10. *Memorials that involve leaving money in memory of someone.* Be aware that this may involve including that person's name on what that money is used for, such as naming a building after him or her.

11. *Endowments that could provide the church with a permanent fund or source of income.* A possibility might be endowed staff positions that would free up budgeted funds for other sources.

I suggest that you form a team of laypersons to conduct this ministry in your church. Look for some person (perhaps retired) who may have worked in the area of deferred giving or some related area and ask him or her to lead this ministry. An ideal situation would be to have a part-time minister to adults on staff that has this knowledge and experience in this area. You will also need the services of an attorney to handle some of these matters from a legal standpoint.

Some would argue against the church's pursuit of deferred funds and any investment funding. They argue that such monies make for lazy givers and will thus hurt overall congregational giving. However, this is relative and depends on congregational leadership and how they communicate and handle such opportunities. I believe that having a deferred giving ratio of 10 to 20 percent of the budget should not adversely affect congregational giving.

I think it would be wise in closing this chapter to remind the reader of the words of missionary Jim Elliot: "He is no fool who gives up what he can't keep in order to gain what he can't lose." Good leadership in the area of church finances produces people who gladly give up what they cannot keep to gain what they cannot lose.

Questions for Reflection, Discussion, and Application

1. Who in your church is primarily responsible for managing finances? As far as you know, has this always been the case? Is this biblical? Does it have to be? What does this responsibility entail?

2. How do you respond to the news that the pastor is responsible to manage the church's finances? Honestly, as a pastor, do you view it as a challenge or a curse? If the latter, why? How might you grow and change to view it as a challenge?

3. What are the key areas of your budget? Does the budget break down into the areas the author recommends for growing, healthy churches? If not, where does it differ? Do the percentages for each area line up with those the author suggests? How might you change your current budget to reflect the information covered in the budgeting section? If you feel that you want to make some of these changes but cannot, what is the problem?

4. Walk your church's budget through the "Monitor Your Budget" section on church budgeting. What did you learn about your budget? How are you doing?

5. Have you articulated a biblical theology of finances and stewardship? If so, is it written down on paper? If not, why do you not have one? Why is it so important to your ministry?

6. Does the section in this chapter on raising finances make sense? What do you agree with and what do you struggle with the most? Do you feel competent to lead a capital funds campaign? Why or why not? If not, what will you do? Are you comfortable with bringing in outside expertise? Why or why not? What are your feelings about cultivating your giving champions? Will you pursue this source of revenue? Why or why not? Are you comfortable with the pastor having access to the giving records of the people? Why or why not?

7. How do you feel about the congregation incurring debt? Do you agree with the author's position? Why or why not?

8. Which of the traditional giving sources does your church currently use? Are there any that it should be using but is not? Which of the additional funding sources might your church adopt? Are you in favor of pursuing deferred giving? How do you think income from deferred funds would affect the congregation's overall giving.

part three

Pursue the Course!

The Practice of Strategic Planning

13

Launching the Boat

Implementing the Strategy

In part 1 we addressed the preparation for strategic planning by preparing to sail. In part 2 we pursued the process of strategic envisioning by setting the course. Now in part 3 we invite the navigator to practice strategic planning—to pursue the course. This involves implementation of the plan or taking action and adjusting your course along the way (chap. 13), which requires evaluation (chap. 14).

Strategic Planning
Part 1. Preparation for strategic planning
Part 2. Process of strategic planning
Part 3. Practice of strategic planning

Ministry navigators can develop the best strategy to get them to their desired port of call; they can recruit the best crew, rent the finest slip, and raise all the necessary funds; however, at some point, they have to launch the boat. If they never set sail and leave port, nothing significant happens.

Most experts on planning and strategic thinking have identified implementation as the greatest problem in the strategizing process. Leaders as strategists may develop good strategic plans, but they do not know how to implement them. Having a strategic plan in writing is one thing; turning it into action is quite another.

Having developed a good organizational strategy, we must take action; we must make it happen.

The temptation for leaders is to wait for exactly the right time and ideal conditions to act. That is the theoretical world. In the real world, however, there is no exactly right time or ideal conditions. At some point you have got to take the plunge, you have got to move, or you will miss the God-given opportunities. The right time to act is now! To fail here is like moving the ball the entire length of the field in American football but not scoring, or going to the altar without getting married. This is the failure to follow through. It is what Moses and God's people in the Old Testament experienced when they made it to the Promised Land the first time but failed to enter (Deut. 1:19–46). The result is the same. The strategy dies for lack of execution.

Just as development of the strategy will take place during its implementation, so implementation will take place to some degree throughout the strategic planning process, especially if you respond to the questions at the end of the chapters and act on your responses. My point is that there will be overlap.

After you develop the five elements of strategy, implementation becomes a primary focus. This chapter presents the first element of the practice aspect of the strategic envisioning process. Its purpose is to communicate how to implement the strategic plan or how to weave it into the very fabric of the organization. It teaches you not only to plan the process but also to do something—to set sail, to follow through on the details. In this chapter we will address four areas affecting implementation excellence: the importance of, the responsibility for, the process of, and the practice of implementation.

Why Is Implementation Important?

Implementation is important to your strategic planning for at least seven reasons.

Accomplishes the Strategic Plan

Not much happens without implementation. Implementation is what closes the gap between ideas and their execution. It translates thought into action. It links strategic thinking with strategic acting. It balances theory with practicality, developing with doing, and planning with practice. And it keeps everything from falling through the cracks.

Research informs us that if we do not practice consistent implementation, then even with the aid of a knowledgeable consultant, approximately one year later, the church begins to return to its old self.[1] I refer to this as the "rubber band effect." If you stretch and then release a fresh rubber band, it instantly flies back to its original shape. However, the longer you stretch the rubber band, over time, the more it will maintain its stretched condition. The same is true of our ministries, and it is the execution step that stretches them over time.

Maintains Ministry Momentum

Every strategic leadership team I have worked with has been excited about the process and what they are accomplishing for the Savior and the congregation. However, when it comes to executing the process, there can be a letdown if it stalls due to "analysis paralysis," cold feet, or indecision on the part of the leadership. Thus it loses vital ministry momentum. So what should you do? Do not procrastinate; move right into the full implementation practice provided in this chapter. Again, the ideal time to implement your strategic thinking is now.

Wards Off Complacency

We know that one of the great enemies of Christ's cause in general and strategic planning in particular is congregational complacency. We see it especially in so-called successful churches. It is usually summarized by some old-timer who rises to the occasion with, "If it ain't broke, don't fix it!" People, even good church people, cling to the status quo. Even when the ministry is crumbling around them, they assume the ostrich position—they bury their heads in the sand and insist that everything is okay. And that is complacency at its worst. Execution, however, holds out a continued sense of urgency along with a monitored follow-up to put the strategic plan in action.

Addresses the Problem of Time

Often time is a major culprit in delaying the accomplishment of the church's strategic thinking. Over time people's excitement and enthusiasm begin to wane. Over time the fog of complacency drifts in and hides the iceberg of decline and death. Over time pastors and staff become preoccupied with other matters, and the process gets buried. Strategic execution does not let this happen. It aids you in doggedly pursuing the process, regardless of time. It assigns and monitors deadlines. It keeps you on time.

Keeps the Team on Track

There are so many things that confront the church in general and its leadership in particular. I refer to them as "sidetracks" because they serve to get you off the main track of execution. Putting out ministry fires can do this. These are distractions that do not serve to support the strategic process. Constant pressure from change resistors and skeptics can derail the process. The pastor's and staff's pursuit of their passions, such as preaching, teaching, and other matters that tempt them away from the process, can interfere with execution. Strategic implementation, however, is paced so as to keep everyone on track and on purpose.

Nourishes Faith in the Process

During implementation, good things happen. People come to faith, and people of faith increase their faith. What "could be" and "should be" become "what is."

And it is this ministry accomplishment that excites and motivates people. They literally see things happening as their dreams one by one become reality. In turn this serves to nourish their faith in the process. It strengthens their identification with the process and keeps their hopes for the church alive.

Heightens Optimism

When people see good things happening and bad things corrected, it has a positive effect. They begin to focus less on the bad and more on the good. This also serves to keep the critics at bay and naysayers in their place, because it is hard to argue against success in the spiritual realm.

> **Implementation**
>
> Accomplishes the strategic plan
> Maintains ministry momentum
> Wards off complacency
> Addresses the problem of time
> Keeps the team on track
> Nourishes faith in the process
> Heightens optimism

Who Is Responsible for Implementation?

When we ask, Who is responsible for implementation? we are asking, Who will make sure it happens? This addresses not so much who does the hands-on work of implementation but who makes sure that the process does not fall through the cracks, that it gets done. The answer is the same as for the development process. The leadership team, consisting of the pastor, the staff, a board if the church has one, and the development teams (DTs), is responsible for implementation.

The Pastor

All that I said about the leadership team in chapter 3 on development applies here to the implementation of the strategy, especially to the pastor. Thus he must remain committed to the process and to implementing it. He must continue to be patient with the process, because just as development took time, so will implementation. He will need to make sure that nothing interferes with the implementation of the plan. And he needs to focus on the 20 percent of what he does to produce the 80 percent of what gets done.

The Staff

If the church has staff other than the senior pastor, they will need now to take responsibility for the implementation of the plan, especially those portions that apply to their areas of expertise.

The Board

As with development, the board (if the church has one) will work closely with the senior pastor to monitor and make sure the plan is implemented.

The Development Teams

While some development will continue to take place, much of the work of the development teams has been completed, and now they must shift their focus to implementing the mini-strategies (community outreach, disciple making, and so forth) they have been working on. They will take responsibility along with some people from the congregation for implementing the envisioning results. There is no way that the pastor or staff by themselves would have the time or the expertise to implement the plan. They are desperately dependent on the DTs to be a part of the process or it won't happen. Scripture affirms the general importance of congregational involvement in Ephesians 4:11–13.

How Will You Implement the Strategic Plan?

Now that we know the reason implementation is so important and who is responsible to make it happen, we turn to the process of implementation—executing the plan. The implementation process consists of four steps.

Step 1. Implement Each Objective and Its Goals

IDENTIFY YOUR OBJECTIVES AND THEIR GOALS

First, we must identify the objectives and goals of the strategic plan or know what they are. We accomplished this earlier in the development phase (see chap. 3), when we formulated an objective and its specific goals needed to effectively develop mini-strategies (small s) that make up the overall Strategic plan (big S). We came up with twelve objectives, two of which are optional.

1. Recruit a lead implementation team who will direct and oversee the planning process.
2. Draft a prayer team who will pray for the teams as well as the process.
3. Recruit a communication team who will take pains to communicate the process and improve the church's overall communication process.
4. Draft a community outreach team who will develop a strategy to reach out to the church's community.
5. Recruit a disciple-making team who will develop a strategy for making disciples.
6. Draft a congregational mobilization team who will develop a strategy to mobilize the congregation.
7. Recruit a staff development team who will design a strategy to grow and develop the church's staff.
8. Recruit a ministry setting team who will design a strategy to assess the ministry's location and facilities.

9. Recruit a finance or stewardship team who will draft a strategy to raise and monitor finances.
10. Draft a creative/innovative team who will develop a strategy to help the church adapt quickly and creatively to its changing culture.
11. Recruit an optional governance team that will draft a strategy to equip the governance board, if the church has one, to lead with excellence.
12. Recruit a leadership development team who will craft a strategy for developing leaders at every level of the church. This too may be an optional objective for some churches.

Each of these objectives has a number of goals. To see these goals and their objectives, turn to appendix D for a sample. We at The Malphurs Group think this is a good representation of the objectives and goals for any church. However, you may need to adjust them to your particular context. Regardless, it is at this point that you have identified and developed these objectives and their goals and are ready to implement them.

Prioritize Your Objectives and Their Goals

Once you have formulated your list of specific implementation objectives and goals, next you must prioritize them. Here is the point: you cannot do everything at the same time, and not everything is of equal importance. Ask yourselves which goals should be done first, second, third, and so on. The highest priorities are those most important things that need to be done right away. Determining strategic priorities allows the church to focus all its resources—people, energy, finances, creativity, and so on—on what needs to be done now. To fail to set priorities means that *everything* will become a priority. When everything is a priority, nothing is and nothing gets done.

How do you determine what is and is not a priority? The answer is threefold.

1. You must bathe your situation in prayer. Ask God to show you the priorities, remembering that he may have already done this, and they are obvious.
2. Determine what goals will have the greatest impact on the church's ability to accomplish its mission and implement its strategy.
3. Determine which of these will have the most immediate impact. Ask, Which will bring quick but significant and enduring results?

You will tackle this with the various DTs. Write the goals on a whiteboard or a piece of paper and ask your team to assign each item a number indicating its priority for accomplishment. They may also want to mark each with an HP for high priority, MP for medium priority, or LP for low priority. Any way you do it, the process will generate some good discussion and healthy debate.

Next, determine how many goals you can actively implement at the same time. The answer for most churches is four to five, depending on the number of people on each team. Thus you will begin with the first four or five goals. As you launch or even accomplish a goal, bump the next one on the list up into the top four or five and begin to focus on it along with the rest.

Articulate the Actions That Will Realize These Goals

Finally, once the ministry formulates its implementation goals and prioritizes them, you will need to articulate the specific measurable actions that will realize these prioritized goals.

Measurable action is a best practice that is essential or core to congregational development. It is not enough for a church to have a strategic plan containing specific targets. Churches must evidence measurable action toward meeting the goals or hitting those targets.

For example, one highly prioritized goal will likely be to implement a congregational mobilization process. To accomplish this the following specific measurable actions are necessary: recruit a pastor or lay leader of mobilization, recruit and train a lay mobilization team, design a mobilization process, select the mobilization tools (assessments and so forth), and design ministry descriptions for each ministry position in the church. Create a matrix on which you place these actions in chronological order, deciding which action to take first, second, and so on.

A Congregational Mobilization Ministry

Specific Actions	Responsible Persons	Deadlines	Necessary Resources
Recruit a lay leader			
Recruit and train a team			
Design a mobilization process			
Select the mobilization tools			
Design ministry descriptions			

Step 2. Determine Who Will Implement Each Objective and Its Goals

Assign responsible persons to take charge of and accomplish the objectives and their goals and write their names on the matrix above. The job of the pastor and his lead development team is to identify the champions who will carry the leadership torch for each objective. Most will be the same people who make up the development teams (DTs)—the pastor, any staff, strategic development team people, board members, and members of the congregation in general. (You may need to recruit a few more people for these teams as there will always be dropouts.) These people will take off their ministry development hats and don their ministry implementation hats. However, they will keep their ministry development hats close by as they will never be completely done with development. The process will need to be tweaked constantly.

A Congregational Mobilization Ministry

Specific Actions	Responsible Persons	Deadlines	Necessary Resources
Recruit a lay leader	Pastor John Smith		
Recruit and train a team	Tom Jones		
Design a mobilization process	Tom Jones and team		
Select the mobilization tools	Tom Jones and team		
Design ministry descriptions	Tom Jones and team		

Step 3. Decide on Launch Dates

Decide when the goals must be launched and enter the dates on the matrix. This means setting implementation dates or deadlines that are the future benchmarks for success. You should know by now who are the doers and who are the procrastinators. Both will need deadlines for implementation as with development. And time continues to be of the essence.

Setting launch dates determines when each developed objective will go public and become operational. There are at least three options.

1. *The staggered launch date.* Because the teams are staggered in their development process, anywhere from a couple of weeks to a month, they may be staggered in their implementation process as well. This is important, because launching all the mini-strategies at the same time could prove overwhelming.
2. *The same launch date.* This is when all the strategies launch at the same time, which some people prefer. Again, make sure this does not overwhelm your people, which is a judgment call on your part.
3. *The special launch date.* There may be certain strategies that need to have been implemented yesterday. For example, the congregation may have maxed out its facility and is losing people because they have no place to put them. These strategies may be developed early and launched as soon as they are developed.

As with the development process, you may want to create a time line that will help you follow each team's implementation progress. We recommend that teams employ a Gantt chart like the one below to help schedule and accomplish this.

A Congregational Mobilization Ministry

Specific Actions	Responsible Persons	Deadlines	Necessary Resources
Recruit a lay leader	Pastor John Smith	2/15	
Recruit and train a team	Tom Jones	3/15	

Specific Actions	Responsible Persons	Deadlines	Necessary Resources
Design a mobilization process	Tom Jones and team	4/15	
Select the mobilization tools	Tom Jones and team	5/15	
Design ministry descriptions	Tom Jones and team	5/15	

Step 4. Provide the Necessary Resources

Like everything else, it takes resources to implement your specific goals. Once it has been determined what resources the teams will need to accomplish their objectives, the resources should be entered on the matrix. These resources are time, finances, facilities, tools, equipment, and so forth. Sometimes we ask our champions and their teams to perform certain functions, but we do not properly equip them to accomplish the functions well. In these situations we must not be surprised when implementation does not go well or does not happen at all. The best judge of these necessary resources is the champion, someone who has done the ministry in the past, or a savvy team member.

A Congregational Mobilization Ministry

Specific Actions	Responsible Persons	Deadlines	Necessary Resources
Recruit a lay leader	Pastor John Smith	2/15	5–6 hours
Recruit and train a team	Tom Jones	3/15	12 hours and $200 (materials)
Design a mobilization process	Tom Jones and team	4/15	4 hours plus a consultant fee
Select the mobilization tools	Tom Jones and team	5/15	1 hour
Design ministry descriptions	Tom Jones and team	5/15	4 hours

Implementation Process

Step 1. Implement each objective and its goals

Step 2. Determine who will implement each objective and its goals

Step 3. Decide on launch dates

Step 4. Provide the necessary resources

Some Important Implementation Practices

In this final section I am distinguishing between the four-step implementation process above and some key practices of implementation. These practices supplement the process and will make the difference between successful implementation and failure. Ignore them and you jeopardize the process. There are a number of key implementation practices that will help your teams execute the objectives and goals that make up their mini-strategies.

Pray for the Implementation Process

It almost goes without saying that you must pray and ask God to guide, direct, and ultimately implement the planning process. This is the very first step and a key implementation practice. Everything must be bathed in prayer. In Matthew 7:7–8 Jesus says that you have not because you ask not. We do not want the implementation process to fail simply because we failed to ask God to use us to deliver the process.

Communicate Your Accomplishments

A key practice is communication. You must communicate to the congregation the ministry goals and their accomplishments. There are at least three reasons for this: The first is obvious to anyone who has read the second chapter of this book. You want your people to know the goals that you are working on so they can support you and also work toward their accomplishment. (I have said this a lot in this book and probably cannot say it enough.) Second, you want them to pray for the team and the accomplishment of the goals. Third, they need to see what is happening—the actual accomplishment of the goals. This will send a strong message that God is working out his purposes through their church (Phil. 2:13). To do this, put your goals where they can be seen, such as on the church's website, in newsletters and bulletins, on bulletin boards, and announce them in the service.

Establish Accountability

One way to ensure accountability is to establish MIR meetings. MIR stands for monthly implementation review, which describes what the meeting is about. At least once a month the DTs take whatever time is needed—an hour or more—to follow up and make sure that the strategy is on track for implementation. This makes it one of the most important meetings of the month. You could accomplish this through a face-to-face meeting or better a conference call. Since the MIR meeting occurs only once a month, the leadership must make sure that it is a priority, that it does take place, and that the responsible people—the DT leaders—are present.

This meeting is held to review the implementation step, not any other aspect or business of the ministry. The MIR looks primarily at two areas: progress and problems. First, ask questions that allow the implementation team to monitor what is taking place and the progress that they have or have not made in implementing the strategy. Then ask, How are you doing? Have the various responsible people taken charge of their goals? Are you making progress? How do you know? Does it look as if you will meet your deadlines? Do you have the necessary resources? Obviously the review will lead to a certain amount of accountability. What is reviewed is most likely to get done. Those who come unprepared to this meeting will have to account for their lack of progress. A lack of personal discipline or "foot dragging" is unacceptable. Those who are progressing well should be affirmed.

Second, the MIR attempts to surface and deal with problems that implementers are facing. The participants should discuss their problems, whether the problems seem insurmountable, which goals will take more or less time than originally thought, any unanticipated factors, and any help that is needed to solve the problems. The team will need to become aware of resources that will help handle the problems. The pastor who leads the MIR is responsible for reporting progress to the board (assuming there is a board) at the monthly or quarterly board meeting. He is accountable to them for progress in implementation.

Address Any Implementation Barriers

Anytime you attempt to execute a process, there will be certain barriers that get in the way and attempt to block it. However, you must not wait until you have supposedly removed all the barriers before you commence the process. That will not happen, and you will never get to the process. There will always be barriers, so you deal with the barriers as you initiate the process. This involves the strategic leadership team in a four-step process.

Step 1. Define an implementation barrier. For you to address implementation barriers, you must know what they are. I define them as embedded practices, policies, or persons (anything or anyone) that block effective activation of your strategic plan. They may be intellectual, emotional, relational, or financial, and I will give you some examples in the next step. My experience is that most lie at the emotional level.

Step 2. Identify your implementation barriers. Implementation barriers are such things as the status quo, complacency, sacred cows, the stress of change, vested interests, and many others along with the people who tenaciously cling to them. I have designed and provided for you in appendix E an Implementation Barriers Audit that you can take to help you identify your specific implementation barriers. You and your team need to take this audit, compare your results, and come up with a consensus list of your church's barriers.

Step 3. Address the implementation barriers. You must not duck the barriers to implementation but face them head-on. The tendency is to try to implement around them, but they have a way of surfacing when you least expect them, and they can stop the process dead in its tracks. The pastor should not have to address these barriers by himself. It will take the mutual support of the strategic leadership team and a strong governing board to face and overcome barriers.

As stated above, you will not be able to address all of them at the same time, and you must not let this delay the implementation process, or it will never happen. However, you will need to address the major ones as you work through the process. Prioritize your barriers. Give the highest priority to those that need to be addressed right away.

Step 4. It is important that you push ahead and not give ground. Respect objectors, but openly disagree. Confront and correct. Never tolerate sinful behavior (anger, gossip, threats, accusations, or intimidation).

Monitor Progress

To keep your implementation process on track, closely monitor team performance. To accomplish this you do not need to require endless paper reports. Few like to do this and most will drag their heels. Instead, use the MIRs (monthly implementation reviews) to monitor progress. Also when we at The Malphurs Group consult with a church, we ask the SLT and DTs to take the first ten to fifteen minutes of our meetings to update us on their progress. A third way is to call the team leaders and ask for a brief update on their progress. An additional byproduct of monitoring progress is accountability. When teams know they'll be asked about their progress, they tend to make progress.

Evaluate the Process

If you want to know how you are doing, and you do, then you need to evaluate what you are doing. This involves evaluating both the people involved and the process itself. There is an old saying that applies here: what gets evaluated, gets done. What you expect, you need to inspect. Chapter 14 addresses how to evaluate your process.

Involve the Congregation in the Process

There is no way that the pastor alone or a staff could implement the overall strategy. It would be a daunting task and attempting it would be futile. This is the reason we have development teams that are made up of the church's leaders. However, they will not be able and should not attempt to do all the implementation either. You do not want to have a process that relies solely on the leadership development teams for its implementation. It is imperative that you recruit the congregation to be a part of the process. This reverts back to one of the mini-strategies—mobilizing the congregation for ministry. The standing rule is the Pareto principle, which says that 20 percent of the people will do 80 percent of the ministry. If this is true of your implementation of the strategy, then it will not happen. Instead, set a goal of 30 or 40 percent of the congregation, or eventually more, who are involved in the ministry. And the time to begin this was yesterday.

Motivate Your Teams

Certain practices will motivate your people, and some will not. It really depends on the person you want to motivate. Thus the church leadership is wise to take a number of approaches to motivation, encouraging others besides the pastor and staff to be motivators. For any staff in particular, you might give them an extra day off. Try some of the following for the staff and lay volunteers. Ask someone who ministers under the leadership of a person to express what that person has meant to them. Give out tickets to a sporting event. Give out coupons for coffee at a coffee shop such as Starbucks. Make heroes out of them. Praise them in public. Buy them a good book. Give them a gift certificate. Send them a personal note or letter of appreciation. Provide them with a plaque or certificate that could go on their wall. If a woman, send her flowers. Actually, the only limit to how you and others might motivate your teams is your innovative, creative abilities.

Research Any Potential Legal Issues

You might think it strange that legal issues would be important to the practice of implementation. However, every church is a legal entity that has to abide by the law in general and its own laws in particular. The latter are found in its constitution and bylaws. And more often than not there will be someone in the church who knows the constitution and bylaws well and will attempt to use them to block change and implementation in the church.

One area of legal concern is that of committees. The Malphurs Group recommends that you drop the committee concept and go instead with teams. The difference is that committees talk about ministry while teams do ministry. However, most churches' constitution and bylaws will limit the church to committees. Thus you may want to change the constitution and bylaws or simply call committee teams when you refer to them.

Another area is specific committees. Many churches have a personnel and finance committee. And the problem is that these committees might conflict with a mini-strategy. An example would be the mini-strategy that addresses developing a strategy for the church's finances, which might clash with the church's finance committee. Which has the authority to make decisions regarding the church's finances? We advise that you merge the two. At the beginning of strategic planning as you recruit the teams, ask the finance committee to be or be on the team that designs the strategy for the church's finances.

Implementation Practices

1. Pray for the implementation process.
2. Communicate your accomplishments.
3. Establish accountability.
4. Address any implementation barriers.
5. Monitor progress.
6. Evaluate the process.
7. Involve the congregation in the process.
8. Motivate your teams.
9. Research any potential legal issues.

Questions for Reflection, Discussion, and Application

1. Are you convinced that implementation of the strategic plan is important? Why or why not? If so, did you come up with some reasons that the author did not mention?

2. Honestly, do you struggle with procrastination when it comes to implementation? Why or why not? If so, what will you do about this?

3. Who in your ministry will take responsibility for implementation? What other people will play a role?

4. What is your definition of an implementation barrier? What or who are some of the implementation barriers in your church? What will you do about them? Do you as pastor have the full support of the strategic leadership team and the board in addressing these barriers? Will they stand behind you?

5. What are some of the things that a pastor needs to delegate to someone else on staff or in the church? Create a "stop doing" list. Determine your 20 percent that accomplishes the 80 percent.

6. Do you have a list of your implementation goals similar to the ones in appendix D? Do you sense a need to prioritize them? If so, what are the top four or five goals?

7. How will you communicate these goals to the congregation so that they know something is happening when the goals are accomplished?

8. What are your objectives and their goals? Who will be responsible for each goal? What deadlines should you assign each? Will you use a time line? Would a Gantt chart be helpful? What resources will be needed (money, equipment, facilities, and so on)?

9. How often will your MIR meetings take place? When? How long do you plan to meet? What are your expectations for this time? Is accountability one of them? How will you respond to people who come unprepared or may be falling behind?

10. What is the difference between the process of implementation and the practices of implementation according to the author. Is this important? What are some examples of the latter?

14

Evaluating the Course

How We Are Doing

Performance appraisal is the final element in the strategic planning or envisioning process. It assumes that the strategic leadership team in general and the development teams in particular are forming the spiritual foundation of the church; have discovered its core values; have developed a mission, a vision, and a strategy; and are implementing the strategy. With all of this in place, the ministry seeks to answer the fundamental question, How are we doing? Without valid critique, the ministry, as well as the process, is quick to sink to the bottom. However, regular critique allows the navigator and the crew to make critical navigational corrections that will keep the ministry ship off the bottom and on course.

Therefore every leader must ask, Am I evaluating my ministry effectiveness, and do we evaluate the effectiveness of the church? If the church's mission is to make disciples, the evaluative request of the senior pastor is, Show me your disciples! Personal ministry and church ministry appraisal are necessary to refine any work for God. When you avoid honest, objective assessment, you are opting for comfort over courage and ministry mediocrity over meaningful ministry.

This final chapter will cover an objection, the purposes, the biblical basis, and the process of good evaluation.

An Objection to Evaluation

The idea of having someone evaluate you as a leader and pastor or evaluate the ministry of your church can be frightening and intimidating. Who in their right mind would invite personal or ministry critique? Some would object that we should not evaluate the church or its people because it is a spiritual not a secular undertaking. Only God should appraise a spiritual ministry such as a church. Who are we to judge God's anointed? I would counter that we must not allow fear and personal feelings of intimidation to get in the way of honest, objective feedback. That a ministry is a spiritual endeavor is more an argument for than against healthy critique.

Far too many churches have offered up ministry mediocrity under the guise of "It's a spiritual undertaking for God!" Scripture encourages God's people to give and do their best for him. Israel was to bring their best animals for sacrifice (Lev. 22:20–22; Num. 18:29–30). When they did not bring the best, it was an indication that their hearts had wandered from God (Mal. 1:6–8). In Ephesians 6:5–8 and Colossians 3:23–24 Paul teaches that God expects us to give only our best in our work. We are to do our work as if we are working for God. When Jesus turned the water into wine at Cana, it was the best wine (John 2:10). If God gave his best for us when he gave his Son (3:16), how can we not give our best for him?

Navigators are critiqued whether they like it or not. Every time they take their boat out, people are watching and judging their performance. They are asking, Is this person a sailing novice? Does he have any idea what he is doing? Would I want to sail with this person? Though unsettling at times, this critique can serve to make you a better sailor, depending on how you handle it.

Even if a church doesn't invite critique, critique will take place. It takes place every Sunday on an informal level. People are very discriminating. On the way home from church, a husband naturally asks his wife, "What did you think about the sermon?" Or, "Do you like the new Sunday school class?" Some go so far as to have roast pastor or roast church for Sunday lunch. Seeker-church pastors are quick to remind us that when lost people visit our services, they do so with a critical eye. If ministry evaluation takes place on an informal level, why not move it to a formal level so that we can benefit from it rather than be a victim of it?

Some Purposes of Evaluation

Not everyone is convinced of the need for personal and ministry appraisal. Those who are convinced of the need should have a rationale for careful, objective feedback. The purposes of evaluation demonstrate the need. At least seven purposes of evaluation exist.

Prompts Ministry Alignment

As we have seen, the values, mission, vision, and strategy of a church are very important, and many leaders need to spend more time thinking and rethinking them. However, it is critical to the organization that they move on to aligning their ministry with the values, mission, vision, and strategy. There is a wide gap between a ministry that has drafted statements of values, mission, and vision and a ministry that is visionary and mission directed. Accomplishing alignment bridges the gap, preserving the ministry's core values, reinforcing its vision, and catalyzing constant movement toward the mission.

In consulting with churches, I have discovered that those who are struggling most likely have a ministry alignment problem. A spiritually healthy, biblically balanced church has all these essential elements in alignment. When you are stuck and struggling, it is because one or more is out of alignment.

To accomplish realignment, get unstuck, and move toward success, we must first discover what is out of alignment, and this involves evaluation. Leaders and their people look around the church, talk to other people, gain feedback, and critique what is taking place. A sample evaluative question is, If this is our mission as a church, what are the obstacles that are in the way of accomplishing this mission? Where are we stuck? Where are we out of alignment? The General Ministry Troubleshooting Guide at the end of the introduction should help you with alignment issues. Once you know where you are stuck, go to the appropriate chapter in this book that deals with that issue.

Prioritizes Ministry Accomplishment

I referred earlier to the saying in some ministry circles—what gets evaluated gets done. We evaluate some things and do not evaluate others. What we choose to evaluate sends a message to our people. It says this is important, whereas something else is not as important, because it isn't evaluated. For example, if every Sunday several people in the congregation evaluate the worship service and the sermon, this signals to those involved—the worship team and the pastor—that these are high-priority areas of ministry. The result is that the worship team ensures that the worship service is the best it can be.

Encourages Ministry Appraisal

A third purpose for evaluation is ministry appraisal. People need to know the answer to the question, How am I doing? It is not unusual for a person to spend a year or more in ministry, thinking that all is at least okay or even good, only to discover, when he or she is abruptly dismissed, that things were not good. This is unfair to the person. He or she should have been warned.

Some churches respond to poor job performance in another way. They simply refuse to deal with individuals who do not have the abilities to do their job, who constantly show poor work habits, or who may be abusive. These churches feel that they are being nice to these people, or feel sorry for them, or worry about what others will think if they dismiss them. The problem with this thinking and practice is that it makes everyone else's job more difficult. Others have to pick up the slack or in some cases take unnecessary abuse. Long-term bending over backwards for and coddling of this kind of worker weakens, frustrates, and diminishes the entire organization.

A fair approach is regular ministry appraisal when a supervisor or mentor identifies problems and deficiencies as well as strengths. When this is done, the person knows where the problems lie and what he or she must do to improve. These areas are reviewed again at the next appraisal. If no progress is made or can be made, the church has proper grounds for dismissal, for discipline, or for shifting the individual to another ministry within the church.

Coaxes Ministry Affirmation

In my experience as a consultant, pastor of three churches, and interim preacher in numerous churches across several different denominations, I have learned that the people who make up the average church tend not to affirm those who are serving them well, whether on a pastoral or lay level. They appreciate excellence in ministry but are slow to affirm those who achieve it. They seem more critical than complimentary. I believe that they assume the individuals who serve well are aware of their accomplishments and the impact they are having. However, this is usually not the case. Proverbs 16:24 says, "Pleasant words are a honeycomb, sweet to the soul and healing to the bones." Who does not look forward to the day when the Savior will say, "Well done, good and faithful servant"?

I recall how in one church that I was consulting with, a lady who led the children's ministry looked at me and the others assembled and said, "It sure would be nice if on occasion someone said 'thank you' and showed a little gratitude for what we do. But that just does not happen around here."

How can we regularly affirm those in our churches who minister well? How can we make sure that it does not fall through the cracks—that it happens around here? The answer is regular evaluation. Most turn up their nose at evaluation because it frightens and even intimidates them. However, identifying problems is only one side of evaluation. The other side is affirmation. If we evaluate workers several times a year, then even when no one else affirms them, they will receive needed, valued affirmation during those times.

Emboldens Ministry Correction

Affirmation is one side of the appraisal coin; correction is the other. The word sounds ominous and conjures up images of difficult times, times of discipline and chastisement. Some hear the word *correction* and envision a harsh father with a strap in his hand. While correction frightens most of us, it is a much needed but most often neglected aspect of leadership and pastoral ministry. No one wants to do the correcting or chastising or be the object of them, but in a fallen world it has become a necessary fact of life. Scripture teaches that God corrects and even disciplines us for our good (Heb. 12:10).

When assessment takes place, we discover that all of us have areas that need correction. We have blind spots. They are things we may not perceive as problems, but they hamper our ministry efforts. These could include a distracting mannerism, tone of voice, or gesture that detracts from a pastor's message; an annoying sense of humor; or inappropriate clothing for the job. Most people can correct these after they are made aware of them, but it will not happen unless some kind of appraisal system is in place to call attention to the problem.

Correction is also needed when the sinful nature, as Paul calls it in Galatians 5:16–21, is allowed to dominate. The acts of the sinful nature indicate that one is not being led by the Spirit (vv. 17–18). This happens far too often in ministry. How do leaders know when the sinful nature predominates in their life? Hopefully someone will confront them. This is not likely to happen, however, unless a regular performance-appraisal system provides the opportunity to identify and deal with the problem.

An important aspect of correction is staff evaluation. When a staff person is not performing up to reasonable expectations, a superior needs to address the problem. State exactly what the problem is and what must be done to correct it. Also make yourself available to help the person. Reevaluate after a month or two. If the staff person shows no improvement, pursue this further. If the situation does not change, you may need to let the person go (fire him or her). However, the advantage of evaluation with correction is that the individual will likely resign before it gets to a dismissal. This is good for two reasons. First, people in the church who might find fault cannot, because the person resigned. Second, it is less likely anyone would attempt to sue you or the ministry if he or she has resigned.

Elicits Ministry Improvement

Inviting and accepting critique are difficult, but the result can and must be learning that leads to improvement. We must ask ourselves how we can get better. Obtaining objective feedback from someone who is more experienced and qualified in our area of ministry is invaluable for those who desire to be the best at what they do for the Savior.

As hard as it is to hear, we desperately need people in our life who will bravely and honestly tell us when something is not working. This is how we get better at what we do. If we choose to immerse ourselves in a comfortable, nonconfrontational ministry cocoon, we will likely create ministry that is much less than it could be for Christ. We need people—hopefully but not necessarily loving people—who provide an objective, informed perspective of what we are attempting for Christ.

I cannot emphasize enough the importance of good ministry appraisal. The benefits far outweigh the disadvantages. However, some liabilities do exist, and you must watch for these. First, evaluation has the potential to terrify volunteers, especially those in up-front positions. The thought that someone is critiquing them is often unnerving. So initially cut them some slack, and make sure they understand why you do evaluation. Second, in situations where you ask someone to evaluate you, you are giving that person a certain amount of authority over you—be careful whom you choose. Third, too much evaluation can create an environment of constant criticism in the church. Be careful of becoming more critical in a negative sense than you were before you started the evaluation process. Fourth, an overemphasis on assessment can destroy enthusiasm, creativity, and spontaneity in the ministry.[1]

Promotes Ministry Change

There, I said it—the C word. However, I do not apologize for using it. I argue that a church that does not change is out of the will of God. This is because Christianity from start to finish is all about change or spiritual transformation. You read this in chapters 2 and 9 where I discussed spiritual formation, growth, and maturity.

To get better at what we do and to grow spiritually, we must change. In some churches this will require deep change. These churches have changed very little in the last twenty to thirty years, and extensive change is needed if they are to survive. However, I would question the effort it would take, because the change itself would probably cause their demise.

The Purposes of Evaluation
Prompts ministry alignment
Prioritizes ministry accomplishment
Encourages ministry appraisal
Coaxes ministry affirmation
Emboldens ministry correction
Elicits ministry improvement
Promotes ministry change

The key is incremental change, or what I referred to earlier as "tweak change." You accomplish tweak change through regular, timely evaluation, tweaking the ministry here and there. At its most basic level, each week you ask, How can I do it better next time? After a year or more, you will discover that you are not the same church. You are a spiritually stronger church, and few will be aware of the changes.

What the Bible Teaches about Evaluation

The purposes of evaluation are convincing. However, we must ask, Is evaluation biblical? We do not have to find a biblical reference before we pursue some activity such as evaluation, so the question is, Does it contradict Scripture? The answer for evaluation is no, it does not. Does the Bible address the practice of evaluation? The answer is yes, it does, as you will see in the following.

Evaluation is not foreign to the Scriptures. While no examples exist in the New Testament of a church passing out some kind of performance appraisal, that does not mean that Christians did not appraise their people and ministries, nor does it mean that we do not have the freedom to do so.[2] Luke regularly supplies us with progress reports and church updates in Acts 2:41, 47; 4:4; 5:14; 6:1, 7; 9:31, 35, 42; 11:21, 24; 14:1, 21; 16:5; and 17:12. In 1 Timothy 3:1–13 Paul gives the qualifications for deacons and elders. That means that some kind of evaluation was made, or such qualifications would not have made sense. In 1 Corinthians 11:28 Paul preached healthy self-examination to the members of the church at Corinth. He encouraged them to examine themselves before taking the Lord's Supper. This would result in the proper proclaiming of the Lord's death (v. 26) and preclude judgment (vv. 29–32). Again, in 2 Corinthians 13:5–6 he tells the people of the church to examine and test themselves to see whether they are in the faith. To fail such a test would have been a calamity. But he seems to indicate that not to test oneself would be an even greater calamity. Then in Revelation 2–3 God evaluates six of his churches, looking for what they are doing well and not so well. Just as an unwillingness to measure one's spiritual condition makes spiritual growth nearly impossible, so failure to measure a church's effectiveness makes its growth nearly impossible.

Evaluation Process
Step 1. Assign a leader over the process
Step 2. Determine whom you will evaluate
Step 3. Determine what you will evaluate

The Process of Evaluation

Now that we understand the purposes and importance of evaluation, we need to ask, What is the process of evaluation? There are three steps: assign a leader over the process, determine whom you will evaluate, and decide what you will evaluate.

Step 1. Assign a Leader Over the Process

It is important to put a competent leader in charge of the evaluation process. Someone has to be responsible for evaluation, or like so many other good things in ministry, it will not happen. In a small church this often is the pastor. I suggest, however, that he find a gifted, talented layperson who can take full responsibility for the appraisal process and then report the findings to the pastor. People who can do this exist in practically every ministry. They are not always aware of their abilities in the area of appraisal or may not be aware that the church needs their help. Many people experience evaluation and review in their job, and some of these, no doubt, may be responsible for doing it. Find these people, train them to exercise this ministry in the church, and then release them to ministry.

In larger churches a pastor, an executive pastor, an administrative pastor, or an administrative staff person could take responsibility for the evaluation program. Many of the new-paradigm churches have begun to recruit and use pastors for assessment. Using titles such as pastor of evaluation and assessment or pastor of involvement, these people serve in a twofold capacity. First, they help laypeople discover their divine designs and then help them use those designs in service to God. Second, they are responsible for performance appraisal.

Step 2. Determine Whom You Will Evaluate

Once a staff or lay leader of the process is in place, he or she will need to work with others—the staff in particular—in determining which people and what ministries will be evaluated. I call the people the "ministers" and refer to what they accomplish as "ministries." I will focus here on the ministers. There are several questions for you to answer before evaluating the ministers: Who are the ministers? Who evaluates them? How do they evaluate them? How often do they evaluate them?

WHO ARE THE MINISTERS?

The ministers of the church are the members of any boards, pastoral and administrative staff, lay ministry leaders, and full- and part-time workers in each ministry area. I use the term *ministers* to refer to all of these people—not just those who have been ordained or minister full time. At my last pastorate we attempted to assess all of these people at some time during the year. It is important to apprise people of this when they first agree to be involved in some way on the ministry team. It was not the first thing I mentioned, but I did cover this when we recruited individuals for service.

Because appraisal can be most intimidating to people, especially volunteer laymen and laywomen, I suggest that the pastor or senior pastor take some time with the topic of evaluation so the people fully understand its importance and process. Make it the occasional topic of a sermon. Explain its purpose and benefits when you give and receive evaluation. I tried to sell our people on evaluation so that they believed in it and wanted to be evaluated. I wanted it to be a positive, growing experience for them. Though all of us feel varying degrees of intimidation before an appraisal, if we are doing our jobs as unto the Lord, then the actual appraisal will turn out to be a time of affirmation more than correction. We should find out more about what we are doing well than about what we are not doing well.

WHO EVALUATES THE MINISTERS?

People are the gist of any appraisal system, doing evaluation and being evaluated. The people who do the evaluation can be divided into two groups: the insiders and the outsiders.

The Insiders

The *insiders* are the ministry constituents. They are the people who have shown a long-term interest in the church. They consist primarily of the ministry's members and regular attenders.

The members are the key to the church's present and future. They are the staff, boards, and laypeople who believe in and have committed themselves to the ministry through their membership. They have bought into the church's values, mission, vision, and strategy. At my last church the board critiqued themselves and others. Naturally the staff was heavily involved in assessment. They and the board were the engines that drove all assessment. They set the example. If they are not willing to critique and be critiqued, we cannot expect others to do what they will not do.

Every church also has a number of regular attenders. They are people who have not joined for various reasons. Some, for example, are not sure if they agree with the church's core concepts. Others are slow to commit because they shy away from commitments in general or they have been abused in other churches and need a little time and space before coming on board.

I believe that we should ask them to evaluate the ministry as well. They may view the church in a totally different light than the members do. Often members are blind to certain inadequacies that others see clearly. For example, nonmembers may like the pastor's sermons but not want to join a church that does not maintain its facilities. However, the members have become accustomed to poor facilities and no longer notice that they are in such poor condition.

We expect others in leadership positions to appraise themselves and the ministries they lead. The person who leads the nursery ministry, for example, is responsible for personal and departmental critique. The person who leads the youth ministry, staff or otherwise, is responsible to critique himself or herself and those who minister in the youth area.

You could also invite other members and nonmembers to critique your ministry. Provide communication cards in the worship service so that your people can easily communicate with you. These cards provide a readily accessible vehicle for feedback of any sort. Periodically ask certain members and nonmembers to evaluate the worship services or the sermons.

Another excellent approach to assessment is to have those who are over you, under you, and beside you on the organizational chart evaluate you. This is known as 360-degree evaluation.

The Outsiders

The *outsiders* are the church's visitors. They consist of several different kinds of people. Some are churched Christians who have been active in other churches in the area, but for some reason they are looking for a new church home. Others are unchurched people, both Christians and non-Christians.

A phenomenon of the last half of the twentieth century and early in the twenty-first century has been the growth in the number of unchurched people across North America as well as much of Europe. In the United States the number of unchurched ranges from 60 to as high as 80 or 90 percent of the population. The South has the highest number of churched people, and the Northwest and some portions of the Northeast have the lowest number. In Europe the number of unchurched people is even higher. When I lived and ministered in Amsterdam (once considered the crown jewel of the Reformation), for example, Christians in that city estimated the unchurched to be 97.5 percent of the population.

Some churches are not only aware of unchurched people but have designed their strategies to include reaching out to the unchurched, as well as addressing the needs of the churched. That was a part of our strategy and mission at my last church. We found that when unchurched people attended, they came to the morning worship service. This was because many prefer anonymity, and the worship service provided that.

Since some churches seek to reach the unchurched, they would be wise to ask for their evaluation of the church and all that it does. We need to know if we are doing something that needlessly turns lost people off to spiritual things. We must never compromise the gospel. If unchurched lost people are going to stumble over anything, we want it to be the gospel (1 Cor. 1:23) and not a matter of church culture. The only way we can know this is to ask them to appraise what we are doing.

How Do They Evaluate the Ministers?

There are a number of ways that the outsiders and the insiders in particular can evaluate the church's ministers. Use one or a combination of the following evaluation tools.

Job Descriptions

The first is using the job or ministry descriptions. At my last pastorate, we took time with these and worked hard on them so that our people knew precisely what our expectations were. We used them for recruitment and guidance in ministry and also for evaluation. In addition, we took each job description and converted it into an appraisal questionnaire. The ministry description for our director of biblical instruction and his ministry appraisal are the third and fourth items in appendix N. The fifth item in appendix N is the general appraisal of the director of biblical instruction. It asks the evaluator to appraise such things as the director's job knowledge, quality of work, productivity, character, and other areas pertinent to the position. Every person evaluated is involved in designing his or her evaluation questionnaire. This has relieved much of the anxiety for some over the appraisal process.

Strengths and Weaknesses Audit

A strengths and weaknesses audit is also useful. This is the model the Lord used when evaluating the seven churches in Revelation 2–3. You ask the evaluator to list the minister's strengths followed by his or her weaknesses. You could also include with these some suggestions for improvement.

The minister's character, competence, and chemistry should also be evaluated. A person's competence relates to how well he or she is accomplishing the ministry tasks. Chemistry refers to relational fit. A question could be, for example, Does the person relate well emotionally to the other staff?

360-Degree Evaluation

Finally, one of the best ways is to use the 360-degree approach mentioned above.

How Often Are Ministers Evaluated?

Theoretically you would often evaluate your ministers formally throughout the year. Reality and the ministry load dictate that you do it once a year. I agree, however, with W. Edwards Deming, the patron saint of the Total Quality Revolution, who has argued that in the corporate world if managers had to go a whole year before evaluating employees, a review would be ineffective. Instead, he believed evaluation needs to be an ongoing, not merely a yearly, process. For example, workers need immediate feedback when they do something well and when they do something poorly. Waiting a year to tell them is too long. This is unofficial evaluation that is as valuable as official evaluation and must be ongoing.

If a minister receives a poor evaluation, you will want to evaluate this person often. After the initial evaluation that identifies a significant problem or problems, I would suggest the following. First, make sure that the individual understands precisely what the problem is. Second, put in place a plan for improvement. Ask what the minister and/or the church can do to help correct the problem. Finally, arrange to meet with him or her again in a reasonable amount of time—three to six months later—to chart progress. Should this person not improve for whatever reason, chances are good that he or she will resign and move on to a more suitable situation. As I said earlier, this is a win-win situation for both the person and the church. The person has the opportunity to find a place for more effective minstry that leads to a sense of ministry fulfillment and greater satisfaction. The church does not have to incur the wrath of those in the church who were ministered to by this person. It also does not have to fire the individual and thus risk potential litigation.

Step 3. Determine What You Will Evaluate

You will need to evaluate the ministries along with the ministers. We need to evaluate not only our people but also what they produce in ministry—their ministry fruit (John 15:16). There are several questions to ask as you set up your evaluation process for ministries.

WHO EVALUATES THE MINISTRIES?

Ministry evaluators come primarily from the staff and the congregation. The staff must regularly evaluate the ministries, especially the ones for which they are responsible. Thus the senior pastor will evaluate the overall ministry of the church in general as well as his areas of expertise and personal responsibility in particular, such as his preaching. A staff person in charge of biblical instruction is responsible for evaluating the biblical instruction ministry, and so on.

The congregation may be invited to evaluate the ministries as well as the staff who are responsible for them. They could use a congregational survey, mentioned below. This way the staff can know how the congregation—those who are the recipients of the ministries—is being helped or hindered in its growth toward maturity.

HOW WILL THEY EVALUATE THE MINISTRIES?

There are at least four ways to evaluate the church's ministries—evaluate the primary and secondary ministries, count heads, and conduct a congregational survey. In addition, you may develop special forms to evaluate some specific area where you believe some feedback is helpful or vital.

1. *Evaluate the primary and secondary ministries.* In chapter 9 I addressed the church's primary and secondary ministries. You will recall that the primary activities are those ministry means that you implemented or were already in place that directly accomplish the characteristics of maturity (the ministry ends). Some examples would be a worship service (including preaching), a Sunday school, a small group ministry, and so on. These you placed in as-similation order along the vertical axis (from top to bottom) on the maturity matrix. The secondary ministries are those ministry means that indirectly accomplish and support the characteristics, such as a men's Bible study, support groups for those struggling with addictions, Vacation Bible School, and so on.

   One way to evaluate activities is to set up a specific evaluation format. There are numerous possibilities. I would include in such an evaluation a question asking if the ministry activity is accomplishing its purpose. (Is it helping people incorporate a characteristic of maturity into their lives, which in turn helps the church accomplish its mission and vision?) I would also evaluate the ministry's strengths and weaknesses. And I would ask the people who are part of the ministry to evaluate its overall effectiveness.

2. *Count heads.* One method used in the first-century church was counting heads. According to Acts 2:41 and 4:4, Luke was counting heads. The reason was that he was updating the church regarding how they were doing spiri-tually, and counting heads should reflect that. To count heads each week, someone must literally count heads and keep good records. This shouldn't be too difficult.

   This is simply monitoring attendance of the primary ministries. For ex-ample, some church's have three primary ministries—a worship-preaching session, a Bible study or Sunday school, and a small group. Simply count the number of people in attendance at these three events. Next, review the figures and compare them to the prior weeks and even the prior year. Are the numbers up or down or the same? And what needs to be done if they are down? What changes, if any, are needed?

3. *Conduct a congregational survey.* You will recall that I encouraged the use of congregational surveys in chapter 9 (p. 207). Please turn to that portion of the chapter and quickly review the information. I consider evaluating your primary and secondary ministries and counting heads as mandatory ways for accom-plishing good evaluation. Conducting a congregational survey, though optional, is beneficial, mainly because it involves the congregation in the process.

4. *Evaluate specific areas of ministry interest.* At my last church we wanted to know how people—especially visitors—felt about the morning worship

service, so we designed a special form that has undergone some revision since the original (the first item in appendix N). We also developed a form for our members and regular attenders (second item in appendix N). We believed that if our various ministries were to improve and bring honor to the Savior, it was imperative that we place them under the microscope of appraisal.

How Often Will They Evaluate the Ministries?

I suggest that you use the congregational survey semiannually or annually. And I would evaluate the primary ministries at least monthly and count heads weekly. Should serious problems surface as the result of a ministry evaluation, you should place that ministry on "evaluative probation" and work with the leader of the ministry to correct the problem.

Questions for Reflection, Discussion, and Application

1. Are your present operating ministry practices, strategies, structures, and systems in alignment with your core values, mission, and vision? How do you know? Why or why not? Do you have some type of formal ministry appraisal currently in place? If yes, what is it? If no, would one enhance the accomplishment of your ministry?

2. What are your personal feelings about having someone evaluate you and the ministry you lead? Why do you feel this way? Will your feelings encourage or discourage the implementation of a performance appraisal system?

3. Do people in your ministry know how they are doing? Do you know how you are doing? Does the church regularly affirm its people? If yes, how? If no, why not? Does the church regularly correct its people? If yes, how? If no, why not? Does your ministry elicit improvement from your members? If yes, how? If no, why not?

4. Having read this chapter and the section on the purposes of evaluation, are you convinced of the need for appraisal in your ministry? Why or why not? Will you follow through and implement an appraisal process in your ministry? Why or why not?

5. Who are the people who might do evaluation? Do you have enough people? Are they insiders, outsiders, or both? Why would you want outsiders, especially lost people, to appraise your ministry or certain parts of it?

6. Make a list of whom and what you would like to see evaluated in your ministry. Did you include yourself? Why or why not? Are you attempting to appraise too much or too little? What are the disadvantages of either extreme?

7. Who would be the best person to take responsibility for performance appraisal? Why? Would some of the appraisal forms in appendix N help you design your own forms?

8. Who will evaluate each team member? Will you attempt to implement a 360-degree evaluation system? Why or why not? Who will review each evaluation with the person evaluated? Are they the best or only people available?

9. Go back to the list you made in question 6 above. How often will you evaluate each person and product? Is it often enough to make evaluation worthwhile? Is it too frequent and thus unrealistic?

Appendix A

Readiness for Change Inventory

Directions: Each item below is a key element that will help you evaluate your church's readiness for change. Strive for objectivity—involve others (including outsiders) in the evaluation process. Circle the number that most accurately rates your church.

1. **Leadership.** The pastor and the church board (official leadership) are favorable toward and directly responsible for change. Also, any influential persons (unofficial leadership: the church patriarch, a respected member, etc.) are for change—score 5. If moderately so—score 3. Only the secondary level of leadership (staff other than the pastor and board, Sunday school teachers, etc.) is for change, while unofficial leadership opposes it—score 1.

    5   3   1

2. **Vision.** The pastor and the board have a single, clear vision of a significant future that looks different from the present. The pastor is able to mobilize others (staff, boards, and the congregation) for action—score 5. The pastor but not the board envisions a different direction for the church— score 3. The pastor and board have not thought about a vision, and they do not believe that it is important—score 1.

    5   3   1

3. **Values.** The church's philosophy of ministry (its core values) includes a preference for innovation

and creativity. Though proven forms, methods, and techniques are not quickly discarded, the church is more concerned with the effectiveness of its ministries than with adherence to traditions—score 5. If moderately so—score 3. The church's ministry forms and techniques have changed little over the years, while its ministry effectiveness has diminished—score 1.

    5   3   1

4. **Motivation.** The pastor and the board have a strong sense of urgency for change that is shared by the congregation. The congregational culture emphasizes the need for constant improvement—score 3. The pastor and/or the board (most of whom have been in their positions for many years) along with the congregation are bound by long-standing traditions that are change resistant and discourage risk taking—score 1. If somewhere between—score 2.

    3   2   1

5. **Organizational Context.** How does the change effort affect the other programs in the church (Christian education, worship, missions, etc.)? If the individuals in charge are all working together for improvement and innovation—score 3. If only some are—score 2. If many are opposed to change and/or are in conflict with one another over change—score 1.

    3   2   1

6. ***Processes/Functions.*** Major changes in a church almost always require redesigning processes and functions in all the ministries of the church, such as Christian education and church worship. If most in charge of these areas are open to change—score 3. If only some—score 2. If they are turf protectors or if they put their areas of ministry ahead of the church as a whole—score 1.

3   2   1

7. ***Ministry Awareness.*** Does the leadership of your church keep up with what is taking place in the innovative evangelical churches in the community and across America in terms of ministry and out-reach effectiveness? Does the leadership objectively compare the church's ministry with that of churches very similar to it? If the answer is yes—score 3. If the answer is sometimes—score 2. If no—score 1.

3   2   1

8. ***Community Focus.*** Does the church know and understand the people in the community—their needs, hopes, aspirations? Does it stay in direct contact with them? Does it regularly seek to reach them? If the answer is yes—score 3. If moderately so—score 2. If the church is not in touch with its community and focuses on itself—score 1.

3   2   1

9. ***Evaluation.*** Does the church regularly evaluate its ministries? Does it evaluate its ministries in light of its vision and goals? Are these ministries regularly adjusted in response to the evaluations? If all of this takes place—score 3. If some takes place—score 2. If none—score 1.

3   2   1

10. ***Rewards.*** Change is easier if the leaders and those involved in ministry are rewarded in some way for taking risks and looking for new solutions to their ministry problems. Rewarding ministry teams is more effective than rewarding solo performances. If your church gives rewards—score 3. If sometimes—score 2. If your church rewards the status quo and has only a maintenance mentality—score 1.

3   2   1

11. ***Organizational Structure.*** The best situation is a flexible church where change is well received and takes place periodically, not every day. If this is true of your church—score 3. If your church is very rigid

in its structure and either has changed very little in the last five years or has experienced several futile attempts at change to no avail—score 1. If between—score 2.

3   2   1

12. ***Communication.*** Does your church have a variety of means for two-way communication? Do most people understand and use it, and does it reach all levels of the congregation? If all of this is true—score 3. If only moderately true—score 2. If communication is poor, primarily one-way and from the top down—score 1.

3   2   1

13. ***Organizational Hierarchy.*** Is your church decentralized (there are few if any levels of leadership between the congregation and the pastor or the board)? If so—score 3. If there are people on staff levels or boards/committees who come between the congregation and the pastor or the board, then more potential exists for them to block essential change—score 1. If between—score 2.

3   2   1

14. ***Prior Change.*** Churches will most readily adapt to change if they have successfully implemented major changes in the recent past. If this is true of your church—score 3. If some change has taken place—score 2. If no one can remember the last time the church changed or if such efforts at change failed or left people angry and resentful—score 1.

3   2   1

15. ***Morale.*** Do the church staff and volunteers enjoy the church and take responsibility for their ministries? Do they trust the pastor and/or the board? If so—score 3. If moderately so—score 2. Do few people volunteer, and are there signs of low team spirit? Is there mistrust between leaders and followers and between the various ministries? If so—score 1.

3   2   1

16. ***Innovation.*** The church tries new things. People feel free to implement new ideas on a consistent basis. People have the freedom to make choices and solve problems regarding their ministries. If this describes your church—score 3. If this is somewhat true—score 2. If ministries are en-snared in bureaucratic red tape and if permission

from "on high" must be obtained before anything happens—score 1.

3   2   1

17. **Decision Making.** Does the church leadership listen carefully to a wide variety of suggestions from all the congregation? After it has gathered the appropriate information, does it make decisions quickly? If so—score 3. If moderately so—score 2. Does the leadership listen only to a select few and take forever to make a decision? Is there lots of conflict during the process, and after a decision is made, is there confusion and turmoil?—score 1.

3   2   1

Total score: _____

If your score is:

47–57: The chances are good that you (the senior pastor or key leader) may implement change, especially if your scores are high on items 1–3.

28–46: Change may take place but with varying success. Chances increase with higher scores on items 1–3. Note areas with low scores and focus on improvement before attempting change on a large scale.

17–27: Change will likely not take place. Note areas with low scores and attempt to improve them if possible. Consider starting a new church and implement your ideas in a more change-friendly context.

Appendix B

Leader-Manager Audit

Directions: As you take this audit, note that there are no correct or incorrect answers. Read each statement quickly and circle the item (A or B) that *best* represents your ministry role. Do not spend too much time on any question; instead, go with your initial impulse.

1. In my approach to change, I . . .
   A) Favor change B) Favor predictability and order

2. In leading an organization or ministry, I . . .
   A) Do the right things B) Do things right

3. When viewing a job or ministry, I see . . .
   A) The whole B) The parts

4. My general outlook on life and ministry is . . .
   A) Optimistic B) Realistic

5. In my job or ministry, I operate on the basis of . . .
   A) Faith B) Facts

6. In my role, I might be described as . . .
   A) An influencer B) A coordinator

7. When I view my job or ministry, I think in terms of . . .
   A) Opportunity B) Accomplishment

8. In my work or ministry, I seek . . .
   A) Effectiveness B) Efficiency

9. In my ministry, I would describe myself as a . . .
   A) Visionary B) Realist

10. In my work and/or ministry, my focus is on . . .
    A) Ideas B) Functions

11. In my work or ministry, I can be counted on to provide . . .
    A) Direction B) Organization

12. In my leadership role, I see myself as . . .
    A) A persuader B) An implementer

13. In my job or ministry, I would describe myself as a . . .
    A) Risk-taker B) Stabilizer

14. When communicating to a group, people say that I speak . . .
    A) Persuasively B) Informationally

15. One of my desires for my job or ministry is to see . . .
    A) Growth B) Harmony

16. In my ministry at the church, I . . .
    A) Take risks B) Exercise caution

316

17. I have the spiritual gift(s) of . . .
    A) Leadership   B) Administration

18. In my work and ministry, I am . . .
    A) Proactive   B) Responsive

19. One of my strengths is . . .
    A) Motivating people B) Organizing people

20. I'm best at . . .
    A) Setting direction   B) Solving problems

Instructions for scoring:

1. Total the number of **A**s that you circled: _____.

2. Total the number of **B**s that you circled: _____.

3. The highest score above represents your ministry role. If you circled more **A**s, your role is that of a leader. If you circled more **B**s, your role is that of a manager or administrator. Which are you?_____

Name: _____

Position and/or ministry in the church:_____

_____

_____

Appendix C

Covenant of Commitment

Listed below are the primary expectations for the strategic planning team. Please read them and sign at the bottom with the appropriate date. (See Nehemiah 9:38.)

To the best of my ability with the help of my Savior, I commit to the following:

1. To pray for the church, the team, and the process
2. To be a positive participant who will enthusiastically support the process
3. To be a team player (not necessarily a "yes" person)
4. To support team consensus decisions even when I don't agree
5. To be at the meetings as much as possible
6. To participate in the group processes, such as storyboarding
7. To keep confidential matters confidential
8. To commit to the total time necessary for the process (six to nine months)
9. To use my gifts and abilities to support and enhance the process
10. To be involved in the development and implementation phases
11. To be prepared for each team session (reading and other assignments)
12. To proactively promote the work of the team with the congregation

Signature:

Date:

Comments: _____

_____

_____

_____

_____

Appendix D

Strategic Development Worksheet

Directions: The following is a list of twelve ministry objectives along with their development teams that review the strategic planning process. (Note that the last two objectives are optional.) For each of the objectives do the following seven things.

1. Assign each objective to a leader/champion who will recruit a team from the strategic leadership team (SLT) and the congregation for its development.
2. Note that each objective lists a number of measurable goals that when accomplished will form your strategy for each ministry objective. They will also serve to keep you on track and focused on your ministry tasks.
3. Each team needs to prioritize their goals and look for potential "short-term wins."
4. Determine who on the team will work through and develop each goal.
5. Observe the deadline (date) for the completion of the goals.
6. You may add or subtract goals (be sure to clear this with the Lead Development Team).
7. Use the space in front of each goal to check off completed goals and/or to prioritize the goals.

Objective 1: What: Recruit a lead development team and begin the process. (Who: Lead Development Team [LDT]. When: completion date _____).

Team leader: _____
Team members:_____

____ Recruit a leader/champion (could be a lay leader, staff person, or the senior pastor) over the entire development process.

____ The leader will recruit an assistant leader and several other team members from the SLT and congregation to assist him/her.

____ Assist the pastor or person responsible for recruiting the other team leaders who, in turn, will recruit their team persons.

____ Exercise general oversight over the development process.

____ Create an overall process time line and use it to coordinate the various completion dates, etc. (We recommend that you use a Gantt chart as your time line.)

____ Regularly monitor and update the time line.

____ Regularly communicate with each team and its leader (track progress, address problems, etc.).

____ Regularly assess the overall progress (the "big picture") of the development process and keep the pastor informed of the same.

___ "Troubleshoot" when necessary.

___ Schedule and conduct the MIR (monthly implementation review) meetings.

___ Set up and monitor a strategic planning website.

___ Assemble and edit the final draft of the strategic plan (if necessary).

___ Regularly evaluate and seek to improve the overall development process.

Objective 2: What: Pray for the development process (Who: Intercessory Prayer Development Team. When: completion date _____).

Team leader: _____
Team members:_____

___ Determine if such a prayer team already exists.

___ Pray specifically for the SLT while it is meeting, usually Friday evenings and Saturday mornings.

___ Pray for the senior pastor, staff, and SLT as they're involved in the process.

___ Pray for the various development teams and their leaders.

___ Pray for the congregation to accept and be involved in the process.

Objective 3: What: Design a congregational communication plan (Who: Congregational Communication Development Team. When: completion date _____).

Team leader: _____
Team members:_____

___ Draft a core values statement (credo).

___ Decide how you will best communicate in particular your values and mission to the congregation (see "best practices" below).

___ Regularly remind the pastor to communicate the mission and vision to the congregation.

___ Investigate and evaluate how the church currently communicates.

___ Apply the Communication Tool to your board meetings, staff meetings, team ministries, etc. The Communication Tool asks eight questions: what needs to be communicated, by whom, to whom, where, when, how, how often, and why?

___ Recruit a lay or staff person who clears and coordinates what gets communicated publically (often this is the senior pastor or chairman of the board).

___ Determine some "best practices" for communication (website, bulletin board, bulletins, newsletters, emails, sermons, a magazine, announcements, annual congregational survey, new members class, etc.).

___ Investigate other churches in your area that are known for good communication and find out what they are doing that would help you.

___ Decide how best to communicate with those outside the church and design a marketing strategy to get your message to them.

___ Draft the overall church vision statement.

___ Decide along with the senior pastor how you will best communicate your vision in particular to the congregation.

___ Regularly evaluate and improve your communication process.

Objective 4: What: Develop a strategy to reach your community (Who: Community Outreach Development Team. When: completion date _____).

Team leader: _____
Team members:_____

___ Attend the instructional meeting led by the staff or a consultant from The Malphurs Group (TMG).

___ Identify your Jerusalem (Acts 1:8)—set "soft" community boundaries.

___ Discover who lives in your community—demographics and psychographics (Community Report). Consider interviewing some of the people who are in your community.

___ Keep abreast of your community's demographics and psychographics.

___ Identify the issues your community struggles with and how your church will address them.

___ Set a challenging goal (each one reach one each year, for example).

___ Identify some redemptive, community-specific ministries (key initial and long-term ministries that would help you reach your community).

___ Discover your congregation's self-identity—how you view yourselves (missionaries, disciples, servants, witnesses, evangelists, members, etc.).

___ Provide evangelistic training for the congregation (a premier evangelistic training course, a gospel presentation, style of evangelism, etc.).

___ Identify other development teams you need to communicate with and meet or somehow connect with them periodically.

___ Develop a one-paragraph vision statement for community outreach.

___ Cast a compelling vision (once the final vision has been developed).

___ Develop a plan to plant church-planting churches in your Jerusalem (Acts 1:8).

___ When you have addressed most if not all these goals, you'll have your strategy to accomplish community outreach. Draft a statement that will capture and communicate this strategy for community outreach, and present it to the LDT or appropriate person(s) (pastor, executive pastor, SLT, board, etc.) for evaluation, input, and final approval.

___ Regularly evaluate and update long term your community outreach strategy.

Objective 5: What: Develop your strategy to make disciples (Who: Disciple-Making Development Team. When: completion date _____).

Team leader: _____

Team members:_____

___ Attend the instructional meeting led by the staff or a TMG consultant.

___ Identify the characteristics of a mature disciple (e.g., worship, fellowship, biblical instruction, evangelism, and service).

___ Identify your primary ministries—"pathway for making disciples": preaching/worship service, Bible study, small groups, etc.).

___ Determine which characteristics are accomplished currently by each primary ministry and which aren't.

___ Evaluate and tweak or develop the primary ministries (your "disciple-making pathway"). (If you have time, do the same with the secondary ministries.)

___ Create or embrace a figure or image to communicate your disciple-making strategy.

___ Decide how you'll measure or evaluate progress (count heads, etc.).

___ Identify other development teams you need to communicate with. Meet or somehow connect with them periodically.

___ Develop a one-paragraph vision statement for making disciples.

___ When you have addressed most if not all these goals, you'll have your strategy to accomplish disciple making. Draft a statement that will capture the church's strategy for making disciples, and present it to the LDT or appropriate person(s) (pastor, executive pastor, SLT, board, etc.) for evaluation, input, and final approval.

___ Regularly evaluate and update long term your disciple-making strategy.

Objective 6: What: Develop a strategy to mobilize your congregation (Who: Mobilization Development Team. When: completion date _____).

Team leader: _____
Team members:_____

___ Attend the instructional meeting led by the staff or TMG consultant.

___ Articulate and communicate to all the importance of mobilizing your congregation (work with the Communication Development Team).

___ Identify the mobilization problem (not enough workers).

___ Determine or guess what percent of your congregation is mobilized.

___ Set a goal for the percent of the congregation you want to be mobilized.

___ Embrace and communicate the biblical solution for mobilization.

___ Understand and be able to explain the divine design concept.

___ Develop and put in place a three-phase mobilization process: discovery, consulting, and placement or something similar.

___ Train ministry leaders (children, youth, adults, etc.) in the mobilization process so they understand their role in the particular ministry (draft job descriptions, etc.).

___ Decide on the appropriate mobilization tools (gifts inventory, passion audit, temperament tool, etc.). Assess costs for these tools.

___ Develop a one-paragraph statement that captures and communicates your vision for church mobilization.

___ Identify other development teams you need to communicate with. Meet or somehow connect with them periodically.

___ When you have addressed most if not all these goals, you'll have your strategy to mobilize your congregation. Draft a paper that will capture the church's strategy for mobilizing its people, and present it to the LDT and appropriate person(s) (pastor, executive pastor, SLT, board, etc.) for evaluation, input, and final approval.

___ Regularly evaluate and update long term your congregational mobilization strategy.

Objective 7: What: Develop a strategy to build a staff team (Who: Staffing Development Team. When: completion date _____.)

Team leader: _____
Team members:_____

___ Attend the instructional meeting led by the staff or TMG consultant.

___ Determine how many staff you should have (1 for every 150 in worship).

___ Address whether you have a balanced staff (functional and age-specific staff).

___ See that all ministry staff have a job/ministry description.

___ Determine if staff will primarily train lay leaders for ministry.

___ Determine if staff and/or trained lay leaders will equip laypersons for ministry.

___ Develop a staff organizational chart.

___ Create a staffing blueprint for recruiting future staff.

___ Address staff deployment (are staff in the right positions?).

___ Design and conduct a staff evaluation process.

___ Evaluate staff chemistry.

___ Develop a one-paragraph vision statement for building staff.

___ Identify other development teams you need to communicate with. Meet or somehow connect with them periodically.

___ When you have addressed most if not all these goals, you'll have your strategy to build your staff. Draft a paper that will capture the church's strategy for building its staff, and present it to the LDT or appropriate person(s) (pastor, executive pastor, SLT, board, etc.) for evaluation, input, and final approval.

___ Regularly evaluate and update long term your staff building strategy.

Objective 8: What: Develop a strategy to determine your best ministry setting (Who: Setting [location and facilities] Development Team. When: completion date _____).

Team leader: _____
Team members:_____

___ Attend the instructional meeting led by the staff or TMG consultant.

___ Determine how best to address your location issues.

___ Draft a church campus master plan (architect).

___ Evaluate the church's "visitor friendliness" and propose corrections.

___ Evaluate the church's cleanliness and propose corrections.

___ Evaluate whether facilities are functional and propose corrections.

___ Identify any facility "blind spots" and propose corrections.

___ Evaluate current parking and propose corrections.

___ Evaluate seating capacity (use the 80–90% rule) and propose corrections.

___ Evaluate acreage (use 1 acre per 100 people) and propose corrections.

___ Address whether or not the church should consider a relocation.

___ Identify other development teams you need to communicate with. Meet or somehow connect with them periodically.

___ Develop a one-paragraph vision statement for setting.

___ When you have addressed most if not all these goals, you'll have your strategy to best determine your ministry setting. Draft a statement that will capture the church's strategy for determining its best ministry setting, and present it to the LDT or appropriate person(s) (pastor, executive pastor, SLT, board, etc.) for evaluation, input, and final approval.

___ Regularly evaluate and update long term your setting for ministry strategy.

Objective 9: What: Develop a strategy to evaluate and raise significant finances for ministry (Who: Finances/Stewardship Development Team. When: completion date _____).

Team leader: _____
Team members:_____

___ Attend the instructional meeting led by the staff or TMG consultant.

___ Determine who will lead the church in the area of stewardship or finances.

___ Reconstruct the budget around the four major allocation areas (missions and evangelism, staff, ministries, and facilities).

___ Determine the proper allocation (percentage) of funds to each area.

___ Monitor and assess your current giving.

___ Decide how you'll raise funding for ministry (review chap. 12, pp. 255–82).

___ Consider alternative sources for funding (capital campaigns, trusts, etc.).

___ Develop a one-paragraph vision statement for your stewardship ministry.

___ Identify other development teams and/or committees you need to communicate with. Meet or somehow connect with them periodically.

___ When you have addressed most if not all these goals, you'll have your strategy to evaluate and raise finances for your church. Draft a statement that will capture the church's strategy for fund-raising and present it to the LDT or appropriate person(s) (pastor, executive pastor, SLT, board, etc.) for evaluation, input, and final approval.

___ Regularly evaluate and update long term your funding strategy.

Objective 10: What: Build a creative, innovative church that can adapt quickly to culture change (Who: Creativity and Innovation Development Team. When: completion date _____).

Team leader: _____

Team members:_____

___ Determine if the church keeps up with and relates well to the culture (surveys of congregation).

___ Interview people within and outside the congregation and ask what you are doing that's become outdated and irrelevant. (What's not changed in the last five years?)

___ Develop and apply a biblical theology of change (function, form, and freedom).

___ Constantly challenge your views and assumptions concerning what you think is true about your community, your congregation, your ministries, your leaders, and the way you do things inside your organization. Take nothing for granted.

___ Develop a process for generating hundreds of new, strategic ministry ideas each year (lay, team, and staff brainstorming sessions, etc.).

___ Gain congregational permission to experiment with and try new things. (This means they and you will have to become comfortable with failure. However, it's far better to have tried and failed than not to have tried at all.)

___ Consider and evaluate creative and innovative ideas from the congregation and others.

___ Identify innovative and creative churches in America and discover what they are doing and how they may help you in your ministry. Visit one in your area.

___ Allocate funds in the budget to fund new ideas (recommend 1–5% of the ministries budget).

___ Read books and articles on creativity and innovation (for example, *Fast Company*) and on innovative, creative churches.

___ Invite new staff and new members and even outsiders to tell you what they think you need to change to be more effective as a church.

Optional Objective 11: What: Craft a process to develop leaders in the church (Who: Leadership Development Team. When: completion date _____).

Team leader: _____

Team members:_____

___ Attend the instructional meeting led by the staff or TMG consultant.

___ Know and be able to articulate the reasons leadership development is so important to the church.

___ Know and be able to articulate the reasons churches are not developing leaders.

___ Determine if you believe that leaders are born or made.

___ Define leader development.

___ Know Jesus's leader development phases, principles, and steps.

___ Determine if your empowered leaders (board, staff, pastor, patriarch, etc.) will support the leader development process.

___ Decide who will initiate, support, and lead the development process (senior pastor?).

___ Determine who will actually develop leaders.

___ Arrive at a consensus definition of leadership.

___ Identify the various leadership levels in your church.

___ Discover and recruit new, emerging leaders for development.

___ Deploy new leaders into their positions of leadership.

___ Develop new and present leaders for their ministries in the church.

___ Regularly evaluate your leadership development process.

___ Consistently reward those in the leadership development process.

___ Identify other development teams you need to communicate with. Meet or somehow connect with them periodically.

___ Develop a one-paragraph vision statement for leader development.

___ When you have addressed most if not all these goals, you'll have your process for developing leaders in your church. Draft a statement that will capture the leader development process, and present it to the LDT or appropriate person(s) (pastor, executive pastor, SLT, board, etc.) for evaluation, input, and final approval.

____ Regularly evaluate and update long term your leader development strategy.

Optional Objective 12: What: Develop a strategy that equips the board for leadership excellence (Who: Board Strategy Development Team. When: completion date _____).

Team leader: _____
Team members:_____

____ Attend the instructional meeting led by the staff or TMG consultant.

____ Define your governing board.

____ Evaluate current board performance.

____ Limit the board's size to nine people or less.

____ Determine the spiritual qualifications for the board.

____ Determine the relationship between the board, pastor, and staff.

____ Evaluate and establish clear board functions (what it does).

____ Review and set the composition of the board.

____ Identify the characteristics of a healthy board.

____ Establish guidelines with the pastor and board for power checks and balances.

____ Implement a church policies approach.

____ Set up an orientation and training process for new board members.

____ Identify other development teams you need to communicate with. Meet or somehow connect with them periodically.

____ Develop a one-paragraph vision statement for the board.

____ When you have addressed most if not all these goals, you'll have your strategy to equip your board for leadership excellence. Draft a statement that will capture the church's strategy for board excellence, and present it to the LDT or appropriate person(s) (pastor, executive pastor, SLT, board, etc.) for evaluation, input, and final approval.

____ Regularly evaluate and update long term your board development strategy.

Appendix E

Implementation Barriers Audit

Directions: Using the scale below, circle the number that best expresses to what extent the following implementation barriers characterize your church. Work your way through the list quickly, going with your first impression.

1	2	3	4
true	important	partly false	false

		1	2	3	4
1.	*Status quo:* Desire to keep things the way they are.	1	2	3	4
2.	*Complacency:* Pleased with things the way they are.	1	2	3	4
3.	*Tradition:* Favoring only the practices of the past over those of the present.	1	2	3	4
4.	*Prejudice:* Holding negative opinions about others without knowledge of them.	1	2	3	4
5.	*Critical spirit:* Inclined to find fault.	1	2	3	4
6.	*Complaining:* Constantly expressing dissatisfaction.	1	2	3	4
7.	*Inward focused:* Self-centered, primarily caring about one's own interests.	1	2	3	4
8.	*Gossip:* Idle talk about others' affairs.	1	2	3	4
9.	*Power:* Being in a position to control things to one's own advantage.	1	2	3	4
10.	*Sacred cow:* Considering a practice or position so important as to be exempt from all, even justified, criticism.	1	2	3	4
11.	*Safety:* Desire to be free from any potential risk or harm.	1	2	3	4
12.	*Vested interests:* Preserving the current situation for personal advantage.	1	2	3	4
13.	*Position:* Exercising undue control over the congregation.	1	2	3	4
14.	*Prestige:* Using one's good reputation to influence an organization for one's own ends.	1	2	3	4
15.	*Distrust:* A lack of trust in the current leadership.	1	2	3	4

16. ***Stress:*** Feeling undue mental or emotional pressure due to the organization's circumstances.   1   2   3   4

17. ***Nostalgia:*** A desire to return to the past.   1   2   3   4

18. ***Inflexible:*** Refusal to change.   1   2   3   4

19. ***Ignorance:*** Unaware of the current situation.   1   2   3   4

20. ***Comfort:*** In a state of contentment.   1   2   3   4

21. ***Compliance:*** Feeling a need to go along with others.   1   2   3   4

22. ***Disobedience:*** An unwillingness to do what God or others expect of us.   1   2   3   4

23. ***Uncommitted:*** No sense of obligation to God or his church.   1   2   3   4

24. ***Passive:*** Lack of initiative on the part of the organization.   1   2   3   4

25. ***Other implementation barriers:***

Write below all the barriers that you rated with a 1 or 2. Rank these according to priority (with the largest barriers receiving top priority).

Appendix F

Vision Statements

Moses's Vision

> For the LORD your God is bringing you into a good land—a land with streams and pools of water, with springs flowing in the valleys and hills; a land with wheat and barley, vines and fig trees, pomegranates, olive oil and honey; a land where bread will not be scarce and you will lack nothing; a land where the rocks are iron and you can dig copper out of the hills.
>
> Deuteronomy 8:7–10

Northwood Community Church *Dallas, Texas*

Vision is not about reality or what is. Vision is all about our dreams and aspirations or what could be.

At Northwood Community Church, we envision our sharing the good news of Christ's death and resurrection with thousands of unchurched friends and people in the metroplex, many of whom accept him as Savior.

We envision developing all our people—new believers as well as established believers—into fully functioning followers of Christ through people-friendly worship services, Sunday school, special events, and most important, small groups.

We envision becoming a church of small groups where our people model biblical community: a safe place where we accept one another and are accepted, love and are loved, shepherd and are shepherded, encourage and are encouraged, forgive and are forgiven, and serve and are served.

We envision helping all our people—youth as well as adults—to discover their divine designs so that they are equipped to serve Christ effectively in some ministry either within or outside our church. Our goal is that every member be a minister.

We envision welcoming numerous members into our body who are excited about Christ, experience healing in their family relationships and marriages, and grow together in love.

We envision our recruiting, training, and sending out many of our members as missionaries, church planters, and church workers all over the world. We also see a number of our people pursuing short-term missions service in various countries. We envision planting a church in America or abroad every two years.

We envision a larger facility that will accommodate our growth and be accessible to all the metroplex. This facility will provide ample room for Sunday school, small groups, Bible study, prayer, and other meetings. While we do not believe that "bigger is better," numerical growth is a by-product of effective evangelism. Thus, we desire to grow as God prospers us and uses us to reach a lost and dying world.

This is our dream—our vision about what could be!

Aubrey Malphurs

Lakeview Community Church *Cedar Hill, Texas*

Our comprehensive purpose is to honor our Lord and Savior, Jesus Christ, by carrying out his command to make disciples of all nations (Matthew 28:19–20). Specifically, we believe God has called us to focus on reaching those in Cedar Hill and the surrounding areas who do not regularly attend any church.

In order to accomplish this, Lakeview Community Church will be an equipping center where every Christian can be developed to his or her full potential for ministry. This development will come through: creative, inspiring worship; teaching that is biblical and relevant to life; vital, supportive fellowship; and opportunities for outreach into the community in service and evangelism.

As a result, the Cedar Hill area will be different in ten to fifteen years, with the Christian influence being increasingly felt in homes, businesses, education, and politics. We further intend to multiply our worldwide ministry by planting churches, by preparing our people for leadership roles in vocational ministries and parachurch groups, by sending out missionaries, and by becoming a resource center and model for Texas and the nation.

River City Community Church *Louisville, Kentucky*

WE SEE . . .
. . . the light of truth cutting through the darkness!

At River City, we will seek to lead irreligious people from the darkness of separation from God to a relationship with Him by proclaiming clearly and often the truth of eternal life in Jesus Christ. Corporately, we will provide a Sunday morning service that is exciting, interesting, and friendly. We will also have outreach events such as concerts, block parties, sports, and festivals. Individually, the mature, trained followers of Christ will reach out to friends, family, and neighbors.

WE SENSE . . .

. . . the aroma of freedom from a selfish lifestyle!

At River City, believers are encouraged to shed the shackles of harmful and selfish behavior and enjoy the freedom of following Christ. They understand the characteristics of a fully functioning follower and are challenged to become one. In formal teaching times and small groups, believers find the means for learning how to study the Word, pray to God, share their faith, and practice hospitality.

WE HEAR . . .

. . . the sound of laughter breaking down the walls of silence!

At River City, we will be a family that calls people from the loneliness of isolation to the joy of relationships. We will seek to know, serve, encourage, challenge, and love one another. We will welcome all people regardless of race, sex, or history into our family, just as God has welcomed believers into His family by His grace. We will not be afraid to laugh or have fun.

WE FEEL . . .

. . . the strength of a loving hand training us to serve!

At River City, men and women will receive further training in order to become leaders who make disciples. As a result of our worship, evangelism, assimilation, and leadership training, we will become a church of ministers that carries out the Great Commission, meets the needs of one another, builds safer communities, and glorifies the name of Jesus Christ in the city of Louisville, Kentucky.

Saddleback Valley Community Church *Mission Viejo, California*

It is the dream of a place where the hurting, the depressed, the frustrated, and the confused can find love, acceptance, help, hope, forgiveness, guidance, and encouragement.

It is the dream of sharing the Good News of Jesus Christ with the hundreds of thousands of residents in south Orange County.

It is the dream of welcoming 20,000 members into the fellowship of our church family—loving, learning, laughing, and living in harmony together.

It is the dream of developing people to spiritual maturity through Bible studies, small groups, seminars, retreats, and a Bible school for our members.

It is the dream of equipping every believer for a significant ministry by helping them discover the gifts and talents God gave them.

It is the dream of sending out hundreds of career missionaries and church workers all around the world, and empowering every member for a personal life mission in the world. It is the dream of sending our members by the thousand on short-term mission projects to every continent. It is the dream of starting at least one new daughter church every year.

It is the dream of at least fifty acres of land, on which will be built a regional church for south Orange County—with beautiful, yet simple facilities including a worship center seating thousands, a counseling and prayer center, classrooms for Bible studies and training lay ministers, and a recreation area. All of this will be designed to minister to the total person—spiritually, emotionally, physically, and socially—and set in a peaceful inspiring garden landscape.

I stand before you this day and state in confident assurance that these dreams will become reality. Why? Because they are inspired by God!

Clear Lake Community Church *Houston, Texas*

Vision for Their Children's Program

We envision children waking up parents on Sunday morning excited to go to church.

We see lots of smiles, glad to be in a place of belonging, welcomed again by a familiar face. We see the fright of first time melted by an extra caring touch and loneliness replaced by laughter. We see motivated volunteers, passionate about being with kids, gifted to teach, serve, and shepherd.

We see a facility which is "kid focused," that will facilitate learning and having fun for hundreds of kids. We see a clean and attractive environment where excellence and creativity are immediately noticed.

We see concerned moms relieved as they drop off their children and dads without distraction, engaged in the service. We envision a security process which builds confidence with parents.

We see physical care, babies being cuddled and crawlers being chased. We sense a foundation being laid where Sunday morning is an experience of God's love for the youngest baby to the oldest child; a time when seeds of faith can be planted and nurtured.

We hear cheers of older kids, and feel fun in the air as hundreds of kids celebrate and sing of the goodness of God; we hear the quietness of prayer. We envision the stories of the Bible told in creative ways. We see the look of conviction as the gospel penetrates a child's heart. We see caring adults leading discussion and listening during small group time. We dream of kids carrying Bibles and bringing friends.

We see whole families growing closer to God and each other through programs to motivate and equip parents.

In the next five years, we envision hundreds of kids choosing to be baptized and building a faith foundation that will lead to a lifetime of full devotion to Christ and multiplication of kingdom impact.

Will Mancini

Appendix G

Vision Style Audit

Directions: Circle the letter that best describes your preference in a ministry context.

1. I tend to
   a. Dislike new problems
   b. Like new problems

2. I work best with
   a. Facts
   b. Ideas

3. I like to think about
   a. What is
   b. What could be

4. I like
   a. Established ways of doing things
   b. New ways for doing things

5. I enjoy skills that
   a. I have learned and used
   b. Are newly learned but unused

6. In my work I tend to
   a. Take time to be precise
   b. Dislike taking time to be precise

7. I would describe my work style as
   a. Steady with realistic expectations
   b. Periodic with bursts of enthusiasm

8. I have found that I am
   a. Patient with routine details
   b. Impatient with routine details

9. I am more likely to trust my
   a. Experience
   b. Inspiration

10. I am convinced that
    a. Seeing is believing
    b. Believing is seeing

Number of **A**s _____

Number of **B**s _____

Calculation: Total the number of **A**s you circled. Total the number of **B**s you circled.

Interpretation: If you circled more **A**s than **B**s, you are the type of person who catches a vision by visiting another ministry and seeing it for yourself. You focus more on the present than the future. Your vision style is that of a **vision catcher**.

If you circled more **B**s than **A**s, you are the type of person who creates a vision in your head. You focus more on the future than the present or past. Your vision style is that of a **vision creator**.

Note: If you circled the same number of **A**s and **B**s, that means you are not sure which you are. You should take the MBTI or the Kiersey Temperament Sorter, which are more exacting tools, or wait and take the vision audit again at a later time.

Appendix H

Values Statements

Northwood Community Church *Dallas, Texas*

Core Values Statement

The following presents the core values of Northwood Community Church. We desire that they define and drive this ministry in the context of a warm and caring environment.

Christ's Headship

We acknowledge Christ as the Head of our church and submit ourselves and all our activities to His will and good pleasure (Eph. 1:22–23).

Biblical Teaching

We strive to teach God's Word with integrity and authority so that seekers find Christ and believers mature in Him (2 Tim. 3:16).

Authentic Worship

We desire to acknowledge God's supreme value and worth in our personal lives and in the corporate, contemporary worship of our church (Rom. 12:1–2).

Intercessory Prayer

We rely on private and corporate prayer in the conception, planning, and execution of all the ministries and activities of this church (Matt. 7:7–11).

Sense of Community

We ask all our people to commit to and fully participate in biblically functioning small groups where they may reach the lost, exercise their gifts, be shepherded, and thus grow in Christlikeness (Acts 2:44–46).

Family

We support the spiritual nurture of the family as one of God's dynamic means to perpetuate the Christian faith (2 Tim. 1:5).

Grace-Orientation

We encourage our people to serve Christ from hearts of love and gratitude rather than guilt and condemnation (Rom. 6:14).

Creativity and Innovation

We will constantly evaluate our forms and methods, seeking cultural relevance and maximum ministry effectiveness for Christ (1 Chron. 12:32).

Mobilized Congregation

We seek to equip all our uniquely designed and gifted people to effectively accomplish the work of our ministry (Eph. 4:11–13).*

Lost People

We value unchurched, lost people and will use every available Christ-honoring means to pursue, win, and disciple them (Luke 19:10).*

Ministry Excellence

Since God gave His best (the Savior), we seek to honor Him by maintaining a high standard of excellence in all our ministries and activities (Col. 3:23–24).*

*These are aspirational values. While they are not yet our values, we are working hard at making them our core values.

The Jerusalem Church Jerusalem, Israel

The Core Values of the Jerusalem Church

1. We value Bible doctrine (Acts 2:42–43).
2. We value fellowship (Acts 2:42, 44–46).

3. We value praise and worship (Acts 2:42, 47).

4. We value evangelism (Acts 2:40–41, 47).

Northwood Community Church *Dallas, Texas*

Our Faith Statement

Northwood Community Church is an Evangelical Free Church. Thus, the members of Northwood Community Church have adopted the following twelve-point statement of the Evangelical Free Church of America.

1. We believe the Scriptures, both Old and New Testaments, to be the inspired Word of God, without error in the original writings, the complete revelation of His will for the salvation of men, and the divine and final authority for all Christian faith and life.

2. We believe in one God, Creator of all things, infinitely perfect and eternally existing in three persons—Father, Son, and Holy Spirit.

3. We believe that Jesus Christ is true God and true man, having been conceived of the Holy Spirit and born of the virgin Mary. He died on the cross as a sacrifice for our sins according to the Scriptures. Further, He arose bodily from the dead, ascended into heaven, where at the right hand of the Majesty on High, He now is our High Priest and Advocate.

4. We believe that the ministry of the Holy Spirit is to glorify the Lord Jesus Christ, and during this age to convict men, regenerate the believing sinner, indwell, guide, instruct and empower the believer for godly living and service.

5. We believe that man was created in the image of God but fell into sin and is therefore lost and only through regeneration by the Holy Spirit can salvation and spiritual life be obtained.

6. We believe that the shed blood of Jesus Christ and His resurrection provide the only ground for justification and salvation for all who believe, and only such as receive Jesus Christ are born of the Holy Spirit, and thus become children of God.

7. We believe that water baptism and the Lord's Supper are ordinances to be observed by the church during the present age. They are, however, not to be regarded as means of salvation.

8. We believe that the true Church is composed of all such persons who through saving faith in Jesus Christ have been regenerated by the Holy Spirit and are united together in the body of Christ of which He is the Head.

9. We believe that only those who are members of the true Church shall be eligible for membership in the local church.

10. We believe that Jesus Christ is the Lord and Head of the Church, and that every local church has the right under Christ to decide and govern its own affairs.

11. We believe in the personal, premillennial and imminent coming of our Lord Jesus Christ, and that this "Blessed Hope" has a vital bearing on the personal life and service of the believer.

12. We believe in the bodily resurrection of the dead, of the believer to everlasting blessedness and joy with the Lord, of the unbeliever to judgment and everlasting conscious punishment.

Fellowship Bible Church *Dallas, Texas*

Our Values

We have ten core values that guide us. These values describe the culture that we seek to create at FBC. We aspire to be . . .

1. Biblically Faithful: We make Scripture the final authority rather than church tradition. We seek to be innovative and flexible as long as we do not violate Scripture.

2. Culturally Relevant: We try to adapt our ministry to current needs and trends in American life, without compromising biblical absolutes. We attempt to communicate the good news of Jesus Christ to American society in ways it can understand.

3. Grace Oriented: We emphasize God's unconditional acceptance and full forgiveness through Jesus Christ. We attempt to motivate people through love and thankfulness rather than guilt, shame, and duty.

4. Seeker Sensitive: We know that many who are not yet committed to Christ are attracted to our ministry; therefore, we desire to create a non-threatening environment in which they are free to explore the Christian faith at their own pace.

5. Growth Responsive: We appreciate the advantages of a small, intimate congregation, but also feel we should respond to the numerical growth that often results from reaching out to those who are exploring Christianity. We do not set a particular limit on the size of our congregation, but trust God to show the church leadership what our facilities should be and how best to utilize them.

6. Relationally Centered: We stress healthy relationships among Christians. We emphasize small groups as a primary means for Christians to care for each other, develop friendships, and share their lives.

7. People Developing: We seek to help people grow spiritually. We provide biblical instruction, and we encourage believers to discover and exercise their spiritual gifts.

8. Family Affirming: We seek to provide an atmosphere which strengthens marriages and families. We are committed to strong youth and children's programs.

9. Simply Structured: We assign the ultimate leadership of the church to elders and the daily operations of the church to paid staff who are responsible to set up effective programs.

10. Cross Culturally Effective: We reach beyond our own culture as we seek to have an effective impact on other cultures with the gospel.

Lakeview Community Church *Cedar Hill, Texas*

This statement of principles clarifies the attitudes and approaches which will be encouraged in the ministries of Lakeview Community Church. Most of these are not biblical absolutes, but represent our understanding of how to most effectively accomplish our purpose.

A Commitment to Relevant Bible Exposition—We believe that the Bible is God's inspired Word, the authoritative and trustworthy rule of faith and practice for Christians. The Bible is both timeless and timely, relevant to the common needs of all people at all times and to the specific problems of contemporary living. Therefore, we are committed to equipping Christians, through the preaching and teaching of God's Word, to follow Christ in every sphere of life.

A Commitment to Prayer—We believe that God desires his people to pray and that he hears and answers prayer (Matthew 7:7–11; James 5:13–18). Therefore, the ministries and activities of this church will be characterized by a reliance on prayer in their conception, planning, and execution.

A Commitment to Lay Ministry—We believe that the primary responsibility of the pastor(s) and teachers in the local church is to "prepare God's people for works of service" (Ephesians 4:12). Therefore, the ministry of Lakeview Community Church will be placed as much as possible in the hands of nonvocational workers. This will be accomplished through training opportunities and through practices which encourage lay initiation, leadership, responsibility, and authority in the various ministries of the church.

A Commitment to Small Groups—We are committed to small group ministry as one of the most effective means of building relationships, stimulating spiritual growth, and developing leaders.

An Appreciation for Creativity and Innovation—In today's rapidly changing world, forms and methods must be continually evaluated, and if necessary, altered to fit new conditions. While proven techniques should not be discarded at a whim, we encourage creativity and innovation, flexibility and adaptability. We are more concerned with effectiveness in ministry than with adherence to tradition.

A Commitment to Excellence—We believe that the God of our salvation deserves the best we have to offer. The Lord himself is a God of excellence, as shown by the beauty of creation; further, he gave the best that he had, his only Son, for us (Romans 8:32). Paul exhorts servants, in whatever they do, to "work at it with all your heart, as working for the Lord, not for men" (Colossians 3:23). Therefore, in the ministries and activities of Lakeview Community Church we will seek to maintain a high standard of excellence to the glory of God. This will be achieved when every person is exercising his or her God-given spiritual gift to the best of his or her ability (1 Corinthians 12).

A Commitment to Growth—Although numerical growth is not necessarily a sign of God's blessing, and is not a sufficient goal in itself, we believe that God desires for us to reach as many people as possible with the life-changing message of Jesus Christ. Therefore, we will pursue methods and policies which will facilitate numerical growth, without compromising in any way our integrity or our commitment to biblical truth.

Willow Creek Community Church *South Barrington, Illinois*

Willow Creek's 10 Core Values

1. We believe that anointed teaching is the catalyst for transformation in individuals' lives and in the church.

   This includes the concept of teaching for life change—Romans 12:7; 2 Timothy 3:16–17; James 1:23–25.

2. We believe that lost people matter to God, and therefore, ought to matter to the church.

   This includes the concepts of relational evangelism and evangelism as a process—Luke 5:30–32; Luke 15; Matthew 18:14.

3. We believe that the church should be culturally relevant while remaining doctrinally pure.

   This includes the concept of sensitively relating to our culture through our facility, printed materials, and use of the arts—1 Corinthians 9:19–23.

4. We believe that Christ-followers should manifest authenticity and yearn for continuous growth.

   This includes the concepts of personal authenticity, character, and wholeness—Ephesians 4:25–26, 32; Hebrews 12:1; Philippians 1:6.

5. We believe that a church should operate as a unified community of servants with men and women stewarding their spiritual gifts.

   This includes the concepts of unity, servanthood, spiritual gifts, and ministry callings—1 Corinthians 12 and 14; Romans 12; Ephesians 4; Psalm 133:1.

6. We believe that loving relationships should permeate every aspect of church life.

   This includes the concepts of love-driven ministry, ministry accomplished in teams, and relationship building—1 Corinthians 13; Nehemiah 3; Luke 10:1; John 13:34–35.

7. We believe that life-change happens best in small groups.

   This includes the concepts of discipleship, vulnerability, and accountability—Luke 6:12–13; Acts 2:44–47.

8. We believe that excellence honors God and inspires people.

   This includes the concepts of evaluation, critical review, intensity, and excellence—Colossians 3:17; Malachi 1:6–14; Proverbs 27:17.

9. We believe that churches should be led by men and women with leadership gifts.

   This includes the concepts of empowerment, servant leadership, strategic focus, and intentionality—Nehemiah 1–2; Romans 12:8; Acts 6:2–5.

10. We believe that the pursuit of full devotion to Christ and His cause is normal for every believer.

   This includes the concepts of stewardship, servanthood, downward mobility, and the pursuit of kingdom goals—1 Kings 11:4; Philippians 2:1–11; 2 Corinthians 8:7.

Parkview Evangelical Free Church *Iowa City, Iowa*

Parkview's Values

1. Scripture

   A Biblical Message: We are committed to the clear and accurate communication of God's Word in a way that ministers grace and urges obedience (2 Tim. 3:16–17).

2. Creativity

   A Fresh Approach: We are committed to forms of worship and ministry that will best capture and express what God is doing in our generation and culture (Luke 5:33–39).

3. Ministry

   A Team Effort: We are committed to a team model for ministry and organization that equips and empowers every family, member, and leader (Eph. 4:11–16).

Grace Bible Church *Laredo, Texas*

Core Values Statement

- We value the Bible as God's authoritative and accurate source for salvation and Christian living.

  Goal: To develop a biblical worldview in all of our people.

  Objective #1: To equip the people of our church in how to properly study the Bible (Senior Pastor, Spiritual Maturity Pastor).

  Objective #2: To teach the people of our church how the fundamental truths of the Christian Faith impact their daily living (Senior Pastor, Spiritual Maturity Pastor).

  Objective #3: To begin a Spiritual Maturity class offered each Sunday that accomplishes the above objectives (Spiritual Maturity Pastor).

- We value worship that is both accurate and authentic.

  Goal: To provide opportunities and to encourage people to authentically and accurately worship God in both personal and corporate settings.

Objective #1: To thoughtfully arrange our Sunday worship in order to maximize participation and purposefully engage people in God-centered worship (Senior Pastor).

Objective #2: To instruct and encourage people in some of the basic forms of personal worship, such as: prayer, Bible study, meditation, fasting, solitude (Senior Pastor, Spiritual Maturity Pastor).

- We value fellowship that is relational and sacrificial.

Goal: To provide multiple opportunities for people to get involved in biblical community.

Objective #1: To provide a variety of small groups to minister to the differing needs of our community (i.e., singles, couples, recovery groups, parenting, etc.) (Spiritual Maturity Pastor).

Objective #2: To provide a training system that would train group leaders quarterly on the purpose of small groups as well as foster the multiplication of groups (Spiritual Maturity Pastor).

- We value discipleship that is transformational.

Goal: To turn believers into followers.

Objective #1: To encourage people in our church to get involved in a small group (Spiritual Maturity Pastor).

Objective #2: To encourage people in our church to discover their spiritual gifts and begin serving (Equipping Pastor).

Objective #3: To encourage people in our church to begin sharing the gospel with others (Missions & Outreach Pastor).

- We value ministry that is compatible with our people and effective for Christ's church.

Goal: To make every member a minister.

Objective #1: To instruct the people of our church in spiritual gifts and encourage them to use them (Equipping Pastor).

Objective #2: To identify the spiritual gifts necessary for each current ministry in our church and put into a ministry guide to help people identify their ideal ministry match (Equipping Pastor).

- We value evangelism that reaches those outside our church with the gospel of grace.

Goal: To share the gospel with the community of Laredo.

Objective #1: To regularly (at least 2x a year) train our people in sharing the gospel (Missions & Outreach Pastor).

Objective #2: To regularly host events that reach those who don't know Jesus Christ, such as: Felt-needs series, Trunk or Treat, CCN broadcasts, Men's/Women's activities (Missions & Outreach Pastor).

- We value prayer that is passionate and Spirit led.

  Goal: To become a church characterized by prayer.

  Objective #1: For our pastors to regularly pray with other pastors in community (Senior Pastor).

  Objective #2: To encourage our people to participate in the quarterly concerts of prayer (Spiritual Maturity Pastor).

  Objective #3: To encourage and provide multiple venues for people in our church to engage in prayer (Spiritual Maturity Pastor).

Appendix I

Core Values Audits

Church Ministry Core Values Audit

Directions: Using the scale below, circle the number that best expresses to what extent the following values are important to your church (actual values). Work your way through the list quickly, going with your first impression.

1	2	3	4
not important	somewhat important	important	most important

1. **Family:** The relationships between husbands and wives and their children   1   2   3   4

2. **Biblical instruction:** A familiarity with and desire to know the truths of Scripture   1   2   3   4

3. **World missions:** Spreading the gospel of Christ around the globe   1   2   3   4

4. **Encouragement:** Giving hope to people who at times need some hope   1   2   3   4

5. **Giving:** Providing a portion of one's finances to support the ministry   1   2   3   4

6. **Leadership:** A person's ability to influence others to pursue God's mission for the church   1   2   3   4

7. **Cultural relevance:** Communicating truth in a way that people who aren't like us understand   1   2   3   4

8. **Prayer:** Communicating with God   1   2   3   4

9. **Excellence:** Maintaining the highest of ministry standards, which brings glory to God   1   2   3   4

10. **Evangelism:** Telling others the good news about Christ   1   2   3   4

11. **Team ministry:** A group of people ministering together   1   2   3   4

12. **Creativity:** Coming up with new ideas and ways of doing ministry   1   2   3   4

13. **Worship:** Attributing worth to God   1   2   3   4

14. **Cooperation:** The act of working together in the service of the Savior   1   2   3   4

15. **Ministry/service:** Christians actively involved and serving in the ministries of the church (a mobilized congregation)   1   2   3   4

16. **Obedience:** A willingness to do what God or others ask of a person   1   2   3   4

17. **Innovation:** Making changes that promote the ministry as it serves Christ   1   2   3   4

18. **Fellowship:** Spending time with other Christians, encouraging, confronting, caring about them   1   2   3   4

19. **Community:** The desire to reach out to the people who live within driving distance of the church (your Jerusalem)   1   2   3   4

20. **Other values:**

Note all the values that you rated with a 4. Rank these according to priority. The first four to six values are your core values as an organization. The rest, including some of the values you rated as a 3, will make up your organizational culture statement.

Personal Core Values Audit

Directions: Using the scale below, circle the number that best expresses to what extent the following values are important to you (actual values). Work your way through the list quickly, going with your first impression.

1	2	3	4
not important	somewhat important	important	most important

1. **Family:** The relationships between husbands and wives and their children   1   2   3   4
2. **Biblical instruction:** A familiarity with and desire to know the truths of Scripture   1   2   3   4
3. **World missions:** Spreading the gospel of Christ around the globe   1   2   3   4
4. **Encouragement:** Giving hope to people who at times need some hope   1   2   3   4
5. **Giving:** Providing a portion of one's finances to support the ministry   1   2   3   4
6. **Leadership:** A person's ability to influence others to pursue God's mission for the church   1   2   3   4
7. **Cultural relevance:** Communicating truth in a way that people who aren't like us understand   1   2   3   4
8. **Prayer:** Communicating with God   1   2   3   4
9. **Excellence:** Maintaining the highest of ministry standards, which brings glory to God   1   2   3   4
10. **Evangelism:** Telling others the good news about Christ   1   2   3   4
11. **Team ministry:** A group of people ministering together   1   2   3   4
12. **Creativity:** Coming up with new ideas and ways of doing ministry   1   2   3   4
13. **Worship:** Attributing worth to God   1   2   3   4
14. **Cooperation:** The act of working together in the service of the Savior   1   2   3   4
15. **Ministry/service:** Christians actively involved and serving in the ministries of the church (a mobilized congregation)   1   2   3   4
16. **Obedience:** A willingness to do what God or others ask of a person   1   2   3   4
17. **Innovation:** Making changes that promote the ministry as it serves Christ   1   2   3   4
18. **Fellowship:** Spending time with other Christians, encouraging, confronting, caring about them   1   2   3   4
19. **Community:** The desire to reach out to the people who live within driving distance of the church (your Jerusalem)   1   2   3   4
20. **Other values:**

Note all the values that you rated with a 3 or 4. Rank these according to priority. The first six are your core values.

Appendix J

Community Survey

Directions: Using this survey, interview at least one unchurched person in your community. Write down his or her answers in the space provided. (Be aware that most will be too polite to give you the unvarnished truth. So, in your own unique way, give them permission to do so.)

1. What are your impressions about churches in general (good for the community, waste of time, place to find God, boring, etc.)?

_____

_____

_____

_____

2. When and under what circumstances might you visit a church?

_____

_____

_____

_____

3. What felt needs would cause you to attend a church (desire to know God, good business contacts, meet a spouse, etc.)?

_____

_____

_____

4. Deep down, what do you really want out of life? What are your hopes, dreams, aspirations (to find God, financial stability, friendships, find happiness, etc.)?

_____

_____

_____

5. Is there anything about our church that turns people off?

_____

_____

_____

6. What should we as a church do to reach people who don't attend church?

_____

_____

_____

7. We need your help. Would you attend one of our morning services and critique what we do?

_____

_____

_____

Note: This survey can be used anonymously. Provide a copy (minus question 7) and include a self-addressed, stamped envelope so that the person can return it by mail.

Appendix K

Character Assessments

Over the years, leaders have discovered that godly character is critical to effective ministry for Christ. However, no one is perfect, and all of us have our weaknesses and flaws as well as strengths. These character assessments are to help you determine your character strengths and weaknesses so that you can know where you are strong and where you need to develop and grow.

Character Assessment for Men

The characteristics for men are found in 1 Timothy 3:1–7 and Titus 1:6–9.

Directions: Circle the number that best represents how you would rate yourself in each area.

1. I am "above reproach." I have a good reputation among people in general. I have done nothing that someone could use as an accusation against me.

   weak   1   2   3   4   5   6   7   8   strong

2. I am the "husband of one wife." If married, I not only have one wife, but I am also not physically or mentally promiscuous, for I am focused only on her.

   weak   1   2   3   4   5   6   7   8   strong

3. I am "temperate." I am a well-balanced person. I do not overdo it in my use of alcohol, etc. I am not excessive or given to extremes in beliefs, etc.

   weak   1   2   3   4   5   6   7   8   strong

4. I am "sensible." I show good judgment in life and have a proper perspective regarding myself and my abilities (humble).

   weak   1   2   3   4   5   6   7   8   strong

5. I am "respectable." I conduct my life in an honorable way, and people have and show respect for me.

   weak   1   2   3   4   5   6   7   8   strong

6. I am "hospitable." I use my residence as a place to serve and minister to Christians and non-Christians alike.

| weak | 1 | 2 | 3 | 4 | 5 | 6 | 7 | 8 | strong |

7. I am "able to teach." When I teach the Bible, I show an aptitude for handling the Scriptures with reasonable skill.

| weak | 1 | 2 | 3 | 4 | 5 | 6 | 7 | 8 | strong |

8. I am "not given to drunkenness." If I drink alcoholic beverages or indulge in other acceptable but potentially addictive practices, I do so in moderation.

| weak | 1 | 2 | 3 | 4 | 5 | 6 | 7 | 8 | strong |

9. I am "not violent." I am under control. I do not lose control to the point that I strike or cause damage to other people or their property.

| weak | 1 | 2 | 3 | 4 | 5 | 6 | 7 | 8 | strong |

10. I am "gentle." I am a kind, meek (not weak), forbearing person who does not insist on his rights nor resort to violence.

| weak | 1 | 2 | 3 | 4 | 5 | 6 | 7 | 8 | strong |

11. I am "not quarrelsome." I am an uncontentious peacemaker who avoids hostile situations with people.

| weak | 1 | 2 | 3 | 4 | 5 | 6 | 7 | 8 | strong |

12. I am "not a lover of money." I am not in ministry for financial gain, but I seek first his righteousness, knowing that God will supply my needs.

| weak | 1 | 2 | 3 | 4 | 5 | 6 | 7 | 8 | strong |

13. I "manage my family well." If I am married and have a family, my children are believers who obey me with respect. People do not think of or accuse them of being wild or disobedient.

| weak | 1 | 2 | 3 | 4 | 5 | 6 | 7 | 8 | strong |

14. I am "not a recent convert." I am not a new Christian who finds myself constantly struggling with pride and conceit.

| weak | 1 | 2 | 3 | 4 | 5 | 6 | 7 | 8 | strong |

15. I have "a good reputation with outsiders." Though lost people may not agree with my religious convictions, they still respect me as a person.

| weak | 1 | 2 | 3 | 4 | 5 | 6 | 7 | 8 | strong |

16. I am "not overbearing." I am not self-willed, stubborn, or arrogant.

| weak | 1 | 2 | 3 | 4 | 5 | 6 | 7 | 8 | strong |

17. I am "not quick-tempered." I am not inclined toward anger (an angry person), and I do not lose my temper quickly and easily.

| weak | 1 | 2 | 3 | 4 | 5 | 6 | 7 | 8 | strong |

18. I am "not pursuing dishonest gain." I am not fond of nor involved in any wrongful practices that result in fraudulent gain.

| weak | 1 | 2 | 3 | 4 | 5 | 6 | 7 | 8 | strong |

19. I "love what is good." I love the things that honor God.

| weak | 1 | 2 | 3 | 4 | 5 | 6 | 7 | 8 | strong |

20. I am "upright." I live in accordance with the laws of God and man.

| weak | 1 | 2 | 3 | 4 | 5 | 6 | 7 | 8 | strong |

21. I am "holy." I am a devout person, whose life is generally pleasing to God.

| weak | 1 | 2 | 3 | 4 | 5 | 6 | 7 | 8 | strong |

22. I "hold firmly to the faith." I understand, hold to, and attempt to conserve God's truth. I also encourage others while refuting those who oppose the truth.

| weak | 1 | 2 | 3 | 4 | 5 | 6 | 7 | 8 | strong |

When you have completed this character assessment, note the characteristics to which you gave the lowest rating (a 4 or below). The lowest of these are the character goals that you will work on developing.

Character Assessment for Women

The characteristics for women are found in 1 Timothy 2:9–10; 3:11; Titus 2:3–5; and 1 Peter 3:1–4.

Directions: Circle the number that best represents how you would rate yourself in each area.

1. I am "worthy of respect." I find that most people who know me respect me and tend to honor me as a dignified person who is serious about spiritual things.

| weak | 1 | 2 | 3 | 4 | 5 | 6 | 7 | 8 | strong |

2. I am not a "malicious talker." I do not slander people, whether believers or unbelievers.

| weak | 1 | 2 | 3 | 4 | 5 | 6 | 7 | 8 | strong |

3. I am "temperate." I am a well-balanced person. I do not overdo it in my use of alcohol, etc. I am not excessive or given to extremes in beliefs, etc.

| weak | 1 | 2 | 3 | 4 | 5 | 6 | 7 | 8 | strong |

4. I am "trustworthy in everything." The Lord and people find me to be a faithful person in everything.

| weak | 1 | 2 | 3 | 4 | 5 | 6 | 7 | 8 | strong |

5. I live "reverently." I have a deep respect for God and live in awe of him.

| weak | 1 | 2 | 3 | 4 | 5 | 6 | 7 | 8 | strong |

6. I am "not addicted to much wine." If I drink alcoholic beverages, I do so in moderation. I am not addicted to them.

| weak | 1 | 2 | 3 | 4 | 5 | 6 | 7 | 8 | strong |

7. I teach "what is good." I share with other women what God has taught me from his Word and life in general.

| weak | 1 | 2 | 3 | 4 | 5 | 6 | 7 | 8 | strong |

8. I "love my husband." If I am married, I love my husband according to 1 Corinthians 13:4–8.

weak   1   2   3   4   5   6   7   8   strong

9. I "love my children." If I am married and have children, I love those children as well as my husband.

weak   1   2   3   4   5   6   7   8   strong

10. I am "self-controlled." I do not let other people or things run my life, and I am not an extreme or excessive person.

weak   1   2   3   4   5   6   7   8   strong

11. I am "pure." I am not involved emotionally or physically in sexual immorality.

weak   1   2   3   4   5   6   7   8   strong

12. I am "busy at home." If I am a married person, then I take care of my responsibilities at home.

weak   1   2   3   4   5   6   7   8   strong

13. I am "kind." I am essentially a good person.

weak   1   2   3   4   5   6   7   8   strong

14. I am "subject to my husband." If I am married, I let my husband take responsibility for and lead our marriage, and I follow his leadership.

weak   1   2   3   4   5   6   7   8   strong

15. I have "a gentle and quiet spirit." I am a mild, easygoing person who wins people over by a pure and reverent life more than by my words.

weak   1   2   3   4   5   6   7   8   strong

16. I "dress modestly." I wear clothing that is decent and shows propriety.

weak   1   2   3   4   5   6   7   8   strong

17. I "do good deeds." I do those things that are appropriate for women who profess to know and worship God.

weak   1   2   3   4   5   6   7   8   strong

When you have completed this character assessment, note those characteristics to which you gave the lowest rating (a 4 or below). The lowest of these are the character goals that you will work on developing.

Appendix L

Ministry Description

Job Title: Christian Education Director with a focus on Children's Ministries

Job Profile: Ideally the Christian Education Director needs gifts or abilities in the following areas: leadership, discernment, shepherding, administration, encouragement, and teaching.

The director needs a passion for adults as well as kids (works primarily with adults on behalf of the kids). A primary function will be the ability to work with and develop adults and teens as leaders.

This person's ideal temperament is a D/I on the Personal Profile.

The director needs to see life "through the eyes of a child." This person should be in touch with children—their world and culture.

Finally, the director should be a visionary who can take the children's ministry to the next level in its development.

Job Summary: The director is responsible for the children's Sunday school program (nursery through youth), children's church, the annual Vacation Bible School, and the Sunday school and worship nurseries. However, the director will focus primarily on children's ministries.

Duties:

A. Sunday School
   1. Recruit teachers and floaters.
   2. Train teachers and floaters.
   3. Evaluate teachers and floaters.
   4. Encourage teachers and floaters.

5. Assist teachers and monitor Sunday morning program.
6. Maintain supplies and facilities.
7. Select and approve all curriculum.
8. Plan and make preparation for class expansion.
9. Maintain a substitute teacher list.

B. Children's Church
   1. Present church program.
   2. Recruit workers for leadership.
   3. Train workers for leadership.
   4. Select the curriculum.

C. Vacation Bible School
   1. Recruit a director and other leaders.
   2. Choose curriculum and coordinate other materials.
   3. Recruit teachers and workers.

D. Sunday School and Worship Service Nurseries
   1. Recruit directors.
   2. Help recruit people as workers.

E. Miscellaneous
   1. Develop the core values, mission, vision, and strategy for the Christian education program.
   2. Attend board meetings.
   3. Attend staff meetings.
   4. Conduct personal background checks.
   5. Conduct personal reference checks.
   6. Preach as needed.

Reports to: Senior Pastor

Works with: Elder responsible for Christian Education

Appendix M

Setting: Creating a Welcoming Environment

Directions: Check any items below that you feel need to be addressed.

Pre-Visit

___ How do people know your church is in their community? (mailer, website, drive by, invitation, referral, signage, etc.)

___ Is the church easy to locate?

___ As a first impression, does the church's name attract or repel people? Why? (Ask people for their first impressions.)

Exterior Appearance

___ Is the exterior attractive?

___ Are the exterior walls and windows clean?

___ Are the grounds attractive and well kept?

Exterior Logistics

___ How would guests know where to turn in to the parking lot(s)?

___ Is the entryway well marked?

___ Do guests know where to park?

___ Do you have parking attendants? (First contact is the first impression!)

___ Is it easy to find a parking space? (Is there guest parking?)

___ Is 4 percent of your parking for guests?

___ Is guest parking close to the entrance?

___ Do you have greeters outside as well as within the facility?

Interior Logistics

___ Is it easy to locate the nursery?

___ Is it easy to locate classes (children's, adult, etc.)?

___ Is it easy to locate the bathrooms?

___ Do you have volunteers who will take visitors to the nursery, classes, worship center, etc.?

____ Do you have a welcome station/concierge? (Do you provide a packet of information that answers most visitors' questions?)

____ Do you locate ushers/greeters in the worship center?

____ Do you have a "ten-foot rule" (greet anyone you don't know within ten feet)?

____ Do your people understand how guests feel when they visit a church?

____ What do guests see, hear, smell, feel when they visit your church?

____ Do you follow up guests? If so, how?

____ What happens when someone calls the church? Are those who answer the phones warm and helpful? (This may be a guest's first impression of the church and not just anyone can do this!)

Interior Cleanliness

____ Are the bathrooms (especially the women's) clean?

____ Are the nurseries clean?

____ Are the primary worship areas clean?

____ Are the classrooms clean?

____ Are the hallways clean?

____ Is the kitchen clean?

____ Does the congregation have any "blind spots"— areas they no longer notice that need to be cleaned, updated, or repaired?

Interior Special Features

____ Is there a special place in the nursery to "show off" your newborns?

____ Is there a coffee or espresso bar (Starbucks)? Do you have a coffee hour with unstructured fellowship?

____ Is there a system for communicating with parents who drop kids off in the nursery?

____ Is there special lighting for the worship services?

____ Is there front or rear screen projection for video presentations, etc.?

____ Is there a play area like the ones at some McDonald's?

____ What happens on a rainy day? Are there volunteers with umbrellas who will walk people to their cars?

Exterior/Interior Signage

____ Is there signage for parking (guest parking)?

____ Is there signage for the bathrooms?

____ Is there signage for classes?

____ Is there signage for the nursery?

____ Is there signage for the exits?

____ Is there signage for the kitchen?

Facilities Functionality

____ Are the facilities functional? (Do they enable or inhibit ministry?) Consider, for example, room size.

____ Do they contribute to or distract from your ministry functions (worship, etc.)?

Appendix N

Sample Evaluations

Visitor Evaluation

Please help us as a church by evaluating the following areas:

1. Were you warmly greeted as you entered our facility? _____

2. Were you able to find your way easily around our facility? _____

3. How would you rate the following:

	Poor	Fair	Good	Outstanding
Greeters	1	2	3	4
Ushers	1	2	3	4
Music	1	2	3	4
Worship	1	2	3	4
Sermon	1	2	3	4

Comments:

_____

_____

_____

4. Were there any distractions during the worship service? _____

5. Did you find our people to be friendly and accommodating? _____

6. How did you find out about this church? _____

7. Do you have any comments or suggestions for improving our church? _____

8. Will you come back? Why? Why not? _____

Signature (optional):

Date:_____

Sunday Worship Service Evaluation

Evaluator (optional):

Date:_____

Directions: Please help us grow by constructively evaluating each area below. (Use back if necessary.)

Poor	Fair	Good	Outstanding
1	2	3	4

1. *Announcements/Bulletin*

Comments:

_____
_____
_____

Poor	Fair	Good	Outstanding
1	2	3	4

2. *Music/Band/Accompanists/Slides*

Comments:

_____
_____
_____

Poor	Fair	Good	Outstanding
1	2	3	4

3. *Special Events* (communion, dedication, other)

Comments:

_____
_____
_____

	Poor	Fair	Good	Outstanding
	1	2	3	4

4. *Sermon*

Comments on delivery: (mannerisms, speech, other)

_____

_____

_____

_____

_____

Was the topic relevant? How?

_____

_____

_____

_____

_____

Comment on the content. (Was it biblical?)

_____

_____

_____

_____

_____

What was the main point of today's message?

_____

_____

_____

_____

_____

Ministry Description

Job Title: Director of Biblical Instruction

Job Profile: The Director of Biblical Instruction needs abilities or gifts in leadership, discernment, shepherding, encouragement, teaching, and administration. While administering the present program, the director needs to be a visionary who can lead it to the next level. This person should have a passion for adults as well as children and youth because he or she will work primarily with the parents on behalf of children and youth.

Job Summary: The Director of Biblical Instruction is responsible for the children's Sunday school program, children's church, the annual Vacation Bible School, and the Sunday school or Bible studies ministries and worship nurseries.

Duties:

A. Sunday School or Bible Studies
   1. Recruit teachers and floaters.
   2. Train teachers and floaters.
   3. Evaluate teachers and floaters.
   4. Encourage teachers and floaters.
   5. Assist teachers and monitor Sunday morning program.
   6. Maintain supplies and facilities.
   7. Select and approve all curriculum.
   8. Plan and make preparation for class expansion.
   9. Maintain a substitute teacher list.

B. Children's Church
   1. Presents church program.
   2. Recruit parents for leadership.
   3. Train parents for leadership.
   4. Select the curriculum.

C. Vacation Bible School
   1. Recruit a director and other leaders.
   2. Choose curriculum and coordinate other materials.
   3. Recruit teachers and workers.

D. Sunday School and Worship Service Nurseries
   1. Recruit directors.
   2. Help recruit people as workers.

E. Miscellaneous
   1. Develop the core values, mission, vision, and strategy for the Christian education program.
   2. Attend board meetings.
   3. Attend staff meetings.
   4. Conduct personal background checks.
   5. Conduct personal reference checks.
   6. Preach as needed.

Reports to: Senior Pastor

Works with: Elder responsible for biblical instruction

Ministry Appraisal

Director of Biblical Instruction

Circle the appropriate number:

Sunday School

	Poor	Fair	Good	Excellent
1. Recruits teachers and floaters.	1	2	3	4
2. Trains teachers and floaters.	1	2	3	4
3. Evaluates teachers and floaters.	1	2	3	4
4. Encourages teachers and floaters.	1	2	3	4
5. Assists teachers and monitors Sunday morning program.	1	2	3	4
6. Maintains supplies and facilities.	1	2	3	4
7. Selects and approves all curriculum.	1	2	3	4
8. Plans and makes preparation for class expansion.	1	2	3	4
9. Maintains substitute teacher list.	1	2	3	4

Comments:

_____

_____

_____

_____

Children's Church

	Poor	Fair	Good	Excellent
1. Presents church program.	1	2	3	4
2. Recruits parents for leadership.	1	2	3	4
3. Trains parents for leadership.	1	2	3	4
4. Selects the curriculum.	1	2	3	4

Comments:

_____

_____

Vacation Bible School

	Poor	Fair	Good	Excellent
1. Recruits a director and other leaders.	1	2	3	4
2. Chooses curriculum and coordinates other materials.	1	2	3	4
3. Recruits teachers and workers.	1	2	3	4

Comments:

_____

_____

Miscellaneous

	Poor	Fair	Good	Excellent
1. Develops values, mission, etc.	1	2	3	4
2. Attends board meetings.	1	2	3	4
3. Attends staff meetings.	1	2	3	4
4. Conducts personal background checks.	1	2	3	4
5. Conducts personal reference checks.	1	2	3	4
6. Preaches as needed.	1	2	3	4

Comments:

_____

_____

_____

General Appraisal

Director of Biblical Instruction

1. ***Job Knowledge:*** The individual is familiar with the duties, requirements, practices, policies, and procedures of the position.   1   2   3   4

Comments:

_____

_____

_____

2. ***Quality of Work:*** The individual does thorough and accurate work.   1   2   3   4

Comments:

_____

_____

_____

3. ***Productivity:*** The individual produces a reasonable, acceptable amount of work in a timely manner.   1   2   3   4

Comments:

_____

_____

_____

4. ***Organization:*** The individual's files, records, etc. are in order and easily   1   2   3   4
accessible.

Comments:

_____

_____

_____

5. ***Initiative and Resourcefulness:*** The individual is a self-starter who identifies   1   2   3   4
opportunities, improves procedures, and suggests new ideas.

Comments:

_____

_____

_____

6. ***Sociability:*** The individual is cooperative and supportive and gets along well with
people.   1   2   3   4

Comments:

_____

_____

_____

7. ***Communication:*** The individual is a good listener who communicates clearly and
accurately when writing or speaking.   1   2   3   4

Comments:

_____

_____

_____

8. ***Character:*** The individual is a person of integrity (respectful, trustworthy, honest,
not a gossip, humble, etc.).   1   2   3   4

Comments:

_____

_____

_____

Notes

Introduction

1. Quoted in Ken Blanchard and Terry Waghorn, *Mission Possible* (New York: McGraw-Hill, 1997), 82.

2. Aubrey Malphurs, *Planting Growing Churches for the 21st Century*, 3rd ed. (Grand Rapids: Baker, 2004), 11–12.

3. "Last Week? You're Sure?" *Dallas Morning News*, Sept. 21, 1997, G1.

4. In no way am I attempting to diminish the importance of preaching and teaching the Scriptures. The Bible communicates God's Word and will to mankind. Without it, we perish.

5. Charles Handy, *The Age of Paradox* (Boston: Harvard Business School Press, 1994), 51.

6. We learn from history and others' experiences that we do not learn from history and others' experiences.

7. Handy, *The Age of Paradox*, 57.

8. See Aubrey Malphurs, *Maximizing Your Effectiveness* (Grand Rapids: Baker, 1995).

9. I have written *Pouring New Wine into Old Wineskins* (Grand Rapids: Baker, 1993) to help those who find themselves in this situation.

Chapter 1 Preparing the Navigator

1. Gordon E. Penfold, "Turnaround Pastors: Characteristics of Those Who Lead Churches from Life-Support to New Life" (a paper presented to the Great Commission Research Network, November 10–11, 2011). I think that you will find this paper to be very helpful, though researchers who take a more sociological approach to research feel that the sample group is a little small and that the paper lacks good statistical analyses.

2. C. Kirk Hadaway, *Church Growth Principles: Separating Fact from Fiction* (Nashville: Broadman, 1991), 120.

3. See *Developing a Vision for Ministry in the 21st Century* (Grand Rapids: Baker, 1999); *Values-Driven Leadership*, 2nd ed. (Grand Rapids: Baker, 2004); *Strategy 2000: Churches Making Disciples in the Next Millennium* (Grand Rapids: Kregel, 1996); *Developing a Dynamic Mission for Your Ministry* (Grand Rapids: Kregel, 1998).

4. Marc Spiegler, "Scouting for Souls," *American Demographics* 18, no. 3 (March 1996): 49.

5. Some examples are Karl Albrecht, *The Northbound Train* (New York: American Management Association, 1994); Nicholas Imparato and Oren Harari, *Jumping the Curve* (San Francisco: Jossey-Bass, 1994); and Gary Hamal and C. K. Prahalad, *Competing for the Future* (Boston: HBS Press, 1994). An extreme example is Randall P. White, Philip Hodgson, and Stuart Crainer, *The Future of Leadership* (Washington, DC: Pitman, 1996). They see no need for strategic planning.

6. Albrecht, *The Northbound Train*, 57, italics mine.

7. Tom Peters, *Thriving on Chaos* (New York: Harper & Row, 1987), 615.

8. Mike Vance and Diane Deacon, *Think Out of the Box* (Franklin Lake, NJ: Career Press, 1995).

9. Some have found an outside consultant more harmful than helpful. It's critical to the accomplishment of your ministry goals that you do your homework before selecting a church consultant. Thus it's important to know what you should look for in a ministry consultant. What are some of the qualities that distinguish the good ones from others in the field? Here are a few things that you'd be wise to check out.

Christian character. Does the consultant know Jesus Christ as personal Savior? Though non-Christian consultants can provide some excellent help in their chosen areas of expertise, Christian consultants should bring spiritual discernment to the consulting arena as well as expertise. Just as important is a second question: Is he or she living a life marked by Christlikeness? Consultants model behavior for those with whom they minister, and it's critical that it be Christlike behavior.

Proven competence. What is the consultant's primary area or areas of expertise? Some consultants minister in several different areas. However, most are experts and are known for their work in just a few specific areas. Look for one who is competent in the area where you need help, who has a reputation for expertise in it. Sometimes you may have to inquire. A consultant's references will clue you to his or her areas of proven competence.

Theological expertise. You would be wise to examine the consultant's theological credentials. Does the consultant have any academic training in the Bible and theology? Few do, and the popular in-thing today is to pooh-pooh academics. However, a person's academic preparation in theology serves to mold his or her thinking and launches the person into a lifetime of ministry. Our group has discovered that good biblical, theological preparation is vital to the consulting equation because strategic ministry planning is deeply theological. Find out if the consultant has gone to a Bible college and/or seminary. If so, is it a reputable school? Evangelical? What degrees does the consultant have? Does he or she have a solid foundation in Bible and theology that will influence the consulting experience?

Strong references. Does the consultant have references, and how do the references rate his or her services? It's imperative that you touch base with those who have worked with the consultant. To a certain extent, consultants function much as another staff person, and you must check their references much as you would a new staff person. Beware of those that have no references or have questionable references at best.

Special gifting. What are the gifts, talents, and abilities that the consultant brings to your ministry context? Some excellent gifts for consulting are leadership, administration, wisdom, and discernment, mixed with lots of good, practical experience. While you're at it, check on the consultant's passions. (Passion is what you feel strongly and care deeply about.) Passion excites people and rubs off on them. Try to discover what will rub off on your people when they work with the consultant. Will they come away excited or discouraged about what's ahead?

Practical experience. Discern how much experience the consultant has. Is he or she a novice, just beginning to use his or her gifts and abilities in the consulting world? Has the consultant ever pastored a church or worked with a parachurch organization? If so, when and for how long? While it's critical that a consultant start somewhere, maybe that first or second organization shouldn't be yours. How can you know? Ask for and check out his or her references. In addition, here are two disclaimers that you should jot down on your mental list. First, just because a consultant has lots of experience doesn't mean that it's good experience. Though we do learn from bad experience, we learn more from good experiences. Second, contrary to popular opinion, star performers don't necessarily make the best consultants. There's often a big gap between being a great leader and coaching others to do the same. That's the reason so few star athletes become coaches.

Name recognition. What might seem like an unusual qualification is name recognition. When you think about the area in which you need a consultant's expertise, whose name usually comes to mind? Who is known to be a leader in the field? When you ask knowledgeable people, whom do they suggest? There's a reason for this that is summed up in two words: proven expertise. While it doesn't have to be, most often it will be someone who's demonstrated competence by ministering and writing in the field under a credible, recognized publisher. They write because they're passionate about what they do and they want to share their competence with others.

Chapter 2 Preparing the Crew

1. The S temperament characterizes those who are patient, consistent, and loyal. They are good listeners who really care about people. They want to know how change will affect their relationships with people before they will accept it. They are often the pastors of small churches. The C temperament characterizes people who are very conscientious. They are detail-oriented and always look for the facts. They are natural skeptics and initially view any change with skepticism.

2. People who are more traditional in their thinking have the SJ temperament. They believe that the best is in the past and pride themselves on being the conservers of the past. They may view change as a threat.

3. Ray Jutkins, *Power Direct Marketing*, 2nd ed. (Lincolnwood, IL: NTC Business Books, 2000), n.p. as cited at http://www.rayjutkins.com/pdm/pdm10-03.html.

4. John Kotter, *The Heart of Change* (Boston: Harvard Business School Press, 2002).

5. J. Scott Horrell, *From the Ground Up: Foundations for the 21st Century Church* (Grand Rapids: Kregel, 2004), chapter 6.

6. John Kotter addresses this issue well in his book *Leading Change* (Boston: Harvard Business School Press, 1996), 4–5, 35–49.

7. Randy Frazee, *The Connecting Church* (Grand Rapids: Zondervan, 2001), 91.

8. Kotter, *Leading Change*, 13.

9. Eliza G. Collins, *Executive Success: Making It in Management* (New York: John Wiley, 1985), 210.

10. I have developed the concept of servant leadership in much greater detail in chapter 2 of my book *Being Leaders* (Grand Rapids: Baker, 2003).

Chapter 4 Developing a Biblical Mission

1. Stephen Covey, *The Seven Habits of Highly Effective People* (New York: Simon & Schuster, 1989), 139.

2. Warren Bennis, *On Becoming a Leader* (New York: Addison-Wesley, 1989), 183.

3. Peter F. Drucker, *Managing the Non-Profit Organization* (New York: Harper Business, 1990), 3.

4. Peter F. Drucker, *Management: Tasks, Responsibilities, Practices* (New York: Harper & Row, 1973), 75.

5. Ibid., 78.

6. Allan Cox, *Redefining Corporate Soul* (Chicago: Irwin Professional Publishing, 1996), 25.

7. Ibid., 26.

8. Patricia Jones and Larry Kahaner, *Say It and Live It* (New York: Doubleday, 1995), 264.

9. I covered this important hermeneutical principle in the section on change in chapter 2.

10. Randy Frazee with Lyle E. Schaller, *The Comeback Congregation* (Nashville: Abingdon, 1995), 6.

11. Fred Smith, *Learning to Lead* (Waco: Word, 1986), 34.

12. If you desire a more thorough, in-depth coverage of how to communicate the mission or the development of a mission statement, see my book *Developing a Dynamic Mission for Your Ministry*.

Chapter 5 Developing a Compelling Vision

1. If after reading this chapter, you desire a more in-depth treatment of the vision concept, see my book *Developing a Vision for Ministry in the 21st Century*.

2. "The Man Who Brought Marketing to the Church," *Leadership* 16, no. 3 (Summer 1995): 124–25.

3. David Goetz, "Forced Out," *Leadership* 17, no. 1 (Winter 1996): 42.

4. Bill Hybels, *Courageous Leadership* (Grand Rapids: Zondervan, 2002), 31.

5. Ibid.

6. Ibid., 113.

7. Lewis Carroll, *Alice in Wonderland* (New York: Book-of-the-Month Club, 1994), 85.

8. Malphurs, *Developing a Vision for Ministry in the 21st Century*, 11.

9. You may take the MBTI through a private counseling agency or one located at a college or university. You may order the Kiersey Temperament Sorter II from Prometheus Nemesis Book Company, Box 2748, Del Mar, CA 92014; 800-754-0039; fax: 619-481-0535.

Chapter 6 Discovering Core Values

1. I am using congregational or corporate soul in this context as a leadership, not a theological, concept.

2. I have included the Jerusalem church's values as a credo in appendix H.

3. Ken Blanchard and Michael O'Connor, *Managing by Values* (San Francisco: Berrett-Koehler, 1996), 3.

4. Lyle E. Schaller, *Getting Things Done* (Nashville: Abingdon, 1986), 152.

5. If you desire a more complete, in-depth presentation of core values, see my book *Values-Driven Leadership*. However, this chapter contains information that I have learned since writing that book.

6. James C. Collins and William C. Lazier, *Beyond Entrepreneurship: Turning Your Business into an Enduring Great Company* (Englewood Cliffs, NJ: Prentice Hall, 1992), 66.

7. Collins, *Executive Success*, 210.

8. Thomas J. Peters and Robert H. Waterman Jr., *In Search of Excellence* (New York: Warner, 1982), 281.

9. Blanchard and O'Connor, *Managing by Values*, 31, 108, 121.

10. It is common for people to mistake what they value with their values. We value all kinds of things, such as a particular method of evangelism, a preaching style, the way we serve communion, small groups, the way we study the Bible, and so on. But these are not values. Go back to the section "What Are Values?" in this chapter for clarification.

11. James C. Collins and Jerry I. Porras, *Built to Last* (New York: Harper Business, 1994), 74, 219.

12. Ken Blanchard and Phil Hodges, *The Servant Leader* (Nashville: Thomas Nelson, 2003), 50.

13. Collins and Porras, *Built to Last*, 74.

Chapter 7 Introducing the Ministry Strategy

1. James A. Belasco and Ralph C. Stayer, *Flight of the Buffalo* (New York: Warner, 1993), 138.

2. Ibid.

3. Ibid.

4. I do not have the time or space here to develop a theology of strategy. For more on this, see my book *Strategy 2000*, chapter 4.

5. Bob Gilliam, "Are Most Churches Intentionally Making Disciples?" Findings from the Spiritual Journey Evaluation (March 29, 1995): 1.

Chapter 8 Reaching the Church's Community

1. Win Arn, "Average Driving Time to Church," *The Win Arn Growth Report* 1, no. 20.

2. Thom Rainer, "Pastors and Time," *Christian Post*, April 26, 2010, http://www.christianpost.com/article/20100412/pastors-and-time/index.html.

3. Floyd Bartel, *A New Look at Church Growth* (Newton, KS: Faith & Life, 1987), 59.

4. Bill Hybels and Mark Mittleberg, *Becoming a Contagious Christian* (Grand Rapids: Zondervan, 1994), 119–34.

5. C. Peter Wagner, *Church Planting for a Greater Harvest* (Ventura, CA: Regal, 1990), 11.

Chapter 9 Making Mature Disciples

1. I say, "typical, traditional format," understanding that there are those in the church who believe this is how the early church ordered its worship and must be followed today. This is unfortunate for two reasons. First, it simply is not true that this was how the early church ordered its worship. Second, it restricts the church's freedom in how it designs its ministry activities.

2. Lynne and Bill Hybels, *Rediscovering Church* (Grand Rapids: Zondervan, 1995), chapter 11.

3. Frazee, *The Connecting Church*, 105.

4. Ibid., 101.

Chapter 10 Building a Ministry Team

1. Drucker, *Managing the Non-Profit Organization*, 145.

2. I will talk about how to let people go in the last chapter, on ministry evaluation.

3. Aubrey Malphurs, *Leading Leaders* (Grand Rapids: Baker, 2005); *Being Leaders* (Grand Rapids: Baker, 2003).

4. I got the idea for these three terms from Jim Dethmer, a former teaching pastor at Willow Creek Community Church.

5. Gary L. McIntosh, *Staff Your Church for Growth* (Grand Rapids: Baker, 2000), 43. I suspect that these are figures for a middle-class suburban church as opposed to a lower-income inner-city church. Thus you might need to adjust the figures to match your situation.

6. Hybels, *Courageous Leadership*, 85.

7. Larry Bossidy and Ram Charan, *Execution: The Discipline of Getting Things Done* (New York: Crown Business, 2002), 112.

8. In the job descriptions at Northwood, we carefully spell out all the ministry responsibilities. Consequently, we cannot randomly dump new responsibilities on staff without first discussing it with them. Also, we discuss increased compensation for increased responsibilities.

9. This concept came from Patrick Lencioni, *The Five Dysfunctions of a Team* (San Francisco: Jossey-Bass, 2002), 195–202.

10. This idea came from Bossidy and Charan, *Execution*, 102–5.

11. Malphurs, *Maximizing Your Effectiveness*, 112–14.

12. Sue Mallory, *The Equipping Generation* (Grand Rapids: Zondervan, 2001).

13. Rick Warren, *The Purpose-Driven Church* (Grand Rapids: Zondervan, 1995), 143.

14. Aubrey Malphurs and Will Mancini, *Building Leaders* (Grand Rapids: Baker, 2004).

Chapter 11 Assessing the Ministry Setting

1. Aubrey Malphurs and Michael Malphurs, *Church Next* (Grand Rapids: Kregel, 2003).

2. Greg L. Hawkins and Cally Parkinson, *Reveal: Where Are You?* (Chicago: Willow Creek Resources, 2007), 21.

Chapter 12 Raising and Managing Finances

1. Hybels, *Courageous Leadership*, 98.

2. Ibid., 100.

3. Ibid.

4. *Leadership Network Advance,* no. 70 (April 8, 2008), 2.

5. George Barna, *How to Increase Giving in Your Church* (Ventura, CA: Regal, 1997), 92–93.

6. Ibid., 118.

7. "God, Money, and the Pastor," *Leadership* (Fall 2002), 30–31.

8. Ibid., 51.

9. Randy Alcorn, *The Treasure Principle* (Sisters, OR: Multnomah, 2001).

10. Lyle E. Schaller, *The New Context for Ministry* (Nashville: Abingdon, 2002), 233.

11. Barna, *How to Increase Giving in Your Church*, 33.

Chapter 13 Launching the Boat

1. C. Kirk Hadaway, "Do Church Growth Consultations Really Work?" in David A. Roozen and C. Kirk Hadaway, eds., *Church and Denominational Growth: What Does and Does Not Cause Growth and Decline?* (New York: Abingdon, 1993), 149–54.

Chapter 14 Evaluating the Course

1. I have gleaned most of these from Rod MacIlvaine, the pastor of Grace Community Church of Bartlesville, Oklahoma.

2. Actually, the New Testament does not tell us a lot about what the early church practiced. I believe that God did this because he knew that we would try to mimic it and become needlessly bound up in the first-century culture.

Index

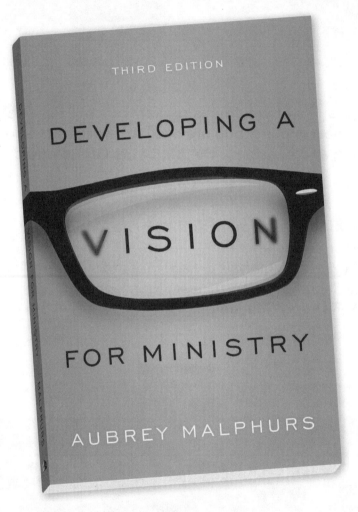

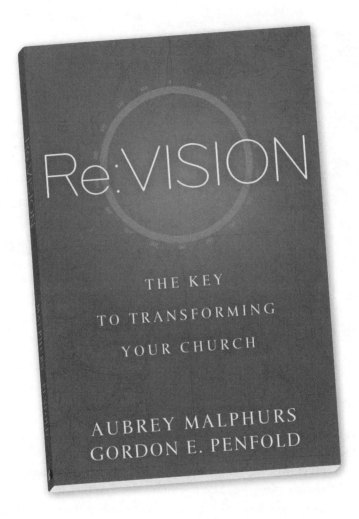

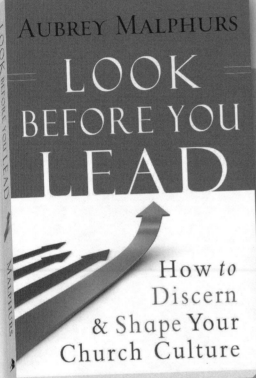

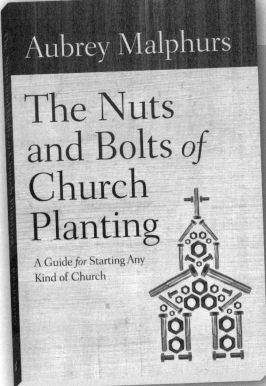

DISCIPLE EVERYONE
IN YOUR CHURCH

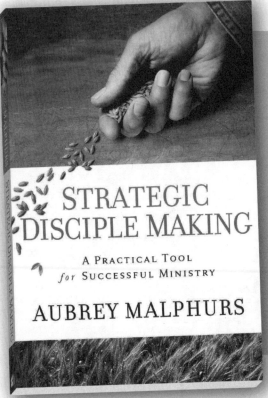

Many understand discipleship as a one-on-one relationship with a mentor that takes place with a select few in the church. However, Jesus's mandate in Matthew 28:19–20 is that the church make disciples of all its people, not just a select few. In *Strategic Disciple Making*, veteran church consultant Aubrey Malphurs teaches churches a process that implements the biblical teaching on discipleship in a simple but practical way as the centerpiece of their ministries.

Maximize Financial Health *in* Your Church

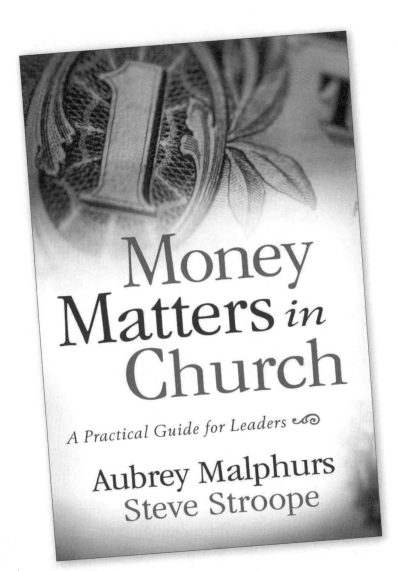

Money Matters *in* Church

A Practical Guide for Leaders

Aubrey Malphurs
Steve Stroope

Connect with

Sign up for announcements about new and upcoming titles at

www.bakerbooks.com/signup

 ReadBakerBooks

 ReadBakerBooks